COUNSELOR SUPERVISION

PRINCIPLES, PROCESS, and PRACTICE

Second Edition

Loretta J. Bradley, Ph.D.
Associate Professor
Department of Educational Psychology
Counselor Education Program
Texas Tech University
Lubbock, Texas

In collaboration with

John D. Boyd, Ph.D.
Independent Practice of Clinical Psychology
Associate Clinical Professor
of Behavioral Medicine and Psychiatry
University of Virginia
Charlottesville, Virginia

 **ACCELERATED DEVELOPMENT INC.**
Publishers
Muncie   Indiana

COUNSELOR SUPERVISION

Principles, Process, and Practice

Second Edition

Technical Development: Tanya Dalton
Delores Kellogg
Marguerite Mader
Sheila Sheward

Library of Congress Cataloging-in-Publication Data

Bradley, Loretta J. 1941-
Counselor supervision: principles, process, and practice

Loretta J. Bradley in collaboration with John D. Boyd
2nd ed. p. xvi + 504   cm.
Earlier ed.: Counselor supervision/John D. Boyd. 1978.
Includes index.
1. Counselors—supervision of. I. Boyd, John Donald, 1944-
II. Boyd, John Donald, 1944- Counselor supervision. III. Title
BF637.C6B65   1989   158'.3--dc19   88-82675
ISBN 0-915202-81-6

ACCELERATED DEVELOPMENT Inc., PUBLISHERS
3400 Kilgore Avenue, Muncie, Indiana 47304-4896
(317) 284-7511

PREFACE

The purpose of this book is to provide information about the principles, process, and practice of counselor supervision for both clinical and administrative supervisors. Although the title of the book conveys counselor supervision, the book is relevant for supervisors in such related disciplines as employee assistance coordination, human resource training in business and industry, family therapy, psychiatry, psychology, and social work.

Overview of the Book

The book is divided into three major parts consisting of Part I Counselor Supervision: Essentials for Training; Part II Models of Supervision; and Part III Approaches, Preparation, and Practices. Each of the major areas are composed of different chapters that comprise a total of twelve chapters in the book.

The book begins with the first chapter of supervision including the basic principles, roles, and functions involved in effective supervisory practice for administrative and clinical supervisors. Part I consists of Chapter 1 which provides a basic model and Chapter 2 which describes the essentials necessary for a supervisory relationship.

Part II provides models of supervision. Five chapters are devoted to supervisory models. Chapter 3 focuses on the psychotherapeutic model. Chapter 4 on the behavioral model, Chapter 5 on the integrative model. Chapter 6 on the systems model, and Chapter 7 presents a developmental model. Chapters 3-6 were originally described by John Boyd in his book *Counselor Supervision* (Boyd, 1978). These chapters and the supervisory overview have been modified to bring the chapters up-to-date with current information and references. Boyd's description of supervisory approaches was and continues to be widely accepted as evidenced by continuous positive feedback and wide adoption by counselor educators.

Part III contains five chapters focusing on the practice of supervision. Chapter 8 illustrates the implementation of the developmental model into supervisory practice. Several practical illustrations help this chapter take the supervisor beyond the model to new understandings of supervisee functioning. Using case illustrations, Chapter 9 describes experiential supervision. Group supervision is the focus of Chapter 10. Ethical principles in supervision provides the theme for Chapter 11. The last chapter, Chapter 12, presents a model for supervision training.

Audience

This book is intended for both clinical and administrative supervisors. It should be very beneficial to supervisors seeking additional supervisory information or for the supervisor-in-training, whether enrolled in university graduate training programs or seeking professional development as a counselor supervisor. For clinical supervisors enrolled in graduate supervision classes, this book is intended as a primary text. For the administrative supervisor employed in an agency, the book is intended as a primary tool for in-service training and professional development. For the practicing supervisor regardless of setting, the book is envisioned as a guide for implementing the supervisory process.

Although the title counselor supervision might suggest the book is only intended for counselors, in reality the book is written to serve a variety of human service providers. In addition to counselors and counseling psychologists, the book will be beneficial to clinical psychologists, directors of human resource providers in business and industry, directors of pupil personnel service, family therapy supervisors, psychiatrists, and social workers.

REFERENCE

Boyd, J.D. (1978). *Counselor supervision: Approaches, preparation and practices.* Muncie, IN: Accelerated Development.

ACKNOWLEDGEMENTS

I want to express my sincere appreciation to Dr. John Boyd for his collaborative assistance. Without Dr. Boyd's advice and encouragement, I wonder if this book would have become reality. His advice and encouragement will always be remembered. I am indeed indebted to Dr. Boyd for his writing about supervision models. With minor modifications, his earlier writing on supervision approaches provides the foundation for four of the five Chapters in Part II and Chapter 1 in Part I.

To Dr. Roger Aubrey, I will always remain grateful for his encouragement and support which provided the original impetus for the writing of this book. To Dr. Joseph Hollis, I offer my thanks for his timely advice, support, and suggestions. To my former colleagues (1978-87) at Peabody College of Vanderbilt University and my present colleagues (1987) at Texas Tech University, I express my thanks for the supervisory experiences that I received. Additionally I want to thank Ms. Billye French for her encouragement and for her excellent professional assistance with the typing of the book.

Finally and perhaps most importantly, I want to express my appreciation to my family. I am grateful to my husband, Dr. Charles Bradley, and my sons, Brian and Brett, for their support and understanding. Without their cooperation, this book would not have become reality.

Loretta J. Bradley, Ph.D.

CONTENTS

LIST OF FIGURES

PART I

COUNSELOR SUPERVISION: ESSENTIALS FOR TRAINING

CHAPTER 1

OVERVIEW OF COUNSELOR SUPERVISION

Counselor supervision is a term which can be found throughout counseling literature (Alonso, 1983; Blocher, 1983; Borders & Leddick, 1987; Falvey, 1987; Hansen, Robins, & Grimes, 1982; Hart, 1982; Hess, 1986; Loganbill, Hardy, & Delworth, 1982; Stoltenberg & Delworth, 1987). The term supervision can be divided into two words, super and vision. These two terms imply that supervision is a process in which an experienced person (supervisor) with appropriate training and experience supervises a subordinate (supervisee). Hart (1982) defined supervision as "an ongoing educational process in which one person in the role of supervisor helps another person in the role of supervisee acquire appropriate professional behavior through an examination of the supervisee's professional activities" (p. 12). Implicit in this definition is the ongoing relationship between supervisor and supervisee, the professional role identity to be acquired and the focus on the behavior to be acquired by the supervisee.

The term supervision appears in the title of the Association for Counselor Education and Supervision, one of the divisions of the American Association for Counseling and Development. About twenty years ago, the Association for Counselor Education and Supervision (ACES) established a Committee on Counselor Effectiveness. In the report of the ACES Committee on Counselor Effectiveness (ACES, 1969) a three part definition defined who a supervisor is, what supervision seeks to achieve, and what constitutes supervision. Accordingly counselor supervision was defined as (1) being performed by experienced, successful counselors (supervisors) who have been prepared in the methodology of supervision; (2) facilitating the counselor's personal and professional development, promoting counselor competencies and promoting accountable counseling and guidance services and programs; and (3) providing the purposeful function of overseeing the work of counselor trainees or practicing counselors (supervisees) through a set of supervisory activities which include consultation, counseling training and instruction, and evaluation.

In recent years, a distinction has been made between administrative (Falvey, 1987) and clinical supervision (Borders & Leddick, 1987). The distinction has largely centered around the tasks performed by the supervisor. In describing administrative supervision, researchers (Abels & Murphy, 1981; Austin, 1981; Black, 1975; Hart, 1982; Simon, 1985; Slavin, 1985) have typically described it as occurring in bureaucratic organizations (e.g., universities, human service organizations). In administrative supervision, the supervisor helps the supervisee function effectively as a part of the organization with the overall intent to help the organization run smoothly and efficiently. The administrative supervisor usually stresses organizational accountability, case records, referrals, and performance evaluations. In contrast, clinical supervision focuses on the work of the supervisee in relation to the services received by the client. In clinical supervision, the supervisor focuses on such areas as client welfare, counseling relationship, assessment, diagnosis, clinical intervention, prognosis, and appropriate referral techniques. Perhaps the distinction between the two is best summarized by Hart (1982) who stated "administrative supervision is aimed at helping the supervisee as part of an organization, and clinical supervision focuses on the development of the supervisee specifically as an interpersonally effective clinician" (p. 13). The focus of administrative supervision is therefore on tasks that directly affect the organization whereas in clinical supervision the focus is on the supervisee's clinical interventions that directly affect the client. This book will focus on both administrative and clinical supervision and distinctions will be made where appropriate within each chapter.

SUPERVISOR

Every profession includes master practitioners who can guide and direct less-experienced colleagues and pre-service trainees. Master practitioners function within apprenticeships and internships by promoting a transfer of learning from instructional settings to the actual environment where the profession is practiced. Moreover, these individuals are key factors in continued personal/professional development which extends throughout a professional's career.

In the helping services and specifically in counseling, these master practitioners often are called "supervisors." They also are known by other labels, such as administrative supervisor, clinical supervisor, human resource supervisor, director of guidance, head counselor, chief psychologist, and/or pupil personnel services director. Whatever the official title, the criterion for being a supervisor is that an individual performs the function of counselor supervision. Supervisors are responsible for supervising the work of student-counselors and/or a staff of practicing counselors.

The academic preparation and background experiences have been investigated recently by Richardson and Bradley (1986) and previously by Riccio (1961, 1966) and the ACES survey (1969). Results from these studies indicate that nearly all supervisors in colleges and universities have attained doctoral degrees and the majority of supervisors in field settings (i.e., agencies, state departments, and schools) have grained a significant level of education beyond the master's degree. Despite these high levels of educational attainment, the alarming fact remains that only a token number of supervisors, regardless of work setting, have received specific preparation for supervision.

A reasonable assumption is that counselor supervisors in general achieved their supervisory positions on the basis of educational level, tenure, and successful counseling experiences.

However, counseling experience and an accumulation of academic credits must be viewed as insufficient qualifications, by themselves, for supervisors of counselors. Preparation in supervision methodology must become an entrance criteria if supervision practice is to be validated. Undergraduate preparation of supervisors is usually in the fields of education and psychology, while graduate preparation and advanced academic work are in counselor education, counseling psychology, or other helping service disciplines. Supervisors tend to be situation oriented; they gain counseling experience in a particular setting and are likely to remain there for supervisory practice.

The literature on supervision and supervisory job functions generates some information about the personality attributes of a supervisor. The supervisor must be a serious, committed professional who has chosen counseling and supervision as a long-term career (Hart, 1982; Hess, 1986). This assumption implies that the supervisor is energetic and ambitious but not in an egotistical or opportunist manner. Instead, the supervisor is committed to and ambitious about developing and maintaining accountable helping services.

The supervisor must possess the core conditions of empathy, respect and concreteness as well as the action-oriented conditions of genuineness, confrontation, and immediacy (Blocher, 1983; Moses & Hardin, 1978; Patterson, 1983). In addition to the core conditions, other descriptions of the good supervisor include concern for the growth and well-being of the supervisee (Blocher, 1983; Hess, 1986; Mueller & Kell, 1972) as well as the welfare of the client (Bernard, 1987; Corey, Corey, & Callanan, 1987; Cormier & Bernard, 1982). Other positive supervisor characteristics include integrity, courage, sense of humor, capacity for intimacy, sense of timing, openness to self-inspection (Loganbill, Hardy, & Delworth, 1982), responsibleness (Leddick & Dye, 1987; Tennyson & Strom, 1986) and nonthreatening, nonauthoritarian approach to supervision (Allen, Szollos, & Williams, 1986; Bordin, 1983; Dodge, 1982; Reising & Daniels, 1983; Worthington, 1984) as well as the capacity to be flexible, tolerant, and open to various styles and levels of learning (Cross & Brown, 1983; Grater, 1985; Stoltenberg, Solomon, & Ogden, 1986; Worthington, 1984).

Competence and success with a broad range of helping activities are essential criteria for the selection of supervisors, although realistically the supervisor cannot be expected to be omnipotent; thus skills and expertise may be unevenly distributed. In addition to such professionally demonstratable qualities, a supervisor must possess confidence and professional assurance. A hesitant, unsure supervisor cannot offer the kind of leadership that is needed in supervisory positions. In a profession where nurturance is sometimes more prevalent than ego strength, those in leadership roles must be self assured. This is particularly true in agencies and schools where counselors are subordinate to other administrators. The supervisor must be confident and strong when working with those who have administrative power over counselors, as well as when grappling with the difficult decisions that arise in supervision.

A supervisor should have both the professional and the personal respect of colleagues and associates in the work environment. Professional respect is founded in competence and ability, first as a good counselor and then as a capable supervisor. Personal respect relates to whether the supervisor is totally accepted as a person by his or her associates and is based upon values, attitudes, ethics, and other moral indices that are reflected through professional behavior.

Finally, the supervisor must have the characteristic of advocacy—the ability to serve as an advocate for counselors. All individuals need reinforcement, and counselors as a group suffer from a lack of professional affirmation. Supervisees need to feel that the supervisor believes in their ability or potential to be capable counselors.

To summarize, the supervisor is a well-prepared individual who has entered the supervisory position after a successful tenure as a counselor. The supervisor is regarded as a capable professional from whom other counselors can learn and is respected as a person of exemplary character. The supervisor is an advocate for counselors and is dedicated to their personal and professional development.

PURPOSE OF COUNSELOR SUPERVISION

A purpose is that which is set before as a general goal to be attained. Statements of purpose characteristically are overlapping, but these statements are extremely important because they register intent and set direction. From purposes may come objectives.

Counselor supervision has three main purposes:

1. facilitation of the counselor's personal and professional development,

2. promotion of counselor competencies, and

3. promotion of accountable counseling and guidance services and programs.

Singularly and collectively, these purposes provide a rationale for the work of supervisors.

Personal and Professional Development

The first purpose of supervision is a dual one—to facilitate personal and professional development of counselors. Wrenn's (1962, p. 168) strong statement provides a rationale of the personal development aspect of this dual-faced purpose.

> The counselor as a person is that most important single factor in counseling. He needs to understand himself psychologically in order to be effective in helping others.

Another statement by Wrenn (1973, p. 272) also adds support to the rationale.

> A professional must be forever at the job of learning. I am proposing that to learn about one's self and the [noncounseling] world around one is as important as it is to read new texts and attend summer school. Perhaps it is more important.

Assuming agreement that facilitation of counselors' personal development should be a purpose of supervision the next questions are how much and what kind of emphasis to place on personal development? Answers to these questions are a matter for conjecture, but the following guidelines may be helpful in arriving at a partial resolution.

1. Generally, counselor supervision should not attempt to intrude on the personal development of counselors. Supervision should offer the counselor an optimal opportunity to self-initiated personal development, and encourage the counselor to take advantage of the opportunity.

2. Supervisory intervention into the counselor's personal development should be undertaken only when psychological distress is obviously and deleteriously affecting the counselor's performance. "Facilitation" of personal development is, however, a continuing supervisory effort.

3. The counselor's personal and professional development are interrelated concepts. Damage to or facilitation of one of these concepts has a reciprocal effect on the other. Furthermore, facilitating personal development can be construed as contributing indirectly to all purposes of supervision.

4. The foremost purposes of counselor supervision are facilitating professional development, increasing competencies, and promoting accountability in guidance and counseling. An assumption is that selection and preparation have produced well-adjusted counselors, thus allowing the facilitation of personal development to become a second priority purpose of supervision.

Since the concept of personal development inherently is vague, the supervisor must be able to put the concept into concrete terms so that supervisory techniques and strategies can be applied. No attempt is made here to give the concept tangibility because personal development is being treated as a general purpose. In Chapter 3, the "psychotherapeutic approach" to supervision the concept will be treated more concretely.

Professional development, an interrelated part of the dual purpose of supervision, is a concept that must be clearly defined if the supervisor is to functionalize its intent. In a broad sense, professional development encompasses all that makes the counselor a professional—including increasing and improving competencies. In the context of this presentation, however, a more narrow definition is used, since competency improvement is designated as a separate supervisory purpose. Professional development, as here defined, refers to four tasks which have been adapted from Becker and Carper, 1956; Hart and Prince, 1970; Zerface and Cox, 1971; and Stefflre, 1964:

1. The counselor must accept the name and image of the profession as part of his or her self concept. This task causes problems for counselors because their preparation may lead to a wide variety of positions, each with a different job or professional title (e.g., child/adult development specialist, counseling psychologist, guidance counselor, human development counselor, human resource specialist, or school counselor.

2. One must have a commitment to, and a clear perception of, the professional role and function. Counselors do not typically enter positions where their role and function have already been established. In fact, establishing this operational base is one of the most important and difficult functions of the newly-employed counselor (Hart & Prince, 1970). Occasionally, situational conditions can be so restrictive that the environment is unfit for good professional practice (Zerface & Cox, 1971).

   A frequently slighted facet of the counselor's role and function is support of the profession and contribution to its growth and strength. Counselors are in dire need of professional affirmation but, ironically, the only way to receive this affirmation is to produce it! Participation in local, state, and national professional associations is a start.

3. The counselor must be committed to goals of the institution in which counseling and guidance services are performed. This commitment does not preclude the

counselor's influence on establishment or alteration of institutional goals.

4. The counselor will recognize and appreciate significance of the profession for individuals, groups, institutions, and society as a whole. A true profession exists to meet the needs of society, and professional accountability begins with recognition of these needs, understanding how the profession meets them, and an assessment of the profession's impact.

An integral component in the supervisory purpose to facilitate personal and professional development is the assumption of responsibility by both the counselor and the supervisor for achieving this development. As Ekstein and Wallerstein (1958) noted, counselor preparation should help the counselor separate himself/herself from formal preparation and carry on a continuous process of independent learning. Similarly, responsible self development (Arnold, 1962; Blocher, 1983; Hess, 1986; Reising & Daniels, 1983; Tennyson & Strom, 1986) is a theme permeating the purposes of supervision.

Competency Development

The second purpose of supervision, to increase counselor competencies, incorporates helping the counselor acquire, improve, and refine the skills required by the counselor's role and function. This purpose unfortunately has become associated more with counselor education programs than with in-service supervision because field supervisors often are reluctant to accept responsibility for colleagues' competency development. Before entering the position of supervisor the master counselor was responsible only for self improvement, and to monitor a colleague's skill level would have been presumptuous. Upon entering the supervisory role, however, the responsibility for supervisee competency development must be accepted, and here the personal characteristics discussed earlier in the Chapter become crucial. Does the supervisor feel confident enough to help others with their skills? Is the supervisor respected as a capable counselor who has something to offer?

Another reason for field supervisors to be uncomfortable with responsibility for supervisee competency development is that most of them have not been prepared in the methodology of supervision. Although supervisors in counselor education programs may lack formal supervisory preparation, they have the advantages of modeling the supervisory behavior of colleagues, being encouraged by eager students to assume a supervisor role, and the controlled conditions of a laboratory setting or a counseling center.

Still another reason why competency development has been almost exclusively associated with formal preparation programs is the assumed existence of a competency ceiling—a point at which the counselor has "learned it all." Such a terminal point is often perceived to be a graduate degree or state certification. A different perspective is needed by both supervisor and supervisee if competency is to be received as something to be upgraded throughout one's professional career. As symbolized in Figure 1.1, the development of counselor competency can be conceptualized as a continual process with several distinguishable levels.

Four finite developmental levels of competence and one infinite level are shown on the continuum. Level 1 represents the skill level which is reached through a master's degree counselor education program. Although such programs strive for the ideal of producing a fully-functioning counselor, more realistically Level 1 may be described as consisting of a repertoire of fundamental skills and a basic foundation of knowledge that extends beyond entry skill boundaries. The repertoire of entry skills are those that the profession and the preparing institution have identified as necessary for competent counselor performance. Attainment and demonstration of these skills should be criteria for awarding a professional degree in counseling. The basic foundation of knowledge at Level 1 provides a background of understanding that enables the counselor to broaden the repertoire of entry skills via experience and supervision. Progress leads to the Level 2 goal of a "fully-functioning counselor."

Level 3 on the continuum is devoted to refinement of the fully-functioning repertoire of skills. At Level 2 the competency

	Master's Degree Preparation	First Year of Counselor Practice	Second Year of Counselor Practice	Third Year of Counselor Practice
	LEVEL 1	LEVEL 2	LEVEL 3	LEVEL 4
Repertoire:	Fundamental Skills	Entry Skills	Fully Functioning	Refined Repertoire	Advanced Skills... Supervision
	Basic Knowledge Foundation			

Figure 1.1. Continuum of counselor supervision.

dimension of quantity (i.e., the number of skills) was the target, but at Level 3, the focus is on quality. The counselor achieves Level 3 by improving existing competencies and moving toward the goal of a repertoire of refined and polished skills.

Advanced skills are the goal at Level 4 of the competency continuum. This level is achieved, after several years of experience, advanced preparation, and supervision by a small percentage of counselors who may be called "master practitioners." The work of "master practitioners" is outstanding in all respects. These individuals possess and perform advanced skills that would be unethical for the neophyte to attempt. Other professionals use such persons as models and depend on them for guidance and leadership because of their demonstrated effectiveness. One of the competencies that may be gained at this level is counselor supervision.

Beyond Level 4 is a continual process of competency development. The neophyte at Level 1 may think that the supervisor, who always seems to know what to do, has reached the ceiling of competency development. However, this is a misconception and perhaps the supervisor should share the truth—that despite advanced preparation, successful performance, and the professional prestige of being a master counselor, always more is to be learned, for the process of competency development never ends.

Promotion of Accountability

To say that the helping professions, and particularly counseling, are presently in an "age of accountability" would be an understatement. Accountability is being demanded by the public that funds these enterprises (Humes, 1972; Pulvino & Sanborn, 1972), and personnel in these professions are trying to demonstrate accountability to that public (and perhaps to themselves). The consequence of not being able to satisfy public expectation could be disastrous for the helping professionals. Counseling is most vulnerable because this field always has been forced to fight for federal, state, and local dollars, and lack of demonstrated effectiveness could reduce or redirect funding, thus changing the support structure of the profession.

To ignore the realities of jeopardized funding and the popularity (however faddish) accountability would be irresponsible but these forces should not be the motivation for helping services and programs to respond to the need for demonstrating accountability. Such forces from outside the professional may serve as cues to raise serious questions about effectiveness, but the motivation for demonstrating accountability must come from within. A profession emerges in response to the needs of society and exists for the purpose of meeting those needs. Accountability is the profession's index of validity evidence that the profession is meeting society's needs. The profession's obligation not society's, is to establish accountability.

As a term, accountability has been given many definitions (Corey, Corey, & Callanan, 1987; Holahan & Gallassi, 1986; Lessinger, 1970; Upchurch, 1985). The core concept relates to accomplishment of purposes and goals which a person or institution has contracted or promised to accomplish. Glass (1972, p. 636) compared this core element of meaning to "the simple economic relationship of vendor and buyer." The public served by helping services is the buyer and counselors are the vendors. An accountable relationship between these two parties would involve

1. complete disclosure concerning the service being sold,

2. a testing of the effectiveness of the service, and

3. a redress if the service is found by the public to be ineffective or falsely advertised.

According to this vendor-buyer paradigm, counselors are accountable to their employers—the public. Counselors must openly and honestly explain their functions and what their services can do. Counselors must test and evaluate their services and share the findings with the public. Lastly, counselors must be responsible for the consequences (good and bad) of their work and make adjustments where their work is ineffective.

Counselor supervision is a means for promoting account-ability in services, programs, and relationships between helping services and the public. Supervised assistance to an individual counselor improves that person's accountability, while supervision applied to a staff of counselors involved in program development, management, and evaluation is a route to program accountability. In both cases, a special set of skills—a technical expertise—is needed by the supervisor if account-ability is to be achieved.

ACTIVITIES OF COUNSELOR SUPERVISION

So far in this Chapter, two parts of a definition of counselor supervision have been covered. The person who performs supervision has been described and the purposes of supervision have been discussed. The third part of the definition states that counselor supervision is the purposeful function of overseeing the work of counselor trainees or less experienced counselors (supervisees) through a set of supervisory activities which include

1. consultation,

2. counseling,

3. training and instruction, and

4. evaluation.

This "nut-and-bolts" definition has two key phrases, the first of which is "purposeful function of overseeing." The concept of function seems the most logical and understandable way of dealing with counselor supervision. A function (noun) is the "action for which a person or thing is specially fitted or used or for which a thing exists" (Webster, 1981, p. 921). In terms of this definition, supervision as a function is the characteristic action or activity involved in implementing a purpose. The word which best describes the characteristic actions and activities of supervision is overseeing—the act of "watching over." Whatever diverse activities comprise the work of counselor supervision, they are subsumed under the principal supervisory function of being aware of and monitoring the work (and development) of counselors.

The second key phrase in this part of the definition of counselor supervision is "through a set of supervisory activities." This phrase indicates that the purposeful function of overseeing is implemented through a number of activities. In contrast to the idea that counselor supervision is a singular entity or activity, it is defined here as a function consisting of four main activities: consultation, counseling, training and instruction, and evaluation. The four activities are depicted in Figure 1.2. Consultation is the principal activity and stance of the supervisor, with training and instruction, counseling, and evaluation completing the list.

COUNSELOR SUPERVISION

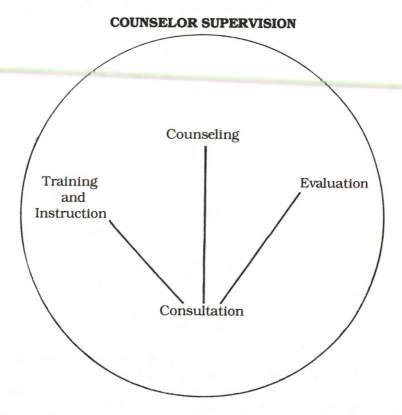

Figure 1.2. Activities comprising the counselor supervison function.

Counselor Supervision:
Consultation

Consultation is performed in many contexts, in which its implementation may be somewhat different. Consultation as an activity to carry out the function of counselor supervision is quite different, for example, from mental health consultation. Identifying characteristics and an implied rationale for supervisory consultation are included in the following items:

1. The consulting supervisor is an authority in his/her respective helping profession—a master counselor who is experienced in performing the counselor's work.

2. If consultees are practicing or post-degree counselors, they are accepted as capable professionals by the consulting supervisor. Presumably a selection process has been applied before employment and counselors have been judged competent. If counselors are still in a counselor preparation program, they are accepted as potentially capable counselors. In either case, if the supervisor cannot accept the consultee in the manner described, supervision will be impaired.

3. A compatible and complementary relationship must exist between roles of the supervisor and the counselor if consultation is to succeed. The role of the consulting supervisor is to help the counselor with personal and professional development, competency development, and establishment and maintenance of accountable services and programs. The role of the counselor is to seek and capitalize upon the supervisor's assistance in the achievement of responsible self development. Development through supervision is a joint responsibility, but the central obligation is on the counselor, since self development is the goal. Sometimes, however, the supervisor may need to establish the environment and the attitudinal framework for self development before the supervisory relationship can be effective. If motivation for self development is dormant and the supervisor must assume all the responsibility for direction of the supervisory process, the activity becomes akin to

autocratic instruction and cannot be called supervisory consultation.

4. Consultation in the context of counselor supervision should lead to objectives which are mutually agreed upon by supervisor and counselor. Objectives tend to fall into the four categories of

   a. personal problems which are interfering with the counselor's work,

   b. concerns about professional development,

   c. acquisition of new skills or improvement of existing competencies, and

   d. program development, maintenance, and evaluation.

   To determine which supervisory consultation objectives are pertinent to a given situation, some type of preliminary assessment is needed. Self assessment by the counselor or cooperative assessment by counselor and supervisor are the preferred types if self development is to be encouraged.

5. To accomplish objectives in supervisory consultation, effective strategies must be applied. Some strategies allow the supervisor to remain in the consulting role. In other strategies the supervisor may need to conduct training sessions and other forms of instruction or render appropriate conditions to shift into counseling. Strategies which lead the supervisor out of the consultation activity and into other supervisory activities should be regarded as acceptable but temporary aberrations. A return to consultation should be later accomplished, thus reaffirming consultation as the dominant activity of supervision.

6. Evaluation has been designated as a supervisory activity separate from consultation, and evaluation will be discussed in that context at a later time. While on the topic of consultation, however, its interrelationship with

evaluation should be clarified. The two aspects of supervision are frequently considered antithetical, with consultation being viewed as a threat-free and non-evaluative working relationship with a counselor (Bernard, 1979; Block, 1981; Bloom, 1984; Brown, Pryzwansky, & Schulte, 1987; Galhessich, 1982; Johnston & Gysbers, 1967; Lewis & Lewis, 1983; Stenack & Dye, 1982; Turner, 1982). As employed within supervision, rarely is the consulting activity completely nonevaluative. Supervision, as previously stated, is the function of overseeing the counselor's work. Evaluation is implied in the overseeing function, and is obviously a necessity for accomplishment of the purposes of supervision. Evaluation can and should be used in conjunction with supervisory consultation without raising the counselor's anxiety level enough to hamper supervision.

Whether the supervisor should evaluate the counselor's performance is a practical rather than just a theoretical question. How can the supervisor nurture counselor self-development while concurrently assuring that supervisory purposes are being achieved? If an autocratic or directive stance, which excludes counselor input is adopted, the objective of self-development is sacrificed. If the supervisor is totally nonevaluative in the relationship with a counselor, the situation may be too benign to be effective. An imperfect but realistic compromise is for the consulting supervisor to encourage counselor self-evaluation, to generate cooperative evaluation wherever efficacious, and to judiciously apply some evaluatory procedures on a unilateral basis.

As depicted in Figure 1.2, consultation should be the predominant stance and activity of counselor supervisor. Consultation is the most viable activity of those to be reviewed. It provides an orientation that allows the supervisor to act immediately when situations call for supervisory action.

Counselor Supervision: Counseling

Several areas of conjecture have already been touched upon in this Chapter, and the activity of counseling raises another.

The question is, "Should the counselor supervisor provide counseling to the supervisee?" Chapter 3 presents a school of thought which views counselor supervision as a counseling-like, therapeutic process, however, this viewpoint seems to obfuscate the issue. The question is not how to supervise, but whether supervision should be permitted to revert to counseling, thereby abandoning for the time being the predominant activity of supervisory consultation.

The issue of whether supervisory consultation should be permitted to revert to counseling may be dealt with in the context of two related questions. Question one is, "Does the supervisee ever need counseling, and/or could the supervisee profit from counseling?" Clearly, the rationale upon which counseling is founded gives an affirmative answer to this question. Counseling exists to help individuals with the developmental tasks, stages, and personal adjustment concerns that beset everyone (Blocher, 1966; Gibson & Mitchell, 1986; Hansen, Stevic, & Warner, 1982; Kell & Burow, 1970; Shertzer & Stone, 1980; Sprinthall, 1971). The professional counselor (supervisee) may at times be facing quite stressful events in his or her life which affect job performance, and particularly then the counselor can profit from counseling.

Question two is, "Who should provide counseling to the supervisee and in what situation?" With few exceptions, the supervisor (a master counselor) is the most qualified person in the supervisee's professional environment to provide counseling. Furthermore, the supervisory relationship is by definition the right context for facilitating personal development. The issue is not whether to include counseling in the set of supervisory activities but when and how the supervisor should utilize counseling?

Typically, the supervisor will be engaged in the consulting activity with the supervisee when cues emerge from the supervisee indicating that he/she wishes to discuss a particular concern. When such cues become apparent, the supervisor can follow the counselor's lead. No abrupt changes need to occur in the supervisor-supervisee relationship because establishment of a positive, interpersonal relationship has already been accomplished in consultation. Gradually, the interaction focuses on a concern that is more personal to the counselor and which is outside the defined objectives of consultation, and counseling ensues. Several counseling sessions may be devoted to the concern, or, if extensive treatment is needed, the supervisor can make a referral to another agency or counselor. Assuming that extensive treatment is not usually needed, counseling will be short term in duration and the transition back into consultation can be achieved through the supervisor's adept management of the interaction.

Counselor Supervision:
Training and Instruction

There are few established approaches for training and instruction in counselor supervision, and yet training and instructional activities are two of the more common supervisory procedures. Resulting from the variety of supervisory procedures and differing views over approaches to supervision, Hosford (ACES, 1969, p. 26) stated that

> the only area of agreement, and that for which some research is available, is the consensus that the supervisory process is a learning experience in which the principles of learning apply.

Although this statement was made almost twenty years ago, it is applicable today. This single area of agreement could explain the wide application of training and instruction as a supervisory activity.

Developmental models (Alonso, 1983; Blocher, 1983; Grater, 1985; Hart, 1982; Heppner & Roehlke, 1984; Hess, 1986; Sansbury, 1982; Stoltenberg, 1981; Stoltenberg & Delworth, 1987; Wiley & Ray, 1986) suggest that training and instruction should vary according to the developmental level of the counselor (supervisee). For example, inexperienced counselors prefer that the supervisor give them specific information about how to do counseling. Beginning counselors prefer teaching approaches that emphasize direct (structured) instruction such as didactic presentations, direct observations of the supervisor demonstrating effective counseling, and written materials describing counseling interventions (Borders & Leddick, 1987; Leddick & Dye, 1987).

In contrast, more experienced counselors want less emphasis on the mechanics and tasks of supervision and more emphasis on sharing ideas and thoughts (Borders & Leddick, 1987; Cross & Brown, 1983; Worthington, 1984; Worthington & Stern, 1985). As counselors gain experience and confidence in their counseling skills, their behavior becomes more autonomous, and they take more responsibility for and direct involvement in the supervisory process. They begin to view the supervisor as a consultant or collaborator for a specific case or problem and soon realize the supervisor also learns from the supervisory experience. Additionally experienced counselors prefer discussions of theoretical issues, more responsibility for case conceptualization and collaborative supervisory sessions than do inexperienced counselors (Borders & Leddick, 1987; Heppner & Roehlke, 1984; Leddick & Dye, 1987).

While researchers (Bradley & Richardson, 1987; Hansen, Robins, & Grimes, 1982; Holloway, 1984, Martin & McBride, 1987; Robyak, Goodyear, Prange, & Donham, 1986) have reported that supervision techniques differ, some interventions emerge more frequently than others. For example in teaching basic helping skills, support has been reported for microtraining (Baker, Scofield, Munson, & Clayton, 1983; Forsyth & Ivey, 1980; Ivey, 1980; Richardson & Bradley, 1984), modeling and reinforcement (Akamatsu, 1980; Froehle, Robinson, & Kurpius, 1983; Hosford & Barmann, 1983; Martin & McBride, 1987), role playing and simulation (Akamatsu, 1980; Gladstein & Feldstein, 1983; Scott, Cormier, & Cormier, 1980), video and audio taping (Kagan, Krathwohl, & Miller, 1963; Smith, 1984; Stewart & Johnson, 1986), direct observation (Bernard, 1981; Constantine, 1984; Coopersmith, 1980; Nelson, 1978; Walker, 1985; West, 1984), and case conceptualization (Hulse & Jennings, 1984; Loganbill & Stoltenburg, 1983; Stoltenburg & Delworth, 1987). In addition to learning basic techniques, counselors value support, encouragement, and understanding (Bordin, 1983; Moses & Hardin, 1978; Reising & Daniels, 1983; Worthington, 1984) as well as honest, constructive feedback (Allen, Szollos, & Williams, 1986; Smith, 1984) from their supervisors.

A rationale for effective use of training and instructional activities in the context of supervision should begin with the setting of objectives for these activities within the total framework of supervisory consultation. Strategies would then be selected or constructed to reach the objectives, and they would be of two types:

1. self-managed learning program, and

2. those involving the supervisor as an active trainer.

In a self-managed training program the supervisor remains in a consultative stance and assists the counselor (supervisee) in progressing through the program, whereas strategies of active instruction and training put the supervisor outside the consultation activity. The differentiating criterion between the consultative stance and that of active trainer is counselor input. A shared responsibility for learning, with maximal input from the counselor, characterizes consultation. Conversely, the supervisor, when functioning as an active trainer, carries most of the responsibility, with the flow of information and direction being principally from supervisor to counselor, and with counselor input at a minimum.

When engaged in consultation, the supervisor can digress to engage temporarily in active training and then return to consultation, just as was done with the counseling activity. One can also feasibly be engaged in the consulting activity with a number of individual counselors (supervisees) while concurrently conducting an in-service training program for the group. Determining when and how to use instruction and training versus consultation is a matter of professional judgment. As an alternative to choosing one or the other, the supervisor can alter the character of an instructional program and incorporate some of the advantages of consultation. Counselors' input can be solicited by letting them select instructional goals, by including counselors as peer trainers, and by using counselors own tapes and cases as instructional material.

Counselor Supervision:
Evaluation

The importance of evaluation to the supervisory function has been stressed. Evaluation is essential for accountable supervision and for accountable counseling in both administrative (Beck & Hillmar, 1986; Falvey, 1987; Fink & Kosecoff, 1978; Gilbert, 1982; Lewis & Lewis, 1983; Madaus, Scriven, & Stufflebeam, 1983) and clinical supervision (Borders & Leddick, 1987; Corrigan & Schmidt, 1983; Hart, 1982; Stoltenburg, Solomon, & Ogden, 1986; Stoltenberg, & Delworth, 1987; Tyler & Weaver, 1981). Potential roadblocks in the path of evaluation include lack of skills in performing evaluation (Falvey, 1987; Goodyear & Bradley, 1983; Hansen, Robins, & Grimes, 1982; Lewis & Lewis, 1983), confusion about the compatibility of supervision and evaluation, and anxiety-evoking qualities attributed to evaluation (Dodge, 1982; Yager & Beck, 1985). The first two roadblocks mentioned are easier to overcome than the third. Skills can be acquired through training; a conceptualization of the appropriate relationship between supervisory consultation and evaluation can be clarified, but the debilitating fear associated with evaluation is the most pervasive roadblock. This fear has led to the anti-evaluation syndrome of those who think that more learning and performance can take place if evaluation and its accompanying threat are removed from learning/performance situations. An oversight in anti-evaluation reasoning however is that evaluation itself need not be anxiety-evoking. Rather, the real antecedents of fear are misperceptions about evaluation.

Evaluation was never intended to be a fearful activity. To the contrary, evaluation was meant to be an eagerly sought activity that answers the basic accountability question that should be asked by every professional, "Am I accomplishing my objectives?" The coup in supervision is to manage the evaluation so that perceptions of those being evaluated create positive motivation rather than anxiety.

Several conditions prerequisite for low-threat evaluation are inherent in the consulting guidelines that were proposed previously. The foremost condition is that the targets for evaluation are known to both supervisor and counselor (supervisee), and the counselor has input into selection of these targets. This condition does more to relieve anxiety than any other. Another condition is that the counselor is aware of the evaluative procedures being conducted,and performs some of them (self-evaluations). In a nutshell, evaluation in conjunction with consultation by the supervisor should be performed cooperatively whenever possible (Drapela, 1983; Harvey & Schramske, 1984; Stenack & Dye, 1982). Finally, the goal of evaluation should be perceived as documentation of success in obtaining objectives and the identification of areas for improvement. Evaluation is proactive rather than being aimed at punishing counselors whose work is not reaching objectives.

Whatever evaluative methods the supervisor employs, three things need to be evaluated: the work of each supervisee, helping service programs, and supervision itself. The scope of this task is beyond the capability of any one supervisor, a condition which provides another reason for sharing evaluation with counselors.

Evaluation of each counselor's progress toward objectives is completed most ethically in individual sessions; program evaluation is performed most efficiently by a division of labor among a counseling staff, and evaluation of supervision can be done by the supervisor with feedback from supervisees and superiors. In each of these areas, evaluation is incorporated into the general planning operation. The supervisor and counseling staff plan a program of services geared toward criterion-referenced objectives, and the supervisor prepares a planned program of supervisory activities. Evaluation thus permeates most the supervisor's work.

SUMMARY

Counselor supervision has been defined as the function of overseeing the counselor's work for the purpose of facilitating personal and professional development, improving competencies, and promoting accountability in services and programs. To accomplish these purposes the supervisor engages in the four activities of consultation, counseling, training and instruction, and evaluation. Consultation includes establishment of the objectives and strategies of supervision and is the supervisor's predominant activity. Strategies for consultation may allow the supervisor to remain consistently in the consulting activity, or they may involve the activities of counseling and training/instruction, during which the supervisor digresses temporarily from the consultant stance. Evaluation is another major activity of supervision that is often a companion to consulting and training/instruction.

Counselor supervision has been presented as a professional specialty with a methodology requiring highly developed skills. Successful counseling experience is a necessary but insufficient prerequisite for supervision, and should be supplemented with advanced preparation in supervisory methods.

The importance of supervision to the future of helpgiving services should again be stressed. Counselor supervision is an indispensable component of counselor preparation programs. Coupled with the counselor's self-development process, counselor supervision is a key to accountable helping services and attainment of a counselor's professional potential. Saying that counselor supervision can be one of the most instrumental factors affecting future development of the helping service professions is not an exaggeration. Furthermore, counselor supervision can have a similarly facilitative effect on counselor-offered services in other disciplines.

REFERENCES

Abels, P., & Murphy, M. (1981). *Administration in human services: A normative systems approach.* Englewood Cliffs, NJ: Prentice-Hall.

Akamatsu, T.J. (1980). The use of role-play and simulation techniques in the training of psychotherapy. In A.K. Hess (Ed.), *Psychotherapy supervision: Theory, research and practice.* New York: John Wiley.

Allen, G., Szollos, S., & Williams, B. (1986). Doctoral students' comparative evaluations of best and worst psychotherapy supervision. *Professional Psychology: Research and Practice, 17,* 91-99.

Alonso, A. (1983). A developmental theory of psychodynamic supervision. *The Clinical Supervisor, 1,* 23-36.

Arnold, D.L. (1962). Counselor education as responsible self development. *Counselor Education and Supervision, 1,* 185-92.

Association for Counselor Education and Supervision, Committee on Counselor Effectiveness. (1969). Commitment to Action in Supervision: Report of a National Survey of Counselor Supervision.

Austin, M. (1981). *Supervisory management for the human services.* Englewood Cliffs, N.J.: Prentice-Hall.

Baker, S., Scofield, M., Munson, W., & Clayton, L. (1983). Comparative effects of training basic counseling competencies through brief microskills practice versus mental practice. *Counselor Education and Supervision, 23,* 71-83.

Beck, A.C., & Hillmar, E.D. (1986). *Positive management practices.* San Francisco, CA: Jossey-Bass.

Becker, H.S., & Carper, J.W. (1956). Development of identification with an occupation. *American Journal of Sociology, 41,* 289-298.

Bernard, J.M. (1979). Supervisory training: A discrimination model. *Counselor Education and Supervision, 19,* 60-8.

Bernard, J.M. (1981). In service training for clinical supervisors. *Professional Psychology, 12,* 740-8.

Bernard, J.M. (1987). In L.D. Borders and G.R. Leddick, *Handbook of counseling supervision.* Washington, D.C.: Association for Counselor Education and Supervision.

Black, J. (1975). *The basics of supervisory management: Mastering the art of effective supervision.* New York: McGraw-Hill.

Blocher, D.H. (1966). *Developmental counseling.* New York: Ronald Press.

Blocher, D.H. (1983). Toward a cognitive developmental approach to counseling supervision. *The Counseling Psychologist, 11,* 27-34.

Block, P. (1981). *Flawless consulting.* San Diego, CA: University Associates.

Bloom, B.L. (1984). *Community mental health: A general introduction (2nd ed.).* Belmont, CA: Brooks/Cole.

Borders, L., & Leddick, G. (1987). *Handbook of counseling supervision.* Alexandria, VA: Association for Counselor Education and Supervision.

Bordin, E.S. (1983). A working alliance-based model of supervision. *The Counseling Psychologist, 11,* 35-42.

Bradley, L., & Richardson, B. (1987). Trends in practicum and internship requirements: A national study. *The Clinical Supervisor, 5,* 97-105.

Brown, D., Pryzwansky, W., & Schulte, A. (1987). *Psychological Consultation.* Boston: Allyn and Bacon.

Constantine, S. (1984). Live supervision of supervision in family therapy. *Journal of Marital and Family Therapy, 10,* 95-97.

Coopersmith, E. (1980). Expanding uses of the telephone in family therapy. *Family Process, 19,* 411-7.

Corey, G., Corey, M., & Callanan, P. (1987). *Issues and ethics in the helping professions.* Pacific Grove, CA: Brooks/Cole Publishing Company.

Cormier, L., & Bernard, J. (1982). Ethical and legal responsibilities of clinical supervisors. *Personnel and Guidance Journal, 60,* 486-90.

Corrigan, J.D., & Schmidt, L. (1983). Development and validation of revisions in the Counselor Rating Form. *Journal of Counseling Psychology, 30,* 64-75.

Cross, D.G., & Brown, D. (1983). Counselor supervision as a function of trainee experience: Analysis of specific behaviors. *Counselor Education and Supervision 22,* 333-341.

Dodge, J. (1982). Reducing supervisee anxiety: A cognitive-behavioral approach. *Counselor Education and Supervision, 22,* 55-60.

Drapela, V. (1983). Counseling consultation and supervision: A visual clarification of their relationship. *Personnel and Guidance Journal, 62,* 158-162.

Ekstein, R., & Wallerstein, R.S. (1958). *The teaching and learning of psychotherapy.* New York: Basic Books.

Falvey, J. (1987). *Handbook of administrative supervision.* Alexandria, VA: Association for Counselor Education and Supervision.

Fink, A., & Kosecoff, T. (1978). *An evaluation primer.* Washington, D.C.: Capitol Publications.

Forsyth, D., & Ivey, A. (1980). Microtraining: An approach to differential supervision. In A.K. Hess (Ed.), *Psychotherapy supervision: Theory, research and practice.* New York: Wiley.

Froehle, T., Robinson, S., & Kurpius, D. (1983). Enhancing the effects of modeling through role-play practice. *Counselor Education and Supervision, 22,* 197-207.

Galhessich, J. (1982). *The profession and practice of consultation.* San Francisco, CA: Jossey-Bass.

Gibson, R., & Mitchell, M. (1986). *Introduction to counseling and guidance* (2nd ed.). New York: Macmillan.

Gilbert, T.F. (1982). A question of performance—Part I: The probe model. *Training and Developmental Journal, 36,* 20-30.

Gladstein, G., & Feldstein, J.C. (1983). Using film to increase counselor empathic experiences. *Counselor Education and Supervision, 23,* 125-32.

Glass, G.V. (1972). The many faces of educational accountability. *Phi Delta Kappan, 10,* 636-9.

Goodyear, R., & Bradley, F. (1983). Theories of counselor supervision: Points of convergence and divergence. *The Counseling Psychologist, 11,* 59-67.

Grater, H.A. (1985). Stages in psychotherapy supervision: From therapy skills to skilled therapist. *Professional Psychology, 16,* 605-10.

Hansen, J., Robins, T., & Grimes, J. (1982). Review of research on practicum supervision. *Counselor Education and Supervision, 22,* 15-24.

Hansen, J., Stevic, R., & Warner, R. (1982). *Counseling theory and process.* Boston, MA: Allyn & Bacon.

Hart, D.H., & Prince, D.J. (1970). Role conflict for school counselors: Training versus job demands. *Personnel and Guidance Journal, 48,* 374-80.

Hart, G. (1982). *The process of clinical supervision.* Baltimore, MD: University Park Press.

Harvey, D., & Schramske, T. (1984). Effective supervision and consultation: A model for the development of functional supervision and consultation programs. *Counselor Education and Supervision, 23,* 197-204.

Heppner, P., & Roehlke, H. (1984). Differences among supervisees at different levels of training: Implications for a developmental model of supervision. *Journal of Counseling Psychology, 31,* 76-90.

Hess, A.K. (1986). Growth in supervision: Stages of supervisee and supervisor development. In F.W. Kaslow (Ed.), *Supervision and training: Models, dilemmas and challenges.* New York: Haworth.

Holahan, W., & Galassi, J.P. (1986). Toward accountability in supervision: A single case illustration. *Counselor Education and Supervision, 25,* 166-73.

Holloway, E. (1984). Outcome evaluation in supervision research. *The Counseling Psychologist, 12,* 167-74.

Hosford, R., & Barmann, B. (1983). A social learning approach to counselor supervision. *The Counseling Psychologist, 11,* 51-8.

Hulse, D., & Jennings, M.L. (1984). Toward comprehensive case conceptualizations in counseling: A visual integrative technique. *Professional Psychology, 15,* 251-9.

Humes, C.W. (1972). Accountability: A boon to guidance. *Personnel and Guidance Journal, 51,* 21-6.

Ivey, A.E. (1980). *Counseling and psychotherapy: Skills, theories and practice.* Englewood Cliffs, NJ: Prentice-Hall.

Johnston, J.A., & Gysbers, N.C. (1967). Essential characteristics of a supervisory relationship in counseling practicum. *Counselor Education and Supervision, 6,* 335-40.

Kagan, N., Krathwhol, D., & Miller, R. (1963). Simulated recall in therapy using videotape: A case study. *Journal of Counseling Psychology, 10,* 237-43.

Kell, B.L., & Burow, J.M. (1970). *Developmental Counseling and Therapy.* Boston, MA: Houghton Mifflin.

Leddick, G., & Dye, H.A. (1987). Effective supervision as portrayed by trainee expectations and preferences. *Counselor Education and Supervision, 27,* 139-55.

Lessinger, L.M. (1970). *Every kid a winner. Accountability in Education.* New York: Simon and Schuster.

Lewis, J.A., & Lewis, M.D. (1983). *Management of human service programs.* Monterey, CA: Brooks/Cole.

Loganbill, C., Hardy, E., & Delworth, U. (1982). Supervision: A conceptual model. *The Counseling Psychologist, 10,* 3-42.

Loganbill, C., & Stoltenberg, C. (1983). The case conceptualization format: A training device for practicum. *Counselor Education and Supervision, 22,* 235-41.

Madaus, G., Scriven, M., & Stufflebeam, D. (1983). *Evaluation methods: Viewpoint on educational and human service evaluation.* Boston, MA: Kluwer-Nijhoff Publishing.

Martin, G.E., & McBride, M. (1987). The results of the implementation of a professional supervision model on counselor trainee behavior. *Counselor Education and Supervision, 27,* 155-67.

Moses, H., & Hardin, J. (1978). A relationship approach to counselor supervision in agency settings. In J. Boyd, *Counselor Supervision.* Muncie, IN: Accelerated Development.

Mueller, W.J., & Kell, B.L. (1972). *Coping with conflict: Supervising counselors and psychotherapists.* New York: Appleton-Century-Crofts.

Nelson, G. (1978). Psychotherapy supervision from the trainee's point of view: A survey of preferences. *Professional Psychology, 9,* 539-50.

Patterson, C.H. (1983). A client-centered approach to supervision. *The Counseling Psychologist, 11*, 21-5.

Pulvino, D.J., & Sanborn, M.P. (1972). Feedback and accountability. *Personnel and Guidance Journal, 51*, 15-20.

Reising, G.N., & Daniels, M.H. (1983). A study of Hogan's model of counselor development and supervision. *Journal of Counseling Psychology, 30*, 235-44.

Riccio, A.C. (1961). The counselor educator and the guidance supervisor: Graduate training and occupational mobility. *Counselor Education and Supervision, 1*, 10-7.

Riccio, A.C. (1966). Counselor educators and guidance supervisors: A second look at graduate training. *Counselor Education and Supervision, 5*, 73-79.

Richardson, B.K., & Bradley, L.J. (1984). Microsupervision: A skill development model for training clinical supervisors. *The Clinical Supervisor, 2*, 43-54.

Richardson, B., & Bradley, L. (1986). *Community agency counseling: An emerging speciality within counselor preparation programs.* Washington, DC: American Association for Counseling and Development.

Robyak, J., Goodyear, R., Prange, M., & Donham, G. (1986). Effects of gender, supervision, and presenting problems on practicum students' preference for interpersonal power bases. *Journal of Counseling Psychology, 33*, 159-63.

Sansbury, D. (1982). Developmental supervision from a skills perspective. *The Counseling Psychologist, 10*, 53-57.

Scott, A.J., Cormier, W.J., & Cormier, L.S. (1980). Effects of covert modeling and written material on the acquisition of a counseling strategy. *Counselor Education and Supervision, 19*, 259-69.

Shertzer, B., & Stone, S. (1980). *Fundamentals of counseling (3rd ed.).* Boston, MA: Houghton Mifflin.

Simon, S. (Ed.). (1985). *Managing finances, personnel, and information in human services.* New York: Haworth Press.

Slavin, S. (Ed.). (1985). *Social administration: The management of the social services.* New York: Haworth Press.

Smith, H.D. (1984). Moment to moment counseling process feedback using a dual channel audiotape recording. *Counselor Education and Supervision, 23*, 346-9.

Sprinthall, N.A. (1971). *Guidance for Human Growth.* New York: Van Nostrand Reinhold.

Stefflre, B. (1964). What price professionalism? *Personnel and Guidance Journal, 42,* 654-59.

Stenack, R.J., & Dye, H.A. (1982). Behavioral descriptions of counselor supervision roles. *Counselor Education and Supervision, 21,* 295-304.

Stewart, R.M., & Johnson, J.C. (1986). Written versus videotaped precounseling training of clients for counseling. *Counselor Education and Supervision, 25,* 197-210.

Stoltenberg, C. (1981). Approaching supervision from a developmental perspective: The counselor-complexity model. *Journal of Counseling Psychology, 28,* 59-65.

Stoltenberg, C., & Delworth, U. (1987). *Supervising counselors and therapists: A developmental approach.* San Francisco: Jossey-Bass.

Stoltenberg, C., Solomon, G., & Ogden, L. (1986). Comparing supervisee and supervisor initial perceptions of supervision: Do they agree? *The Clinical Supervisor, 4,* 53-61.

Tennyson, W., & Strom, S. (1986). Beyond professional standards: Developing responsibleness. *Journal of Counseling and Development, 64,* 298-302.

Turner, A.N. (1982). Consulting is more than giving advice. *Harvard Business Review, 60,* 120-9.

Tyler, J., & Weaver, S. (1981). Evaluating the clinical supervisee: A survey of practices in graduate training programs. *Professional Psychology, 12,* 434-7.

Upchurch, D.W. (1985). Ethical standards and the supervisory process. *Counselor Education and Supervision, 75,* 90-8.

Walker, J.R. (1985). Group facilitation supervision through a one-way mirror. *Journal of Counseling and Development, 63,* 578-80.

Webster's Third New International Dictionary. (1981). Springfield, MA: G & C Merriam.

West, J.D. (1984). Utilizing simulated families and live supervision to demonstrate skill development of family therapists. *Counselor Education and Supervision, 24,* 17-27.

Wiley, M., & Ray, P. (1986). Counseling supervision by developmental level. *Journal of Counseling Psychology, 33,* 439-45.

Worthington, E.L., Jr. (1984). Empirical investigation of supervision of counselors as they gain experience. *Journal of Counseling Psychology, 31,* 63-75.

Worthington, W., & Stern, A. (1985). Effects of supervisor and supervisee level and gender on the supervisory relationship. *Journal of Counseling Psychology, 32,* 252-62.

Wrenn, C.G. (1962). The Counselor in a Changing World. *American Personnel and Guidance Journal.*

Wrenn, C.G. (1973). *The world of the contemporary counselor.* Boston: Houghton Mifflin.

Yager, G., & Beck, T.D. (1985). Beginning practicum: It only hurt until I laughed! *Counselor Education and Supervision, 25,* 149-57.

Zerface, J.P., & Cox, W.H. (1971). School counselors, leave home. *Personnel and Guidance Journal, 49,* 371-75.

Chapter 2

SUPERVISION:
AN INTERPERSONAL
RELATIONSHIP

Mary Deck, Ph.D.

Jim Morrow, Ph.D.

As the title suggests, this chapter focuses on the inter-personal nature of the supervisory relationship. Further, supervision is viewed as a helping relationship which parallels counseling and consulting relationships. No distinction is intended or made between clinical supervision of counselors-in-training or administrative supervision of credentialed counselors unless specifically mentioned.

Loganbill, Hardy, and Delworth (1982) defined supervision as "an intensive, interpersonally focused, one-to-one relationship in which one person is designated to facilitate the development of therapeutic competence in the other person" (p.4). Within the supervisory relationship, the supervisor struggles to discover how to assist the supervisee in remaining open to his/her own experiences (Altucher, 1967). The supervisor strives to enable the supervisee to "view all of himself—needs, conflicts, life experiences—as potentially helpful to his clients" (Kell & Mueller, 1966, p. 18). Learning and growing as a counselor "is both an emotional and an intellectual experience, and of the two, the emotional part is the most crucial. The important learning occurs in situations where one's feelings are engaged" (Altucher, 1967, p. 165). Learning to be a counselor is accomplished through learning about one's own feelings, emotions, and traumas rather than through didactic discussion about fear, confusion, hope, and hopelessness (Arbuckle, 1963). The supervisory relationship is the vehicle through which such personalized learning occurs (Loganbill et al., 1982).

Within the supervisory relationship, the focus is not only on the activities of counseling and supervision but on feelings which emerge within the counseling and supervisory relationships (Bordin, 1983; Eckstein & Wallerstein, 1958; Moses & Hardin, 1978; Patterson, 1983). Moreover, "experiencing of the *relationship itself* can be the significant learning experience" (Loganbill et al., 1982, p. 29) as the relationship is a potent source of learning about the complexity of human interactions. The mix of attitudes, conflicts, anxieties, and dynamics which intensify the supervisor's and supervisee's encounters within the relationship is the grist of the learning mill. From the previous discussion, one can clearly deduct that the power of this intense, one-to-one relationship is considered by a number of experienced supervisors/authors to be the critical aspect of supervision.

Supervisees also attach much importance to the interpersonal relationship in supervision. Hutt, Scott, and King (1983) reported supervisees' perceptions of positive and negative supervisory experiences. Their findings support the significance of the supervisory relationship. Supervisees who report negative supervisory experiences perceive their relationship with the supervisor to be the source of their negative feelings. They report that learning is hampered by the negative atmosphere within the relationship, and they find themselves feeling powerless and seeking ways to minimize risks. While supervisees report that some content learning occurs in negative experiences, it is clouded by negative process learning. Supervisors' behaviors in negative supervision are characterized by mistrust, disrespect, and lack of honest self-disclosure.

Conversely, supervisees report that in positive experiences supervisors offer support, encourage exploration of behaviors, attitudes and feelings, and openly discuss conflict and work toward resolution. In positive experiences, supervisees' mistakes are not regarded as failures and self-worth is not jeopardized. Supervisor self-disclosure appears to be a link in moving the relationship when the supervisee is inhibited, resistant, or conflicted. From supervisees' reports, the qualities of warmth, acceptance, understanding, respect, and trust are exhibited by supervisors in positive experiences.

CONDITIONS OF THE SUPERVISORY RELATIONSHIP

For the supervisee, supervision entails being in a "you are up; I am down" (Rioch, 1980) relationship. The relationship is uneven from the onset. Unlike the client who may choose to be in a therapeutic relationship, the supervisee is often in a supervisory relationship because of educational and/or professional requirements. This "have to" circumstance, with its accompanying evaluative component and status hierarchy, exacerbates the intensity of the relationship for the supervisee. Just as the supervisee embarks warily into the unknown of the relationship, so does the supervisor enter the relationship knowing that "no supervisor is invulnerable to threat from those he supervises" (Kell & Mueller, 1966, p. 101). Both supervisor and supervisee enter the relationship with fears, hopes, and expectations (Hart, 1982; Mueller & Kell, 1972). Considering the very human nature of the supervisory process, no surprise is obtained by the intensity of the relationship being frequently iterated (e.g., Eckstein & Wallerstein, 1958; Loganbill et al., 1982; Moskowitz & Rupert, 1983).

To place two persons from unequal positions into an intense, personal relationship requires that the supervisory relationship be built upon the basic core conditions of all helping relationships—empathic understanding, genuineness, respect, and concreteness (Blocher, 1983; Moses & Hardin, 1978; Patterson, 1983). Moreover, to fully realize the potential of this intense interaction requires the necessary integration of the two universal components of supervisory relationships—

support and confrontation (Marshall & Confer, 1980). This is clearly pointed out in Mueller and Kell's (1972) statement; "if conflict is to be encountered actively and with optimism [confrontation]—then that relationship must be founded in trust, openness, warmth, and honest collaboration [support]" (p. 7).

Moses and Hardin (1978) identified facilitative and action-oriented relationship conditions within supervision. Under facilitative conditions, they listed the core conditions of empathy, respect, and concreteness; action-oriented conditions are genuineness, confrontation, and immediacy. Although these facilitative and action-oriented conditions are most often associated with counseling relationships, they apply equally in supervisory relationship.

Empathy, Respect, and Concreteness

Empathy involves communicating to the supervisee an understanding of her/his subjective frame of reference, e.g., conveying an understanding of the supervisee's fear of being unable to respond appropriately to a client's tears or of the self-doubt experienced by the supervisee when meeting with a reluctant client. The supervisor's acknowledgement and verbal expression of the difficult struggle and often painful process, in which the supervisee must engage to grow and learn, communicates empathy and understanding (Blocher, 1983). A supervisor's empathy with the supervisee, according to Moses and Hardin (1978), parallels what Rogers (1957) named the "as if" experience; that is empathy is understanding the super-visee's world "as if" it were the supervisor's, but without ever losing the "as if" quality.

Respect conveys the unconditional acceptance of the supervisee as a person and the belief that the supervisee can work through the anxieties, discomforts, and difficulties of learning to gain competence in counseling, e.g., accepting the supervisee's anger and disappointment when a client cancels an appointment or accepting the underlying fears of the super-visee's questions regarding the values of taping and transcripts. Through awareness of the supervisee's style of presentation and developmental level, by careful attention to the supervisee's experiences in the counseling process, and through recognition of the care and concern the supervisee feels toward the client, the supervisor communicates respect (Blocher, 1983).

Concreteness is the specific expression of feelings, behaviors and experiences relative to the supervisee, e.g., sharing with a supervisee an observation that he/she was smiling at the client when the client related a painful situation or noting that the supervisee's relaxed posture and natural, steady voice tone seemed to calm the client. Providing concrete, honest feedback requires empathy and respect as concomitant conditions. Being concrete provides clear, specific information which the supervisee can utilize to gain greater self-awareness, to maintain effective behaviors and attitudes, and to implement needed change. Through these three dimensions, empathy, respect, and concreteness, the supervisor expresses care and interest in the supervisee as a developing professional and as a person.

Genuineness, Confrontation, and Immediacy

The action-oriented conditions—genuineness, confrontation, and immediacy—involve the supervisor in helping the supervisee to develop a deeper understanding of the counseling process and to act on this understanding (Moses & Hardin, 1978). Action-oriented conditions are optimally employed once the relationship is well grounded in mutual trust and open communication, resulting from the facilitative conditions of empathy, respect, and concreteness.

Genuineness requires that the supervisor be him/herself without playing roles or games with the supervisee. The supervisor need not feel compelled to spontaneously share and tell all; potentially harmful comments need not be communicated (Moses & Hardin, 1978). The supervisor should be guided by an understanding of the supervisee and sincere concern for his/her growth. For example, the supervisor may share a past success in order to assist the supervisee, but such sharing is not appropriate if it is a hidden power play or an attempt at one-upmanship.

In confrontation, the supervisor shares his/her perceptions of incongruence in the feelings, attitudes, or behaviors of the supervisee in order to assist the supervisee to develop awareness of such incongruence. Confrontation should arise from the supervisor's desire to help the supervisee gain self-understanding and assume responsibility for change. On the other hand, confrontation is not appropriate when it meets the supervisor's need to punish, criticize, or gain power over the supervisee. A caring and professional invitation to self-explore distortions and discrepancies will be better received than a forced or coerced directive to self-dissect one's work. For example, a timely confrontation may be to stop a video tape at a point where the supervisee's behavior is flirtatious. The supervisee's viewing of the concrete behavior provides the supervisor an opportune situation for inviting the supervisee to consider how his/her behavior may be impacting the client. Thus, the supervisor assists the supervisee in discerning how his/her behavior may influence the client-counselor relationship. It must be noted that assessment of the supervisee's readiness for confrontation is crucial to its effective utilization.

Immediacy is focusing on the "here and now," the present interactions between the supervisor and supervisee. A supervisee may experience difficulties in relationship to clients and recreate similar dynamics in his/her interactions with the supervisor. This mirroring or "parallel process" (Hart, 1982) offers the astute supervisor the opportunity to employ immediacy, thereby assisting the supervisee in resolving difficulties with clients through the examination of the corresponding supervisory interaction. Immediacy also may be an appropriate focus when the supervisory relationship appears to be stalled or at an impasse (Mueller & Kell, 1972). For example, a supervisee who doubts the supervisor's empathy and trustworthiness may express his/her doubts through a questioning of the value of empathy. The aware supervisor might wonder if this statement has implications for the supervisory relationship. Using immediacy, the supervisor responds and openly asks the supervisee whether he/she is experiencing doubts about the supervisor's understanding of the supervisee. Immediacy is a powerful learning tool which can assist the supervisee to more fully comprehend interpersonal dynamics.

Using confrontation or immediacy demands that the supervisor also incorporate the dimensions of empathy, respect, concreteness, and genuineness within the focus of the current interaction. As with confrontation, the timeliness and utilization of immediacy is chosen to serve the supervisee and not the supervisor.

Qualities of Supervisors

In addition to the core relationship conditions, characterization of good supervision includes descriptions of the supervisor as nonthreatening, tactful, nonauthoritarian, supportive, understanding, accepting, and expressive of confidence in the supervisee (Miller & Oetting, 1966). On the other hand, poor supervision is characterized by supervisors who are biased, rigid, domineering, critical, and defensive. Similarly, citings of positive supervisor characteristics include the following: potency, courage, sense of timing, sense of humor, capacity for intimacy, openness to fantasy and imagination, and consideration (Loganbill et al., 1982); ability to create a relaxed atmosphere (Bordin, 1983); a willingness to examine one's own attitudes and feelings, and a willingness to consult when feeling ineffective or dissatisfied with the supervisory process (Hawthorne, 1975); an assumption of interest and capability on the part of the supervisee (Altucher, 1967); and a strong commitment to the growth and development of the supervisee (Blocher, 1983).

SOURCES OF SUPERVISEE ANXIETY

The supervisee enters the relationship both desiring to change and fearing change. Those changes required for a supervisee to grow and develop as a counselor create anxiety—that common, naturally occurring phenomenon prevalent among supervisees. Supervisee anxiety can be generated by any number of issues which affect the dynamics of the supervisory relationship. For example, all of the following can impinge on the supervisory relationship: the supervisee's questions, fears, and uncertainties relative to starting in a training or employment position; irrational thoughts pertaining to whether he/she will be competent and gain others' approval; and the concerns stemming from being in a subordinate role to the supervisor. Discussions of anxieties relative to these topics are presented in the following sections.

Beginner's Quandaries

Anxiety is a pervasive state of being for supervisees who are beginning practica or internships and for supervisees beginning employment or moving to a different employment setting (e.g., Eckstein & Wallerstein, 1958; Hart, 1982; Schmidt, 1979). Supervisees are adult learners who have habitual, ingrained patterns of behavior. They have been independent and accustomed to autonomy. Some supervisees come from previous settings in which they enjoyed recognition and respect, and often were in positions of authority. Therefore, coming into a relationship where the focus is on acquiring new learning and relinquishing autonomy and independence is very threatening to most supervisees (Kadushin, 1968).

The unknown which surrounds new experiences precipitates anxious feelings, as does the "grapevine" information which quickly spreads through training and agency networks (Cohen, 1980). Supervisees begin to hear varying tales regarding supervisors and supervision experiences. Institutional myths surround supervision and are passed from one group of supervisees to the next. Testimonials or comments ranging from "your every move is watched from behind a little hidden room" to "supervision changed my life" create bewildering, frightening and confusing images for incoming supervisees.

New supervisees have concerns related to the logistics of when and where client contact will begin and who clients will be. Time and family commitment issues loom as the supervisees engage in the demands of professional expectations and responsibilities. Questions related to supervision are presented: How skilled is the supervisor? Who is the supervisor as a person? How will the relationship develop? What will be the subsequent evaluation by the supervisor? Beginning trainees have specific fears over such skills as how to begin interviews, what to do when a client does not talk or talks incessantly, and how to reschedule appointments. Global anxiety, even more frightening and consuming, is generated by fears over competence and ability to relate with and assist clients.

A humorous, albeit exaggerated, perspective of how beginning trainee anxiety relates to competency and intimacy issues is presented by Yager and Beck (1985). Through a series of short vignettes, the authors illustrated that anxieties are part of the normal development of counselors-in-training. For example, one of the competency-related vignettes, "Silence Is Not Golden" (p. 153), follows, pointing out the supervisee's terrified over-reaction to silence.

A first interview

> **CLIENT:** Well, I was on my way to visit a friend in Canada. I think it was, uh . . . [pause for 10 seconds as client stares glumly at the floor].

> **COUNSELOR:** Could it be Toronto or Montreal?

> **CLIENT:** No, I was trying to remember how it was that I met Diane. Let's see . . . [pause for 5 seconds].

> **COUNSELOR:** Maybe it was at a campground on the way, or in a tavern?

One of the present authors (M. Deck) utilizes these vignettes with counselors-in-training through role play. Supervisees laugh and release tension as they identify with the situations, and, subsequently, they begin to share their own anxiety stories.

Credentialed counselors as new supervisees in an employment setting have specific concerns related to clientele, caseload, case management procedures, referral sources, and administrative hierarchies. Supervisees' general concerns relate to roles, expectations, the skill of the supervisor, and adjustment within an already established environment.

Performance and Approval Anxiety

Supervisees' anxieties are often centered in concerns related to evaluation and others' perceptions of them. Dodge (1982) identified two types of supervisee anxiety, performance or competence anxiety and approval or respect anxiety. Some commonly held irrational beliefs relate to competence and approval anxiety: "I must always be a perfect counselor. If not, I am a failure," and/or "I must have my supervisor's approval. If I don't, it's just more evidence that I'm not a good counselor" (Dodge, p. 58). Other irrational beliefs relate to supervisees' anxiety through their emotional responses to clients and may be expressed as anger at a client, e.g., "The client ought to do as I suggest"; boredom with a client, e.g., "It's awful that this person is so uninteresting"; or, guilt related to a client, e.g., "I don't like this client and I should" (Schmidt, 1979).

To combat anxiety, supervisees mobilize coping mechanisms and defense patterns. Dodge (1982) offered the following examples of defensive strategies supervisees employ to protect themselves.

1. Silence or hesitation. Silence is a response utilized when the supervisee fears being wrong or not being respected and heard. Silence or hesitation is also a way to maintain a low profile and avoid possible rejection or the appearance of incompetence.

2. Intellectualization. Discussing tangential issues or theoretical issues is a method for appearing to be involved in supervision without taking personal risks.

3. Anger or aggression. This response pattern may result when the supervisee interprets negative feedback as an evaluation of self-worth.

4. Fear compounded by anxiety. The supervisee responds to a basic, original fear, e.g., taping a session, and exacerbates the fear with catastrophizing the outcome.

5. Termination. An extreme defensive behavior is to terminate supervision, drop out of the training program or leave the profession.

Supervisees who cling to irrational beliefs and maintain their defensive patterns create a self-defeating cycle, decreasing their ability to improve skills, to concentrate and reason, and to fulfill performance responsibilities to clients (Dodge, 1982).

Dominance Anxiety

The supervisee enters the supervisory relationship in a "you are up; I am down" stance (Rioch, 1980). The supervisor's dominant position within the relationship can stir anxieties in the supervisee relative to various issues, such as evaluation (Hart, 1982; Robiner, 1982), sexual attraction (Robiner, 1982; Rozsnafszky, 1979), and dependency (Rioch, 1980).

Through evaluation, the supervisor's power has far reaching, anxiety producing implications for the supervisee. For the counselor-in-training, anxiety may be intensely focused on immediate outcomes of the supervisor's evaluation, e.g., assessment of skill levels with present clients, assignment of a course grade, or recommendations for continuation or termination of a program of study. Trainees are also concerned with the future implications of the supervisor's evaluation for recommendations for advanced study, licensure and certification requirements, and references for employment. Credentialed supervisees experience anxiety related to evaluation in terms of salary increases, promotions and advancement within the profession, as well as collegial, peer assessment of ability and skills.

Issues related to sex—attraction, harassment and liaisons— are a source of anxiety in supervisory relationships, as they are in all human relationships. The emotional dominance a supervisor wields over a supervisee can increase anxiety if the supervisor attempts to gratify sexual needs through the supervisory relationship (Rozsnafszky, 1979). Rozsnafszky described sexual behaviors in male and female supervisors resulting in "psychonoxious supervision," i.e., supervision in which immature supervisors meet their own needs rather than fostering the growth and change of supervisees. Sexual behavior categories of male supervisors include the Teddy Bear, Macho Mouth, The Fox, Dale Carnegie Touchers, and the Super Guru; female categories are Daisy Miller, Beauty Unaware, Big Mother, and Seductive Mother. An example of the immature male supervisor is the Teddy Bear, who is the least dangerous of the male types according to Rozsnafszky. The Teddy Bear primarily supervises women on whom he develops adolescent crushes. He appears the gentleman, while maintaining flirtatious behavior to meet his need for conquest. The female counterpart to the Teddy Bear is Daisy Miller, who uses her innocent, although seductive, flirtatious behavior to get what she wants. Rozsnafszky emphasized that the emotional power a supervisor holds over a supervisee requires that maturity and integrity be essential characteristics of the supervisor.

As a supervisee attempts to reduce the anxiety created by dependency in the "you are up, I'm down" stance, he/she may employ a number of methods to achieve balance in the relationship. Rioch (1980) offered the following retaliatory strategies used by the supervisee to secure balance. The supervisee may note errors in supervision, report lack of success in utilizing the supervisor's suggestions, or act passive and uninvolved to reflect his/her perception of the ineffectiveness of the supervisor. Another supervisee may deal with the anxiety by overestimating the power of the supervisor, hence "pairing" with the supervisor and adopting the illusory belief that without the supervisor the learning and outcomes would not be as productive. A likely response for the supervisee who enjoys the dependency/"I'm down" role is to stay protected by relinquishing responsibility to the supervisor. To counteract dependency, a supervisee may choose fight/flight and either employ devious, sulky, and combative tactics or flee through the avoidance of confrontation. An example of a devious fighting strategy may be the supervisee who belittles the qualifications of the supervisor to the client, while the flight strategy might be the supervisee's scheduling of a client when supervision is scheduled in an attempt to delay a possible confrontation with the supervisor.

SUPERVISOR ANXIETY

Anxiety is not the sole province of the supervisee; supervisors, too, suffer anxiety. Supervisory anxiety can be attributed to various sources, including the need to be loved and admired, discomfort with competition and evaluation, personal loneliness, unresolved former stresses in supervision, and unresolved tension between the supervisor and the institution (Alonso, 1983; Hart, 1982). Hess (1986) proposed a three-stage model of supervisor development in which supervisor anxiety prevails in the beginning stage. The new supervisor has been found to have difficulties with supervisee resistance, designing interventions, understanding cases, and knowledge of research and techniques (McColley & Baker, 1982).

A novice supervisor often faces abrupt role change status in a relatively short period of time and may have difficulty shifting gears (Hart, 1982; Hess, 1986). Moving from counselor to supervisor, or from supervising in one setting to another, or from being graduate student to supervisor may cause the beginning supervisor to give way to feelings of insecurity regarding competence and preparation for the newly acquired responsibilities. Lack of experience and training combine to present issues for new supervisors regarding expectations, authority, and evaluation. Typical reactions might be "I'm still just learning myself"; "I have no training to be a supervisor"; "I'm too inexperienced to be a supervisor"; "I don't feel comfortable in the role of master counselor or expert"; "I've never supervised in an agency setting before."

Fresh from the ranks of graduate education or having just shifted from direct client service to supervision, the new supervisor may closely identify with the supervisee (Styczynski, 1980). Styczynski suggested that such identification may result in tendencies to be overly supportive and to hesitate to confront. On the other hand, the supervisor may become rigid and demanding in an effort to separate him/herself from the supervisee. Therefore, a beginning supervisor may have diffi-culty setting realistic expectations for either him/herself or the supervisee or both. Expectations may be too stringent creating frustration and disappointment in both parties or may be too low, thus limiting the supervisee's learning. Similarly, it may be safer for a beginner to stay with concrete techniques and approaches rather than to explore process and interpersonal concerns in the relationship (Hess, 1986).

A supervisee's expertise, advanced knowledge, varied life experiences and/or high level of personal integration can threaten and arouse anxiety within a supervisor (Hart, 1982). A very intimidating experience can be to supervise a person who can draw from more clinical or life experiences than oneself. The supervisor may react by raising standards, failing or ceasing to reward performance, and feeling envious. Equally as intimidating is the supervisee who is defensive, seductive, or verbally persuasive. Each of these behaviors may elicit a supervisor's anxieties.

Anxiety may revolve around motivations prompting one to be a supervisor. Needs for authority and control and to be "loved, admired, sought after, validated, and even feared" (Alonso, 1983, p. 28) increase the likelihood of a supervisor meeting personal needs within the relationship; thus, creating anxiety for the supervisor and supervisee. A beginning supervisor may foster his/her own anxiety striving to achieve an identity, especially if seeking to be known as the "most liked," "most difficult," or "most available" supervisor (Styczynski, 1980).

A beginning supervisor whose experience includes extensive client contact may have difficulty with the third person perspective required of the supervisor; subsequently, supervision may initially seem less rewarding than direct service (Styczynski, 1980). The supervisor may become disappointed with supervision and feel impatient and frustrated with the setbacks and fluctuations in a supervisee's progress (Hart, 1982).

On a more optimistic note, Styczynski (1980) pointed out that new supervisors can impact the supervisory relationship positively through being more empathetic, retaining familiarity with the positive and negative aspects of training or agency procedures, radiating enthusiasm, and being willing to invest time and energy into the supervisory process. However, these positive behaviors can contribute to the intensity of the relationship and induce anxiety. One of the present authors (M. Deck) as a new supervisor in a beginning supervision session stressed (to excess, in retrospect) the demands of the practicum. Later, the supervisee informed MD that after that first meeting, the supervisee left feeling as if MD had conferred with God just prior to the session. Zeal is intensive at its best and worst.

As the supervisor becomes more experienced and mature, Hess's (1986) three-stage model of supervisor development suggests that at the second stage supervisors become less concerned with power related issues, such as evaluation and personal validation, and become more committed to the growth of supervisees. Likewise, Hess contended that upon reaching the third stage, the supervisor has an integrated supervisor identity and is sought by supervisees for the excitement of what he/she offers. Evaluation has become an integral, ongoing aspect of his/her supervisory style and occurs in a nonthreatening, direct manner. Less concern is experienced "about" the supervisory relationship and as a result more of a relationship with the supervisee is enjoyed. A check and balance system operates permitting the supervisee's agenda to be the focus of the supervisory session, thus creating more involvement and greater professional development for the supervisee. At this stage, the supervisor's professional pride and personal integrity are integrated and the supervisor takes pleasure in seeing the supervisee excel and even exceed the supervisor's own ability.

GAMES SUPERVISEES AND SUPERVISORS PLAY

In order to minimize the anxiety and reduce the conflict that are inherent within the supervisory relationship, supervisees and supervisors may rely on "games" to gain control. Kadushin (1968) defined supervisory games as "recurrent interactional incidents between supervisor and supervisee that have a payoff for one of the parties" (p. 23). Kadushin proposed four series of games supervisees play. A brief definition of each game within the four series follows:

Series 1: Manipulating Demand Levels

Two against the agency or seducing the subversive.

A game in which the supervisee attempts to reduce the supervisor's enforcement of agency rules and regulations by focusing attention on the needs of the client population.

Be nice to me because I am nice to you.

A game of flattery aimed at ingratiating the supervisor to soften the evaluative focus on the supervisee's client contacts.

Series 2: Redefining the Relationship

Protect the sick and infirm or treat me, don't beat me.

A game in which the supervisee exposes details regarding his/her personal concerns in lieu of clinical work in order to appeal to the therapist in the supervisor.

Evaluation is not for friends.

A game which redefines the relationship into a more social, informal interaction with the expectation that friends are less accountable.

Maximum feasible participation.

A game which stresses a peer-peer relationship, granting the supervisee extensive decision-making power to determine what he/she needs to know.

Series 3: Reducing Power Disparity

If you knew Dostoyevsky like I know Dostoyevsky.

A game designed to highlight the supervisee's intellectual powers and ability to educate the supervisor.

So what do you know about it?

A game in which the supervisee alludes to his/her own wealth of information in an area in which the supervisor has little expertise or life experience.

All or nothing at all.

A game which involves the supervisee's seeking broader visions and questioning the greater meaning of life with the intent to make the supervisor feel he/she has abandoned idealism and lofty dreams.

Series 4: Controlling the Situation

I have a little list.

A game in which the supervisee brings in a series of work related concerns to control and direct the supervisor's attention away from the supervisee.

Heading them off at the pass.

A game of supervisee self-flagellation designed to solicit reassurance from the supervisor.

Little old me.

A game of gaining strength through the supervisee's feigning weakness and seeking a prescription from the supervisor with the question, "What would you do?"

I did like you told me.

A hostile, angry game in which the supervisee follows the advice of the supervisor with "spiteful obedience" to put the supervisor on the defensive.

It's all so confusing.

A game of seeking suggestions and guidance from a number of authorities in an attempt to erode supervisor's authority.

What you don't know won't hurt me.

A game of selective sharing with the supervisor to present a favorable picture and keep distance between the supervisee and supervisor.

Bauman (1972) also delineated games that supervisees play as forms of resistance to supervision. He described five games which he terms submission, turning the tables, the "I'm no good" approach, helplessness, and projection. **Submission** is a dependency game in which the supervisee believes that clients need direction from the counselor and, likewise, the counselor needs direction from the supervisor. **Turning the tables** is a diversionary game which keeps the focus on anything outside the supervisee. The **"I'm no good"** approach is a game of "pleading fragility" in which the supervisee appears brittle and easily broken. **Helplessness** is another dependency game in which the supervisee becomes the sponge for all the omnipotent knowledge the supervisor has to offer. **Projection,** a game of self-protection, is one in which the supervisee blames external inhibitions for lack of effectiveness, e.g., blaming a poor session on the fact that the supervisor was observing.

Supervisors, too, have their games (Hawthorne, 1975; Kadushin, 1968). Supervisors may rely on games when they feel their positions are threatened, when they are uncertain or uncomfortable with authority, if they are hesitant to utilize their authority, or when they feel hostility toward the supervisee. Supervisors' games are categorized into two types, abdication and power (Hawthorne, 1975). **Abdication games** involve the giving up of responsibility and **power games** keep the relationship closed while fostering a helplessness in the supervisee.

Hawthorne (1975) and Kadushin's (1968) supervisee games follow with a brief description:

Games of Abdication

They won't let me.

A game which indicates a willingness from the supervisor to permit action but is in reality an avoidance of decision making through projection of responsibility onto agency or institutional rules or authorities.

Poor me.

A game in which the supervisor excuses not keeping supervision commitments due to the excessive demands of other tasks and implies that the supervisee make no additional demands.

I'm really one of you or I'm really a nice guy.

Approval seeking games with the first variation designed to gain approval by siding with the supervisee's point of view; the later variation designed to gain approval based on personal qualities.

One good question deserves another.

A game of answering a question with a question as a ploy to stall for time or to avoid answering, deciding, or disclosing information to the supervisee.

Games of Power

Remember who's boss.

A game of explicit reminders of power (e.g., memos and evaluations) and implicit reminders of authority (e.g., "my trainees," "my unit") designed to maintain no contradictions and an omnipotent position.

I'll tell on you.

A game of threat in which the disciplinary action is carried out but by a higher power, allowing both the retention of power and the abdication of responsibility.

Parent (Father/Mother) knows best.

A game of validation of supervisor's experience and wisdom designed to preserve and guide the helpless, dependent supervisee.

I'm only trying to help or I know you can't really do it without me.

A game of lowered expectations with assumptions of supervisee incompetence or failure disguised in a cloak of help and caring.

I wonder why you really asked that question.

A game of redefinition to retain control and imply that the supervisee' question is psychological resistance; thus staying in power yet avoiding validation of the supervisee's viewpoint or hypothesis.

Games are an easily identifiable way of examining various sources of anxiety and personal conflict within the relationship. For games to be operative, collusion is necessary within the relationship (Kadushin, 1968). To avoid supervisee and supervisor games, the supervisor must be self-aware; willing to risk anger, hostility, and rejection; willing to be fallible; prepared to deny the fruits of flattery, omniscience, and being liked; and ready to focus on honest, open, direct communication (Kadushin).

DEVELOPMENTAL STAGES OF THE SUPERVISORY RELATIONSHIP

Developmental models of supervisee growth have been proposed (e.g., Hogan, 1964; Littrell, Lee-Borden, & Lorenz, 1979; Loganbill et al., 1982; Stoltenberg, 1981) and are receiving empirical support (e.g., Heppner & Roehlke, 1984; Hill, Charles, & Reed, 1981; McNeill, Stoltenberg, & Pierce, 1985; Reising & Daniels, 1983). As the supervisee progresses in his/her development toward a counseling identity, the course of the supervisory relationship changes as well (e.g., Altucher, 1967; Hart, 1982; Loganbill et al., 1982; Stoltenberg, 1981). Friedman and Kaslow (1986) proposed six normative relationship stages for psychotherapists-in-training and new professionals. Although the stages are identifiable and discernible as such, Friedman and Kaslow pointed out that they overlap considerably and that retrograde movement is inherent within the developmental process. Furthermore, they note that to predict the length of time required for a trainee to progress through the stages is impossible; however, they make the assumption that the process of achieving a professional identity never takes less than four years and may take many more. Therefore, what is highly likely is that supervisees will not achieve an integrated professional identity during the training process, and realistically, some counselors will never accomplish movement through the six stages.

A summarization and application of Friedman and Kaslow's (1986) stages in the supervision of counselors follows.

Stage 1: Excitement and Anticipatory Anxiety

This stage precedes the supervisee's seeing the first client and is characterized by his/her sense of awe at the newness and prospect of learning to be therapeutic. With no specific client-related tasks on which to focus, the supervisee experiences diffused anxiety.

The supervisor can use this incubation period as a time to establish the working relationship with the supervisee (Borders & Leddick, 1987). It is the time to provide the supervisee with information regarding training or agency regulations and to clarify logistical details regarding supervision place, time, and so forth. Inviting the supervisee to share expectations and concerns regarding the supervisory process provides a basis for understanding the supervisee. The supervisor might employ queries, such as: "Tell me the kind of supervisory experiences you have had before." "What questions do you have about this experience?" "How do you view supervision?" A supervisor's communication of accurate empathy with the supervisee's anxiety and vulnerability in this brief, but chaotic, period initiates the formation of a trusting, open relationship. The supervisor provides the supervisee with a "holding environment" (Friedman & Kaslow, 1986), providing information and encouraging exploration of feelings and anxieties.

Stage 2: Dependency and Identification

When the supervisee sees the first client, Stage 2 begins with the supervisee exhibiting a high degree of dependency due to lack of confidence, skill, and/or knowledge. The supervisee develops an idealized perception of the supervisor, often emulating the style, attitude, and even posture of the supervisor. The dependency of this stage is frequently voiced in the barrage of "how to" questions as the supervisee seeks cookbook instructions from the supervisor on specific issues related to client contact.

During this time, a supervisee experiences an emotional drain at the end of one or two sessions. Trying to be therapeutic, a supervisee struggles to grasp the internal realities of the client and prematurely attempts to detect pathology. It is a period of self-doubt and ambivalence; yet these feelings are often masked by the supervisee's choosing not to reveal doubts and client-session information out of fear of appearing immature, silly, incompetent, or vulnerable.

A warm, accepting, and supportive supervisor helps the supervisee maneuver through this confusing and insecure period. Supportive measures include an empathic under-standing of the supervisee's interpersonal struggles, plaudits for productive interventions, constructive critiques, encouragement with difficult clients, and opportunities to explore alternatives (Marshall & Confer, 1980). The supervisor can help the supervisee to anticipate, organize, and plan strategies for anxiety-producing situations in this stage; thus fostering a less dependent, and subsequently, a healthier relationship. If the supervisor has input into client selection for the supervisee, he/she may selectively screen out those more difficult clients who might overwhelm the supervisee and/or disillusion the unsure supervisee who questions the value of the therapeutic process.

Stage 2 ends when the supervisee recognizes he/she has had impact, usually of a personal rather than a professional nature, on the client. That is, as a result of the client's feeling of attachment or reliance on the supervisee, the supervisee realizes that the client regards him/her as a counselor. However, the supervisee has yet to own this self-identity.

Stage 3: Activity and Continued Dependency

Beginning with the client's show of faith in the supervisee as a counselor, this phase is a time of fluctuation in self-assessment and vacillation in dependency on the supervisor. A supervisee will over- or underestimate his/her capacity to intervene with clients. Exercising more independence and responsibility with clients, the supervisee will revert to dependency in times of crisis. A supervisee is likely to use psychological jargon and diagnosis at will, without having acquired the ability to integrate such information in work with clients. Seeking out numerous opinions on interventions and strategies is typical.

This can be a trying period for the supervisor as the supervisee is asserting more independence but progressing at inefficient and uneven rates. Clearly, this may not be the time for the supervisor to reflect on the rewards and joys of supervision. A supervisor will need tolerance and patience with the supervisee. An important procedure for the supervisor is to convey acceptance, stability, and predictability within the relationship. Limiting and focusing critical commentary and setting judicious limits are also important considerations for maintaining the relationship.

Stage 4: Exuberance and Taking Charge

As the supervisee realizes he/she really is a counselor and that the process "really works," Stage 4 is entered with exuberance, energy, and enthusiasm. As client contact has accrued, and the didactic and experiential facets of the learning process come together, the supervisee begins to organize and synthesize information into a personalized style and framework. By this stage, a counselor-in-training may have entered into his/her own personal therapy, thereby gaining increased personalized knowledge about the therapeutic process and becoming more aware of the dynamics within the counseling and supervisory relationships. The supervisee's relationship with clients becomes warmer, more genuine, and interventions are more authentic. As the supervisee matures in his/her professional development, less bonding occurs with the supervisor.

During this phase, the supervisor must resist being overinvolved or overcontrolling with the supervisee. This is a creative, productive, satisfying period for the supervisee. By recognizing the professional identity of the supervisee, the supervisor assists the supervisee's internalization of the counselor identity. The supervisee now prefers more consultative and intellectually challenging supervision over the more supportive relationship of earlier stages.

Stages 5: Identity and Independence

Characterized as "professional adolescence," this is the stage of separation and conflict. As with adolescents, it is a more conflictual and turbulent period for some supervisees than for others. Hence, when supervisee-initiated power struggles erupt at this stage, they are considered normal. The supervisee asserts independence by basing decisions on his/her clinical judgment and internalized frame of reference. Withholding information from the supervisor and seeking peer supervision are also signs of independence. Recognizing where his/her strengths exceed the supervisor's, the supervisee rejects or devalues the "less-than-perfect" supervisor.

A painful stage for some supervisors, this stage requires the acceptance of the autonomy and freedom the supervisee is asserting, while retaining final responsibility for interventions conducted by the supervisee. The supervisor must be willing to negotiate and find methods to support and affirm the supervisee's competence without limiting the individuation needed for professional growth. As the supervisee resists and devalues the supervisor's role, the supervisor needs to remain nondefensive and to value his/her previous contributions to the professional the supervisee has become.

Stage 6: Calm and Collegiality

The welcome entry of the supervisee into the peer collegiality of faculty or employee staff is the final stage of development and may be the point at which supervision is no longer required or formally offered. Therefore, as a professionally employed counselor, when Stage 6 has been reached the supervisee may need to actively seek supervision as an avenue of ongoing professional development and growth. By voluntarily investing in the supervisory relationship and working to make the experience beneficial, the supervisee indicates willingness to engage in self-scrutiny, to take risks, and to explore clinical issues and treatment. Less preoccupation with evaluation concerns occurs in Stage 6 than prevailed in earlier stages. Peer supervision is sought for its professional enhancement rather than as an act of defiance typical of the previous stage. In Stage 6, the supervisee also may become the supervisor and begin the process of helping the next generation.

CONCLUSION

With their vulnerable human frailties and their equally human potential for growth and healing, supervisor and supervisee form the intensely personal relationship which is at the center of the supervisory process. Anxiety and conflict are unavoidable and may arouse any number of emotions and responses within the relationship. Both supportive and confrontational conditions are requisites in transforming the anxiety-prone and conflictual relationship into one which fully promotes and fosters the developing competence and growth of the supervisee. As the supervisee gains confidence, ability, and identity as a counselor, the relationship between the supervisor and supervisee also shifts, changes, and ideally grows into a shared journey in which both persons contribute to mutual professional development, a continued expansion of self-awareness, and an ongoing desire to learn and improve.

REFERENCES

Alonso, A. (1983). A developmental theory of psychodynamic supervision. *The Clinical Supervisor, 1*(3), 23-36.

Altucher, N. (1967). Constructive use of the supervisory relationship. *Journal of Counseling Psychology, 14,* 165-170.

Arbuckle, D. S. (1963). The learning of counseling: Process not product. *Journal of Counseling Psychology, 10,* 163-168.

Bauman, W. F. (1972). Games counselor trainees play: Dealing with trainee resistance. *Counselor Education and Supervision, 11,* 251-256.

Blocher, D. H. (1983). Toward a cognitive developmental approach to counseling supervision. *The Counseling Psychologist, 11,* 27-34.

Borders, L. D., & Leddick, G. R. (1987). *Handbook of counseling supervision.* Alexandria, VA: Association for Counselor Education and Supervision.

Bordin, E. S. (1983). A working alliance based model of supervision. *The Counseling Psychologist, 11*, 35-42.

Cohen, L. (1980). The new supervisee views supervision. In A. K. Hess (Ed.), *Psychotherapy supervision: Theory, research and practice* (pp. 78-84). New York: John Wiley.

Dodge, J. (1982). Reducing supervisee anxiety: A cognitive-behavioral approach. *Counselor Education and Supervision, 22*, 55-60.

Eckstein, R., & Wallerstein, R. S. (1958). *The teaching and learning of psychotherapy*. New York: Basic Books.

Friedman, D., & Kaslow, N. J. (1986). The development of professional identity in psychotherapists: Six stages in the supervision process. In F. W. Kaslow (Ed.), *Supervision and training: Models, dilemmas, and challenges* (pp. 29-49). New York: Haworth.

Hart, G.M. (1982). *The process of clinical supervision*. Baltimore: University Park Press.

Hawthorne, L. (1975). Games supervisors play. *Social Work, 20*, 179-183.

Heppner, P. O., & Roehlke, H. J. (1984). Differences among supervisees at different levels of training: Implications for a developmental model of supervision. *Journal of Counseling Psychology, 31*, 76-90.

Hess, A. K. (1986). Growth in supervision: Stages of supervisee and supervisor development. In F. W. Kaslow (Ed.), *Supervision and training: Models, dilemmas, and challenges*. New York: Haworth.

Hill, C. E., Charles, D., & Reed, K. G. (1981). A longitudinal analysis of changes in counseling skills during doctoral training in counseling psychology. *Journal of Counseling Psychology, 28*, 428-436.

Hogan, R. A. (1964). Issues and approaches in supervision. *Psychotherapy: Theory, research, and practice, 1*, 139-141.

Hutt, C. H., Scott, J., & King, M. (1983). A phenomenological study of supervisees' positive and negative experiences in supervision. *Psychotherapy: Theory, research, and practice, 20*, 118-123.

Kadushin, A. (1968). Games people play in supervision. *Social Work, 13*, 23-32.

Kell, B. L., & Mueller, W. J. (1966). *Impact and change: A study of counseling relationships*. New York: Appleton-Century-Crofts.

Littrell, J. M., Lee-Borden, N., & Lorenz, J. (1979). A developmental framework for counseling supervision. *Counselor Education and Supervision, 19*, 129-136.

Loganbill, C., Hardy, E., & Delworth, U. (1982). Supervision: A conceptual model. *The Counseling Psychologist, 10,* 3-42.

Marshall, W. R., & Confer, W. N. (1980). Psychotherapy supervision: Supervisees' Perspective. In A. K. Hess (Ed.), *Psychotherapy supervision: Theory, research, and practice* (pp. 92-100). New York: John Wiley.

McColley, S. H., & Baker, E. (1982). Training activities and styles of beginning supervisors: A survey. *Professional Psychology, 13,* 283-292.

McNeill, B. W., Stoltenberg, C. D., & Pierce, R. A. (1985). Supervisees' perceptions of their development: A test of the counselor complexity model. *Journal of Counseling Psychology, 32,* 630-633.

Miller, C. D., & Oetting, E. R. (1966). Students react to supervision. *Counselor Education and Supervision, 6,* 73-74.

Moskowitz, S. A., & Rupert, P. A. (1983). Conflict resolution within the supervisory relationship. *Professional Psychology: Research and Practice, 14,* 632-641.

Moses, H. A., & Hardin, J. T. (1978). A relationship approach to counselor supervision in agency settings. In J. Boyd (Ed.), *Counselor supervision* (pp. 437-480). Muncie, IN: Accelerated Development.

Mueller, W. J., & Kell, B. L. (1972). *Coping with conflict: Supervising counselors and psychotherapists.* New York: Appleton-Century-Crofts.

Patterson, C. H. (1983). A client-centered approach to supervision. *The Counseling Psychologist, 11,* 21-25.

Reising, G. N., & Daniels, M. H. (1983). A study of Hogan's model of counselor development and supervision. *Journal of Counseling Psychology, 30,* 235-244.

Rioch, M. J. (1980). The dilemmas of supervision in dynamic psychotherapy. In A. K. Hess (Ed.), *Psychotherapy supervision: Theory, research, and practice* (pp. 68-76). New York: John Wiley.

Robiner, W. (1982). Role diffusion in the supervisory relationship. *Professional Psychology, 13,* 258-267.

Rogers, C. R. (1957). The necessary and sufficient conditions of therapeutic personality change. *Journal of Consulting Psychology, 21,* 95-103.

Rozsnafszky, J. (1979). Beyond schools of psychotherapy: Integrity and maturity in therapy and supervision. *Psychotherapy: Theory, research, and practice, 16,* 190-198.

Schmidt, J. P. (1979). Psychotherapy supervision: A cognitive-behavioral model. *Professional Psychology, 10,* 278-284.

Stoltenberg, C. (1981). Approaching supervision from a developmental perspective: The counselor complexity model. *Journal of Counseling Psychology, 28,* 59-65.

Styczynski, L. E. (1980). The transition from supervisee to supervisor. In A. K. Hess (Ed.), *Psychotherapy supervision: Theory, research, and practice* (pp. 29-39). New York: John Wiley.

Yager, G. G., & Beck, T. D. (1985). Beginning practicum: It only hurt until I laughed! *Counselor Education and Supervision, 25,* 149-157.

PART II
MODELS
OF
SUPERVISION

Chapter 3

PSYCHOTHERAPEUTIC MODEL OF SUPERVISION

The psychotherapeutic approach to counselor supervision is a synthesis and extension of views that conceptualize supervision as being similar to counseling and psychotherapy (Altucher, 1967; Arbuckle, 1965; Bernier 1980; Brammer & Wassmer, 1977; Eckstein, 1964; Eckstein & Wallerstein, 1958; Heppner & Handley, 1981; Kell & Mueller, 1966; Lister, 1966; Moore, 1969; Mueller & Kell, 1972; Patterson, 1964, 1973, 1983; Rice, 1980; Rogers, 1951, 1957). According to this approach, counselor supervision is a therapeutic process focusing on the intrapersonal and interpersonal dynamics in the counselor's relationships with clients, supervisors, colleagues, and others.

Of the supervisory approaches to be covered the psychotherapeutic approach is ranked first in seniority. This approach was the first to be advocated and has always had a large following, although its proponents have never been in total theoretical accord. Historically, the training model for psychoanalysis, with its required analysis for trainees, probably had an early influence on other schools of psychotherapy and the upstart profession of counseling. Those who prepared counselors discovered and promulgated an important principle. As stated by Altucher (1967, p. 165) "learning to be a counselor is both an emotional and intellectual experience, and of the two, the emotional part is the most crucial."

FOCUS ON DYNAMICS

The psychotherapeutic approach to counselor supervision could well be called a "dynamic approach" because interpersonal and intrapersonal dynamics are its focus and *modus operandi.* An individual's dynamics are considered a criterion of psychological adjustment, and the dynamic interplay between helper and helpee is the instrument for therapeutically induced change. The counselor must be aware fully of these dynamics and use them for the other's benefit. Psychotherapeutic supervision aims at helping counselors attain this awareness and acquire skill in utilizing dynamics.

Conceptualizing psychotherapeutic supervision is difficult because writers have described the approach in piecemeal fashion and have often failed to explicate underlying theory. Thus some writers and practitioners explain how dynamics operate in supervision from a psychoanalytic viewpoint; others may treat dynamics from a phenomenological perspective. At the end of this Chapter a case study from the cognitive theory of supervisory dynamics is presented.

To gain an overall perspective of the psychotherapeutic approach and to facilitate explanation, Figure 3.1 has been drawn to depict focal dynamics in the supervisory situation. As illustrated, the dynamics which are examined in supervision are provided by three people: the counselor, the person (helpee) who is interacting with the counselor, and the supervisor. The numbers in Figure 3.1 identify the dynamics occurring among and within these three parties, and these are the focal points of psychotherapeutic supervision. Numbers, 1, 2, and 3 depict interpersonal dynamics, and intrapersonal dynamics are identified by numbers 4, 5, and 6.

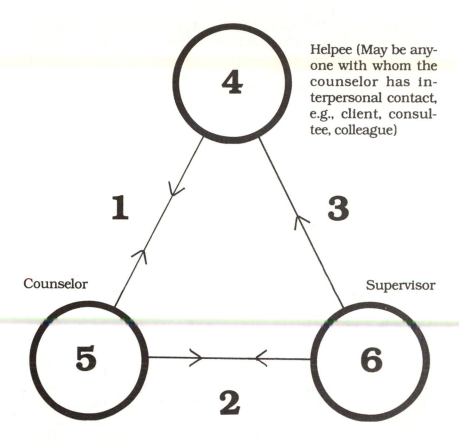

Helpee (May be anyone with whom the counselor has interpersonal contact, e.g., client, consultee, colleague)

Counselor

Supervisor

Figure 3.1. Counselor supervision dynamics.

Interpersonal Dynamics

The interpersonal dynamics which occur between the counselor and helpee are a primary focus in psychotherapeutic supervision (Figure 3.1, dynamic 1). Communication travels by non-verbal as well as verbal interpersonal behavior. The counselor is responsible for being a sensitive receiver of both explicit and implied communication and a sender of communication that will have a beneficial effect upon the one being counseled. Supervision should help the counselor be an effective interpersonal communicator.

Interpersonal dynamics between counselor and supervisor (Figure 3.1, dynamic 2) are a second focus which has much in common with the counselor-client interaction. Within the supervisory process the supervisor has the same responsibility toward the counselor as does the counselor to the client in counseling. The supervisor is responsible for dealing with received and sent interpersonal dynamics in such a manner that the counselor learns how to interact effectively. Counselor learning takes place as the supervisor is accepted as a model of interpersonal behavior within supervision.

The third set of interpersonal dynamics in Figure 3.1 relates to the supervisor's responsibility for the quality of the psychological contact with the helpee. Concerning this respon- sibility, Altucher (1967) has noted that the supervisor's first commitment is to the counselor, and that a consequence of allowing neophyte counselors to work with clients is less adequate service. Patterson (1964) agreed, but suggested that an adequately trained (but neophyte) counselor will rarely damage the client irreparable in a single interview before the supervisor can intervene. Supervisors have a three-fold respon- sibility of allowing only adequately-prepared counselors to do supervised practice, of monitoring their performance closely, and supervising without taking responsibility away from them. A supervisor's ethical responsibility to protect the welfare of those who are being counseled need not be compromised unduly by the "less adequate" service of trainees. Although less adequate than the service of experienced counselors, supervisee performance can and must be competent.

Intrapersonal Dynamics

Intrapersonal dynamics consist of covert behaviors and sensory processes such as feelings, thoughts, and perceptions. Included in the intrapersonal realm are attitudes and beliefs— cognitive routines for attributing meaning to stimuli. Many other terms are used to refer to intrapersonal dynamics. From a phenomenological foundation, Rogers (1951) might refer to intrapersonal activity as organismic functioning: perceptions, thoughts, and feelings that could be clustered into aspects of the self. Another common term associated with the intra- personal realm is "experiencing" (Lister, 1966; Hansen &

Barker, 1964). Experiencing can be defined as a sensory awareness of psychologically influenced psychological activity.

Terminology used to describe intrapersonal dynamics in scholarly discourse can be confusing, but this difficulty may not be as prevalent or significant in supervisory practice. Terminology is relatively unimportant as long as the supervisor and counselor can communicate clearly.

Within the psychotherapeutic approach, nature and amount of supervisory attention given to intrapersonal dynamics varies, depending upon the counselor, supervisor, and situation. Some counselors pay less attention to intrapersonal aspects than do others, and the same is true for supervisors who vary on their particular style of supervision. The degree of attention given to intrapersonal dynamics is also a function of how appropriate such a focus would be in the situation under study. For example, when supervising an educational counseling session, fewer opportunities would exist for fruitful intrapersonal focus than would be present in supervising a counselor who is resolving a personal conflict with a colleague.

Of the three sources of intrapersonal activity with which the psychotherapeutic supervisor can grapple (Figure 3.1, dynamics 4, 5, 6), the least threatening for the counselor and supervisor is the intrapersonal realm of the helpee (dynamic 4). The supervisor's main task in respect to these dynamics, which will be discussed later in this Chapter, is to help the counselor understand the other person's internalized responses and the influences on his or her overt behavior.

Counselors' intrapersonal dynamics (Figure 3.1, dynamic 5) are often very threatening to them, and, consequently, may be well guarded by resistive defenses which are difficult to handle in supervision (Bauman, 1972; Cross & Brown, 1983; Dodge, 1982; Guttman & Haase, 1972; Liddle, 1986; Shaver, 1985) Ironically though, the counselor's anxiety surrounding these dynamics may offer a cue to the supervisor, indicating which ones need supervisory attention (Dobbs, 1986; Mueller & Kell, 1972).

Psychotherapeutic supervision must "zero in" on the counselor's intrapersonal dynamics, particularly those which evoke anxiety, because these covert elements are a direct and powerful influence on the counselor's interpersonal behavior. Therapeutic utilization of one's interpersonal dynamics in a counseling relationship is virtually impossible if corresponding awareness and control of covert dynamics are not present.

Another intrapersonal focus in psychotherapeutic supervision is the supervisor (Figure 3.1, dynamic 6). The supervisor's overt behavior is influenced by intrapersonal dynamics, and professional control (not to be confused with supression or repression) must be maintained in both realms. If uncontrolled and unconscious intrapersonal dynamics are primary antecedents for the supervisor's conduct, supervision will become a freewheeling relationship in which both counselor and supervisor are striving to satisfy their own needs. Instead, professional intent should guide the supervisor toward behaving (supervision methodology) in a way that will be optimally beneficial to the supervisee.

Dynamic Interactions and Patterns

Although the foregoing discussion has treated the six dynamic foci of psychotherapeutic supervision as discrete elements, operationally they are expressed in patterns. Patterns develop when a number of dynamics have contingencies which link them together. A specific pattern may be somewhat characteristic of the individual's typical interactions, or it may be idiosyncratic to the immediate human relationship. In the former case, a dynamic pattern, if recognized, is a particularly revealing clue that guides efforts of the counselor or supervisor. Identification of and intervention in patterned dynamics is the essence of therapeutic supervision methodology.

Patterning may be illustrated in the case of an insecure beginning counselor interacting with a defensive client. The counselor attempts to perform capably, but the client does not respond in a reinforcing manner. Many of the client's statements and mannerisms may be perceived by the counselor as indicating that he/she is doing a poor job of counseling. These perceptions, some of which may be unrealistic or exaggerated, cause the counselor's anxiety to rise, thus further inhibiting effective performance.

The pattern may become even more of a problem if the client begins to act in a way that capitalizes upon the counselor's insecurity. For example, if the client were threatened by the counselor, an aggressive reaction might be to say something about the counselor's neophytic status or lack of helpfulness. This action would thwart the counselor, and effectively safeguard the client from being confronted with any more threatening material. Just such a client confrontation would be necessary for therapeutic counseling to be effective, and good results would occur only if the dynamic pattern were broken.

Another common illustration of a dynamic pattern occurs when counselors express incapability and dependence, causing the supervisor to accept his/her responsibility. In this case the counselors' intrapersonal dynamics are expressed and if the supervisor does allow his or her nurturance needs to be tapped, then the supervisor's overt response is one of the helpgiving. This pattern would undermine supervision because the counselor would never be given the opportunity to gain competence and self-confidence.

Mueller and Kell (1972) described several other dynamic patterns that frequently arise in their work. One pattern is for the client, particularly a female client, to present herself as fragile and easily hurt. When the counselor approaches the client's anxiety-laden material, she may cry, and the counselor then concludes that he/she has erred in following this direction. If the counselor thereupon becomes guilty and apologetic, the client may shortly attack the counselor for being ineffective. In this pattern, the client's behavior initially fends off the counselor, then administers punishment for not helping. For the dynamically naive counselor, such a turn of events would create an impasse in the counseling process.

Another common pattern is when an angry, hostile client attacks the counselor, who responds with a counter attack. This deadlock of reciprocal hostility probably would lead to termination of the counseling session unless the counselor could gain insight into his or her own dynamics and then begin to understand how the client elicited hostility.

"Parallel reenactment" is one of the most interesting dynamic patterns in therapeutic supervision. This pattern consists of the supervisee replaying, within the supervisory setting, significant dynamics of the helping relationship. The counselor will act toward the supervisor just as the helpee was perceived to have acted toward him/her. Frequent instances are (1) the helpee expresses dependence on the counselor and the counselor expresses dependence on the supervisor, (2) the helpee becomes angry with the counselor and the counselor becomes angry with the supervisor, and (3) the helpee dominates the counselor and the counselor tries to dominate the supervisor.

Why parallel reenactment occurs is open to debate. Perhaps the ocurrance is just happenstance, since the main dynamic dimensions of human relationships are few and universal, and possibilities exist that a certain percentage of instances would illustrate similar dimensions that could be interpreted as dynamic parallelism. A contrary hypothesis by Mueller and Kell (1972) is that the counselor actually experiences conflicts which are perceived as paralleling those of the helpee. This feeling or perception may be the motivation, not necessarily conscious, that is responsible for reenactment.

GOALS OF THERAPEUTIC SUPERVISION

Discussion of dynamic points and patterns in psychotherapeutic supervision identifies foci but does not define what the supervisor should try to accomplish. What are the goals of psychotherapeutic supervision?

Mueller and Kell (1972) have offered a two-part goal for dynamically oriented supervisors, a goal that should be acceptable to most theoretical persuasions. Their supervisory process goal is for the counselor to learn what is therapeutic, and the product goal is for the counselor to behave in a manner that has a therapeutic effect on the client or other party. Relating this two-part goal to the dynamic triangle of Figure 3.1, at least four sequential subgoals exist that the supervisor attempts to accomplish: ***dynamic awareness, understanding dynamic contingencies, change in dynamics,*** and ***therapeutic utilization of dynamics.***

Dynamic Awareness

Learning what is therapeutic begins with discovering (becoming aware of) interpersonal and intrapersonal dynamics. This first subgoal, which opens the counselor's eye to the existence of dynamics, is low fidelity in nature and is followed by learning that dynamics influence human relationships. Through such awareness the counselor learns that everyone has a covert world of thoughts, feelings, and attitudes and that human interaction, by its nature, involves interpersonal pathways of communicatory behavior.

Awareness is basic to power—power to change or prevent change during counseling (May, 1972, p.99). Awareness is the first step in gaining personal control of the dynamics in a helping relationship and in using them therapeutically.

Understanding Dynamic Contingencies

After awareness of dynamics has been achieved, the next step is understanding the operations of these dynamics within helpgiving and supervision. Understanding comes about through assessment of dynamics within two contingencies: (1) the influence of intrapersonal dynamics on interpersonal behavior, and (2) the influence of interpersonal behavior on intrapersonal dynamics. Using the counselor-client dyad from Figure 3.1 as an illustration, assessment involves the following questions:

1. How does the counselor's intrapersonal behavior (# 5) influence his/her interpersonal behavior (# 1) toward the helpee?

2. How does the interpersonal behavior of the counselor (# 1) influence the helpee's intrapersonal dynamics (# 4)?

3. How do the helpee's intrapersonal dynamics (# 4) influence his/her interpersonal behavior (# 1) toward the counselor?

Answers to these questions would unravel the patterns of interacting dynamics in the counselor-client relationship. Similar questions and answers pertaining to the supervisor-counselor dyad would provide a helpful diagnostic picture at that level. Assessment and diagnostic unraveling of this kind constitutes a large portion of the methodology of therapeutic supervision. To the supervisor unacquainted with the therapeutic approach, too much emphasis may seem to be placed on the goal of understanding dynamics, and too much time may seem to be spent in examining the dynamics of the supervisory triangle (Figure 3.1). However, the supervisor must comprehend the theoretical rationale underlying the goal and methodology of psychotherapeutic supervision if an appreciation of the approach is to be attained and if skill in application of its principles is to be acquired. Numerous writers, such as Cashdan (1973) and Leary (1957), have offered a dynamics-oriented theory for psychotherapy. Kell and Mueller (1966), Kell and Burow (1970), and Mueller and Kell (1972) have provided a theoretical rationale for dynamically oriented supervision, with support from Altucher (1967) and Moore (1969). Briefly, their position is that interpersonal and intrapersonal dynamics are subject to the general principles of social learning theory. The dynamics which an individual has developed through past learning experiences tend to be reasserted in future situations, particularly when conditions are perceived to be similar to those of the original learning situations. Research by Heller, Myers, and Kline (1963), Hosford & Barmann (1983), Kurpius, Benjamin & Morran (1985), Mueller (1969), Raush, Dittman, and Taylor (1959), and Raush (1965) have supported this theoretical contention.

Thus, when a client demonstrates certain dynamics in the helping relationship, the counselor can hypothesize that these are indicative of at least a part of the individual's dynamic make-up, established through time. The performance tells the counselor how the client is likely to react dynamically in other relationships. For the client to hide dynamic difficulties from a competent counselor is impossible, because the dynamics played out in the counseling relationship relate to the client's problems outside the counseling relationship. Kell and Burow (1970, p. 15) suggested that "clients present most of their problems in a compacted, cryptic form in the first interview." If the counselor identifies the client's problematic dynamics as they occur in helpgiving, this diagnostic knowledge can guide the counselor in utilizing dynamics within the helping relationship.

Correspondingly, dynamic difficulties in the counselor's helping efforts can be found in the helpgiving and supervisory relationship. These difficulties will hinder supervision and the counselor's future helpgiving, if not resolved. In summary, focusing on intrapersonal and interpersonal dynamics is a way for the counselor to unlock others' problems, and in parallel fashion, the same approach can be applied to unlocking a counselor's difficulties in helping his/her relationships with others.

Change In Dynamics

Dynamic difficulties of the counselor, discovered with the aid of the supervisor, must be resolved if counselor performance is to improve. Such change is a goal shared by dynamically oriented counseling and supervision. In counseling, the dynamic change is necessary to improve the client's intrapersonal functioning (maladaptive emotion, perception, and ideation), as well as his/her interpersonal dynamics (social behavior). Changes in a counselor's dynamics as a consequence of supervision are ordinarily not as significant for the improvement of life functioning as are changes in the client as a result of counseling. This assumption is based on the fact that admittance to counselor preparation includes personal adjustment screening, so most counselor-trainees can be expected to be reasonably well adjusted people. However, problem aspects of a counselor's dynamic functions which may not be much of a difficulty in everyday life can, nonetheless, be significant hindrances to helpgiving. Latent conflicts may be activated during counseling, and others that are avoided in day-to-day living may be in the forefront of therapeutic activity. Such trouble spots in a counselor's pattern of dynamics are prime targets for change.

Therapeutic Utilization Of Dynamics

The culminating skill in psychotherapeutic supervision is therapeutic utilization of dynamics. Three kinds of dynamic utility are sought:

1. the counselor's experiencing/control of personal dynamics,

2. the counselor's planned influence on the dynamics of others, and

3. the counselor's management and utilization of dynamics in situations where no direct involvement exists.

The rationale for specifying control of personal dynamics as a factor affecting dynamic utility has been voiced by Mueller and Kell (1972, p.5): "Learning what is therapeutic is an insufficient goal of supervision unless both parties recognize that a major part of what is therapeutic is the way in which the therapist uses himself." Counselors use themselves by "experiencing," described by Lister (1966) as a kind of intrapersonal communication which aids one to detect and modify within the immediate present subtle, moment-by moment nuances of feelings . . . .which disrupt communication with others.

When the counselor "experiences" in the manner described by Lister, he/she is controlling personal dynamics for the benefit of the other party, as well as therapeutically influencing the other's dynamics. The counselor's dynamics have a contingent relationship to the dynamics of others with whom the counselor relates, and therefore, through self-control, the counselor is simultaneously extending the influence of therapeutic control to these others.

The word "control" is not a popular one in the counseling profession. Counselors like to think of themselves as genuine people who do not exert ingenuine controls over their own honest feelings and thoughts, and, who, in the interest of preserving integrity, do not attempt to manipulate or control the behavior of others. Yet, by possessing the knowledge of how dynamics interact, the counselor has a responsibility to use this knowledge for the benefit of helpees. In this context of responsible helpfulness "dynamic control" is employed. The following illustration will clarify the concept.

Certain clients use sly deprecating statements to "put down" the practicum counselor. The client's passive-aggressive verbalizations normally awaken either anxiety or anger in the counselor. In the former case the counselor interpersonally reacts by trying to prove to the client that he/she is competent, and in the latter case (anger) the counselor reacts with counter aggression and "puts down" the client. Counselors who are relatively secure and have mastered the experiencing process react differently, however. They usually recognize their anxiety or anger, refuse to succumb to it, and react with an approved counseling technique—such as reflecting the client's emotion and facilitating self awareness. These "experiencing" counselors feel the same intrapersonal dynamics of anxiety or anger, but control them, and react in a therapeutically designed manner rather than in response to their own felt needs. Their dynamic "control" is certainly manipulative, in the influential sense, but the affect upon the client is therapeutic, and this is the crucial determinant in assigning value to terms such as "control" and "manipulation." Being able to overcome one's own needs in order to act in the interests of others is the height of personal and professional integrity in helpgiving. Moreover, as empirical support for the importance of therapeutic utilization continues to accumulate (Dietzel & Abeles, 1975; Hansen, Robin & Grimes, 1982; Holloway, 1984; Holloway & Wampold, 1983; Kaplan, 1983) experiencing and personal control of dynamics become necessary components in the counselor's repertoire of competencies.

In contrast to the spontaneous experiencing technique is the counselor's influence on helpee dynamics in a planned and deliberate manner. Before encountering a helpee, the counselor can decide to behave interpersonally in such a way that helpee dynamics are affected therapeutically. To illustrate consider the case of an insecure colleague or client who continually solicits the counselor's help in negotiating avoidance of a responsibility. The counselor could assess this pattern and decide to deliberately control this person's dynamics therapeutically by encouraging and fostering responsible action.

Management and control of dynamics when the counselor is not directly involved with helpees is another application of dynamic utilization. This is accomplished as the counselor assesses dynamic evoking properties of non-counseling situations and constructively influences them for the dynamic benefit of others. Such influencing could occur in building the composition of a discussion group, consulting with a teacher who has problems with class morale, and helping to alter policies or activities of an institution.

Therapeutic utilization of dynamics is the final goal of psychotherapeutic supervision, reached through awareness, understanding, and usually some form of change in one's personal dynamics. Cross and Brown (1983) and Lister (1966) have suggested that experience and maturity are necessary for the development of dynamic utilization, but, even if this high-level skill does require a number of years to develop, it can be initiated through dynamic supervision. The dynamics-oriented supervisor facilitates birth of this skill in a counselor through the skill he or she applies during supervision. By expertly utilizing the dynamics of the supervisory relationship, the supervisor will help the counselor acquire skill in applying those dynamics in the helpgiving relationship.

METHODOLOGY

Didactic knowledge of methodology acquired through the usual modes of reading, lecture, and discussion is, more often than not, insufficient preparation for application of that methodology. The transition from knowledge to performance is difficult and Jakubowski-Spector, Dustin, & George (1971) have cited the need for "transfer training" to facilitate it. The methodology of psychotherapeutic supervision is quite susceptible to the barrier between knowledge and performance. Furthermore, practicing field-supervisors tend to regard the psychotherapeutic approach as being applicable only to psychotherapy in a clinic setting. In this Chapter the methodology of psychotherapeutic supervision is presented in a pragmatic and uncomplicated way, and it is related to real-life situations in supervision practice. Hopefully this presentation will encourage readers to accept the psychotherapeutic approach as a practical one.

Two basic methods exist for implementing the psychotherapeutic approach to supervision, with each comprised of numerous skills and techniques. The first method is a standardized procedure called *interpersonal process recall* (IPR), and the second is *unstructured and intensive therapeutic supervision.*

Interpersonal Process Recall (IPR)

The IPR procedure was developed initially through the work of Kagan and Krathwohl (1967). Research and further development of IPR has produced an impressive body of literature (Archer & Kagan, 1973; Dendy, 1971; Grzegorek, 1971; Kagan, 1980; Kagan & Schauble, 1969; Kagan, Schauble, Resnikoff, Danish, & Krathwohl, 1969; Resnikoff, Kagan, & Schauble, 1970; Schauble, 1970; Spivack, 1970, 1972). In supervision, the IPR procedure exposes the counselor to a recorded playback of an interaction he or she had with a client. The playback can be an audio recording or video recording, although the latter is deemed more potent for eliciting intrapersonal affective material (Carlson, 1980; Kagan & Krathwohl, 1967; Fuller & Manning, 1973). The playback exposure is augmented by assistance from a recall supervisor who utilizes inductive questioning to direct the counselor's attention to the intrapersonal and interpersonal dynamics of the interaction. The intent of the playback and the recall questions is to encourage counselors to identify and recall dynamics, thereby leading them to recognize some of their feelings and thoughts which interfered with effective communication in the recorded situation. The following questions are illustrative of those that a supervisor might use to lead a counselor into self-confrontation (Dendy, 1971):

1. What do you think he/she was trying to say?

2. What do you think he/she was feeling at this point?

3. Can you pick-up any clues from his/her nonverbal behavior?

4. What was running through your mind when he/she said that?

5. Can you recall some of the feelings you were having then?

6. Did anything prevent you from sharing some of your feelings and concerns about the person?

7. If you had another chance, would you like to have said something different?

8. What kind of risk would have occurred if you said what you really wanted to say?

9. What kind of a person do you want him to see you as?

10. What do you think his/her perceptions are of you?

Recall by the counselor can be supplemented with "client recall" and "mutual recall" to form a full IPR treatment. In client (or helpee) recall the same exposure and line of questioning are employed, with the counselor observing the helpee as he/she participates in the recall session. The helpee benefits from the recall, and the counselor is offered the rare opportunity of entering into the helpee's experience in the original situation, as recalled. Recall observation helps the counselor to "become aware of and sensitive to subtle meanings underlying the [helpee's] verbal and nonverbal behavior" (Kagan & Krathwohl, 1967, p. 93).

Mutual recall is held with the counselor and helpee following their respective individual recall sessions. In mutual recall both parties are encouraged to recall their covert experiences and to share them with one another as they observe or listen to the playback. Mutual recall illuminates the reciprocal interaction of dynamics, and the counselor becomes sensitive to the bilateral nature of human interactions.

Kagan and Krathwohl (1967, p. 96) summarized the objectives full treatment IPR in counseling supervision as

> assisting the trainee to see himself as he really is and how he looks to his counselees, to help him understand himself and to be aware of his own feelings throughout the counseling session, to enable the trainee to "check-out" his personal perceptions of his client and to appropriately communicate these impressions to the client, and to open the trainee to the channels of communication both verbal and non-verbal, existing between himself and his client.

These objectives include two of the four goals that were stated previously for psychotherapeutic supervision: *dynamic awareness* and an *understanding of dynamic contingencies.* These two are prerequisites for the more advanced goals of *dynamic change* and *therapeutic utilization of dynamics.* The IPR procedures described here do not directly attend to these two advanced goals, seemingly for two reasons. An assumption in psychodynamic theory is that awareness and understanding often are sufficient for dynamic change, and guidance-to-awareness through IPR may give counselors insights sufficient to change and become more therapeutic. Another practical reason for limiting IPR's focus principally to awareness and understanding is that the procedure has been employed most frequently with beginning counselors. Video recall sessions contain some highly instructive material which is beyond the grasp of beginning counselors: the concerns of the helpees, the subtleties of their communication, the nature of the counselor's impact on them, and a host of valuable insights (Kagan & Krathwohl, 1967). Because the totality of this material is beyond the novice counselor, limiting the procedure to "attainable goals" makes sense. IPR is thus an appropriate method for initiating psychotherapeutic supervision, although it need not be restricted to use with student-counselors. Kagen and Krathwohl (1967) suggest that IPR can be used with more experienced counselors because counseling experience by itself does not guarantee that a counselor will have adequate insight into dynamics. IPR therefore is a particularly proper method for use with experienced counselors who have not been exposed to psychotherapeutic supervision.

Since the methodology of IPR requires that the supervisor have advanced skills, prospective recall-supervisors are recruited from among competent counselors who then undergo thorough training. IPR supervision training begins with the candidate learning the rationale, function and technique of recall. The supervisor-trainee then works with an experienced IPR supervisor in recorded counseling sessions to become sensitive to the specific cues which indicate that recall questions should be asked. Kagan and Krathwohl (1967) suggested the following cues for productive IPR questions:

> abrupt shifts in theme during the interview; shifts in body posture; changes in voice level, tone or pace; use of vocabulary which describes

intense affect; changes in visual focus (especially glances at the counselor after the client has made a statement); instances in which either person clearly misinterpreted the other or appeared to not hear the other; possible use of metaphoric communication (e.g., "my counselor at school gets me angry"); inappropriate affect, such as a laugh following a serious comment. (p. 15)

These and similar cues may be indicative of heightened underlying emotionality and are potential insight points. Following training in identification of cues, taped and live IPR sessions are critiqued until the supervisor-trainee reaches a level of competence justifying the final learning experience of supervised practice.

IPR methodology has been presented as a somewhat standard procedure, but it can be altered innovatively. Gimmestad and Greenwood (1974) employed multiple recallers (counselor trainees) in their IPR work and reported that this procedure extends participation and learning to a greater number. IPR also can be applied in counseling and has been reported as effective in facilitating client progress (Kagan, Krathwohl, & Miller, 1963; Kagan & Schauble, 1969, Kagan, Schauble, Resnikoff, Danish, & Krathwohl, 1969; Resnikoff, Kagan & Schauble, 1970; Schauble, 1970). Dynamic insight is therapeutic for clients as well as counselor-trainees.

Still another innovative adaptation of IPR is "affect simulation." In this procedure a client is exposed to a film which encourages him/her to simulate interpersonal relations. Both the client and film are videotaped while the client views the film. Shortly after this taping, the client views the videotape of his/her reactions to the film, and a counselor trained in recall technique helps the client examine dynamics. The client's videotaped behavior becomes the focus for counseling, and the goals of dynamic supervision are criteria for success. Anticipated benefits are that the client will become more aware and understand personal dynamics, that troublesome dynamics will be changed, and that new dynamics behavior will be incorporated into the personality.

Psychotherapeutic Supervision: Unstructured Method

The unstructured implementation of psychotherapeutic supervision has been described by Altucher (1967), Arbuckle

(1965), Ekstein and Wallerstein (1958), Hansen and Barker (1964), Kell and Mueller (1966), Lister (1966), Moore (1969), Mueller and Kell (1972), Patterson (1964), and Rogers (1957). The collective thinking of these authors is that the essence of counselor supervision is in the relationship and intensive interaction between supervisor and counselor as they examine and explore together the intrapersonal and interpersonal dynamics of the counselor's interactions with clients, consultees, colleagues, and the supervisor. The counselor brings something to the supervisor for discussion, such as an audio or video tape of a counseling session, or a professional problem or conflict with a colleague. If the counselor's selected concern involves any kind of human interaction, a potential exists for dynamic methodology to be helpful.

Unstructured Method Contrasted With IPR. An effective way to describe the unstructured method of psychotherapeutic supervision is to identify and contrast it with Interpersonal Process Recall (IPR). IPR is most often used with beginning counselors, or those who are receiving their introduction to dynamic supervision. The unstructured approach also can be employed with beginners at a low level of intensity, but its full potential is reached with more experienced counselors. In IPR the treatment is of relatively low threat, and the relationship between the counselor and supervisor is task oriented. The recall supervisor "leads" the counselor into self confrontation, and resistance usually is not confronted. Contrarily, since the unstructured approach capitalizes on the supervisor-counselor relationship as a source of dynamics for study and resolution, anxiety and discomfort in both parties are more likely to be evidenced. Because of more dynamic confrontation, resistance will probably come up and be dealt with interpretively by the supervisor as a therapeutic necessity.

The goals of IPR are essentially awareness and understanding of dynamics, and these are shared by unstructured psychotherapeutic supervision; but, in addition, the unstructured approach places an emphasis on counselor and client dynamic change at impasse points and a subsequent therapeutic utilization of dynamics by the counselor. These two additional goals necessitate supervisory skills which are similar but beyond those based in IPR. Not only does the supervisor expose the counselor to dynamics, but the supervisory process becomes therapeutically intensive for the supervisee, since there is examination and exploration in depth of the meaning of dynamics, and the supervisor-counselor interaction becomes a "working-through" emotional experience.

IPR is somewhat structured and procedural, although the recall supervisor can be flexible in the asking of recall questions. On the other hand, unstructured psychotherapeutic supervision does not follow a set of standardized procedures and the supervisor reacts "moment-by moment." A definite strategy is behind the supervisor's actions, but the stimuli offered by the counselor determine how the strategy will be implemented.

Unstructured Therapeutic Supervision: Relationship Conditions

The essence of unstructured psychotherapeutic supervision lies in the relationship between the supervisor and supervisee. Facilitative conditions such as empathy, genuineness, warmth, trust, and positive regard are of paramount importance. The supervisee will be examining personal dynamics and a supervisory relationship characterized by such facilitative conditions will be conducive to accomplishing this task. Bordin (1983); Patterson (1983); Pierce, Carkhuff, and Berenson (1967); Pierce and Schauble (1970); and Smith, Glass and Miller (1980) have stressed that the counselor can grow and learn by experiencing these conditions in a therapeutic supervisory relationship.

Even though general support exists for establishing and maintaining facilitative conditions in unstructured therapeutic supervision, theoretical disagreement also exists regarding the emphasis to be placed on these conditions. Should the supervisor maintain a focus on the supervisee and concentrate mainly on providing a counseling-like interaction? Does a violation of facilitativeness occur when sometimes focusing on the dynamics of parties to whom the supervisee is relating, as a means of teaching the supervisee how to understand and relate to others?

The dynamic model of therapeutic supervision presented in this Chapter is in agreement with Lambert (1974). Lambert suggested that the supervisor need not keep a rigid and constant focus on the supervisee's dynamics, since to do so would ignore all other sources of dynamic learning. Whereas the overall level of facilitative conditions and the postsupervision self perception of the counselor are important process objectives, a flexible and personalistic supervisory style will facilitate learnings in addition to self development. In a word, psychotherapeutic supervision is more than merely the providing of facilitative conditions.

Unstructured Therapeutic Supervision: For Dynamic Awareness

The methodology for helping counselors achieve dynamic awareness via the unstructured approach is the same as for IPR. Supervisory technique consists simply of *focus* and *response,* with the supervisor focusing on the dynamics of the interaction and making responses which lead the supervisee to give attention to these dynamics. For example, after talking over a counseling case or viewing a portion of it, the counselor might say something to the supervisor in reference to the client's responses, such as "He/she talked a lot about making this decision, and I wasn't sure if it was an immediate one or far in the future." Rather than follow the counselor's focus which might skirt dynamics, the supervisor would turn the focus to dynamics by asking, "Did you see any evidence of anxiety about making the decision? Can you remember how he acted when talking about it?" In this example the supervisor is helping the counselor become aware of external evidence of internal dynamics. One comment like this may not have an effect on the counselor, but repeated dynamic focusing upon strategic spots will shape the direction of the supervisory session.

The strategy behind the supervisors' technique of focus and responses is to lead the counselor without eleciting undue anxiety. Even though a certain degree of anxiety is inevitable, the first stage of unstructured psychotherapeutic supervision attempts to minimize it by beginning the focus on counselor-client interpersonal dynamics. From this beginning, a paradigm for focus and response which would gradually lead the counselor to anxiety confrontation would be the following:

1. interpersonal dynamics of the other party,

2. intrapersonal dynamics of the other party,

3. counselor interpersonal dynamics,

4. counselor intrapersonal dynamics, and

5. interpersonal and intrapersonal dynamics of supervision.

The supervisor depends on certain cues within these five paradigm categories that indicate where and when to focus and respond. Some of these cues were mentioned in the discussion of IPR, but many more exist. These cues are the most subtle of intrapersonal dynamics. They are not expressed intentionally, and although the counselor and helpee usually are unaware of them, they can have a dramatic effect on the behavior of both and the helping process. Lister (1966, p. 56) identified cues which show the supervisor that the counselor is experiencing discomfort, probably in reaction to the helpee or to something the helpee has said:

1. Missing an obvious "opening" for an interpretation or reflection.

2. Unusual difficulty in formulating a response to client statements; overelaborate and argumentative responses as if driving home a point.

3. Marked changes in voice tone and speech patterns.

4. Nervous motor behavior such as shifting posture, moving chair, and so forth.

In the following statement Mueller and Kell (1972, p. 52) identified cues that they interpreted as behavioral evidence of a therapeutic impasse, i.e., a state in which anxiety on the part of counselor, helpee, or both has brought helpgiving progress to a standstill:

An abundance of seemingly irrelevant materials during sessions, an unsatisfying recycling process, repeated expressions of dissatisfaction with progress, ambivalence, gestures toward a premature termination, loss of goal directedness, confusion, and the diffuse expressions of anger and hostility are some indices of impasse. Such impasses have been stimulated by either the client or the therapist, although we are inclined to think that clients often have a major hand in their instigation.

On the other hand, the therapist's apparent inability to bring his/her creative process to bear on client material, his/her failure to see connections, his/her acceptance of surface behaviors without sensitivity to underlying trends, and his/her seeming lack of awareness of the parallel reenactment of client problems during sessions with him/her often indicate that the therapist is immobilized and that it is his/her anxiety that is primarily responsible for the creation of impasses.

The therapeutic technique of focus and response, following a paradigm of gradual anxiety confrontation, is ordinarily an effective way of helping supervisees discover dynamics. But with the unusually defensive supervisee, an "anxiety avoider" in Mueller and Kell's (1972) typology, or the affectively blunted individual, the goal of dynamic awareness is very difficult to achieve. These supervisees will require more than average experiential treatment, and affective simulation is an excellent beginning. Through this procedure the supervisor can control dynamically evocative stimuli and be relatively sure of the consequent dynamics experienced by the supervisee. This type of control enables the supervisor to be particularly persistent, intensive, yet non-confrontive with recall questions.

A counselor's failure to achieve dynamic awareness through a prolonged period of psychotherapeutic supervision is a fairly reliable predictor of ineffective performance on the job. While dynamic awareness does not ensure effective counselor performance, lack of it is a serious limitation. Therefore, if dynamic awareness is a stumbling block for the counselor, his/her suitability for the helping professions should be examined.

Unstructured Psychotherapeutic Supervision
For Understanding Dynamic Contingencies

The techniques selected for helping a counselor understand dynamic contingencies and see the dynamic patterns created thereby should be matched to the counselor's characteristics. Some techniques that are effective with one counselor may be useless with another. For counselors who genuinely are eager for supervision and can tolerate anxiety arising from dynamic exposure, inductive techniques which lead to understanding of dynamic contingencies and patterns are preferable.

A few random inductive techniques (reflection, restatement, clarification) may be sufficient to help the counselor see broad patterns, but the supervisor can go a step further by focusing discretely on the dynamics of a single pattern through a paradigm which parallels the sequence of the actual dynamic contingencies. For example, the supervisor could follow this line of leads:

1. How did you feel when the other person did that?

2. What's the next thing you did after you felt this way?

3. How do you think this affected the other person; what did he/she feel like; what went through his/her mind? How did he/she react?

4. Did the person act this way at any other point of the interaction? What was going on then, what were you doing?

This complete sequence of leads would not be necessary with a responsive supervisee, but it shows the path to understanding a dynamic pattern. Another inductive technique that Moore (1969) has reported is to present to the counselor an example of a dynamic pattern that is analogous to one with which the counselor is dealing. The supervisor explains the example and puts particular focus on those dynamic aspects which are analogous to those of the counselor's situation. As the counselor thinks about the example, without anxiety, its analogous properties should gradually become apparent and a more objective analysis of the counselor's dynamic pattern should result.

When inductive and analogy techniques do not produce an understanding of dynamic contingencies and patterns, and the supervisee defensively resists learning, an alternative route is required. Two strategies are recommended, the first being a set of techniques which are loaded with modeling. Sometimes these are less threatening and more penetrating than inducement and analogy. Examples are

1. reading case studies of dynamic patterns,

2. watching films of counselors who are constructively dealing with their anxiety,

3. group supervision whereby the target supervisee observes others disclosing and assessing the dynamic patterns in their helping relationships, and

4. the modeling influence of the supervisor as he/she discloses past dynamic resolutions and expresses the significance of dynamics in the present relationship with the supervisee.

Permeating all four techniques is the supervisor's implied message that dynamics and anxiety are factors to be uncovered, approached, and resolved if they are problematic, and that the supervisor will assist in this process.

A second strategy to be attempted after these other techniques have failed is to be interpretative and confrontive. Interpretation is an explanation to the supervisee of dynamic patterns in his/her helping or supervisory relationship. This is done objectively, without blame, and the first attempts may be tentative, i.e., exposing or sharing an interpretative perception. Tentative interpretations are less threatening than the firm, assured ones that can come later.

Confrontation is a presentation to the supervisee of discrepancies in his/her behavior. For example, if the supervisee disclaims having anger toward a client but occasionally shows this anger through a raised voice or clenched fist, the supervisor would raise this discrepancy for examination.

Unstructured Psychotherapeutic Supervision
For Counselor Dynamic Change

Supervision techniques for dynamic awareness and understanding of contingencies leads to many changes in the counselor's intrapersonal and interpersonal dynamics (Peters, Cormier, & Cormier, 1978). This type of easily attained dynamic change is often taken for granted and is attributed to the "natural" experience of learning how to counsel. To illustrate, if the supervisor helps a beginning counselor to understand the possible relationship between his/her frowns and the helpee's feeling of disapproval, very likely the counselor will demonstrate more smiles in the next interview. Similarly, ideational changes, such as lowering exaggerated expectancies for success or eliminating anticipations of disastrous failure, also can take place merely through experience and dynamic awareness.

Those dynamic changes which occur within the counselor as a result of awareness and understanding of dynamic contingencies are of low threat to the counselor. Secure counselors, who rarely experience high degrees of threat and tend to approach and deal with anxiety-evoking situations, can make the greatest use of IPR and unstructured supervision techniques. For them, this methodology is sufficient to induce dynamic change. Whenever secure counselors are exposed to evidence of intrapersonal and interpersonal dynamics, they perform a quick reality check to verify the evidence, and, if reality verifies the evidence, they accept it and begin to change self perceptions. On the other hand, when counselors who are high in anxiety are exposed to dynamic information which is contrary to self perceptions and threatening to self esteem, this exposure evokes defenses which will block acceptance of, or identification with, the information. The high-threat counselor may superficially and intellectually exhibit awareness and understanding but will not acquire the true insight which is mandatory for dynamic change.

"Dynamic insight" is an incorporation into the self of information which previously was not known and which is probably somewhat contradictory to one's perceptions of self, others, and the world. Insight in the low-threat counselor often occurs concurrently with dynamic awareness and understanding, but fails to occur under the same conditions in the high-threat counselor. Secure counselors gain insight easily; high-threat counselors rarely do.

The experience of gaining dynamic insight can take a variety of forms, the classic one being a sudden and emotionally exhilarating acceptance of a piece of information about oneself which causes a new conceptualization to come into being. This experience may be described as "having a lightbulb turned on in a darkened room."

Insight experiences may be painful since confrontation with a feared piece of knowledge can raise one's anxiety to a very unpleasant level. Defenses are stretched to the limit, but the turning point comes when the feared dynamic information is no longer distorted or avoided. The individual then is emersed in anxiety for a brief period, only to find that the feeling quickly subsides and the dreaded information is perceived to be not so awful after all. As a result, the individual tends to feel weak and drained emotionally, but more free and whole than before.

A supervisee working with a counselor educator years ago during her graduate studies had just such an insightful experience in relation to her inability to deal with clients who were emotionally distressed. Particular difficulty occurred in situations involving clients coping with the death of loved ones. One day, after becoming upset during observation of a client who was expressing distress over the death of two family members, the counselor-supervisee again spoke of how terrible it was for people to have to face such trauma. The supervisor responded with an interpretative and confrontative lead which finally broke through the supervisee's defenses: "Whom have you lost—that is (the loss) causes you so much pain?" With that, the supervisee broke down in tears and several therapeutic sessions followed centering on unresolved grief and guilt over her father's death. Insight into her intrapersonal dynamics, and their expression and resolution, enabled her to deal more empathically, rather than sympathetically, with the clients' personal problems. Since that first dynamic conflict regarding death of a loved one, the author has encountered several others and has come to realize that such a loss is one of the most traumatic events in a person's life. The successful resolution of these losses is a difficult developmental task which faces each human being.

Abrupt insights, such as the one offered in the previous paragraph make interesting reading, but insight more often occurs in undramatic ways. Insight can occur slowly as small pieces of information are gathered and integrated to form a particular understanding about one's dynamics. Supervisee resistance may accompany "slow insight," and a begrudging acceptance is not uncommon. "Post-hoc insight" may even take place following supervision, when defenses are lowered and the supervisee rethinks the supervisory experience.

To encourage acquisition of dynamic insight through unstructured psychotherapeutic supervision, the supervisor "intervenes"—focusing, exploring, and expanding supervisee dynamics through techniques such as interpretation and confrontation. When using interpretation and confrontation for insight, the objective is to help the counselor assume true ownership and responsibility for dynamics. Awareness without insight is shown when the counselor can intellectually describe problematic dynamics, but continues to experience them in helpgiving situations. This situation is quite common and is an indication to the supervisor that methodology must become interventionist in nature, and thereby move the counselor toward insight.

The following excerpt, taken from an authentic supervision session, illustrates the schism that can lie between awareness and insight. The case involves a school counselor who exhibited a biased attitude toward college-bound counselees and prejudice toward vocationally-oriented students. The counselor exhibited these attitudes by

1. spending most of his time with college-bound students,

2. refusing to offer more than token guidance services to vocationally-oriented students, and

3. offending vocationally-oriented students with remarks of a condescending and prejudicial nature.

Supervisor: *Tom, we've talked before about your preference to work with college-bound students, and that you seem to act less interested, even irritated sometimes, with job-oriented students...*

Counselor: (Cutting in.) *Yea, I know...it's one of those things you have to do... work with the other half... I realize that.*

Supervisor: *Do you mean that you've been trying to do more work with vocational students?*

Counselor: *Uh, yeah, sure. I know it has to be done.*

Supervisor: *Has to be?*

Counselor: (Silence and a confused facial expression.)

Supervisor: *Tom, you obviously don't like to work with vocationally-oriented students, and it's a chore to force yourself to do it. Am I right?*

Counselor: (Silence, but an affirmative facial expression.)

Supervisor: *I guess we agreed upon this point the last time we talked, but, just agreeing or intellectually realizing your preference hasn't changed it. . .and the attitude continues to affect your behavior toward vocational students.*

Counselor: *Well, I'm just tired of trying to relate to some of these... students who just don't give a damn about their future, the school. . .or anything. Why should I be expected to work with students who don't care?*

In this supervisory interaction the supervisee is superficially aware of his prejudicial attitude, but does not have dynamic insight. Insight in this instance would probably be based on many of the following realizations:

1. I do have a prejudicial attitude toward vocational students. I don't like them or respect them as much as college-bound students.

2. I don't like vocational students because they don't like me as well as do college-bound students. Also, college-bound students come from my socio-economic class, their parents are my friends—the kind of people who appreciate my work.

3. My dislike for vocational students puts me on edge in their presence, and I do treat them curtly, without much warmth. It is my perception of them that precipitates my irritable emotions and behavior. I am responsible for my reactions.

4. Sometimes I exaggerate the aversiveness of vocational students. I "awfulize" about them. I also demand that they be just the kind of people I think they should be. I get carried away sometimes.

5. Regardless of whether vocational students like me or the school, they do have a right to an education, and it is my job to provide guidance services to them.

6. In spite of the resistance which I sometimes receive from vocational students, they have a need for guidance services, in many cases it is a more desperate need than college-bound students.

The supervisory techniques for promoting the counselor's acquisition of these insights include those for facilitating dynamic awareness. However, when insight has not been gained through facilitative techniques the supervisory interaction must become more "interventionist" by using the techniques of interpretation and confrontation. An interventionist interaction is offered in the following excerpt to show how such techniques could be employed by the supervisor. Note is to be made that these same techniques can be used in many different ways, depending upon the supervisor's theoretical orientation.

Counselor: Well, I'm just tired of trying to relate to some of these. . .students who just don't give a damn about their future, the school. . .or anything. Why should I be expected to work with students who don't care?

Supervisor: Tom, I'm not going to tell you what you should do, that is your decision and only you are responsible for your attitudes and behavior. But I do know this, if you continue to be at odds with the vocational students, it will be necessary for the administration to remove you from this position; and I think you can see why if you think about it, you are getting along and providing guidance services only to a portion of the students.

Counselor: (Silence.)

Supervisor: The real tragedy in this situation is that your prejudice toward vocational students is not necessary and doesn't make sense!

Counselor: (Silence.)

Supervisor: (Waiting for a response from the counselor. When it does not come:) You're just a victim of faulty thinking and circumstances.

Counselor: What do you mean?

Supervisor: Well, I've heard you say that the vocational students don't like you, and I know that student approval is important. In fact, I think you are downright angry because they don't like you.

Counselor: So what!

Supervisor: So when you come into contact with vocational students you already have a reserve of anger ready to dump onto them. You feel rejected and lash back.

Counselor: *Are you telling me that I don't have a right to my feelings?!*

Supervisor: *No, Tom, you have a right, and I certainly understand what it's like to feel that way, but I just think that **you** create this anger by demanding that vocational students be the kind of people you think they should be. And when they don't live up to your demands, and on top of that when they don't like you, then you blame them and dump anger onto them. Do you see what I'm getting at?*

Counselor: (Nod.)

This initial supervisory intervention is just the beginning of insight for the counselor. The supervisor directively broke through the counselor's defenses with confrontations and interpretations of the covert attitudes and thoughts which precipitate the counselor's anger. All the while the supervisor kept the counselor in a responsible role, never allowing him to rationalize his unprofessional actions, yet understanding and not condemning him for human fallacy.

The dynamic insights gained by supervisees through such intervention is therapeutic in its effects, and its benefits generalize to the supervisees' lives outside of counseling and supervision. In the previous excerpts regarding prejudice toward vocational students, effective supervision could influence the counselor to be more accepting and tolerant of people in his private life. However, one must remember that counselor supervision is not counseling, and a distinction between the two should be maintained. Mueller and Kell (1972, p.77) have emphasized this distinction:

> When the therapist begins to express how he felt at times of impasse, the supervisor and therapist could be inadvertently diverted into extensive excursions into the emotional life of the therapist, studying the historical development of those feelings, and their current meaning. However, we feel that the beneficial effects of such a therapeutic venture can still be experienced by the therapist and will have more meaning to him if they are directed back to his relationship with his client. Essentially, the supervisory process begins at the point of conflict that has arisen out of the therapist's relationship with the client (or other) and it should terminate in the restoration of that relationship without unnecessary derailment.

Dynamic theory posits that an individual who has gained insight can change covert and overt behavior. This is a point of conjecture though, and perhaps a more representative prevailing attitude of counselor supervisors would be to say that insight enables "some" individuals to change dynamics. Even when insight successfully promotes intrapersonal dynamic change, one is not assured that interpersonal behavior change will follow. The supervisee may still be deficient in counseling competencies and may need skill development to fill these deficits. Chapter 4 addresses this task.

Unstructured Psychotherapeutic Supervision For The Therapeutic Utilization of Dynamics

Thus far three goals of dynamic supervision have been discussed in terms of methodolgy to be employed. Assuming achievement of these goals, the counselor has become aware of dynamics, understands at least some of the dynamic contingencies and patterns operative in his/her helpgiving and supervisory interactions, and has made changes in counterproductive dynamics. Now the counselor is beginning to function at a fairly sophisticated level in a dynamic sense, but the last goal of therapeutic supervision is yet to be achieved. This final goal, the therapeutic utilization of dynamics, is the counselor's skill of using and maintaining the three previously learned dynamic processes (awareness, diagnostic understanding, and change) in all forms of helping interactions.

Although the counselor's more troublesome dynamics and patterns may be resolved through psychotherapeutic supervision, a need for diligence always will exist, lest he/she become complacent. As long as the counselor engages in helping interactions, dynamics will arise to inhibit the process. The counselor may encounter aggressive persons who elicit defensiveness, sexually solicitous people who evoke attractions, dependent individuals who seek someone to carry their problems, and so on. In such cases the counselor must not react intrapersonally or interpersonally in an irresponsible manner, for such undisciplined reactions sustain problematic dynamics and are not therapeutic. The counselor must be aware of the natural tendency to be anxious, to be attracted, or to jump to the rescue; but, rather than yield to such inclinations, he/she must assess how best to act, and then act appropriately to utilize dynamics therapeutically.

Supervisors help their supervisees learn to skillfully use dynamics by employing such skills themselves within supervision, and by teaching supervisees to use the skills in counseling. During supervision the supervisor should continually disclose his/her own dynamics, encourage the counselor to do likewise, and, in general, approach the dynamics of supervision in an exploratory and problem-solving manner. A model of dynamic control is provided by the supervisor, and the counselor is encouraged to manage dynamics rather than avoid them or succumb to them unprofessionally. Kell and Mueller (1966, p.99) suggest that the supervisor has qualities which cause others to believe that he/she can control dynamics but is willing to support others as they engage in exploration, experimentation, and learning to control their dynamics.

The counselor also is assisted during supervision to plan dynamic strategies for use in counseling and other direct interactions. With the supervisor's help, the counselor decides how to interact with the other party in a way that will be most helpful to that person. An illustrative counseling case comes to mind when speaking of planned dynamic strategies. The case involved a female client in the eleventh grade who sought attention following initial contact during routine course scheduling procedures. The student, without apparent justifications, expressed feelings of inferiority and self condemnation, and she publicly displayed anxiety attacks in the classroom and other social situations. Exploration of her problems revealed a suppressed positive self esteem which was not disclosed for fear of disapproval. Observation of her interpersonal style revealed a solicitation of peer and teacher sympathy through the masquerade of being filled with insecurity. This masquerade behavior had succeeded in eliciting sympathy from peers, teachers, parents, and her counselor.

The dynamic strategy employed in this case was for the counselor to control sympathetic inclinations, and to socially reinforce only the student's demonstrations of positive self-reference and constructive, independent action. Furthermore, after establishing rapport, the counselor confronted and interpreted, in the counseling situation, the student's interpersonal style, i.e., "act insecure and weak so that others will approve of me."

The strategy of dynamic utilization was a success, as indicated by cessation of anxiety attacks and gradual increase in expressions of self confidence and esteem. Through interaction with the counselor, and later in the larger school environment, the student learned that a positive self-concept is more self-fulfilling and socially reinforced than a "weeping willow act."

Planning strategies for management of dynamics in situations where the counselor is only indirectly involved is yet another characteristic of advanced stages of therapeutic supervision. The supervisor helps the counselor diagnose dynamics in these situations, and then assists in constructing and implementing strategies to improve dynamic interaction.

A recent example of dynamic management illustrates the kind of counselor activity that the supervisor can help to plan. A group of teachers were distressed at the difficulty they were having with "disrespectful" students. In the role of mental health consultant, the counselor met with the group and utilized some of the procedures which already have been described in this Chapter. Dynamics that normally occur in an interaction between a disrespectful student and a teacher were diagnosed and questions of an IPR nature were addressed so the teachers would become aware of their dynamic patterns.

1. What thoughts and feelings precipitate disrespectful behavior from a student?

2. What exactly are the disrespectful behaviors, what message are they intended to communicate?

3. What message is received by the teacher from the student's disrespectful behavior?

4. What are the teacher's intrapersonal dynamics in response to disrespect?

5. How does the teacher act (interpersonally) toward the student when experiencing such thoughts and feelings?

6. How does the teacher's action affect the student?

After dynamic patterns and their significance had been explored, strategies for interacting with disrespectful students were developed—strategies designed to be dynamically appropriate treatments. This approach to the management of dynamics through teacher consultation involved diagnosis, awareness and understanding, and reconstruction of dynamic patterns.

Summary

The methodology of psychotherapeutic supervision consists of numerous techniques which can be categorized into two basic methodological categories: IPR and the unstructured method. In supervisory practice the techniques from these two categories can be employed compatibly and integratively to achieve the goals of psychotherapeutic supervision. Figure 3.2 is an integrated listing of psychotherapeutic supervisory techniques as they relate to supervision goals and supervisee effect. The chart may be helpful to trainees and practitioners of the psychotherapeutic approach as they attempt to choose the "right" technique for their particular situation. Choice of methodology requires that the supervisor be aware of his/her goals, the intended effect on the supervisee, and the unique characteristics of the supervisee that may influence his/her receptivity to supervisory techniques.

PSYCHOTHERAPEUTIC SUPERVISION: EMPIRICAL SUPPORT

Research in counseling and psychotherapy has been plagued with methodological problems (Hansen, Robins, & Grimes, 1982; Kaplan, 1983; Ryan, 1978; Whiteley, 1967; Woolsey, 1986). Major difficulties hamper planning and employment of an experimental design that controls all intervening variables within the settings and situations of counseling. Another common problem is the difficulty in establishing a

Supervision Goal	Therapeutic Technique	Supervisee Effect
Dynamic Awareness	IPR proper and adaptations of IPR	Discovery and consequent awareness of one's interpersonal and intrapersonal dynamics
	Focus and response; gradual anxiety confrontation	
	Affect simulation	
Understanding Dynamic Contingencies and Patterns	IPR proper and adaptations of IPR	A general understanding that intrapersonal dynamics precipitate interpersonal dynamics, and a personal understanding of how this contingency operates in one's own helpgiving situations
	Inductive techniques	Inductively achieved realization of dynamic patterns
	Analogy technique	Understanding one's own dynamic pattern by comparing it to an analogous pattern
	Techniques for defensive supervisors	
	Read case studies Films Group supervision Supervisor modeling	Understanding via modeling and identification with supervisor and peers
	Interpretation Confrontation	Forced exposure to threatening dynamic patterns
Dynamic Change	Facilitative technique for dynamic insight	Self discovery of insight; low threat experience
	Interpretation and confrontation for dynamic insight	Supervisor induced insight; low threat experience
Therapeutic Utilization of Dynamics	Supervisor employing and modeling the skill of dynamic utilization within supervision	Imitative and experiential learning
	Monitoring of the counselor's dynamics during helpgiving and assistance/ guidance in using dynamic-based skills	Supportive guidance and facilitation as the counselor utilizes himself/herself as a therapeutic tool

Figure 3.2. Psychotherapeutic supervision methodology.

criterion which is a valid index of the dependent variable—accessibility and measurability often dictate selection of criteria. Specification, control, and measurement of independent variables—i.e., the treatment process—constitute yet another complicated set of problems (Burck, Cottingham, & Reardon, 1973).

However difficult these problems seem to be for researchers in the field of counseling, they are even more troublesome for those attempting supervision research. Since supervisory treatment is, as yet, poorly understood, descriptive investigations and quasi-experimental studies have constituted the bulk of the research effort in this area. After a decade or so of asking, "What are we doing?", there is reason for optimism in the recent increase of experimental studies aimed at assessing the effectiveness of supervision.

A continuing problem in supervision research however is the limited number of valid dependent variables to be investigated. The independent variable of counseling, already described as difficult to specify, measure, and validate, are the dependent variables in supervision research. Thus, if one does not know that a particular counseling skill produces positive effects in clients, it is foolish to use it as a dependent variable in research on supervision. So few counseling skills have received strong empirical support that the list of dependent variables for research on supervision is quite limited.

Research in psychotherapeutic supervision is particularly susceptible to the problems mentioned, but, rather than dwell on the difficulties, a more proactive approach is to identify what has been learned. Although the limitations of past research must be recognized, one can draw some conclusions, speculate about areas where evidence is inconclusive, and plan for more and better research to broaden knowledge about counselor supervision.

In the following pages, a brief summary of research findings bearing on three aspects of psychotherapeutic supervision will be presented: counselor expectancies of supervision, effectiveness of Interpersonal Process Recall, and effectiveness of experiential supervision.

Expectations of Supervisees

The counselor's expectations of supervision is an intra-personable variable which fits into the psychotherapeutic approach. Knowing these expectancies will help the supervisor predict the counselor's reaction to supervision, and will enable the supervisor to make a presentation that is likely to be received favorably.

Very few investigations have dealt with the topic of expectancies for supervision, but three studies have provided descriptive information. Delaney and Moore (1966) used the *Supervisor Role Analysis Form* to assess the supervision expectancies of 123 pre-practicum students. A component analysis of the data yielded fifteen factors, nine of which could be related to the instructional nature of the interaction. The investigators concluded from their findings that the supervisee sample viewed the supervisor's role as dealing largely with teaching.

Hansen's (1965) investigation of the supervision expectancies of thirty NDEA trainees, using the *Barrett-Lennard Relationship Inventory*, revealed results compatible with those of Delaney and Moore. Their sample of trainees did not have high expectations for a facilitative relationship in supervision, and reported having received a more facilitative experience than had been expected.

Gysbers and Johnston (1965) administered the *Supervisor Role Analysis Form* to fifty-one counselor-trainees before, during, and after a practicum supervisory experience. Results showed that these counselor-trainees expressed a desire for instruction in techniques at the beginning of the practicum, but were less dependent and more autonomous toward the supervisor at the end of the experience. Friedlander and Snyder (1983) using practicum students (n=82) as participants, investigated their general expectations for the supervisory process. She found the student trainees expected their supervisors to be significantly more trustworthy than expert, more expert than attractive, and more evaluative than supportive. Similar results were obtained by Allen, Szollos, and Williams (1986) and Stoltenberg, Solomon and Ogden (1986).

Information gathered from these three inquiries must be viewed cautiously, but it tends to be consistent with the theoretical notion of Hogan (1964) and Reising and Daniels (1983). Hogan suggested that there are four identifiable levels represented in the development of psychotherapists (counselors), and the first level fits the descriptive data on practicum counselors from the previously cited studies: the beginner is dependent, insecure, uninsightful of self and impact on others, anxious, but also motivated. The accumulated academic experience of such trainees, probably including one year of graduate-level academic study in counselor education, may incline them to expect direct instruction from, and a somewhat distant relationship with, a supervisor. Likewise, considering the supervisee's professional immaturity and lack of experience, the dependency revealed by Gysbers and Johnston (1965) is not expected.

If we assume that these cautious conclusions have some validity, the next question is "How will a nervous, instructionally-hungry supervisee react to dynamic supervision?" Not much research evidence to answer this question is available. An inquiry by Miller and Oetting (1966) reported responses to two open-ended questions asked of a small group of supervisees. The investigators reported that the counselors (supervisees) disliked a therapy-like supervisory approach, but they did want the supervisor to be sensitive to their feelings and ideas. An early study by Hansen (1965) and a more recent study by Reising and Daniels (1983) supported this finding. This modest body of evidence suggests that even though the psychotherapeutic approach may not provide as much didactic instruction as the supervisee is accustomed to receiving, the facilitative relationship is valued.

The next logical question is whether therapeutic supervision is effective if supervisee expectancies and desires are contrary. Birk (1972) investigated this question by permitting subjects to register preference for a supervisory approach (didactic or experiential) and then treating this factor as an independent variable in her experimental design. In terms of the dependent measure of empathic response to supervisees, subjects who received their preferred type of supervision did not achieve significantly better performance than did subjects who received the non-preferred type of supervision. Findings in this one study support the probability that preference for a supervisory approach does not significantly influence results of supervision—particularly if supervision effects were perceived as positive by the supervisee.

While preference has not been shown to be a significant expectancy variable, perceived supervisor competence may be another one with potential implications. Hester, Weitz, Anchor, and Roback (1976) found supervisor skillfulness to be a main contributor to supervisee attraction to a supervisor, more influential than supervisor-supervisee attitude similarity.

These findings are similar to those of Beutler, Johnson, Neville, Elkins, and Jobe (1975) who concluded that a therapist's credibility is more important, when predicting outcomes of psychotherapy, than is attitude similarity between therapist and client. Perhaps future research in supervision will produce findings showing that perceived helper credibility is a most important variable in helpee expectancy for outcome.

Effectiveness of Psychotherapeutic Supervision

The most crucial question to be answered about psychotherapeutic supervision concerns its effectiveness. Until recently, only the subjective evaluations of practitioners could be cited to support claims for effectiveness. Psychotherapeutic supervision seemed to work in practice. Recently, research on psychotherapeutic supervision has increased, and two directional trends are apparent. One is the investigation of Interpersonal Process Recall (IPR) and the other is the study of experiential supervision.

IPR Effectiveness. Development and validation of IPR began with an initial research project by Kagan and Krathwohl (1967). Through an experimental design, the investigators compared a group of supervisees receiving an IPR program to a similar group receiving a more traditionally dyadic form of dynamic supervision. Criterion gain-scores on the *Counselor Verbal Response Scale* showed that IPR produced significantly greater gains, but that both the IPR and traditional supervision groups made significant improvement.

Numerous IPR studies have appeared since the procedure was developed. Experimental studies by Dendy (1971). Grzegorek (1971), and ARcher and Kagan (1973) illustrated IPR's efficacy in terms of criterion gains on the *Counselor Verbal Response Scale, Empathic Understanding Scale, Affective Sensitivity Scale, Personal Orientation Inventory, Barrett-Lennard Relationship Inventory*, and the *Wisconsin Relationshp Orientation Inventory*. In some studies the IPR treatment was not superior to other supervisory treatments, but measurable gains were a consistent finding (Ward, Kagan, & Krathwohl, 1972). IPR has been used effectively with clients in counseling to promote growth in the direction of therapeutic goals (Kagan, 1980; Kagan, Krathwohl, & Miller, 1963; Resnikoff, Kagan, & Schauble, 1970; Schauble, 1970), although an investigation by Van Noord and Kagan (1976) did not find stimulated recall and affect stimulation to be more efective than traditional therapy.

Substantive research supports IPR as a viable supervisory procedure to improve relationship and facilitative skills of counselors. Archer and Kagan (1973) demonstrated the efficiency of IPR as they extended supervision to paraprofessionals, when preparing them to be competent IRP trainers. Although further research into the instrumental factors and long range effects of IPR is needed (Kingdon, 1975; Van Noord & Kagan, 1976), the IPR procedure seems to be an innovative and valuable contribution to counselor supervision.

Effectiveness of Experiential Supervision. As described in this Chapter, psychotherapeutic supervision is a helping process focusing on the intrapersonal and interpersonal dynamics in the counselor's relationships. The "therapeutic quality" of the process comes from insight into dynamics and from the experienced relationship with the supervisor. In respect to this latter component, a special type of psychotherapeutic supervision has arisen which places optimum importance on the supervisory relationship. *Experiential supervision* does not attempt to teach the supervisee about dynamics; instead, the experiential supervisor offers a therapeutic relationship which facilitates self growth and learning. Instrumental in the supervisory relationship is the quality of facilitative conditions (empathy, genuineness, regard, concreteness) offered by the supervisor.

Payne, Winter, and Bell (1972) assessed and compared the effectiveness of technique-oriented supervision, experiential supervision, and a placebo treatment in terms of the amount of skill acquired in offering empathic statements. Their results were not supportive of experiential supervision, since only the technique-oriented supervisory approach produced a significant improvement in counselors' levels of empathy. Similar results obtained by Payne and Gralinski (1968) showed that counselors receiving technique-oriented supervision and control treatment were higher in the learning of empathy than those receiving counseling-oriented supervision. Payne, Weiss, and Kappa (1972) and Birk (1972) also found didactic supervision to be superior to experiential supervision for achieving the criterion of counselor-learned empathic behavior. Ronnestad (1977) compared the three supervisory techniques of modeling, feedback, and experiential intervention in teaching counseling students to communicate empathic understanding. Post treatment ratings of counselors' empathic responding showed that the modeling method was more effective than the feedback method and the feedback method was more effective than the experiential method.

In contrast to the previously cited lack of supportive findings for the experiential approach to supervision, an experimental study by Pierce and Schauble (1970, p. 186) produced the following results:

1. supervisees who received supervision from supervisors who themselves were functioning at high levels on the facilitative core dimensions . . . grew significantly on these dimensions;

2. supervisees who had supervisors functioning at low levels on these dimensions did not gain; and

3. supervisees of the high-level supervisors were functioning significantly better on the core dimensions than the supervisees of the low-level supervisors at the end of the supervision period.

A follow-up study nine months later showed that supervisees of the high-level supervisors continued to function more effectively on the core dimensions than did supervisees of the low-level supervisors, and that neither group of supervisees had changed significantly in respect to the core dimensions (Pierce & Schauble, 1971).

One is tempted to conclude from the findings of Pierce and Schauble that the supervisees of high-level supervisors actually "grew" in terms of the core dimensions as a direct consequence of the facilitative conditions received in experiential supervision, but Lambert (1974, p. 55) has aptly noted that the investigators

> did not measure the level of facilitative conditions offered trainees, but assumed that it was equal to that offered clients in a counseling relationship. In fact, they gave no evidence supporting their assumption that supervisors offer identical levels of facilitative conditions in counseling and supervision.

Pierce and Schauble's (1970) investigations do support the supervision of highly facilitative (in counseling) supervisors, but the efficacy of instrumental conditions within the supervisory treatment was not addressed.

Lambert (1974) went on to investigate the extent to which the same facilitative qualities which appear in counseling also appear in the supervisory process. Through a factorial analysis of the counseling and supervision of five experienced and facilitative (in counseling) counselors, he found that no significant differences between levels of genuineness and respect in counseling and supervision existed, but empathy and specificity were significantly higher in counseling than in supervision. On the *Hill Interaction Matrix* a significantly greater proportion of therapeutic-work statements in counseling than in supervision was reported. Lambert interpreted his findings as an indication that the assumption cannot be made that therapists function at the same levels in both supervision and counseling. The supervisory processes he studied, which were unspecified in terms of the intended approach, were more didactic than were those employed by the same subjects during counseling.

Payne and Gralinski (1968) also have investigated the effect of experiencing facilitative conditions within supervision. In their experimental design, level of empathy, as operative within experiential supervision, technique-oriented supervision, and a control treatment, did not significantly influence supervisees' post-supervision performance of empathic counseling behavior. Wedeking and Scott (1976) also found supervisee empathy in counseling to be unaffected by the supervisor's empathy in supervision.

Very little research supports a claim for the effectiveness of experiential supervision, or for the hypothesis that experiencing facilitative conditions within supervision will enable the supervisee to offer these same therapeutic ingredients to others. Precisely, empirical findings suggest that the singular treatment by experiential supervision is ineffective for the learning of facilitative counseling skills. Although Carkhuff (1969a, p. 156) has compiled a large number of studies which associate high-functioning supervisors with supervisee gain in performing facilitative skills, the supervision and/or training they offered to supervisees included more learning principles than only those associated with phenomenal experience. Carkhuff's (1969, p. 153) recommendation is that

> hopefully, the trainer is not only functioning at high levels on these dimensions but is also attempting to impart learnings concerning these dimensions in a systematic manner, for only then will he integrate the critical sources of learning—the didactic, the experiential, and the modeling.

A later restatement of this same notion (Carkhuff, 1972) cited the finding of a study of Vitalo (1970) which suggested that both the facilitative level of the trainer/supervisor and systematic social reinforcement were necessary to produce the verbal-conditioning effect by which trainees learn to make facilitative responses.

Conclusions drawn by Carkhuff have not been validated by subsequent research. Brady, Rowe, and Smouse (1976) replicated the Vitalo study and failed to find similar results. They interpreted their findings as supporting the contention that contingent reinforcement is the most potent aspect of effective verbal conditioning, and that the role of facilitative conditions has not been shown to be instrumental.

Indirectly in support of the instrumental role, however, is the finding by Dowling and Frantz (1975) that facilitative models generate significantly more imitative learning of ethnocentrism than do unfacilitative models. Although this study cannot be directly generalized to experiential supervision, it does suggest that, within certain subject-situation-variable paradigms, the role of facilitative behavior can be conducive to learning some classes of behavior.

The lack of support for instrumental learning effects of facilitative conditions does not mean that they do not have a place in counselor supervision, although it does raise a serious question about the viability of experiential supervision. Facilitative conditions have not been shown to be a "sufficient" treatment for the kinds of counselor learning which should take place within supervision, but it can be speculated that a facilitative supervisory relationship is a good climate for learning. The supervisor attends to the insecurities and efforts of the supervisee, relieves anxiety, and creates a working relationship within which other learnings can occur. In such a context the facilitative conditions seem appropriate and desirable.

PRACTICAL APPLICATION: ILLUSTRATIVE CASES

The practice of psychotherapeutic supervision has largely been confined to university settings, and one seldom hears of dynamic methodology being used in field supervision. In the case of IPR this is somewhat justified, since that procedure requires laboratory equipment and is geared for beginning counselors. However other kinds of dynamic methodology could just as easily be employed in field settings as in the university, and there probably are adaptations of IPR that would be applicable to field work. Why hasn't psychotherapeutic supervision "caught on"? A possible reason is that field supervisors, the majority of which have not received preparation for supervision, consider psychotherapeutic supervision to be a highly sophisticated treatment, one to be expected from university professors but not from practitioners in the field. What these supervisors don't realize is that for those who have had experience in dealing with dynamics in counseling, the shift to dealing with them in supervision is not overly difficult.

The most unjustified reason for not using dynamic methodology is the argument that it is neither applicable nor useful in the "real" world of counselor practice. This argument indicated a complete lack of awareness of interpersonal and intrapersonal dynamics. The work of the counselor is constantly involved with dynamics; they are tools of the trade, utilization of which is an index of the counselor's competency and personal development.

Some synoptic cases of psychotherapeutic supervision, drawn from actual supervisory practice, are presented here to illustrate that dynamics are operative in most of the counselor's work with people, and that a wide variety of supervisory methods can be developed and applied toward meeting the goals of psychotherapeutic supervision.

Case 1: An Uptight Counselor

A counseling director was having difficulty with a counselor who recently had entered counseling after two unsuccessful years as a classroom teacher. The director noticed that the counselor was not relating well to students in her new capacity, and weekly supervisory sessions were begun on the pretext of helping the new counselor get off to a good start. The director and counselor listened to audio-tapes of several typical interviews, and the director observed that the counselor dominated her counseling sessions with cognitively oriented, closed-ended questions. She dominated supervisory sessions in a similar fashion and her tension was evident. The director gradually led her into exploring her feelings in general about counseling, and her emotional reactions to counselees in particular. The counselor discovered painfully that she was threatened by close interpersonal contact. She thought students didn't like her, and reacted with defensive authoritative behavior.

As the threat of supervision dissolved, so did her anxiety in counseling. She slowly gained confidence and found that students like her much more when she related in a person-to-person manner. Consequently, she developed a greater degree of self esteem.

Case 2: An Insecure Beginner

The counselor in this case was enrolled in a counseling practicum course. He was a courteous and somewhat shy student whom everyone liked. In counseling with his practicum client he quickly established rapport and was off to a good start, but the supervisor noticed later that the counselor was being manipulated by the client to the detriment of counseling progress. Crucial topics were being avoided by the client, who placed responsibility for solving concerns on the counselor. Client contradictions were overlooked by the counselor, and the tone of the counseling relationship was controlled totally by the client.

The supervisor conducted Interpersonal Process Recall with the client and counselor so their thoughts and feelings during counseling could be recalled and examined. Through IPR the counselor became aware of his feelings of inadequacy, his desire to have the client like him, and how these dynamics were affecting his interpersonal counseling behavior. Client recall revealed disappointment in the counselor's lack of assertiveness, with this disappointment having been masked effectively by the client's controlling behavior—a response to his fear of "being told that I'm maladjusted."

Subsequent to IPR, the counselor's behavior was more congruent and effective. Insight into himself and the client enabled the counselor to act out of a professional intent, rather than solely from personal needs.

Case 3: A Problem With Consultation

A school counselor was having difficulty with parental consultation. The supervisor found that the counselor was satisfied with some consultation sessions and parents gave approving feedback about the helpfulness of these sessions, but other sessions were disastrous. The counselor and parents emerged from these interactions with anger toward each other, and on one occasion the parents had reported their irate dissatisfaction to the school superintendent who asked for an investigation into the counselor's conduct.

The supervisor arranged to have regular meetings with the counselor to work on the consultation problems. At first there was considerable resistance from the counselor, but the supervisor's skill at establishing a non-threatening relationship reduced anxiety and together they explored the counselor's past consultation cases. Clearly, the counselor had no trouble interacting with friendly parents, but confrontive and demanding parents evoked the counselor's anxiety and anger, and the consequential reaction was to "tell them off." The counselor felt a need to defend the school and its personnel from the implied accusations of defensive parents. Coming from a family of educators and having a strong commitment to public education, the counselor was offended personally by such parents.

A thorough exploration of intense feelings, strong attitudes, and the interpersonal behavior they spawned helped the counselor see where consultation problems began. Supervision was directed at helping the counselor learn to control intrapersonal dynamics and behave in a way that promoted progress toward consulting goals. The counselor discovered that the best way to gain public recognition for the integrity of educators was through effective professional behavior with even the most offensive consultees. The experience was rewarding when the counselor first succeeded in converting an argumentative parent into a cooperative working partner.

Case 4: A "Difficult" Colleague

A staff of counselors included one member who was arrogant and hostile toward colleagues. The behavior of this individual bordered on the unethical, but there was never conclusive evidence of professional misconduct. Yet, conflicts and continual reports of the counselor's discrediting and untruthful statements caused a serious staff morale problem.

The supervisor asked the counselor to meet for individual supervision, and at that time gave the counselor an opportunity to express perceptions of the staff and individual colleagues. One hope was that the counselor could discuss feelings and attitudes that may have prompted aggressive behavior, but the counselor was reticent and the supervisor was forced to present the problem directly in as non-threateningly a way as possible. The supervisor also suggested that they work on improving the counselor's relationship with colleagues. This choice was a forced one, and the problem would have become more severe if the counselor had refused supervision. However, the supervisee begrudgingly agreed to participate in supervision, holding fast to the attitude that the problem existed only in the minds of others.

A series of supervisory sessions followed and each one was strained. The counselor never admitted having any negative feelings or attitudes toward colleagues and treated supervision as a "requirement," but the supervisor was able to concentrate on overt conflicts that occurred within the staff. Interpersonal dynamics and their probable intrapersonal impact on others were explored. Concurrently, the supervisor consulted with other staff members concerning the handling of intrastaff conflicts.

Gradually the counselor's interactions with colleagues improved. The facilitative relationship of supervision and the examination of interactions had a positive effect on the counselor. Although the counselor had refused direct exploration of intrapersonal dynamics, arrogance and hostility faded as interactions improved.

Case 5: Applying Rational Emotive Therapy (RET) To Counseling Supervision*

The theory and practice of RET (Ellis & Grieger, 1977; Grieger & Boyd, 1980) provides yet another point of departure for therapeutic supervision. The cornerstone of RET is the thesis that it is the individual's current, irrational ways of interpreting and evaluating life events, rather than the events themselves, that cause and maintain the individual's emotional and behavioral disturbances. In other words, individuals generally control their own destiny, particularly their emotional destiny,

---

*This supervisory case is offered by R.M. Grieger, Ph.D., an Associate Fellow and training faculty member of the Institute for Advanced Study in Rational Psychotherapy. Dr. Grieger also is an Associate Professor in the School of Education, University of Virginia.

by the way they "personalize" their experiences. Given this premise, which has a great deal of empirical support, the major thrust of RET is three fold:

1. to help people get in touch with the basic values, beliefs and philosophies they hold that prompt them to evaluate events as they do;

2. to induce them to give up those erroneous beliefs and values that lead to emotional distress; and

3. to help them learn more adaptive and valid beliefs and values to replace those which are disturbing or maladaptive.

By way of example, take the young college student who loses his girlfriend and reacts with depression. He stays home much of the time, avoids going out with other girls or frequenting places where they used to go together, stops attending to his school work, and in general feels miserable. Most people would falsely conclude that this young man's loss caused these reactions. RET theory explains his differently. What happened to him emotionally didn't automatically follow from his loss, but from his evaluation of the loss. Specifically, to feel miserable, he had to evaluate his girlfriend's departure in the following manner: "I must have her. I can't exist without her. Life will be absolutely awful since she's gone. Since I lost her, I must be a worm whom no one can love." If he had concluded something like, "I really care for her. Since I care for her, I am very sorry she doesn't care for me too, but, life goes on and I'll make it ok." he would not have felt depressed but only sad and frustrated. Thus, this young man caused his own depression by interpreting and evaluating his loss in the ways that he did.

What do these RET tenets mean for counselor education and supervision? They help the counselor-in-training develop a better understanding of ideational and emotional dynamics of clients' problems and help the counselor decide just how to intercede strategically. More germaine to this discussion, however, RET provides a focus for helping the counselor-in-training deal with his/her own emotional reactions within the counseling session.

Most beginning counselors, and a good many experienced ones as well, find working with clients an emotional experience that they do not always understand and often do not know how to manage. One common emotional reaction, particularly with beginners, is anxiety. This usually results from the counselor's belief that he/she must do well with a client to gain the approval of supervisors or peers, and then perceiving himself or herself as an inadequate counselor ignores the fact that disturbed people do disturbed things, and illogically demands that the client work hard, inhibit resistances, and generally make steady progress. Then, when the client does not or cannot fully cooperate, the counselor evaluates the client negatively.

In an RET perspective on psychotherapeutic supervision, the supervisor, among other things, attends to the emotional reactions of the counselor and, more importantly, to the evaluative thoughts behind these emotional reactions. The supervisor first helps the counselor get in touch with his/her feelings and thoughts, and then initiates a discussion of the validity and appropriateness of these evaluations, while helping the counselor adopt a more constructive, empathic perspective of the client.

To conclude this RET supervision case, an authentic supervisor-counselor interchange will be cited to illustrate the points made previously. George had counseled Susan for approximately two months and was getting nowhere. He had tried just about everything he knew to establish a trusting relationship and was at his wit's end. To be sure, Susan was a difficult client. She generally was suspicious, resistant and argumentative. Note in the following transcript the tact that the supervisor took in focusing on George's anger and on what lay behind that anger.

> **Supervisor:** *Let's stop the tape here, George. Now, reflect on what was taking place right then between you and Susan. What were your feelings?*
>
> **George:** *Well, like I didn't know where to go.*
>
> **Supervisor:** *But, I bet you were not without feeling and were stuck only in respect to techniques. What was that feeling?*

George: *Anger.*

Supervisor: *Yeah. That really came through loud and clear. Were you aware of it?* (George nods yes). *Well, let's talk about that some, because I've been hearing that for some time now and, at least the way you're expressing it, I'm not sure it is constructive. Do you hear the same thing?*

George: *OK. I guess I am angry at her.*

Supervisor: *Good. You're in touch with it. Now, what evaluative thinking were you doing about Susan to get **yourself** so mad?*

George: *Probably something like, "Damn it. We've been working for two months now and. . .what can I do!"*

Supervisor: *You've been working hard with her for two months and she. . .What?*

George: *Should **cooperate!***

Supervisor: *Right. You've concluded in your head that she **should** be cooperating with you. That sounds like a demand on your part that she act sensibly with you. That's your premise, right? I wonder why she should do that with you. After all, she is pretty disturbed and pretty good at screwing up her life. Why is it she **should** act sanely with you? Are you special?*

George: *I does sound kind of silly of me.*

Supervisor: *Yeah, it does when you think about it. See how **your** evaluative, demanding thoughts lead to **your** getting **yourself** angry? Now, what's a better attitude to take?*

George: *How about something like: "She's really disturbed and, because of her disturbance, she probably will be a difficult client for me and will get in* *her own way of getting better. So, it's ok for her to be the way she is. But, how can I break through her resistances?" How's that?*

Supervisor: *Makes sense to me. But, does it make sense to you?*

George: Yeah.

Supervisor: *If you really take that track, you will certainly not feel angry and will probably be more effective in dealing with her. As it is, she really sucks you into her games.*

George: *Right.*

Supervisor: *Now, let's talk about ways you might respond to her argumentativeness.*

In this interchange the supervisor saw that George was angry at the client, and that this anger was blocking his effective counseling performance. The supervisor helped George identify his problematic feelings (anger), and then forced him to discover the irrational self-talk with which he was precipitating the feelings. Next, the supervisor disputed this self-talk and showed it to be illogical. Lastly, the supervisor helped George to replace the illogical self-talk with a rational sentence, one that may allow for inevitable frustration and irritation over the client's lack of cooperative behavior, but would not spawn the original intense anger which inhibited counseling progress. The cognitive restructuring sequence ends as the supervisor and counselor search for appropriate counseling responses to replace the counselor's anger responses.

REFERENCES

Allen, G.J., Szollos, S.J., & Williams, B.D. (1986). Doctoral students' comparative evaluations of best and worst psychotherapy supervision. *Professional Psychology, 17* 91-99.

Altucher, N. (1967). Constructive use of the supervisory relationship. *Journal of Counseling Psychology, 14,* 165-170.

Arbuckle, D.S. (1965). Supervision: Learning, not counseling. *Journal of Counseling Psychology, 12,* 90-94.

Archer, J., & Kagan, N. (1973). Teaching interpersonal relationship skills on campus: A pyramid approach. *Journal of Counseling Psychology, 20,* 535-540.

Bauman, W.F. (1972). Games counselor trainees play: Dealing with trainee resistance. *Counselor Education and Supervision, 11,* 251-256.

Bernier, J.E. (1980). Training and supervising counselors: Lessons learned from deliberate psychological education. *Personnel and Guidance Journal, 59,* 15-20.

Beutler, L.E., Johnson, D.T., Neville, C.W. Jr., Elkins, D., & Jobe, A.M. (1975). Attitude similarity and therapist credibility as predictors of attitude change and improvement in psychotherapy. *Journal of Consulting and Clinical Psychology, 43*(6), 90-92.

Birk, J.M. (1972). Effects of counseling supervision method and preference on empathic understanding. *Journal of Counseling Psychology, 19,* 542-546.

Bordin, E.S. (1983). A working alliance based model of supervision. *The Counseling Psychologist, 11*(1), 35-43.

Brady, D., Rowe, W., & Smouse, A.D. (1976). Facilitative level and verbal conditioning: A replication. *Journal of Counseling Psychology, 23*(1), 78-80.

Brammer, L.M., & Wassner, A.C. (1977). Supervision in counseling and psychotherapy. In D.J. Kurpius, R.D. Baker & J.D. Thomas (Eds.), *Supervision of applied training.* Westport, CT.: Greenwood, pp. 43-82.

Burck, H.D., Cottingham, H.F., & Reardon, R.C. (1973). *Counseling and Accountability.* New York: Pergamon Press, Inc.,

Carkhuff, R.R. (1969). *Helping and human relations, Volume I.* New York: Holt, Rinehart & Winston.

Carkhuff, R.R. (1972). The development of systematic human resource development models. *The Counseling Psychologist, 3*(3), 4-11.

Carlson, J. (1980). Audiotape and videotape procedures: A study of subject's reactions. *Journal of Counseling Psychology, 27,* 605-610.

Cashdan, S. (1973). *Interactional psychotherapy.* New York: Gruen and Stratton.

Cross, D.G., & Brown, D. (1983). Counselor supervision as a function of trainee experience: Analysis of specific behaviors. *Counselor Education and Supervision, 22,* 333-341.

Delaney, D.J., & Moore, J.C. (1966). Student expectations of the role of practicum supervisor. *Counselor Education and Supervision, 6,* 11-17.

Dendy, R.F. (1971). A model for the training of undergraduate residence hall assistants as paraprofessional counselors using videotape playback techniques and interpersonal process recall. Unpublished doctoral dissertation. Michigan State University.

Dietzel, C.S., & Abeles, N. (1975). Client-therapist complementarity and therapeutic outcome. *Journal of Counseling Psychology, 22*(4), 264-272.

Dobbs, J.B. (1986). Supervision of psychology trainees in field placements. *Professional Psychology, 17,* 296-300.

Dodge, J. (1982). Reducing supervisee anxiety: A cognitive-behavioral approach. *Counselor Education and Supervision, 22,* 55-60.

Dowling, T.H., & Frantz, T.T. (1975). The influence of facilitative relationship on imitative learning. *Journal of Counseling Psychology, 22*(4), 259-263.

Ekstein, R. (1964). Supervision of psychotherapy: Is it teaching? Is it administration? Or is it therapy? *Psychotherapy: Theory, Research and Practice, 1,* 137-138.

Ekstein, R., & Wallerstein, R.S. (1958). *The teaching and learning of Psychotherapy.* New York: Basic Books.

Ellis, A., & Grieger, R. (1977). *Rational-emotive therapy: Handbook of theory and Practice.* New York: Springer.

Friedlander, M.L., & Snyder, J. (1983). Trainees' expectations for the supervisory process: Testing a developmental model. *Counselor Education and Supervision, 22,* 342-348.

Fuller, F.F., & Manning, B.A. (1973). Self-confrontation reviewed: A conceptualization for video playback in teacher education. *Review of Educational Research, 43,* 469-528.

Gimmestad, M.J., & Greenwood, J.D. (1974). A new twist on IPR: Concurrent recall by supervisory group. *Counselor Education and Supervision, 14*(1), 71-73.

Grieger, R., & Boyd, J. (1980). *Rational-emotive therapy: A skills-based approach.* New York: Van Nostrand Reinhold.

Grzegorek, A.E. (1971). A study of the effects of two types of emphasis in counselor training used in conjunction with simulation and videotaping. Unpublished doctoral dissertation. Michigan State University.

Guttman, M.A.J., & Haase, R.F. (1972). Generalization of microcounseling skills from training period to actual counseling setting. *Counselor Education and Supervision, 12,* 98-108.

Gysbers, N.C., & Johnston, J.A. (1965). Expectations of a practicum supervisor's role. *Counselor Education and Supervision, 4,* 68-74.

Hansen, J.C. (1965). Trainees expectations of supervision in the counseling practicum. *Counselor Education and Supervision, 4,* 75-80.

Hansen, J.C., & Barker, E.N. (1964). Experiencing and the supervisory relationship. *Journal of Counseling Psychology, 11,* 107-111.

Hansen, J.C., Robins, T.H., & Grimes, J. (1982). Review of research on practicum supervision. *Counselor Education and Supervision, 22,* 15-24.

Heller, K., Myers, R., & Kline, L. (1963). Interviewer behavior as a function of standardized client role. *Journal of Consulting Psychology, 27,* 117-122.

Heppner, P.O., & Handley, P.G. (1981). A study of the interpersonal influence process in supervision. *Journal of Counseling Psychology, 28,* 437-444.

Hester, L.R., Weitz, L.J., Anchor, K.N., & Roback, H.B. (1976). Supervisor attraction as a function of level of supervision skillfulness and supervisees' perceived similarity. *Journal of Counseling Psychology, 23*(3), 254-258.

Hogan, R.A., (1964). Issues and approaches in supervision. *Psychotherapy: Theory, Research and Practice, 1,* 139-141.

Holloway, E.L. (1984). Outcome evaluation in supervision research. *Counseling Psychologist, 12*(4), 167-174.

Holloway, E.L., & Wampold, B.D. (1983). Patterns of verbal behavior and judgments of satisfaction in the supervision interview. *Journal of Counseling Psychology, 30,* 227-234.

Hosford, R.E., & Barmann, B. (1983). A social learning approach to counselor supervision. *The Counseling Psychologist, 11*(1), 51-58.

Jakubowski-Spector, P., Dustin, R., & George, R. (1971). Toward developing a behavioral counselor education model. *Counselor Education and Supervision, 10,* 242-250.

Kagan, N. (1980). Influencing human interaction Eighteen years with IPR. In A.K. Hess (Ed.). *Psychotherapy supervision: Theory, research and practice* (pp. 262-283). New York: Wiley.

Kagan, N., & Krathwohl, D.R., (1967). *Studies in human interaction: Interpersonal process recall stimulated by videotape.* East Lansing, Michigan: Educational Publishing Services.

Kagan, N., Krathwohl, D.R., & Miller, R. (1963). Stimulated recall in therapy using videotape: A case study. *Journal of Counseling Psychology, 19,* 237-243.

Kagan, N., & Schauble, P.D. (1969). Affect simulation in interpersonal recall. *Journal of Counseling Psychology, 16,* 309-313.

Kagan, N., Schauble, P.G., Resnikoff, A., Danish, S.J., & Krathwohl, D.R. (1969). Interpersonal process recall. *Journal of Nervous and Mental Disease, 148,* 365-374.

Kaplan, D.M. (1983). Current trends in practicum supervision research. *Counselor Education and Supervision, 22,* 215-226.

Kell, B.L., & Burow, J.M. (1970). *Developmental counseling and therapy.* Boston: Houghton Mifflin.

Kell, B.L., & Mueller, W.J. (1966). *Impact and change: A study of counseling relationships.* New York: Appleton-Century-Crofts.

Kingdon, M.A. (1975). A cost-benefit analysis of the interpersonal process recall technique. *Journal of Counseling Psychology, 22*(4), 353-357.

Kurpius, D.J., Benjamin, D., & Morran, D.K. (1985). Effects of teaching a cognitive strategy on counselor trainee internal dialogue and clinical gypotesis formulation. *Journal of Counseling Psychology, 33,* 263-271.

Lambert, M.J. (1974). Supervisory and counseling process: A comparative study. *Counselor Education and Supervision, 14,* 54-60.

Leary, T. (1957). *Interpersonal diagnosis of personality.* New York: Ronald Press.

Liddle, B. (1986). Resistance in supervision: A response to perceived threats. *Counselor Education and Supervision, 26*(2), 117-128.

Lister, J.L. (1966). Counselor experiencing: Its implications for supervision. *Counselor Education and Supervision, 5,* 55-60.

May, R., (1972). *Power and innocence.* New York: W.W. Norton.

Miller, C.D., & Oetting, E.R. (1966). Students react to supervision. *Counselor Education and Supervision, 6,* 73-74.

Moore, M. (1969). The client's voice in supervision. *The Art and Science of Psychotherapy, 5,* 76-78.

Mueller, W. (1969). Patterns of behavior and their reciprocal impact in the family and in psychotherapy. *Journal of Counseling Psychology Monograph, 16* (2, Pt. 2).

Mueller, W.J., & Kell, B.L. (1972). *Coping with conflict.* New York: Appleton-Century-Crofts.

Patterson, C.H. (1964). Supervising students in the counseling practicum. *Journal of Counseling Psychology*, *22*, 47-53.

Patterson, C.H. (1973). *Theories of counseling and psychotherapy*. New York: Harper and Row.

Patterson, D.H. (1983). A client-centered approach to supervision. *The Counseling Psychologist*, *22*(1), 21-25.

Payne, P.A., & Gralinski, D.M. (1968). Effects of supervisor style and empathy upon counselor learning. *Journal of Counseling Psychology*, *15*, 517-521.

Payne, P.A., Weiss, S.D., & Kappa, R.A. (1972). Didactic, experiential, and modeling factors in the learning of empathy. Journal of *Counseling Psychology*, *19*, 425-429.

Payne, P.A., Winter, D.E., & Bell, G.E. (1972). Effects of supervisor style on the learning of empathy in a supervision analogue. *Counselor Education and Supervision*, *22*, 262-269.

Peters, G., Cormier, L., & Cormier, W. (1978). Effects of modeling, rehearsal, feedback, and remediations on acquisition of a counseling strategy. *Journal of Counseling Psychology*, *25*, 231-237.

Pierce, R., Carkhuff, R.R., & Berenson, B.G. (1967). The differential effects of high and low functioning counselors upon counselor-in-training. *Journal of Clinical Psychology*, *23*, 212-215.

Pierce, R.M., & Schauble, P.G. (1970). Graduate training of facilitative counselors: The effects of individual supervision. *Journal of Counseling Psychology*, *17*, 210-215.

Raush, H.L. (1965). Interaction sequences. *Journal of Personality and Social Psychology*, *2*, 487-499.

Raush, H.L., Dittmann, A.T., & Taylor, T.J. (1959). The interpersonal behavior of children in residential treatment. *Journal of Abnormal and Social Psychology*, *58*, 9-26.

Reising, G.N., & Daniels, M.H. (1983). A study of Hogans' model of counselor development and supervision. *Journal of Counseling Psychology*, *30*, 234-244.

Resnikoff, A., Kagan, N., & Schauble, P. (1970). Acceleration of psychotherapy through stimulated videotape recall. *American Journal of Psychotherapy*, *24*, 102-111.

Rice, L.N. (1980). A client-centered approach to the supervision of psychotherapy. In A.K. Hess (ed.), *Psychotherapy supervision: Theory, research, and practice*, (pp. 136-147), New York: Wiley.

Rogers, C.R. (1951). *Client-centered therapy*. Boston: Houghton Mifflin.

Rogers, C.R. (1957). The necessary and sufficient conditions of therapeutic personality change. *Journal of Consulting Psychology, 21*, 95-103.

Ronnestad, M.H. (1977). The effects of modeling, feedback, and experiential methods on counselor empathy. *Counselor Education and supervision, 16*(3), 194-201.

Ryan, T.A. (Ed.), (1978). *Systems models for counselor supervision*. Washington, D.C.: American Personnel and Guidance Association.

Schauble, P.G., (1970). The acceleration of client progress in counseling and psychotherapy through interpersonal process recall. Unpublished doctoral dissertation. Michigan State University.

Shaver, A.H. (1985). Effects of observation and evaluation on anxiety in beginning counselors: A social facilitation analysis. *Journal of Counseling and Development, 63*, 279-285.

Smith, M.L., Glass, G.V., & Miller, T.J. (1980). *The benefits of psychotherapy*. Baltimore: John Hopkins.

Spivack, J.D., (1970). The use of developmental tasks for training counselors using interpersonal process recall. Unpublished doctoral dissertation. Michigan State University.

Spivack, J.D. (1972). Laboratory to classroom: The practical application of IRP in a master's level pre-practicum counselor education program. *Counselor Education and Supervision, 12*, 3-16.

Stoltenberg, C.D., Solomon, G.S., & Ogden, L., (1986). Comparing supervisee and supervisor initial perceptions of supervision: Do they agree? *The Clinical Supervisor, 4*(3), 53-61.

Van Noord, R.W., & Kagan, N., (1976). Stimulated recall and affect simulation in counseling: Client growth reexamined. *Journal of Counseling Psychology, 23*(1), 28-33.

Vitalo, R.L., (1970). Effects of facilitative interpersonal functioning in a conditioning paradigm. *Journal of Counseling Psychology, 17*, 141-144.

Ward, G.R., Kagan, N., & Krathwohl, D.R., (1972). An attempt to measure and facilitate counselor effectiveness. *Counselor Education and Supervision, 11*, 179-186.

Wedeking, D.F., & Scott, T.B., (1976). A study of the relationship between supervisor and trainee behaviors in counseling practicum. *Counselor Education and Supervision, 15*(4), 259-266.

Whiteley, J.M., (Ed.), (1967). *Research in counseling*. Columbus, Ohio: Charles E. Merrill.

Woolsey, L.K., (1986). Research and practice in counseling: A conflict of values. *Counselor Education and Supervision, 26*, 84-95.

CHAPTER 4

BEHAVIORAL
MODEL OF
SUPERVISION

Counselor supervision from a behavioral approach is a direct corollary to the Behavioral Counselor Education Model proposed by Jakubowski-Spector, Dustin, and George (1971), and similar views by Delaney (1969), Hackney (1971), Hackney and Nye (1973), Hackney and Cormier (1979), Krumboltz (1966a, 1966b, 1967), Levine and Tilker (1974), and many others who subscribe to the following four propositions.

1. Proficient counselor performance is more a function of learned skills than a "personality fit." Personality is actually a constellation of situation-specific behaviors, some of which may be appropriate for the counselor's role while others may not be appropriate. The purpose of counselor education is to teach appropriate counselor behaviors (skills) to trainees and to help them extinguish inappropriate behavior from their professional actions.

2. The counselor's professional role and job description is comprised of identifiable tasks, each one requiring skill behaviors. Counselor education should enable counselor-trainees to develop these skills, and supervision should assist the counselor in applying and refining the skills.

3. Counselor skills can be behaviorally defined, and these behaviors respond to the principles of psychological learning theory just as other behaviors.

4. Counselor supervision should employ the principles of psychological learning theory within its methodology.

Behavioral supervision is thus a process of helping counselors develop, apply, and refine those skill-behaviors that comprise the counseling craft. This is done through multiple modalities based on psychological learning theory. Although other terms like "didactic", "technique-oriented" and "instructional" have been used in place of behavioral supervision, the later term is most frequently observed in the literature. While behavioral supervision is not totally revolutionary, it does add more scientific rigor and psychological application to the older, directive supervision approaches.

FOCUS AND GOALS

The focus of behavioral supervision is upon the skill behaviors of the counselor (supervisee) (Boyd, 1978; Delaney, 1972; Fuqua, Johnson, Anderson & Newman, 1984; Linehan, 1980; Strosahl & Jacobson, 1986). These skill behaviors are broadly conceptualized to include the counselor's thinking, feeling, and acting behaviors. Skills exist at various levels of difficulty ranging from fundamental to advanced. Some skills frequently may be used (e.g., reflection, tacting response) while other skills are to be utilized only when a particular problem or assignment arises (e.g., relaxation, thought control, and covert sensitization).

The **goal** of behavioral supervision is always the **person-specific skill needs of the supervisee.** Each supervisee should be treated as an individual with needs that are particular to him/her. Generally speaking the minimal broad goal for any supervisee would be a level of skill functioning representing the competent performance of the counselor's role and function; beyond this minimal level the goal would be a level of functioning above present performance yet within realistic expectation. The "person-specific" nature of a behavioral supervision goal is a necessary ingredient in effective methodology, and each counselor will be at a somewhat different level of skill development. Assessment of this level will be discussed later.

The ideal supervisee would be one who has gained the skills necessary for "fully functioning performance," making possible Hackney's (1971, p. 103) notion that

> the relationship between supervisor and (supervisee) should take on more of the qualities of a professional relationship characterized by consultative interactions rather than skill-acquisition relationships. The differences that exist between supervisor and (supervisee) in a consultation-professional model should be differences in experience rather than differences in counseling skills.

Hackney's suggestion that the learning of basic skills (e.g. reflective responses and open-ended leads) should occur prior to supervision would be a desirable sequence. But readers should not assume that skill development does not belong in supervision, because the development and refinement of high-level skills (e.g., interpretation, confrontation, behavior-change strategies) can and should continue throughout the counselor's career—and this development can be promoted through consultative supervision and colleague interaction. Further, a realism is that some supervisees for one reason or another will enter supervision with significant skill deficiencies and inappropriate behaviors. The supervisor may encounter basic skill deficiencies such as a lack of affective listening and empathic responding, an inability to help others set goals or make decisions, and an ignorance of strategies such as assertive training, vocational exploration, and the building of study skills. Inappropriate counselor behaviors that would probably accompany deficiencies include self-referent thoughts and "mind-wandering" during helpgiving, and a profusion of advice-giving wherein offered solutions are based upon the counselor's personal experience.

The person-specific supervisory goal for a counselor having such deficiencies and inappropriate behaviors would be to help the counselor begin to perform the deficient skills and cease performing the inappropriate behaviors. If skill deficiencies and inappropriate behaviors are too serious for supervision, the supervisee must attain the goal through other routes that do not include helping duties. For a counselor-in-training the best solution may be a recycling through practicum preparation courses, or special work outside of class to acquire the needed skills and overcome inappropriate behavior. Practicing counselors with significant skill problems pose a particularly difficult problem. The supervisor may need to construct a temporary job which avoids the counselor's skill problems so that the counselor can be employed while participating in remedial training. A leave of absence for further training is another route; and termination of the counselor's duties is the last resort if all else fails. The point being made in these steps with the low-skill counselor is that the welfare of helpees is protected while the skills of the counselor are promoted through supervision and/or remedial skill-training.

METHODOLOGY

The process of behavioral supervision involves a five-step methodological sequence. First is the *establishment of a relationship* between the supervisor and counselor. Second is a *skill analysis and assessment* which will lead into the third step—*setting of supervision goals.* Fourth is the *construction and implementation of strategies* to accomplish the goal(s). Fifth supervision is finalized with a *follow up evaluation and generalization of learning.*

SUPERVISORY RELATIONSHIP

In the *psychotherapeutic approach* to supervision the relationship between the counselor and supervisor served as a source of dynamic learning. A dynamically rich supervisory relationship was established, and later the dynamics of this relationship were analyzed to discover how each party was acting and reacting. An "offshoot" of the dynamics approach, *experiential supervision*, treated the supervisory relationship as an opportunity for the counselor to receive psychologically facilitative conditions and to grow therapeutically.

Behavioral supervision does not consider the supervisory relationship itself to be a primary source of experiential learning or therapeutic growth, but the relationship is a very important and instrumental part of the supervisory process. In behavioral supervision, a relationship must exist between the supervisor and counselor that is conducive to learning, otherwise supervision is at a standstill. An understanding, honest, and respectful relationship in behavioral supervision is the route to this conducive learning atmosphere.

Such a "facilitative" relationship can overcome the common problem of supervisee resistance, and although a more straightforward way of handling resistance (Guttman, 1973) may exist, a psychologically comfortable relationship is the best for promoting future supervision progress. Also, a facilitative relationship offers an interaction in which formal learning activities can be conducted (e.g., role playing, modeling, reinforcement). Lastly, Jakubowski-Spector et al., (1971) have made the point that behavioral supervision should attend to the counselor's covert skill-behaviors, and the only way to obtain these data is by self-report. A facilitative relationship is a necessary condition for the counselor's sharing of thoughts and feelings, thus giving the behavioral supervisor needed data for skill assessment and goal setting.

Because the supervisory relationship is so instrumentally important, Delaney (1972) has recommended taking whatever time is necessary to establish the working alliance before moving on to active methodology. Sometimes relationship building will require patience, such as when the counselor's skill deficiencies are obvious and these deficiencies temptingly await the behavioral supervisor's strategies. But rushing the supervision process is a damaging error, and the experienced supervisor knows that establishing a working alliance is the *top priority* when initiating supervision.

SKILL ANALYSIS AND ASSESSMENT

Behavioral supervision is goal directed. Two of the methodological steps in the behavioral supervision process are to set supervision goals (step three) and to employ effective strategies to accomplish the goals (step four). But in order to set goals a skill-behavior analysis and assessment (step two) must be done. This analysis and assessment step can be performed on a particular counselor performance, task, or entire skill repertoire.

Using an unsuccessful consultation session as an illustrative performance target, *skill analysis* proceeds in this fashion. From a consultative stance the behavioral supervisor works with the counselor (supervisee) (perhaps assisting the counselor in self-appraisal) to behaviorally define the discrete skills comprising the consultation performance. *Skill assessment* follows the analysis and consists of evaluating each skill behavior in terms of the counselor's performance capability, and then assigns the behavior to one of the five assessment categories in Figure 4.1.

An illustration of the information that could result from an analysis and assessment of skill behaviors in the counselor's unsuccessful consultation performance can be seen in Figure 4.1. In this case the counselor's performance capability is quite low, an occurrence that is typical when the counselor has not received training or experience in consultation. The counselor cannot initiate consultation, but can respond to consultee initiated contacts. Although sometimes the counselor is at a loss for words, eye contact and supportive statements are assets. Questions help to promote the consultation interaction but are often peripheral to the core of the consultee's problem. Reflections are absent but the counselor has demonstrated this skill in counseling, so generalization to consultation needs to be done. Perhaps the major deficiencies in the counselor's consultation *are not knowing how to target the causal factors in the consultee's problem and being unable to conceptualize the problem adequately.* These two deficiencies make the establishment of goals and strategies with the consultee an impossibility. Compounding skill deficiencies is the counselor's easily aroused anger and resentment which affronts consultees.

Analysis (Discrete Skill-Behaviors)	Assessment Categories (Performance Capability)
1. Expresses anger and resentment in response to consultee's hostility and other behavior	Inappropriate counselor behaviors which interfere with task or skill performance; these should be reduced or extinguished in frequency.
2. Targeting instrumental factors. 3. Conceptualizing the consultee's problem. 4. Establishing a goal and strategy with the consultee.	**Necessary skill-behaviors which are not performed and are absent from the counselor's repertoire, these should be acquired.**
5. Reflecting consultee feelings. 6. Reflecting consultee's troublesome attitudes. 7. Initiating consultant contact.	Necessary skill-behaviors which are present in the counselor's repertoire but are not performed because the counselor cannot apply them in actual practice. The counselor must learn when and how to apply these skills.
8. Verbal responses to consultee's initiated contact. 9. Asking questions	Necessary skill-behaviors which are applied but at a low level of quality. Improvement and refinement is needed in skill application.
10. Visual attending. 11. Supportive statements.	Satisfactory frequency and quality of skill-behavior performance.

Figure 4.1. Skill behavior analysis and assessment.

Analysis and assessment of counselor skills necessitate that the behavioral supervisor have an extensive knowledge of the skills required by the counselor's work. In the previous example of unsuccessful consultation, the counselor could not conduct the analysis and assessment alone because of inexperience with the focal task—consultation. The supervisor could make suggestions regarding consultation because of familiarity with analysis and assessment skills.

The behavioral supervisor would be wise to construct a mental model of the ideal skill repertoire of the fully performing counselor according to function or task and, during analysis and assessment, this model can serve as a guide. Herr (1969) has provided a valuable contribution to the building of such a model for school counseling by drawing 44 functions from policy statements of the American School Counselor Association (i.e., "Statement of Policy for Secondary School Counselors" and "Guidelines for Implementation").

1. Helps to plan and develop the guidance program in relation to the needs of pupils.

2. Helps to plan the curriculum in relation to the needs of pupils.

3. Helps each pupil, through the counseling relationship, to

   a. understand him/herself in relation to the social and psychological world in which he/she lives,

   b. accept him/herself as he/she is,

   c. develop personal decision-making competencies, and

   d. resolve special problems.

4. Assumes the role of leader and consultant in the school's program of pupil appraisal by doing the following:

   a. coordinating the accumulation and use of meaningful information about each pupil;

b. interpreting information about pupils to pupils;

c. interpreting information about pupils to teachers;

d. interpreting information about pupils to parents;

e. interpreting information about pupils to admini-strators, curriculum committees, and other con-cerned professionals for use in educational modifi-cation; and

f. identifying pupils with special abilities or needs.

5. Collects and disseminates to pupils and their parents information concerning the following:

a. school offerings,

b. opportunities for further education,

c. Careers and career-training opportunities, and

d. Financial assistance for post-secondary education.

6. Provides each pupil through systemactic group guidance programs the following:

a. opportunity to relate his/her personal characteristics to educational requirements, and

b. opportunity to relate his/her personal characteristics to occupational requirements.

7. Provides group counseling for those students unable or unready to profit from individual counseling.

8. Coordinates the use of services available beyond those he/she can provide by doing the following:

a. making pupils and their parents aware of the availability of such services,

b. making appropriate referrals,

c. maintaining liaison and cooperative working relationships with other pupil personnel specialists,

d. maintaining liaison and cooperative working relationships with agencies in the community where special services are available, and

e. encouraging the development and/or extension of community agencies for meeting pupil needs that are not already adequately met.

9. Assists in providing placement services for pupils by doing the following:

a. planning with teachers and administrators for the grouping and scheduling of pupils;

b. helping pupils make appropriate choices of school programs and develop long-range plans of study;

c. helping pupils make the transition from one school level to another, from one school to another, and from school to employment successfully; and

d. coordinating his/her placement work with others for the most effective use of the placement services available in the school and the community.

10. Helps parents by doing the following:

a. acting as a consultant to them regarding the growth and development of their children,

b. providing them with information about their children (with due regard to the child's desire for confidentiality),

c. providing them with information about educational and occupational opportunities and requirements,

d. providing them information about counseling programs and related guidance services available to them and their children, and

e. assisting them to develop realistic perceptions of their children's development in relation to their potentialities.

11. **Serves as a consultant to members of the administrative and teaching staffs in the area of counseling by doing the following:**

a. sharing appropriate individual pupil data with them (again with due regard for the child's desire for confidentiality),

b. helping them to identify pupils with special needs and problems,

c. participating in in-service training programs, and

d. assisting teachers to secure materials and develop procedures for a variety of classroom group guidance experiences.

12. Conducts or cooperates with others in conducting local research related to pupils needs and how well school services are meeting those needs by doing the following:

a. contacting graduates and dropouts in follow-up studies,

b. comparing scholastic aptitudes with achievement, selection of courses of study and post high school experience,

c. studying occupational trends in the community, and

d. evaluating the school's counseling and guidance services.

13. Carries out a program of public relations by doing the following:

   a. participating in programs of various community groups;

   b. preparing and disseminating to parents graphic and narrative materials or bulletins and newsletters in order to keep parents and the community informed of guidance objectives and programs; and

   c. furnishing information regarding the counseling and guidance programs to local publishers, radio and TV stations.

Identification of school counselor tasks can begin the supervisor's analysis procedure. Each task would then be defined in terms of discrete skill behaviors which would serve as concrete objectives.

Menne (1975) also has provided a foundation for the setting of skill objectives which comprise counseling. From the questionnaire responses of 175 counselors and therapists from throughout the United States Menne factored out twelve dimensions of counseling competency. In the order of respondents' perceived importance the dimensions were as follows:

Professional Ethics
Self Awareness
Personal Characteristics
Listening, Communicating
Testing Skills
Counseling Comprehension
Behavioral Science
Societal Awareness
Tutoring Techniques
Professional Credentials
Counselor Training
Vocational Guidance

Just as Herr's tasks were defined in behavioral terms, Menne's dimensions also could be translated into skill behaviors. General competency dimensions thus are coverted to specific targets for behavioral supervision strategies.

Another analysis and assessment procedure is to use rating scales rather than a conceptual skill-model. The scale takes the place of the model, and rating pertains to the skills listed on the scale. A revised version of Cogan's (1977) *Survey of Counselor Competencies* is presented in Figure 4.2. The **survey** was originally a research tool, but has been altered so that an analysis and assessment of ninety-nine competencies can be performed. Each competency can be analyzed in terms of importance (critical, important, non-essential) to the counselor's job duties, and then assessed in terms of the counselor's demonstrated or perceived performance capability (satisfactory, non-satisfactory). Two additional rating scales are the *Practicum Student Counselor Form* (Figure 4.3) and the *Practicum Evaluation Form* (Figure 4.4). The two scales provide a means for evaluating the supervisee's performance.

Supervision rating instruments can be advantageous, for they increase the objectivity and ease of analysis and assessment for the supervisor lacking these skills. But disadvantages are also inherent. The analysis dimensions or categories of such instruments may not be as behaviorally definitive as traditional skill-behavior analysis, and scales sometimes present a narrow view of effective counselor performance. Assessment dimensions may also lack concrete criteria for evaluation of performance capability. Nevertheless, rating instruments do provide a gross procedure from which the supervisor can begin analysis and assessment. Readers are encouraged to read the evaluative commentary of Zytowski and Betz (1972, pp. 72-81) and for research purposes use extreme caution in selecting any supervision rating instrument. An instrument which may be an effective supervision tool may not have the psychometric properties necessary for use in research.

Whatever method of analysis and assessment is employed, the translation of counseling and therapy into teachable skills is a challenge which faces supervision. This is a challenge to be

(Continued on page 152)

COUNSELOR COMPETENCY	ANALYSIS Skill Value to Interview			ASSESSMENT Proficiency	
	Non-Essential	Important	Critical	+	−

PERSONAL CHARACTERISTICS

1. SOCIAL RESPONSIBILITY—the counselor states, and his/her past experiences show, that he/she is interested in social change. —— —— —— —— ——

2. PEOPLE ORIENTED—the counselor is people oriented as demonstrated by his/her past experiences and by his/her present social interactions. —— —— —— —— ——

3. FALLIBILITY—the counselor recognizes that he/she is not free from making errors. —— —— —— —— ——

4. PERSONAL PROBLEMS—the counselor's personal problems are kept out of the counseling session. —— —— —— —— ——

5. MODELING—the counselor models appropriate cognitive process, behaviors, and feelings during the counseling session. —— —— —— —— ——

6. NON-DEFENSIVE—the counselor gives and receives feedback to and from his/her clients, peers, and supervisor without making excuses or justifications. —— —— —— —— ——

Other _____ —— —— —— —— ——

Other _____ —— —— —— —— ——

Other _____ —— —— —— —— ——

PHILOSOPHICAL FOUNDATIONS

7. EVALUATION—the counselor's theoretical frame of reference includes a means for describing the cognitive, behavioral and/or affective change(s) that take place in determining the effectiveness of the selected counseling strategy. —— —— —— —— ——

8. DIAGNOSIS—regardless of his/her theoretical orientation, the counselor can identify maladaptive symptomology consistent with his/her theoretical frame of reference. —— —— —— —— ——

Figure 4.2. Counselor competency scale for the analysis and assessment of counselor competencies. (This scale is an altered version of the "Survey of Counselor Competencies," developed by Dennis B. Cogan, Department of Counselor Education, Arizona State University, Tempe, Arizona).

Figure 4.2. (Continued).

	ANALYSIS	ASSESSMENT
COUNSELOR COMPETENCY	Skill Value to Interview	Proficiency

Philosophical Foundations (continued)

Non-Essential
Important
Critical

$\downarrow \quad \downarrow \quad \downarrow \qquad \overset{+}{\downarrow} \quad \overset{-}{\downarrow}$

9. THEORY—the counselor states his/her assumptions about human behavior, through which he/she will incorporate or abstract his/her empirical findings and through which he will make predictions concerning his/her client.

— — — — —

10. THEORY—the counselor explains human behavior from at least two theories of personality.

— — — — —

11. PRIORITIZING—the counselor decides on which problems, when presented with more than one, to deal with first according to his/her theoretical frame of reference.

— — — — —

12. INTERPRETATION—the counselor provides the client with a possible explanation for or relationships between certain behaviors, cognitions, and/or feelings.

— — — — —

13. PROGNOSIS—the counselor can make an evaluation of the client's potential for successful treatment consistent with his/her theoretical frame of reference.

— — — — —

14. INTERACTIONS—the counselor describes the interactions that take place between the counselor and client consistent with his/her theoretical frame of reference.

— — — — —

15. DEFENSE MECHANISMS—the counselor is aware of the defense mechanisms used by the client, the purpose they serve, and can help the client substitute more appropriate ones for less appropriate ones.

— — — — —

16. CATHARSIS—the counselor understands the concept of catharsis.

— — — — —

17. NATURAL CONSEQUENCES—the counselor understands the concept of environmental manipulation.

— — — — —

18. ENVIRONMENTAL MANIPULATION—the counselor understands the concept of environmental manipulation.

— — — — —

19. TEST SELECTION—the counselor selects an appropriate test(s) according to his/her theoretical frame of reference.

— — — — —

Figure 4.2. Continued)

COUNSELOR COMPETENCY	ANALYSIS Skill Value to Interview	ASSESSMENT Proficiency

Philosophical Foundations (continued)

Non-Essential
Important
Critical ↓ ↓ ↓   + ↓   − ↓

20. INFERENCE—the counselor provides an explanation for and the functional use of the client's behaviors, cognitions, and/or feelings consistent with his/her theoretical frame of reference and how they might influence the counseling process. — — — — —

OTHER _____ — — — — —

OTHER _____ — — — — —

OTHER _____ — — — — —

COMMUNICATIONS

21. OPEN-ENDED QUESTION—the counselor asks the client a question that cannot be answered by a yes or no, and the question does not provide the client with the answer. — — — — —

22. MINIMAL VERBAL RESPONSE—the counselor uses "mmmh, oh, yes" to communicate to the client that he/she is listening, without interrupting the client's train of thought or discourse. — — — — —

23. GENUINENESS—the counselor's resonses are sincere and appropriate. — — — — —

24. POSITIVE REGARD—without interjecting his/her own values, the counselor communicates respect and concern for the client's feelings, experiences, and potentials. — — — — —

25. LANGUAGE—the counselor uses terminology that is understood by the client. — — — — —

26. CLARIFICATION—the counselor has the client clarify vague and ambiguous cognitions, behaviors, and/or feelings. — — — — —

27. PARAPHRASING—without changing the meaning, the counselor states in fewer words what the client has previously stated. — — — — —

28. SUMMARIZES—the counselor combines two or more of the client's cognitions, feelings, and/or behaviors into a general statement. — — — — —

Figure 4.2. (Continued)

COUNSELOR COMPETENCY	ANALYSIS Skill Value to Interview			ASSESSMENT Proficiency	
Communications (continued)	Non-Essential	Important	Critical	+	–
29. RESTATEMENT—the counselor conveys to the client that he/she has heard the content of the client's previous statement(s) by restating in exactly or near exact words, that which the client has just verablized.	___	___	___	___	___
30. EMPATHIC UNDERSTANDING—the counselor's responses add noticeably to the expressions of the client in such a way as to express feelings at a level deeper than the client was able to express for himself/herself.	___	___	___	___	___
31. REFLECTION—from non-verbal cues the counselor accurately describes the client's affective state.	___	___	___	___	___
32. PERCEPTIONS—the counselor labeled his/her perceptions as perceptions.	___	___	___	___	___
33. CONFRONTATION—the counselor confronts the client by stating the possible consequences of his/her behaviors, cognitions, and/or feelings.	___	___	___	___	___
34. SUPPORTIVE—the counselor makes statements that agree with the client's cognitions, accepts the client's behavior, and/or shares with the client that his/her feelings were not unusual.	___	___	___	___	___
35. PROBING—the counselor's statement results in the client providing additional information about his/her cognitions, behaviors, and/or feelings.	___	___	___	___	___
36. DISAPPROVAL—the counselor makes a statement that conveys disapproval of one or more of the client's cognitions, behaviors, and/or feelings.	___	___	___	___	___
37. ADVICE GIVING—the counselor shares with the client which alternatives he/she would select if it were his/her decision to make.	___	___	___	___	___
OTHER _____	___	___	___	___	___
OTHER _____	___	___	___	___	___
OTHER _____	___	___	___	___	___
COUNSELING SKILLS					
38. VOICE—the counselor's tone of voice and rate of speech is appropriate to the client's present state and/or counseling session.	___	___	___	___	___

Figure 4.2. Continued.

COUNSELOR COMPETENCY	ANALYSIS Skill Value to Interview	ASSESSMENT Proficiency

Counseling Skills (continued)	Non-Essential Important Critical ↓ ↓ ↓	+ ↓	− ↓

39. EYE CONTACT—the counselor maintains eye contact at a level that is comfortable for the client. ___ ___ ___ ___ ___

40. INITIAL CONTACT—the counselor greets the client in a warm and accepting manner through some accepted form of social greeting (handshake, nod of head, etc.). ___ ___ ___ ___ ___

41. ACTIVITY LEVEL—the counselor maintains a level of activity appropriate to the client during the counseling session. ___ ___ ___ ___ ___

42. PHYSIOLOGICAL PRESENCE—the counselor's body posture, facial expressions, and gestures are natural and congruent with those of the client's. ___ ___ ___ ___ ___

43. COUNSELOR DISCLOSURE—the counselor shares personal information and feelings when it is appropriate in facilitating client movement. ___ ___ ___ ___ ___

44. SILENCE—the counselor does not speak when appropriate in facilitating client movement. ___ ___ ___ ___ ___

45. ACCENTING—from the client's previous statement, behavior, and/or feeling, the counselor repeats or accentuates the same, or has the client repeat or accentuate the statement, behavior, and/or feeling. ___ ___ ___ ___ ___

46. OBJECTIVITY—the counselor has sufficient control over his/her feelings and does not impose his/her values on the client. ___ ___ ___ ___ ___

47. PROBING—the counselor avoids bringing up or pursuing areas that are too threatening to the client. ___ ___ ___ ___ ___

48. RESISTANCE—the counselor is able to work through the client's conscious and/or unconscious opposition to the counseling process. ___ ___ ___ ___ ___

49. VERBOSITY—the counselor speaks when it is necessary, does not inappropriately interrupt the client or verbally dominate the counseling session. ___ ___ ___ ___ ___

50. ATTENDING—the counselor's attention is with the client's cognitions, behaviors, and/or feelings during the counseling session in accord with his/her stated theoretical frame of reference. ___ ___ ___ ___ ___

Figure 4.2. Continued.

COUNSELOR COMPETENCY	ANALYSIS Skill Value to Interview			ASSESSMENT Proficiency	
Counseling Skills (Continued)	Non-Essential	Important	Critical	+	-
51. TRANSFERENCE—the counselor is able to work through feelings directed at him/her by the client which the client originally had for another object or person.	—	—	—	—	—
52. COUNTER-TRANSFERENCE—the counselor is aware of and is able to correct his/her placing his own wishes on the client.	—	—	—	—	—
53. MANIPULATION—the counselor recognizes the client's attempt at influencing the counselor for his/her own purpose.	—	—	—	—	—
54. FACTORS—the counselor explores and is aware of socio-economic, cultural, and personal factors that might affect the client's progress.	—	—	—	—	—
55. DEPENDENCY—the counselor encourages the client to be independent, does not make decisions for the client or accept responsibility for the client's behaviors, cognitions, and/or feelings.	—	—	—	—	—
56. THEORY—the counselor can work with clients from at least two theories of counseling.	—	—	—	—	—
57. ALTERNATIVE EXPLORATION—the counselor, with the client, examines the other options available and the possible consequences of each.	—	—	—	—	—
58. IMPLEMENTATION—the counselor helps the client put insight into action.	—	—	—	—	—
59. DISTORTIONS—the counselor explains to the client his/her previously distorted perceptions of self and the environment.	—	—	—	—	—
60. MOTIVATION—the counselor can verbally confront the client with his/her lack of goal directed behavior.	—	—	—	—	—
61. CASE HISTORY TAKING—the counselor obtains factual information from the client that will be helpful in developing a course of action for the client consistent with is/her theoretical frame of reference.	—	—	—	—	—
62. INSIGHT—the counselor helps the client become more aware of his/her cognitive, behavioral, affective, and spiritual domain.	—	—	—	—	—

Figure 4.2. Continued.

COUNSELOR COMPETENCY	ANALYSIS Skill Value to Interview	ASSESSMENT Proficiency

Counseling Skills (continued)

Non-Essential
Important
Critical   +   -

63. STRUCTURE—the counselor structures the on-going counseling sessions so there is continuity from session to session.

64. INCONSISTENCIES—the counselor identifies and explores with the client contradictions within and/or between client behaviors, cognitions, and/or affect.

65. RE-FOCUSING—the counselor makes a statement or asks a question that redirects the client to a specific behavior, cognition, or feeling.

66. GOALS—the counselor, with the client, establishes short and long range goals which are congruent with societal goals and are within the client's potential.

67. REINFORCEMENT—the counselor identifies and uses reinforcers that facilitate the identified client goals.

68. FLEXIBILITY—the counselor changes long and short term goals within a specific session or during the overall counseling process as additional information becomes available.

69. BEHAVIORAL CHANGE—the counselor can develop specific plans, that can be observed and/or counted, for changing the client's behavior(s).

70. STRATEGY—the counselor's course of action is consistent with the counselor's stated theory of counseling.

71. TERMINATION—the counselor resolves the client's desire for premature termination.

72. EMERGENCIES—the counselor can handle emergencies that arise with the client.

73. TERMINATION—the counselor ends each session and the counseling relationship on time or at a point at which the client is comfortable with the issues that have been explored.

74. TERMINATION—the counselor advises the client that he/she may return in the future.

75. PERIODIC EVALUATION—with the client, the counselor periodically evaluates the progress made toward the established goals.

Figure 4.2. Continued.

COUNSELOR COMPETENCY	ANALYSIS Skill Value to Interview			ASSESSMENT Proficiency	
Counseling Skills (continued)	Non-Essential	Important	Critical	+	−
76. FANTASY—the counselor has the client use his/her imagination to gain insight and/or move toward the client's established goals.	___	___	___	___	___
77. HOMEWORK—the counselor appropriately assigns work to the client that is to be completed outside the counseling session.	___	___	___	___	___
78. PROBLEM SOLVING—the counselor teaches the client a method for problem solving.	___	___	___	___	___
79. TEST INTERPRETATION—the counselor interprets test(s) according to the procedures outlined in the test manual.	___	___	___	___	___
80. ROLE PLAYING—the counselor helps the client achieve insight by acting out conflicts and/or situations unfamiliar to him/her.	___	___	___	___	___
81. DESENSITIZATION—the counselor can apply a purposeful technique to reduce the level of anxiety that the client is experiencing.	___	___	___	___	___
82. DREAMS—the counselor works with client's dreams in a manner consistent with his/her stated theoretical frame of reference.	___	___	___	___	___
83. CONTRACTS—the counselor makes a contractual agreement with the client.	___	___	___	___	___
OTHER _____	___	___	___	___	___
OTHER _____	___	___	___	___	___
OTHER _____	___	___	___	___	___

ADJUNCTIVE ACTIVITIES

COUNSELOR COMPETENCY					
84. CASE NOTES—the counselor is able to communicate in writing in a clear and concise manner initial, ongoing, and summary case notes.	___	___	___	___	___
85. STAFFING—the counselor can staff a case in a clear and concise manner by presenting an objective description of the client, significant information, goals for the client, strategy to be used, and a prognosis for the client.	___	___	___	___	___

Figure 4.2. Continued.

COUNSELOR COMPETENCY	ANALYSIS Skill Value to Interview	ASSESSMENT Proficiency

Adjunctive Activities (continued)

Non-Essential / Important / Critical ↓ ↓ ↓   + ↓   − ↓

86. TEST ADMINISTRATION—the counselor can administer test(s) according to the procedures in the test manual. ___ ___ ___ ___ ___

87. DIAGNOSIS—the counselor identifies cognitions, behaviors, and/or feelings in the client important in making a diagnosis according to the Diagnostic and Statistical Manual of Mental Disorders III-R. ___ ___ ___ ___ ___

88. APPOINTMENTS—the counselor is on time for his/her appointments with clients, peers, and supervisors. ___ ___ ___ ___ ___

89. INFORMS—the counselor provides the client with factual information. ___ ___ ___ ___ ___

90. ORGANIZED—the counselor effectively organizes and completes the assigned work within the prescribed time limits of the setting in which he/she is employed. ___ ___ ___ ___ ___

91. DRESS—the counselor's attire is appropriate to the client population and work setting being served. ___ ___ ___ ___ ___

92. RESPONSIBILITIES—the counselor can clarify the role and responsibilities he/she and the client have in the counseling relationship according to his/her theoretical frame of reference. ___ ___ ___ ___ ___

93. ATMOSPHERE—within the limits of his/her work setting, the counselor provides an atmosphere that is physically and psychologically comfortable for the client. ___ ___ ___ ___ ___

94. CANCELLATIONS—the counselor notifies the client as soon as possible when he/she will be unable to keep an appointment. ___ ___ ___ ___ ___

95. COMPETENCY—the counselor is aware of and does not go beyond his/her counseling abilities. ___ ___ ___ ___ ___

OTHER _____ ___ ___ ___ ___ ___

OTHER _____ ___ ___ ___ ___ ___

OTHER _____ ___ ___ ___ ___ ___

ETHICAL STANDARDS

96. PROFESSIONALISM—the counselor maintains a professional relationship with the client in accord with APA and/or AACD ethical standards. ___ ___ ___ ___ ___

Figure 4.2. Continued.

COUNSELOR COMPETENCY	ANALYSIS Skill Value to Interview	ASSESSMENT Proficiency			

Ethical Standards (continued)

Non-Essential
Important
Critical

↓ ↓ ↓ + ↓ – ↓

97. ETHICS—the counseor adheres to the ethical standards outlined by the APA and/or AACD.   — — — — —

98. CONFIDENTIALITY—the counselor adheres to the ethical standards of confidentiality as outliend by the APA and/or AACD.   — — — — —

OTHER _____   — — — — —

OTHER _____   — — — — —

OTHER _____   — — — — —

Date _____

Professor _____	Practicum Student _____
On-Site Supervisor _____	Practicum Setting _____

PRACTICUM EVALUATION FORM

In an attempt to evaluate the counseling practicum field experience of the above student, please complete this evaluation form and return it to my office. This report will be included in the overall evaluation of the student's progress as a counselor trainee along with various on-campus assessments. Thank you for your valuable assistance in providing this professional service to our program and for your continued support of our practicum students.

Please evaluate the student's performance on each of the following activities (where applicable):

(Place X along scale)

	POOR	GOOD	EXCELLENT	COMMENTS
1. A. Individual Counseling	___	___	___	_____
B. Group Counseling	___	___	___	_____
C. Consultation	___	___	___	_____
D. Testing & Appraisal	___	___	___	_____
E. Relationships with Staff	___	___	___	_____
F. In-Service Training	___	___	___	_____
G. Staffings/Meetings	___	___	___	_____
H. Other (Explain)	___	___	___	_____
2. Overall Performance	___	___	___	_____
3. Potential as a future Counselor	___	___	___	_____

4. If you were in a position to add this person to your staff, would you feel comfortable employing him/her? _____ _____

                                                 Yes   No

Additional Comments: _____

_____

_____

I have had an opportunity to review this evaluation and am aware of its content

_____ _____

Practicum Student   Date

Figure 4.3. Practicum evaluation form.

Practicum Student Counselor _____ Date _____

Directions: Rate the practicum student counselor on each of the items by circling the number which best reflects your evaluation.

	Poor	Adequate	Good
1. The counselor's voice was easily heard.	1 2	3 4	5 6
2. The counselor demonstrated some variation in voice pitch.	1 2	3 4	5 6
3. The counselor did not sound bored.	1 2	3 4	5 6
4. The counselor exhibited a friendly, pleasant disposition.	1 2	3 4	5 6
5. The counselor's verbal comments pursued the topic introduced by client.	1 2	3 4	5 6
6. The counselor focused on the content of the client's problems.	1 2	3 4	5 6
7. The counselor seemed relaxed and comfortable in the interview.	1 2	3 4	5 6
8. The counselor explained the nature and goals of counseling (when appropriate).	1 2	3 4	5 6
9. The practicum counselor established good rapport with client.	1 2	3 4	5 6
10. The counselor communicated interest in and acceptance of client.	1 2	3 4	5 6
11. The counselor was spontaneous in the interview.	1 2	3 4	5 6
12. The counselor's verbal statements were concise and to the point.	1 2	3 4	5 6
13. The counselor refrained from repetition of his/her verbal statements.	1 2	3 4	5 6
14. The counselor (at least once) verbally stated his/her desire to understand client's feelings.	1 2	3 4	5 6
15. The client (at least once) acknowledged that the counselor understood what he/she was trying to communicate (verbally or non-verbally).	1 2	3 4	5 6

Figure 4.4. Practicum student counselor form. (Adapted from forms at Purdue University and Vanderbilt University.)

Figure 4.4. Continued.

	Poor	Adequate	Good
16. The counselor recognized and resisted manipulation by the client.	1 2	3 4	5 6
17. The counselor recognized and dealt with the positive affect of the client.	1 2	3 4	5 6
18. The counselor recognized and dealt with the negative affect of the client.	1 2	3 4	5 6
19. At least once during the interview the counselor provided specific feedback to the client.	1 2	3 4	5 6
20. Several times the counselor shared his/her own feelings with the client.	1 2	3 4	5 6
21. The counselor answered directly and honestly when the client asked about his/her opinion or reaction.	1 2	3 4	5 6
22. The counselor handled values effectively.	1 2	3 4	5 6
23. Did counselor try to impose his/her values on client? (YES or NO)	———————		
24. The counselor seemed aware of his/her own feelings during the session.	1 2	3 4	5 6
25. The counselor used silence effectively in the interview.	1 2	3 4	5 6
26. The counselor seemed to recognize (and interpret) the client's correct messages.	1 2	3 4	5 6
27. The counselor facilitated realistic goal-setting with the client.	1 2	3 4	5 6
28. The counselor encouraged the client to identify some of the consequences resulting from the client's behavior.	1 2	3 4	5 6
29. The client verbally expressed his/her counseling goals.	1 2	3 4	5 6
30. The counselor facilitated realistic goal-setting with client.	1 2	3 4	5 6
31. If the client appeared resistant or unconcerned about achieving change, the counselor discussed this with the client.	1 2	3 4	5 6

Figure 4.4. Continued.

	Poor	Adequate	Good
32. The counselor used intermittent one-word vocalizations to reinforce the client's demonstration of goal directed topics.	1 2	3 4	5 6
33. The counselor encouraged the client to identify and evaluate his/her actions.	1 2	3 4	5 6
34. The counselor discouraged the client from making and accepting excuses (rationalization) for his/her behavior.	1 2	3 4	5 6
35. The counselor used *relevant* case data in planning immediate and long-range goals.	1 2	3 4	5 6
36. The counselor appeared to use *relevant* case data in considering various strategies and their implications.	1 2	3 4	5 6
37. Throughout the session, the counselor was permissive of the client's emotions, feelings, and expressed thoughts.	1 2	3 4	5 6
38. Throughout the session, the counselor reflected and reacted to feelings and thus the session did not remain on an intellectual level.	1 2	3 4	5 6
39. Throughout the session, the counselor and client seemed to communicate in a meaningful way . . . counselor did not rush .	1 2	3 4	5 6
40. When used the counselor explained, administered, and interpreted tests correctly.	1 2	3 4	5 6
41. When appropriate, the counselor confronted in an effective manner.	1 2	3 4	5 6
42. The counselor terminated the session smoothly (e.g., acknowledgement of time limits, client or counselor summarization, did not introduce new topics at end, mutual feedback, some planning for new session).	1 2	3 4	5 6
43. The counselor demonstrated ethical behavior in the counseling activity and during case management.	1 2	3 4	5 6

Figure 4.4. Continued.

	Poor	Adequate	Good

44. **Overall,** (a) I would rate the **counselor's effectiveness** during the session as . . . (put comments on back); (b) the **weak** and strong aspects were . . . (put comments on back); (c) my **suggestions for improvement** are . . . (put comments on back).

Date _____   Evaluator _____

tackled optimistically, for nebulous abilities such as clinical judgment are becoming susceptible to objective inquiry (Garner & Smith, 1976), and the intangibles of contemporary therapists can become tomorrow's training objectives.

Skills and Process

An error can be made in analysis and assessment if the discrete skill behaviors identified are divested of their "process dimension." When this error happens the counselor loses sight of the purpose of the focal task or function, and becomes a mechanical dispenser of skill behaviors. The sequence and flow of skills within a function must be retained, and indeed performing a set of skills in a smooth process manner is a skill in itself (see assessment categories three and four in Figure 4.1.). Nowhere is the process dimension more important than in counseling. As an illustration, consider the abbreviated definitions of the following seven counseling skills:

1. **Goal Setting**—the verbal interaction between counselor and client during which they agree on a goal to work toward (e.g., a particular behavior change, making a decision, gaining information about a career).

2. **Reflection of Feeling and Attitude**—a counselor verbal response that reveals a feeling or attitude which was explictly or implicitly expressed by the client.

3. **Open-Ended Question**—a questioning verbal response which allows the client maximum freedom for content and style of answer.

4. **Implementing Strategies**—the implementation of a plan of action by the counselor and client for the accomplishment of a counseling goal.

5. **Tacting Response Lead**—a counselor's verbal response which "helps the client discuss abstract concepts in more specific terms, or to associate significant behavioral events with certain environmental circumstances" (Delaney & Eisenberg, 1972, p. 82).

6. **Constructing Strategies**—the development of a plan of action by the counselor and client for the accomplishment of a counseling goal.

7. **Conceptual Summary**—a summarization of information revealed in the exploration of client concerns that creates meaningful relationships between disparate information elements.

A reading of these skill definitions probably would do little toward helping the counselor acquire, perform, and apply the skills. Even if a counselor had acquired these skill behaviors and could perform them, this learning would be less than adequate for actual practice until the *purpose* (effect on the client) of the skills was understood, and the *process sequence* of the skills was grasped. Skill-behavior analysis and assessment by the supervisor should enhance the counselor's understanding of purpose and sequence, thus adding a dimension of fidelity to skills and function as indicated in the following elaborations:

1. **Open-Ended Question**—a good technique for starting the counseling session and facilitating client exploration during the session. From the client talk elicited by this technique the counselor can make other good responses (reflection, etc.) and gain information about the client's concerns.

2. **Reflection of Feeling and Attitude**—a particularly useful technique in the beginning of the counseling process for helping the client explore concerns from a personal frame of reference. This process is instrumental in the

client's acquisition of self awareness concerning emotions and attitudes, communicates empathy and acceptance, and helps the client explore concerns at a meaningful level. Affective information from reflections is a building block for problem conceptualization.

3. **Tacting Response Lead**—helps the client be more specific about concerns, and explore them in detail. Precipitory antecedents and consequences can be revealed through tacting so that the client sees some of the instrumental factors in his/her problem. The concreteness generated by tacting enables the client to more objectively appraise and conceptualize the problem, leading to goal setting and resolution strategies. Tacting can occur throughout the counseling session but is particularly effective following self exploration, when the counselor and client zero-in on the tangible aspects of the problem.

4. **Conceptual Summary**—a summarizing statement which brings together seemingly disparate affective and cognitive information revealed in the client's exploration of concerns, enables the client to conceptualize or create a unitary picture of concerns so that goals can be set and strategies constructed and implemented. Short conceptual summaries throughout the counseling process help the client develop a perspective and an all-inclusive one at the end of exploration prepares the client to set goals.

5. **Goal Setting**—done from a conceptualization of concerns by the counselor and client to resolve or ameliorate the client's expressed concerns.

6. **Constructing Strategies**—a plan of action, constructed by the counselor and client, which will accomplish the goals. Each party determines the amount and kind of input he/she will offer toward implementation of the strategy.

7. **Implementing Strategies**—to accomplish counseling goals, and to help the client acquire skills for future

problem resolution and goal accomplishment. If the strategy is effective, the counselor and client subsequently review the counseling process, generalize learnings to other and future situations, and then terminate the alliance.

If a supervisor were assisting a counselor with any of these seven skill behaviors, or the whole counseling function, the elaborations of purpose and sequence would be mandatory. To reiterate, all skill behaviors have a purpose and sequence which determine the fidelity of skill performance.

SETTING SUPERVISION GOALS

After the behavioral supervisor has established a facilitative relationship with the counselor and the analysis/assessment procedure has been performed, the *establishment of supervision goals* is the next and third methodological step. Analysis and assessment provides the information from which supervision goals can be selected. Returning to the analysis and assessment in Figure 4.4, supervision goals will come from the discrete skill behaviors in the analysis section, and the corresponding assessment categories provide information that will help the counselor and supervisor in constructing strategies.

Setting supervision goals is a crucial aspect of the behavioral supervision process where the supervisee's cooperation and motivation can be strengthened or easily weakened by the actions of the supervisor. The counselor should have taken part in analysis and assessment, and now should have even more self directedness in choosing supervision goals. Supervision goals must be acceptable to the supervisor and counselor, but the recommendation is that the supervisor be tolerant of the counselor's choice if the goals are anywhere near realistic. The supervisor may see a skill-goal of a higher priority than the one chosen by the counselor, but to accept the counselor's choice rather than to impose the supervisor's will is often better. Any time the counselor is demonstrating self-initiated development it should be encouraged if possible. Moreover, the skill goals that the supervisor would have chosen may be gained later, or as a result of generalization from supervision directed at the counselor's chosen goals.

Skill behavior goals can be covert *and* overt. Often the supervisor will see an inappropriate overt performance of skills, and later in supervision will learn that the counselor was impaired at the covert rather than overt level. When performing analysis, assessment, and goal setting, the supervisor should keep in mind that overt skill performance usually relies on knowledge and covert skill behaviors. In Figure 4.5 the skill-behaviors of targeting instrumental factors and conceptualizing the consultee's problem are examples at the covert (thinking) level. These covert skills are prerequisites for overt skills which occur later in the counseling process (e.g., goal setting and using strategies).

CONSTRUCTING AND IMPLEMENTING SUPERVISORY STRATEGIES

The fourth step in the methodological sequence of behavioral supervision is construction and implementation of strategies to accomplish the goal(s). Supervision strategies are the action plans that are made and implemented by the counselor and supervisor for the attainment of supervision goals. A single strategy may contain numerous learning activities, or it may be simple in structure. Supervisor offered reinforcement is an example of a simple strategy whereas microtraining involves many learning activities. Strategies are constructed rather than selected, being designed for the counselor as were supervision goals. Factors to consider when constructing a strategy are the following:

1. the counselor's preference for certain learning modes,

2. the effectiveness of the strategy for reaching the goal, and

3. the feasibility of the strategy (e.g., facilities, materials, setting).

Client Exploration of Self and Concerns	Conceptualization of Concern	Setting Counseling Goals	Constructing and Implementing Strategies
Open-ended questions Reflections Tacting	Conceptual Summaries	Goal Setting	Constructing Implementing Strategies Strategies

Figure 4.5. Skill-behaviors in the counseling process. (States of the counseling process overlap, as well as the process positions of the skill-behaviors.)

Two methodological thrusts in supervision strategies exist: *a dependence on the self directedness and personal resources of the counselor, and a reliance predominantly on output from the supervisor.* From the first thrust the supervisor is in the stance of a consultant to the counselor. The counselor assists in constructing the strategy and receives only consultative assistance in carrying out this process. Self monitoring and reinforcement is an example of a self-directed strategy (Holahan & Galassi, 1986). From the second thrust the supervisor operates as a trainer, actively participating in the strategy. Microtraining is an example of a supervisor-directed strategy. An example of microtraining for supervision is presented in an article by Richardson and Bradley (1984).

These two thrusts are not entirely discrete and each of the supervision techniques to be addressed shortly can vary in the degree to which the supervisor acts as a consultant or active trainer. Determining which thrust to lean toward is a professional judgment to be made by the supervisor based upon the three factors mentioned previously. Consistent with earlier suggestions again the recommendation is that self development be promoted as much as possible by the supervision strategy. Where active training and the counselor's dependence upon the supervisor is necessary, the supervisor should use discretion and retain the development of counselor autonomy as a later objective.

Self-Instructional Modules

As suggested earlier, the behavioral supervisor may encounter supervisees who cannot demonstrate the requisite skills for competent counseling practice. If these deficiencies are not beyond short-term remediation procedures, a number of training activities can be employed by the supervisor (Bernstein, Hofmann & Wade, 1986; Keller & Protinsky, 1984; Tennyson & Strom, 1986). Self-instructional modules are one of the most feasible activities because they require a minimal amount of time from the supervisor.

As described by Cormier and Cormier (1976) a self-instructional module *is an instructional unit that contains explicit skill-behavior objectives, evaluation procedures for assessing the extent to which the skill behaviors have been acquired and demonstrated, and the self-directed learning activities which the supervisee will follow to learn the skill behaviors.* Modules can be structured packages that form the components of a classroom or laboratory course, however in counselor supervision what seems more propitious is for the supervisor to have a cache of materials and learning activities from which modules can be designed for each supervisee, with the assistance of the supervisee. Also appropriate are evaluation procedures which stress demonstration of the skill behaviors in role playing or other life-like situations.

The most common module assignment usually concerns the elementary but important skill of empathy communication and problem exploration. Many student-counselors overlook these skills and prematurely try to "solve the client's problem." Yet the importance of empathy in counselor training has been documented (Bowman & Glsen, 1982; Bowman & Reeves, 1987; Brown & Smith, 1984; Gladstein & Feldstein, 1983; Kimberlin & Friesen, 1980). But in this instance and most others, assignment to a skill module usually results in the supervisee making rapid learning progress. Supervisees who have been unable to communicate empathically, and to explore the client's concerns, have quickly acquired and demonstrated these skills.

Empirical support for self-instructional modules in supervision and counselor training is modest, mainly because the topic has not received research attention. Supportive findings have been reported by Cormier, Cormier, Zerega, and Wagaman (1976) for the learning of counseling strategies. Cormier and Cormier (1976) have cited many studies in higher education where self-instructional modules have been used successfully. The potential for self-directed learning in counselor training and supervision looks promising.

Self Appraisal and Skill Monitoring

One supervision activity that obviously reflects a self-development strategy is self appraisal and skill monitoring by the counselor. Self appraisal has the advantage of being a non-threatening procedure, and one that is perpetual if learned well in supervision. Self appraisal and skill monitoring go hand in hand. Studies in self observation have indicated that individuals automatically evaluate the behaviors which they observe, and attempt to influence these behaviors in a desired direction (Cavior & Marabotto, 1976; Dodds, 1986; Fuqua, Johnson, Anderson, & Newman, 1984; Goldfried & Merbaum, 1973; Kurpius, Benjamin, & Morran, 1985; Mahoney & Thoresen, 1974; Miars, Tracey, Ray, Cornfeld, O'Farrell, & Gelso, 1983; Robinson, Froehle, & Kurpius, 1979a; Thoresen & Mahoney, 1974). Hackney and Nye (1973, p. 121) suggested that self monitoring (following initial appraisal) seems to interfere with unwanted behavior by breaking the stimulus-response association and by encouraging performance of the desired response—which then is often reinforced by feedback of progress and a sense of accomplishment.

Little support is found in the literature for unstructured and subjective self appraisal. Such a procedure may be so undisciplined as to be of dubious value. Yet, the counselor who has a clear understanding of the elements of effective performance can appraise and bring performance into line with those guidelines. The key is understanding—an articulation of effective performance (Kanfer, 1970, and Cavior & Marabotto, 1976). Many counselors have a hazy idea of what is good counselor performance. Even those who are performing admirably may never have articulated the skills that comprise good performance. Probably for this reason structured self appraisal has been more popular than the unstructured variety.

Structured self appraisal and skill monitoring utilizes some kind of structure for the counselor to follow in the appraisal and monitoring process. Any framework which helps the counselor attend to the important factors in effective performance is acceptable. A job description outlining the counselor's specific skill behaviors and behavioral criteria with which to evaluate those skills is a particularly useful document.

Modest but positive support exists for the effectiveness of counselors' self appraisal and skill monitoring. Reports by Mathewson and Rochlin (1956) and Walz and Johnston (1963) have cited observed improvement in counseling as a function of structured appraisal of audio taped interviews and unstructured observation of video recorded sessions respectively.

Altekruse and Brown (1969) found that counselors appraising their counseling performance with the *Counselor Self-Inter-action Analysis Instrument* began to use more indirective responses than counselors who used unstructured appraisal. Martin and Gazda (1970) measured significant improvement in the counselor-offered facilitative conditions of empathy, non-possessive warmth, genuineness, and intensity of interpersonal contact as a result of self appraisal employing interaction scales to assess those facilitative conditions. Austin and Altekruse (1972) unexpectedly discovered that a supervisor-absent group of practicum counselors significantly increased their under-standing responses in counseling by the unstructured self appraisal of a leaderless group process. They subsequently suggested that the *Counselor Verbal Response Scale* (their criterion instrument) might be valuable as an appraisal tool to improve self-directed supervision.

Self appraisal and skill monitoring have their limits, they are not cure-alls and will not replace the supervisor's role. But their use can be a valuable and effective technique for the behavioral supervisor.

Peer Supervision

Peer supervision has for some time been recognized as being a valuable aid to the supervisor (Fraleigh & Buchheimer, 1969; Wagner & Smith, 1979) yet this potential has never been tapped and peer supervision has received little development and research. Those few studies conducted have yielded inconsistent findings of questionable value.

Investigations by Arbuckle (1956), Stefflre, King, and Leafgren (1962), and Walton (1974) have studied the attributes which counselor-trainees value in the counselor or peer supervisors with whom they might choose to work. Confidence and strength or dominance is the one common finding in these studies, and this seems understandable. Whether the counselor is in the role of client or supervisee, an uncertainty is present which leads the individual toward sources of directive help-giving and security.

Researchers (Bishop, 1971; Brown & Cannady, 1969; Friesen & Dunning, 1973) have illustrated that the use of peers as raters can be reliable and accurate. One can infer from these investigations that training and structure probably improve rating performance, and that an untrained rater can give destructive feedback to a fellow counselor.

By incorporating this paucity of evidence with other guidelines for behavioral supervision a number of discernible suggestions can be made for the employment of peer supervisors. The first suggestion, voiced by Fraleigh and Buchheimer (1969), is that peer supervision always should be considered supplemental to that of the behavioral supervisor—it is not a substitute.

A second suggestion is to recognize that *peer supervision can be helpful or harmful,* and three factors seem to be the determinants—the *attitude* of the peer supervisor, the *format* of peer supervision, and *training* in peer supervision. The attitude of the peer supervisor must be one of helpfulness, cooperation, and equality rather than an intent on one-upmanship (Fraleigh & Buchheimer, 1969). This attitude contributes to a recommended supervision format where feedback and sharing are the peer's primary functions with evaluation being deemphasized. Within this format the peer supervisor's task is structured yet flexible; using a rating scale is the basic method but a free discussion of ideas is encouraged. Dowd and Blocher (1974) have shown that awareness and reinforcement are separate variables in counselor training, but that their combined effects are stronger than either in isolation. The peer supervisor should thus promote counselor skill-awareness through ratings and shared perceptions. Positive reinforcement could be offered and more discriminative evaluation (positive and negative reinforcement) would be inherent in the rating data.

Of the three determinants in peer supervision, training is the most important because it can affect attitude and prepare the peer supervisor to follow the format. Training should include an explanation of the peer-supervision format, a modeling of peer supervision by the behavioral supervisor, and skill practice.

A third suggestion for peer-supervision is that the behavioral supervisor conduct group supervision before allowing peers to supervise each other individually. The group can be an opportunity for training and practice.

A final suggestion is that peer supervision, like self supervision, has limits. Counselors with serious skill deficiencies and those who are extremely defensive should not be candidates for peer supervision. Further, for counselors to learn where and when advanced and complex counselor skills are required may necessitate the expertise of the behavioral supervisor, and that often peer supervision is insufficient for this goal.

Modeling and Reinforcement

Two of the most powerful principles in psychological learning theory are *modeling and reinforcement.* Research support and the clinical application of these principles has been presented in numerous scholarly works [Bandura, 1969; Bergin & Garfield, 1971; Franks, 1969; Kanfer & Phillips, 1970; Krumboltz, 1966a; Thoresen (Ed.), 1973], and application to counselor training and supervision has received substantial attention in the last few years. Blane (1968), Carlson (1971), Clark (1970), Davidson and Emmer (1966), and Kelly (1971) have shown that various forms of supervisor-or-trainer-controlled reinforcement, offered following the performance of a desired skill behavior, can increase the frequency of that target. Canada (1973) has illustrated the importance of presenting reinforcement immediately after performance instead of a delayed presentation.

Numerous investigators have demonstrated the supervisor's or trainer's successful use of modeling for teaching focal skills to counselors. Among these individuals are Dalton, and Sundblad (1976); Dalton, Sundblad, and Hylbert (1973); Frankel (1971); Froehle, Robinson, and Kurpius (1983); Hosford and Johnson (1983); Payne and Gralinski (1968); Payne, Weiss, and Iappa (1972); Payne, Winter, and Bell (1972); Perry (1975); Peters, Cormier, and Cormier (1978); Robinson, Froehle, and Kurpius (1979b); Rank, Thoresen, and Smith (1972); Ronnestad (1973); Silverman and Quinn (1974); Sodetz (1972); Stone and

Vance (1976); and Uhlemann, Lea, and Stone (1976). In some of these studies citing the efficacy of reinforcement or modeling the two learning effects are integrated, and other cognitive learning processes may have been present. Miller's (1971) findings have suggested that treatments combining both modeling and reinforcement are stronger than either effect in isolation. Instructional power also has been increased by combining modeling with instructions and rehearsal (Stone & Vance, 1976), and role play and supervisory feedback (Wallace, Horan, Baker, & Hudson, 1975).

Modeling and reinforcement are not techniques or activities but psychological learning principles, and the astute behavioral supervisor does not have a cookbook of methods for utilizing them. What the supervisor does need is an understanding of how the principles can operate in supervision. A few practical suggestions will thus be offered.

1. Modeling and reinforcement can be employed within the immediate supervisor-counselor interaction, or in activities outside the supervisory dyad. Critiquing tapes and role playing are examples of activities within the dyad; viewing expert counselors on tape and self-managed reinforcement are examples of activities outside the dyad.

2. The supervisor can be a dispenser of modeling and reinforcement, or persons and activities other than the supervisor can be the media. Choosing the type of presentation for exerted learning influence is a strategy decision, and whatever source is likely to be most influential to the counselor should be chosen. For example, the supervisor's modeling of reflections may not be as potent as a film of Carl Rogers because of the higher status that trainees would probably attribute to Rogers (Mischel & Grusec, 1966; Kloba & Zimpfer, 1976). Videotaped modeling presentations are likely to have more impact than audiotaped models (Ivey, Normington, Miller, Morrill, & Haase, 1968; Stone & Stebbins, 1975; Walz & Johnston, 1963).

3. Modeling and reinforcement should be as focal and concentrated as possible. A concrete skill-behavior is the focal point, and high fidelity modeling and reinforcement should be directed there—not diffused. Modeling loses effectiveness if the viewers' attention is not directed at the focal skills (Bandura, 1969; Eskedel, 1975).

4. Learning complex counselor skills may require complex strategies which **combine** learning principles, involve discrimination training, and are "personalistic" (Lazarus, 1971, p. 31) to the counselor. The supervisor's confidence and ingenuity in constructing an effective strategy is paramount.

5. Modeling is often a sufficient experience for the **acquisition** of a skill, but sometimes the skill must be developed behaviorally through step-by-step training (employing reinforcement) in order for it to be **performed** (Bandura, 1969). Do not assume that viewing a skill is sufficient for subsequently performing it.

Role Playing and Simulation

Role playing and simulation exercises have been standard educational methods in counselor training (Akamatsu, 1980; Gladstein & Feldstein, 1983; Schwebel, 1953; Scott, Cormier, & Cormier, 1980) and their efficacy continues to be supported empirically and practically (Delaney, 1969; Eisenberg & Delaney, 1970; Errek & Randolf, 1982; Jakubowski-Spector et al., 1971; Mann & Mann, 1966; Strosahl & Jacobson, 1986). The impact of these procedures probably lies in the fact that numerous psychological learning principles are operative within them.

Role playing is the exercise of behaving in a contrived experience according to a prescribed role and by altering roles a number of learning situations can be presented to the counselor. In the role of helpee, the counselor attempts to experience the part of the helper and act in that way. Sensitivity to helpees is promoted through this kind of role taking. The helpee role also places the counselor in a position to observe the supervisor and imitatively learn from his/her performance.

The supervisee's performance of the helpee role, whether for empathic experience or modeling of the supervisor, preferably precedes the role performance of counselor. This sequence is preferred because it gives the supervisee an opportunity to observe the skills of an effective counselor (as role played by the supervisor). Subsequent supervisee performance in the role of counselor is facilitated by this previous modeling.

Simulation, as employed in supervision, is a contrived experience which represents an experience that occurs naturally in the counselor's work. The counselor is confronted with nearly the same situational exigencies as in actual practice and is forced to react immediately with learned skills. Simulation in this manner is an effective method for facilitating skill generalization beyond the classroom or supervisory session.

A simulation technique that has received attention is the presentation of filmed or video taped client expressions to counselor-trainees. Kagan and Schauble (1969), Danish (1971), and Spivack (1973) reported that counselors react experientially to filmed clients as they would in a real counseling session, and that counselors can gain self understanding by discovering their responsive affect. Carlson (1980), Danish (1971), Delaney (1969), Smith (1984), Stewart and Jessell (1986), Ward (1985), and Young (1985) go further than self understanding and help counselors practice responding with effective statements to the taped clients. The counselor thus can shape responding skills and receive reinforcement from the supervisor as performance improves.

Simulation and role playing are not restricted to counseling skills. Panther (1971) has successfully taught consulting skills through simulated exercises, and the list of skills that could be targeted is limitless. The supervisor should keep some guidelines in mind though, for simulation and role playing in supervision require expertise. The supervisor must be well acquainted with the situation (environment, persons, influential factors) that is to be simulated so simulation can be as real as possible. As in all behavioral methods, the focal skill must be defined and within the counselor's capability to perform. Complex skills should be divided into easily performed components. The supervisor must be able to demonstrate the skill, and the counselor may want to act the part of other parties in the situation who usually inhibit his/her performance (e.g., uncooperative parent, teacher, or client).

As Hackney (1971) has suggested, counselor supervision cannot become just another laboratory training experience, and the behavioral supervisor must not spend the majority of time in role playing and simulation exercises. But these techniques have a place in supervision as long as counselors encounter situations where they must perform skills they have not acquired or have not learned to apply.

Microtraining

The first documentation of microtraining for counselors was by Ivey et al. (1968). Their microtraining program, called microcounseling, successfully trained beginning counselors in the skills of attending behavior, reflection of feeling, and summarization of feeling. Since this pioneer project, others have found various microcounseling training programs effective with the skills of attending (DiMattia & Arndt, 1974), basic supervision skills (Baker, Johnson, Kopala, & Strout, 1985; Baker, Scofield, Munson & Clayton, 1983; Forsyth & Ivey, 1980; Richardson & Bradley, 1984; Stone, 1981), fundamental social skills (Saltmarsh & Hubele, 1974), communication of test results (Miller, Morrill, & Uhlemann, 1970), a counseling-like verbal response set (Boyd, 1973), and multiple response techniques (Toukmanian & Rennie, 1975). Guttman and Haase (1972) have supported the long-term retention of skills learned through microcounseling training, and the technique has become a particularly practical and valid procedure that personifies good counselor education (Bellucci, 1972).

Microtraining is a direct attempt to systematize training. This methodological approach follows a paradigm of training steps including intensive practice of the focal skill until it is performed satisfactorily. The basic microtraining model is as follows (Ivey, 1971):

1. The trainee attempts to perform the focal skill within a situation where it is appropriate. This attempt at performance could be a simulated, coach-client, role-played exercise.

2. The attempted performance is videotaped.

3. If the performance was of an interpersonal skill, the other party completes an evaluation form, and may be interviewed for additional feedback. When the focal skill does not involve another party this step can be eliminated.

4. The trainee reads a manual describing the focal skill to be learned. The supervisor is available for discussion and clarification of the focal skill.

5. **Video models of an expert demonstrating the skill are shown to the trainee, and these may be positive or negative models. Discrimination training is present as the supervisor and trainee discuss the models.**

6. The trainee and supervisor critique the videotaped attempt (step 1) to perform the focal skill. Discrimination is again present as the trainee identifies examples where the focal skill was performed satisfactorily, poorly, or not at all. The supervisor offers verbal reinforcement for capable skill performance.

7. The supervisor and trainee plan and prepare for another performance of the focal skill.

8. The trainee makes a second attempt to perform the focal skill, and this is videotaped.

9. Feedback and evaluation are made available to the trainee.

The construction of other microtraining programs is possible, but the nine-step model has been found most successful. Ivey (1971, pp. 8-9) offers several propositions upon which the success is based.

First, microtraining *focuses on single skills.* The trainee masters one skill at a time and can see him/herself improve in each one rather than being barraged with a whole set of competencies. Second, microtraining affords opportunity for *self observation and confrontation.* Third, *video models* are provided for imitative learning. Fourth, microtraining can *accommodate any skill* that is demonstrable and behaviorally defined. Fifth, *actual performance* and practice in a life-like situation make microtraining a "real" experience.

Microcounseling seems to capitalize on many of the training/learning variables that have been found instrumental in effective counselor preparation, and supervision is one of these training components that contributes feedback, reinforcement, and shaping influence on the trainee. Authier and Gustafson (1976) discovered another supervisory contribution that may be unique among microcounseling components. Supervision helps the trainee reduce undesirable behavior *in addition* to increasing the use of focal skills. Referring to their results, they stated that

> This would seem to indicate that the supervised group more clearly discriminated the microcounseling skill from its opposite. Thus, it appears that feedback from a skilled observer, in this case the supervisor, may be necessary in learning and discrimination, especially within a very limited time span.(Authier & Gustafson, 1976, p. 708)

Ivey (1971) described microtraining as an "open system"—programs can be constructed within the limits of facilities available and for specific populations in respective settings. Where supervisors are scarce, peer supervision and self appraisal are alternatives. For some skills audio recording can substitute for videotaping. Live demonstrations can replace video models. The possibilities are many for the ingenious supervisor.

Self-Management Techniques

Throughout the behavioral supervision methodology are opportunities for using self-management techniques, and these opportunities would be especially pertinent for the supervisor following a self-development strategy thrust. Self management has been defined by Boyd and LaFleur (1974, p. 2) *as the ability of individuals to make personal behavioral adjustment decisions and actions based on analyses of self and the environment.* A self-management technique in supervision would be a method supervision would be a method by which the supervisee changes his/her own skill behavior with only consultative assistance from the supervisor. The behavioral supervisor helps the counselor analyze and assess the skill behaviors required by role and function, the counselor then decides what adjustments in skill behavior are needed, and self-directed action plans are constructed to make the adjustment.

A concise explanation of self-management techniques has been presented by Boyd and LaFleur (1974), and Kahn (1976), and a more thorough discourse is provided by Bernstein, Hofman, and Wade (1986); Bernstein and Lecomte (1979); Hector, Elson, and Yager (1977); Keller and Protinsky (1984); Mahoney and Thoresen (1974); Tennyson and Strom (1986); and Thoresen and Mahoney (1974). The present coverage of self-managed techniques is limited to the following applications found to be most practical.

Overt-Stimulus Control. Mahoney and Thoresen (1974, p.40) have defined stimulus control as those strategies involving the rearrangement of cues that have come to elicit undesired responses and/or the establishment of cues that will elicit desired responses. These cues may be divided into the overt category—observable cues in the environment, and the covert category—private events within the counselor that generate behavior. The use of overt stimulus control has had successful applicability in counseling and psychotherapy (Mahoney & Thoresen, 1974; Thoresen & Mahoney, 1974) but its utilization in supervision seems more restricted. A plethora of stimuli exists to which supervisees react in a non-therapeutic manner and to attempt to rearrange these stimuli would be unrealistic. A major portion of supervision consists of helping the counselor adapt to and learn to respond therapeutically to stimuli which elicit unconstructive responses from people, the counselor included. So if a counselor is upset by strong emotion in the helpee, for example, obviously to tell the helpee to cease affect is inappropriate; rather, through supervision the counselor learns to respond to helpee emotion in a helpful way.

Some applications of overt stimulus control belong in supervision. Sometimes response inhibition or stimulus avoidance is an immediate but temporary reaction which the counselor can take when cues are overwhelming. Perhaps under certain environmental stimulus conditions the counselor performs unusually well. To capitalize on these conditions is opportunistic.

Establishment of cues to elicit desired responses is perhaps the most useful overt-stimulus control technique, and it represents a mainstay of behavioral supervision. When a counselor is responding inappropriately, or at a technique frequency level that is too low, the supervisor can (1) help the counselor learn to perform the desired skill behavior, and (2) help him/her identify those situational cues to which the skill behavior should be directed. For example, the counselor who asks closed questions learns **how** and **when** to make open-ended leads, and the counselor who uses too few leads learns of more opportunities to use them.

Covert-Stimulus Control. Whenever overt stimuli elicit undesirable responses from the counselor and the conditions are such that to control these cues would be unrealistic, the a covert-stimulus control technique may be the answer. Such techniques are one of the behavioral supervisor's means of dealing with counselor intrapersonal dynamics. Two principal techniques are *modification of cognitive content* and *modification of cognitive process.*

Cognitive modification involves two dimensions—content and process. The **content dimension** concerns ideational content, and the **process dimension** concerns the longitudinal-situational pattern of focal cognitions and their antecedent and consequence contingencies. Regarding the latter, the principles of stimulus control and operant conditioning are used to influence certain cognitions, so that in turn the timing and frequence of these cognitions are manipulated to produce desirable emotion and overt behavior. The works of Albert Ellis (1973), Ellis and Harper (1975), and Aaron Beck (1976) are representative of the content focus in cognitive modification, and those of Meichenbaum and Cameron (1974) and Meichenbaum (1975) are representative and a learning-theory influenced approach. The content and process distinction is not an absolute dichotomy, but more of a theoretical and methodological leaning.

The content emphasis to cognitive modification, as exemplified by applications of Rational Emotive Therapy to counselor supervision, was touched upon earlier in Chapter 3. Changing ideational content is a technique which seems to have more in common with the psychotherapeutic approach to supervision than the behavioral approach, and this is the reason for its discussion in Chapter 3.

The process emphasis however is a more behaviorally-oriented self-management technique in which the supervisee learns to control his/her cognitive process, rather than spending a considerable amount of time with the supervisor in a cognitive restructuring dialogue. Self management of counselor anxiety is one promising area for *cognitive process* control. Research has consistently linked counselor anxiety and poor therapeutic performance (Bergin & Jasper, 1969; Carter & Pappas, 1975; Milliken & Kirchener, 1971), and counselor-trainees are particularly prone to experience anticipatory anxiety and demonstrate its effects (Hagan & Boyd, 1976; Mooney & Carlson, 1976). Self-managed anxiety control methods, employing some form of cognitive stimulus control, have shown efficacy for anxiety reduction in clients (Chang-Liang & Denny, 1976; Dodge, 1982; Hagan & Boyd, 1976; Hui-Ho, Hosford & Johnson, 1985; Kline, 1983; Liddle, 1986; Mooney & Carlson, 1976; Shaver, 1985; Russell, Miller, & June, 1974, 1975; Russell & Sipich, 1973; Sanchez-Craig, 1976; Spiegler, Cooley, Marshall, Prince, & Puckett, 1976) and supervisees (Russell & Wise, 1976). By combining the elements of these anxiety treatments into a comprehensive method, the following eclectic model, Cognitive Stimulus Control of Counselor Anxiety, is suggested.

1. The *awareness treatment* of Carter and Pappas (1975), effective in itself, is a procedure which seems to change cognitive content as well as identify focal stimuli for later control. Awareness may act as a prelude for stimulus control steps. It consists of helping supervisees become aware of feelings and behaviors arising from interpersonal anxieties through supervisor-lead group discussion. Questions by the supervisor, outlined by Sanchez-Craig (1976), may facilitate a cognitive reap- praisal of stressful stimuli; "Is the situation actually that

bad; how can you reinterpret the actions of that person; How can you reinterpret your own reactions in the situation?" (p.8)

2. **Cue-controlled relaxation training** is a logical second step whereby the supervisee learns relaxation and associates the relaxed state with certain self generated cue words (Russell & Wise, 1976).

3. The supervisee is then instructed and encouraged to use the cue-controlled relaxation skill in situations which present anxiety evoking cues (e.g., clients, supervision, peer critique). An alternative self-managed response thus replaces the anxiety-controlled one (Russell & Wise, 1976; Sanchez-Craig, 1976), and a modification in the usual cognitive process takes place.

4. Practice of this self-management procedure should precede implementation in counseling and supervision situations.

Another promising application for cognitive process control is a technique which the author has found valuable in practicum supervision. A descriptively accurate label for this technique is "covert planning and rehearsal." This technique consists of a brief period of mental preparation and imaginal rehearsal immediately before an interview. The supervisor administers the first treatment, and thereafter the supervisee can do it without assistance. Steps in this technique are as follows:

1. In a regular supervision session the counselor and supervisor review the last helping interchange and plan for the next one.

2. Just before the next helping interchange the counselor seeks a quiet setting where he/she can think over the things to be performed in the upcoming session. By closing eyes and imagining these events taking place the counselor can covertly rehearse the required skills. The process of planning rehearsing takes up the time which might normally be spent in anticipating the fearful

properties of the interchange. further, covert rehearsal is an effective procedure for facilitating later overt performance.

3. The counselor is spontaneous in action and uses caution to assure that planning and rehearsal does not replace spontaneous action. If the helpee wishes to direct the interchanges away from the counselor's planned agenda it may be appropriate to follow this lead rather than force the client to follow the counselor's plan.

FOLLOW-UP AND GENERALIZATION OF LEARNING

The fifth methodological step in behavioral supervision is to evaluate the strategies and techniques employed. This follow-up should be done during the strategy and again upon completion to see if it is having the desired effect on the counselor. Adjustments must be made if the strategy and techniques are not having the desired effect.

Evaluation of strategy results is relatively easy because skill goals are behaviorally defined and observable. If the goals have been reached, the strategies are judged effective (although not necessarily efficient). When goals have not been reached an assessment of the reasons for failure should transpire. Potential reasons are as follows:

1. The supervisee does not have the prerequisite knowledge and/or acquired behavior for successful participation in the strategy or strategies. These deficiencies should be filled through remedial work.

2. The supervisee was not motivated to participate in the strategy and reach the skills goals. A discussion of the counselor's desires, attitudes, and commitment to counseling could follow to determine whether or not they are appropriate.

3. The supervisor may have offered too little assistance with the strategy, and more thorough treatment should

be started. Sometimes a self-development strategy is not as effective as one with more supervisor input.

4. During the strategy implementation the counselor and/or supervisor may not have fully understood the strategy and/or goal. By correcting this error and putting heads together the supervisor and counselor can hypothesize what strategy would be more effective and then implement that strategy.

When follow-up has shown a supervision strategy to be accountable, a final task remains before termination. The skills and learning acquired by the counselor, in the context of supervised performance, should be generalized to other performance situations that are likely to present themselves in the future. Generalization of behavior change (Kanfer & Phillips, 1970), and transfer of training to practical settings (Jakubowski-Spector et al., 1971) is the ultimate success criteria for behavioral supervision.

Generalization and transfer are more probable if the counselor has been personally involved in the supervision process and has been allowed, and indeed encouraged, to provide input into supervised learning. The self direction of the counselor is a crucial component in the long-term effects of behavioral supervision.

Another factor in generalization and transfer is the amount of different situations to which the counselor has been exposed—the more the better! Even discussing or simulating situations that demand unfamiliar skills can help the counselor develop "response ability."

Weinrach's (1976) model for the systematic generalization of counseling skills adds a final test even beyond the demonstration of a skill behavior. The supervisee has truly mastered a skill and can generalize it to other situations when he/she can teach it to another person. As mentioned earlier, the "fully functioning" counselor who can do this teaching for all his/her skills is ready to become a supervisor.

BEHAVIORAL SUPERVISION: EMPIRICAL SUPPORT

Behavioral supervision is an arena where the learning theory principles found effective in other circumstances should be subjected to more applied research. The assumption that learning theory will function within supervision and with supervisee behaviors as it has in other environmental situations remains to be shown. Of the many techniques suggested in this section, few have been empirically supported by *actual supervision research.* For techniques which have not received research attention, validity has been generalized from counseling research and practical supervision experience.

A small but credible body of supervision research suggests that, in terms of skill-behavior change (e.g., empathic responding), behavioral supervision is somewhat superior to experiential and psychotherapeutic methods that do not systematically utilize psychological learning theory principles (Birk, 1972; Boyd, 1973; Hansen, Pound, & Petro, 1976; Payne & Gralinski, 1968; Payne, Weiss, & Iappa, 1972; Payne, Winter, & Bell, 1972). As reviewed in this Chapter, some of the activities of behavioral supervision, notably microcounseling, reinforcement, and modeling, have received strong empirical support. Moderate support also exists for simulation exercises, self appraisal, and peer supervision. In most of these activities the exact effect of learning theory principles is unknown, and in fact we often assume that effectiveness is because of learning principles. Research is needed to unravel the tangled and interacting effects.

PRACTICAL APPLICATION: ILLUSTRATIVE CASES

As mentioned previously in this Chapter, the behavioral supervisor can choose to follow a counselor-directed strategy and act as a consultant to the counselor, or a supervisor-directed plan can be chosen and the supervisor will act as an active trainer. Whichever thrust is chosen, a unique strategy is constructed to meet the learning needs of the supervisee. A number of cases will be presented to illustrate the two thrusts and several different strategies.

Case 1. An Unskilled Supervisee

This case involves a practicum supervisor and a beginning practicum student. When the supervisor reviewed the student counselor's performance in role-played exercises, it was apparent that fundamental interaction skills were lacking and inappropriate behavior (social chit-chat) was profuse. The student counselor also was very nervous and defensive.

The supervisor decided that enough time remained in the practicum course for the student counselor to remedy deficiencies and attain required performance objectives, so a recycling back to pre-practicum training was not done. In a critique session the supervisor and student counselor assessed the role-played counseling performance and areas for development were identified. Rather that attempting to reduce the many inappropriate behaviors that were evidenced, the supervisor elected to focus on replacing them with appropriate skills. In this manner less criticism was directed at the defensive student counselor.

A program of simulated training exercises was developed so that the counselor could attain the skills needed in order to begin counseling with actual clients in the practicum course. For several weeks the supervisor worked with the counselor in supervisory-training sessions; the supervisor employed verbal reinforcement, role playing, and modeling to help the counselor. Heavy extra-supervision training assignments were also completed by the counselor. At the end of the remedial training program the counselor entered supervised practice in the practicum course with real clients.

Epilogue. Remedial training within supervision is certainly not the ideal—and it is hopefully the exception. But a realistic fact is that the supervisor will continually encounter supervisees who are not functioning at required skill levels. Remedial work, if the supervisor and counselor are willing, is one alternative in this situation. Termination of supervision, or referral to remedial skill training, are the other alternatives.

Needless to say, the counselor's continuation in supervised practice at a less than adequate skill level is professionally unethical.

Case 2. Microcounseling For A Skill Deficiency

A supervisor and group of practicing counselors evaluated their program of services and decided that program goals could be met more efficiently through group counseling. None of the counselors had received more than a superficial reading knowledge of group counseling, and they recognized their deficiency in group counseling skills.

The supervisor helped the counselors state desired skills in behavioral terms and then designed and conducted a microcounseling training program for the development of these goals. Microcounseling took the counselors through a sequence of:

1. reading literature describing and illustrating the focal skills,

2. viewing videotapes of skill demonstrations,

3. performing the skills in simulated exercises and role-playing sessions, and

4. receiving performance feedback and supervision so that the focal skills could be refined through further practice.

Following microcounseling each counselor initiated a group counseling session with clients and received more supervision as skills were used in a real situation.

Case 3. Self-Managed Improvement

Mrs. X was an uptight practicing counselor who dealt with nervousness by becoming quite verbal and asking repetitive closed-ended questions. Her counseling could be described as authoritative information gathering and advice giving. The supervisor and counselor agreed upon the goals of relaxation and improved verbal techniques as areas for improvement in counseling performance. Mrs. X completed a self-instruction program of relaxation and the supervisor helped her transfer this learning into the counseling setting. Verbal techniques were improved by listening to taped examples of open-ended questions, reflections, and other effective counselor responses, and then systematically reinforcing herself each time she used one of the techniques correctly. Approved responses replaced a large percentage of the poor ones, and coupled with relaxation, Mrs. X improved her counseling. Positive feedback for the supervisor and counselees strengthened her new skills even more.

Case 4. Professional Assertion

A guidance director in a large city school system was discouraged over the lack-luster performance of most guidance staffs in the city schools. An assessment of the problem revealed that counselors expended a large portion of their time in clerical and quasi-administrative duties that were not a part of their job description. Investigation led to the discovery that these duties were assigned to or requested of the counselors by principals and assistant principals.

Among the steps which the guidance director took to rectify the problem was the supervision of head counselors toward the goal of becoming "professionally assertive." The head counselors were not providing the leadership necessary to maintain the counselors' role and function. The counselors were inappropriately subservient to the administration.

Group supervision sessions were held to discuss the problem, and the guidance director led training sessions on the specific skills involved in being professionally assertive in response to stressful situations. The circumstances leading to subservience were simulated and head counselors role played and practiced assertive techniques. These simulations helped develop the ability to maintain the counselors' legitimate role and function.

REFERENCES

Akamatsu, T.J. (1980). The use of role-play and simulation techniques in the training of psychotherapy. In A.K. Hess (Ed.), *Psychotherapy supervision: Theory, research and practice.* New York: John Wiley.

Altekruse, M.K., & Brown, D.F. (1969). Counseling behavior change through self analysis. *Counselor Education and Supervision, 8,* 108-112.

Arbuckle, D.S. (1956). Client perception of counselor personality. *Journal of Counseling Psychology, 3,* 93-96.

Austin, B., & Altekruse, M.K. (1972). The effects of group supervisor roles on practicum students' interview behavior. *Counselor Education and Supervision, 12,* 63-68.

Authier, J., & Gustafson, K. (1976). Application of supervised and nonsupervised microcounseling paradigms in the training of registered and licensed practical nurses. *Journal of Consulting and Clinical Psychology, 44*(5), 704-709.

Baker, S.B., Johnson, E., Kopala, M. & Strout, N. (1985). Test interpretation competence: A comparison of microskills and mental practice training. *Counselor Education and Supervision, 25,* 31-44.

Baker, S.B., Scofield, M.E., Munson, W.W., & Clayton, L.T. (1983). Comparative effects of training basic counseling competencies through brief microskills practice versus mental practice. *Counselor Education and Supervision, 23,* 71-83.

Bandura, A. (1969). *Principles of Behavior Modification.* New York: Holt, Rinehart and Winston.

Beck, A.T. (1976). *Cognitive Therapy and the Emotional Disorders.* New York: International Universities Press.

Bellucci, J.E. (1972). Microcounseling and imitation learning: A behavioral approach to counselor education. *Counselor Education and Supervision, 12,* 88-97.

Bergin, A.E., & Garfield, S.L. (Eds.). (1971). *Psychotherapy and Behavior Change.* New York: John Wiley.

Bergin, A.E., & Jasper, L.G. (1969). Correlates of empathy in psychotherapy: A replication. *Journal of Abnormal Psychology, 74,* 447-481.

Bernstein, B.L., Hofmann, B., & Wade, P. (1986). Counselor self-supervision: Beyond traditional approaches to practicum supervision. *Michigan Journal of Counseling and Development, 17,* 13-17.

Bernstein, B.L., & LeComte, C. (1979). Self-Critique technique training in a competency-based practicum. *Counselor Education and Supervision, 19,* 69-76.

Birk, J.M. (1972). Effects of counseling supervision method and preference on empathic understanding. *Journal of Counseling Psychology, 19,* 542-546.

Bishop, J.B. (1971), Another look at counselor, client, and supervisor ratings of counselor effectiveness. *Counselor Education and Supervision, 10,* 319-323.

Blane, S.M. (1968). Immediate effect of supervisory experiences on counselor candidates. *Counselor Education and Supervision, 8,* 39-44.

Bowman, J.T., & Glsen, J.M. (1982). Predicting ratings of counselor trainee empathy with self-report anxiety measures and skill conductance. *Counselor Education and Supervision, 22,* 154-162.

Bowman, J.T., & Reeves, T.G. (1987). Moral development and empathy in counseling. *Counselor Education and Supervision, 26,* 293-299.

Boyd, J.D. (1973). Microcounseling for a counseling-like verbal response set: Differential effects of two micromodels and two methods of counseling supervision. *Journal of Counseling Psychology, 20,* 97-98.

Boyd, J.D., & LaFleur, N.K. (1974). Self management: A basic counseling goal. *Focus on Guidance, 7,* 1-10.

Boyd, J.D. (1978). *Counselor supervision: Approaches, preparation, practices.* Muncie, In.: Accelerated Development.

Brown, D., & Cannady, M. (1969). Counselor, counselee, and supervisor ratings of counselor effectiveness. *Counselor Education and supervision, 8,* 113-118.

Brown, P.B., & Smith, H.D. (1984). All-inclusive conceptualization as a dimension of trainee empathic responding. *Counselor Education and Supervision, 23,* 341-346.

Canada, R.M. (1973). Immediate reinforcement versus delayed reinforcement in teaching a basic interview technique. *Journal of Counseling Psychology, 20,* 395-398.

Carlson, J. (1980). Audiotape and videotape procedures: A study of subject's reactions. *Journal of Counseling Psychology, 27,* 605-610.

Carlson, K.W. (1971). Reinforcement of empathy: An operant paradigm for the training of counselors. Unpublished doctoral dissertation. Northern Illinois University.

Carter, D.K., & Pappas, J.P. (1975). Systematic desensitization and awareness treatment for reducing counselor anxiety. *Journal of Counseling Psychology. 22*(2), 147-151.

Cavior, N., & Marabotto, C.M. (1976). Monitoring verbal behaviors in a dyadic interaction. *Journal of Consulting and Clinical Psychology, 44*(1), 68-76.

Chang-Liang, R., & Denny, D.R. (1976). Applied relaxation as training in self-control. *Journal of Counseling Psychology, 23*(3), 183-189.

Clark, M.D. (1970). The effects of counselor supervisor's verbal reinforcements upon counselor trainees' verbal behavior. Unpublished doctoral dissertation. Arizona State University.

Cogan, D.B. (1977). Survey of counselor competencies. Unpublished manuscript. Arizona State University.

Cormier, L.S., & Cormier, W.H. (1976). Developing and implementing self-instructional modules for counselor training. *Counselor Education and Supervision, 16*(1), 37-45.

Cormier, W.H., Cormier, L.S., Zerega, W.D., & Wagaman, G.L. (1976). Effects of learning modules on the acquisition of counseling strategies. *Journal of Counseling Psychology, 23*(2), 136-141.

Dalton, R.F., & Sundblad, L.M. (1976). Using principles of social learning for communication of empathy. *Journal of Counseling Psychology, 23*(5), 454-457.

Dalton, R.F., Sundblad, L.M., & Hylbert, K.W. (1973). An application of principles of social learning to training in communication of empathy. *Journal of Counseling Psychology, 20,* 378-383.

Danish, S.J. (1971). Film-simulated counselor training. *Counselor Education and Supervision, 11,* 29-35.

Davidson, T., & Emmer, E. (1966). Immediate effect of supportive and non-supportive supervision behavior on counselor candidates focus of concern. *Counselor Education and Supervision, 5,* 27-31.

Delaney, D.J. (1969). Simulation techniques in counselor education: Proposal of a unique approach. *Counselor Education and Supervision, 8,* 183-188.

Delaney, D.J. (1972). A behavioral model for the practicum supervision of counselor candidates. *Counselor Education and Supervision, 17,* 293-299.

Delaney, D.J., & Eisenberg, S. (1972). *The Counseling Process.* Chicago: Rand McNally and Company.

Dimattia, D.J., & Arndt, G.M. (1974). A comparison of microcounseling and reflective listening techniques. *Counselor Education and Supervision, 14,* 61-63.

Dodds, J.B. (1986). Supervision of psychology trainees in field placements. *Professional Psychology, 17,* 296-300.

Dodge, J. (1982). Reducing supervisee anxiety: A cognitive-behavioral approach. *Counselor Education and Supervision, 22,* 55-60.

Dowd, E.T., & Blocher, D.H. (1974). Effects of immediate reinforcement and awareness of response on beginning counselor behavior. *Counselor Education and Supervision, 13,* 190-197.

Eisenberg, S., & Delaney, D.J. (1970). Using video simulation of counseling for training counselors. *Journal of Counseling Psychology, 17,* 15-19.

Ellis, A. (1973). *Humanistic Psychotherapy.* New York: McGraw-Hill.

Ellis, A., & Harper, R.A. (1975). *A New Guide to Rational Living.* No. Hollywood, California: Willshire.

Errek, H., & Randolf, D. (1982). Effects of discussion and role-playing activities in the acquisition of consultant interview skills. *Journal of Counseling Psychology, 29,* 304-308.

Eskedel, G.A. (1975). Symbolic role modeling and cognitive learning in the training of counselors. *Journal of Counseling Psychology, 22*(2), 152-155.

Forsyth, D.R., & Ivey, A.E. (1980). Microtraining: An approach to differential supervision. In A.K. Hess (Ed.), *Psychotherapy Supervision: Theory, Research and Practice.* New York: John Wiley.

Fraleigh, P.W., & Buchheimer, A. (1969). The use of peer groups in practicum supervision. *Counselor Education and Supervision, 8,* 284-288.

Frankel, M. (1971). Effects of videotape modeling and self-confrontation techniques on microcounseling behavior. *Journal of Counseling Psychology, 18,* 465-471.

Franks, C.M. (1969). *Behavior Therapy: Appraisal and Status.* New York: McGraw Hill.

Friesen, D.D., & Dunning, G.B. (1973). Peer evaluation and practicum supervision. *Counselor Education and Supervision, 12,* 229-235.

Froehle, T., Robinson, S., & Kurpius, D. (1983). Enhancing the effects of modeling through role-play practice. *Counselor Education and Supervision, 22,* 197-207.

Fugua, D.R., Johnson, A.W., Anderson, M.W., & Newman, J.L. (1984). Cognitive methods in counselor training. *Counselor Education and Supervision, 24,* 84-95.

Garner, A.M., & Smith, G.M. (1976). An experimental videotape technique for evaluating trainee approaches to clinical judging. *Journal of Consulting and Clinical Psychology, 44*(6), 945-950.

Gladstein, G., & Feldstein, J.C. (1983). Using film to increase counselor empathic experiences. *Counselor Education and Supervision, 23,* 125-132.

Goldfried, M.R., & Merbaum, M. (Eds.), (1973). *Behavior Change Through Self Control.* New York: Holt, Rinehart, and Winston.

Guttman, M.A.J. (1973). Reduction of the defensive behavior of counselor trainees during counseling supervision. *Counselor Education and Supervision, 12,* 294-299.

Guttman, M.A.J., & Haase, R.F. (1972). Generalization of microcounseling skills from training period to actual counseling setting. *Counselor Education and Supervision, 12,* 98-108.

Hackney, H.J. (1971). Development of a pre-practicum counseling skills model. *Counselor Education and Supervision, 11,* 102-109.

Hackney, H., & Cormier, L.S. (1979). *Counseling strategies and objectives.* Englewood Cliffs, N J: Prentice-Hall.

Hackney, H., & Nye, S. (1973). *Counseling strategies and objectives.* Englewood Cliffs, NJ: Prentice-Hall.

Hagan, L., & Boyd, J.D. (1976). Concept-specific and verbally manifest anxiety in the initial interview. Unpublished report, University of Virginia.

Hansen, J.C., Pound, R., & Petro, C. (1976). Review of research on practicum supervision. *Counselor Education and Supervision, 16*(2), 107-116.

Hector, M.A., Elson, S.E., & Yager, G.G. (1977). Teaching counseling skills through self-management procedures. *Counselor Education and Supervision, 17*(1), 12-22.

Herr, E.L. (1969). The perceptions of state supervisors of guidance of appropriateness of counselor function, the function of counselor, and counselor preparation. *Counselor Education and Supervision, 8,* 241-257.

Holahan, W., & Galassi, J. (1986). Toward accountability in supervision: A single-case illustration. *Counselor Education and Supervision, 25,* 166-174.

Hosford, R., & Johnson, M. (1983). A comparison of self-observation, self-modeling, and practice without video feedback for improving counselor interviewing behaviors. *Counselor Education and Supervision, 23,* 62-71.

Hui-Ho, P., Hosford, R., & Johnson, M. (1985). The effects of anxiety on recall in self versus other-mother observation. *Counselor Education and Supervision, 25,* 48-56.

Ivey, A.E. (1971). *Microcounseling.* Springfield, Illinois: Charles C. Thomas.

Ivey, A.E., Normington, C., Miller, C., Morrill, W., & Haase, R. (1968). Microcounseling and attending behavior: An approach to pre-practicum counselor training. *Journal of Counseling Psychology* (Monograph Supplement), *15,* 1-12.

Jakubowski-Spector, P., Dustin, R., & George, R. (1971). Toward developing a behavioral counselor education model. *Counselor Education and Supervision, 10,* 242-250.

Kagan, N., & Schauble, F.G. (1969). Affect simulation in interpersonal process recall. *Journal of Counseling Psychology, 16,* 309-313.

Kahn, W.J. (1976). Self-management: Learning to be our own counselor. *Personnel and Guidance Journal, 55*(4), 176-180.

Kanfer, F. (1970). Self-monitoring: Methodological limitations and clinical applications. *Journal of Consulting and Clinical Psychology, 35,* 148-152.

Kanfer, F.H., & Phillips, J.S. (1970). *Learning Foundations of Behavior Therapy.* New York: John Wiley and Sons.

Keller, J.F., & Protinsky, H. (1984). A self-management model for supervision. *Journal of Marital and Family Therapy, 10,* 281-288.

Kelly, J.D. (1971). Reinforcement in microcounseling. *Journal of Counseling Psychology, 18,* 268-272.

Kimberlin, C.L., & Friesen, D.D. (1980). Sex and conceptual level empathic responses to ambivalent affect. *Counselor Education and Supervision, 19,* 252-259.

Kline, W.B. (1983). Training counselor trainees to talk to themselves: A method of focusing attention. *Counselor Education and Supervision, 22,* 296-303.

Kloba, J.A., & Zimpfer, D.G., (1976). Status and independence as variables in microcounseling training of adolescents. *Journal of Counseling Psychology, 23*(5), 458-463.

Krumboltz, J.D. (1966a). *Revolution in counseling.* Boston: Houghton Mifflin.

Krumboltz, J.D. (1966b). Stating the goals of counseling. *California Personnel and Guidance Association Monograph.*

Krumboltz, J.D. (1967). Changing the behavior of behavior changers. *Counselor Education and Supervision, 6,* 222-229.

Kurpius, D.J., Benjamin, D., & Morran, D.K. (1985). Effects of teaching a cognitive strategy on counselor trainee internal dialogue and clinical hypothesis formulation. *Journal of Counseling Psychology, 32,* 263-271.

Lazarus, A. (1971). *Behavior Therapy and Beyond.* New York: McGraw Hill.

Levine, F.M., & Tilker, H.A. (1974). A behavior modification approach to supervision of psychotherapy. *Psychotherapy: Theory, Research and Practice, 11*(2), 182-188.

Liddle, B.J. (1986). Resistance in supervision: A response to perceived threat. *Counselor Education and Supervision, 26,* 117-128.

Linehan, M.M. (1980). Supervision and behavior therapy, In A.K. Hess (Ed.), *Psychotherapy supervision: Theory, research and practice.* New York: John Wiley.

Mahoney, M.J., & Thoresen, C.E. (1974). *Self control: Power to the person.* Monterey, CA.: Brooks/Cole.

Mann, J.H., & Mann, C.H. (1966). The effect of role-playing experience on role-playing ability. In B.J. Biddle and E.J. Thomas (Eds.), *Role-theory: Concepts and research.* New York: John Wiley.

Martin, D.G., & Gazda, G.M. (1970). A method of self-evaluation for counselor education utilizing the measurement of facilitative conditions. *Counselor Education and Supervision, 9,* 87-92.

Mathewson, R.H., & Rochlin, I. (1956). Analysis of unstructured self-appraisal: A technique in counselor education. *Journal of Counseling Psychology, 3,* 32-36.

Meichenbaum, D. (1975). Self instructional methods. In G.H. Kanfer & A.P. Goldstein (Eds.), *Helping people change.* Elmsford, N.Y.: Pergamon Press.

Meichenbaum, D., & Cameron, R. (1974). The clinical potential of modifying what clients say to themselves. In M.J. Mahoney & C.E. Thoresen, *Self-control: Power to the person.* Monterey, CA.: Brooks/Cole.

Menne, J.M. (1975). A comprehensive set of counselor competencies. *Journal of Counseling Psychology, 22*(6), 547-553.

Miars, R.D., Tracey, T.J., Ray, P.N., Cornfeld, J.L., O'Farrell, M., & Gelso, C.J. (1983). Variation in supervision process across trainee experience levels. *Journal of Counseling Psychology, 30,* 403-412.

Miller, N.L. (1971). The effects of videotape procedures on counselor trainees' responses. Unpublished doctoral dissertation. Arizona State University.

Miller C.D., Morrill, W.H., & Uhlemann, M.R. (1970). Micro-counseling: An experimental study of pre-practicum training in communicating test results. *Counselor Education and Supervision, 9,* 171-177.

Milliken, R.L., & Kirchener, R. (1971). Counselor's understanding of communication as a function of the counselor's perceptual defense. *Journal of Counseling Psychology, 18,* 14-18.

Mischel, W., & Grusec, J. (1966). Determinants of the rehearsal and transmission of neutral and aversive behaviors. *Journal of Personality and Social Psychology, 3,* 197-205.

Mooney, T.F., & Carlson, W.A. (1976). Counselor trainee emotional response to initial counseling-interview stress. *Journal of Counseling Psychology, 23*(b), 557-559.

Panther, E.E. (1971). Simulated consulting experiences in counselor preparation. *Counselor Education and Supervision, 11,* 17-23.

Payne, P.A., & Gralinski, D.M. (1968). Effects of supervisor style and empathy upon counselor learning. *Journal of Counseling Psychology, 15,* 517-521.

Payne, P.A., Weiss, S.D., & Iappa, R.A. (1972). Didactic, experiential, and modeling factors in the learning of empathy. *Journal of Counseling Psychology, 19,* 425-429.

Payne, P.A., Winter, D.E., & Bell, G.E. (1972). Effects of supervisor style on the learning of empathy in supervision analogue. *Counselor Education and Supervision, 11,* 262-269.

Perry, M.A. (1975). Modeling and instructions in training for counselor empathy. *Journal of Counseling Psychology, 22*(3), 173-179.

Peters, G., Cormier, L., & Cormier, W. (1978). Effects of modeling, rehearsal, feedback and remediation on acquisition of a counseling strategy. *Journal of Counseling Psychology, 25,* 231-237.

Rank, R.C., Thoresen, C.E., & Smith, R.M. (1972). Encouraging counselor trainee affective group behavior by social modeling. *Counselor Education and Supervision, 11*(4), 270-278.

Richardson, B.K., & Bradley, L.J. (1984). Micro-supervision: A skill development model for training clinical supervisors. *The Clinical Supervisor, 2,* 43-54.

Robinson, S., Froehle, T., & Kurpius, D. (1979a). Effects of model and media of modal presentation on skill development of counselor trainees. *Journal of Counseling Psychology, 26,* 74-80.

Robinson, S.E., Froehle, T.C., & Kurpius, D.J. (1979b). Self-instructional modules: Comparison of modeling and feedback media. *Counselor Education and Supervision, 18,* 251-260.

Ronnestad, M.H. (1973). Effects of modeling, feedback and experiential supervision on beginning counseling students: Communication of empathic understanding. Unpublished doctoral dissertation. University of Missouri.

Russell, R.K., Miller, D.E., & June, L.N. (1974). Group cue-controlled relaxation in the treatment of test anxiety. *Behavior Therapy, 5,* 572-573.

Russell, R.K., Miller, D.E., & June, L.N. (1975). A comparison between group systematic desensitization and cue-controlled relaxation in the treatment of test anxiety. *Behavior Therapy, 6,* 172-177.

Russell, R.K., & Sipich, J.F. (1973). Cue-controlled relaxation in the treatment of test anxiety. *Journal of Behavior Therapy and Experimental Psychiatry, 4,* 47-49.

Russell, R.K., & Wise, F. (1976). Treatment of speech anxiety by cue-controlled relaxation and desensitization with professional and paraprofessional counselors. *Journal of Counseling Psychology, 23*(6), 583-586.

Saltmarsh, R.E., & Hubele, G.E. (1974). Basic interaction behaviors: A micro-counseling approach for introductory courses. *Counselor Education and Supervision, 13,* 246-249.

Sanchez-Craig, B.M. (1976). Cognitive and behavioral coping strategies in the reappraisal of stressful social situations, *Journal of Counseling Psychology*, 23(1), 7-12.

Schwebel, M. (1953). Role playing in counselor training. *Personnel and Guidance Journal*, 32, 196-201.

Scott, A.J., Cormier, W.J., & Cormier, L.A. (1980). Effects of covert modeling and written material on the acquisition of a counseling strategy. *Counselor Education and Supervision*, 19, 259-269.

Shaver, A.H. (1985). Effects of observation and evaluation on anxiety in beginning counselors: A social facilitation analysis. *Journal of Counseling and Development*, 63, 279-285.

Silverman, M.S., & Quinn, P.F. (1974). Co-counseling supervision in practicum. *Counselor Education and Supervision*, 13, 256-260.

Smith, H.D. (1984). Moment to moment counseling process feedback using a dual channel audiotape recording. *Counselor Education and Supervision*, 23, 246-249.

Spielgler, M.D., Cooley, E.J., Marshall, G.J., Prince, H.T., & Puckett, S.P. (1976). *Journal of Counseling Psychology*, 23(1), 83-86.

Spivack, J.D., (1973). Critical incidents in counseling: Simulated video experiences for training counselors. *Counselor Education and Supervision*, 12, 263-270.

Sodetz, A.R. (1972). The effect of videotape microtraining on counselor behavior. Unpublished doctoral dissertation. University of Missouri.

Stefflre, B., King, P., & Leafgren, F. (1962). Characteristics of counselors judged effective by their peers. *Journal of Counseling Psychology*, 9, 335-340.

Stewart, R.M., & Jessell, J.C. (1986). Written versus videotaped precounseling training of clients for counseling. *Counselor Education and Supervision*, 25, 197-210.

Stone, G.L. (1981). Effects of different strategies within a microtraining situation. *Counselor Education and Supervision*, 20, 301-312.

Stone, G.L., & Stebbins, L.W. (1975). Effect of differential pretraining on client self-disclosure. *Journal of Counseling Psychology*, 22(1), 17-20.

Stone, G.L., & Vance, A. (1976). Instructions, modeling, and rehearsal: Implications for training. *Journal of Counseling Psychology*, 23(3), 272-279.

Strosahl, K., & Jacobson, N.S. (1986). Training and supervision of behavior therapists. *The Clinical Supervisor, 4,* 183-206.

Tennyson, W.W., & Strom, S.M. (1986). Beyond professional standards: Developing responsibleness. *Journal of Counseling and Development, 64,* 298-302.

Thoresen, C.E. (Ed.) (1973). *Behavior modification in education.* The Seventy-second Yearbook of the National Society for the Study of Education. Chicago: University of Chicago Press.

Thoresen, C.E., & Mahoney, M.J. (1974). *Behavioral self control.* New York: Holt, Rinehart and Winston.

Toukmanian, S.G., & Rennie, D.L. (1975). Microcounseling versus human relations training: Relative effectiveness with undergraduate trainees. *Journal of Counseling Psychology 22*(4), 345-352.

Uhlemann, M.R., Lea, G.W., & Stone, G.L. (1976). Effect of instructions and modeling on trainees low in interpersonal-communication skills. *Journal of Counseling Psychology, 23*(6), 509-513.

Wagner, C.A., & Smith, J.P. (1979). Peer supervision: Toward more effective training. *Counselor Education and Supervision, 18,* 288-294.

Wallace, W.G., Horan, J.J., Baker, S.B., & Hudson, G.R. (1975). Incremental effects of modeling and performance feedback in teaching decision-making counseling. *Journal of Counseling Psychology, 22*(6), 570-572.

Walton, J.M. (1974). Peer perceptions of counselor effectiveness: A multiple regression approach. *Counselor Education and Supervision, 13,* 250-255.

Walz, G.R., & Johnston, J.A. (1963). Counselors look at themselves on video tape. *Journal of Counseling Psychology, 10,* 232-236.

Ward, L.G. (1985). Strategic self-preservation in supervision. *Journal of Counseling Psychology, 32,* 111-118.

Weinrach, S.G. (1976). A model for the systematic generalization of counseling skills. *Counselor Education and Supervision, 15*(4), 311-314.

Young, D.W. (1985). Reliability of videotape-assisted recall in counseling process research. *Counselor Education and Supervision, 24,* 360-365.

Zytowski, D.G., & Betz, E.L. (1972). Measurement in counseling: A review. *The Counseling Psychologist, 3,* 72-86.

CHAPTER 5

INTEGRATIVE MODELS OF SUPERVISION

An integrative approach to counselor supervision may be said to exist when methodology from one or more supervisory approaches is integrated to form a new approach. Given this liberal definition, many different kinds of integrative approaches can be formed by creating various combinations of techniques. Although this "technique-mixing" process is a rather unscientific endeavor, it probably represents the actual practice of supervision more accurately than any other supervisory approach. Helpers are renowned for their nurturant needs and their quest for new and varied techniques to improve their helping effectiveness. Supervisors are no exception.

Most supervisors subscribe to Lazarus' (1971) principle of *technical eclecticism.* Supervisors attempt to arm themselves with a host of techniques drawn from various approaches to counseling and supervision, and then they construct integrative methodological approaches which are comfortable for them and effective for supervisees. The supervisors' rationale for this approach is that an integrative set of techniques prepares one to be more effective across the infinite variety of supervisor situations than does a single approach with a narrow range of techniques. The two approaches presented in this Chapter, the Carkhuff model and psychobehavioral supervision, are based upon the integrative rationale. Each attempts to integrate methodology from the psychotherapeutic and behavioral approaches to counselor supervision.

THE CARKHUFF
SUPERVISORY-TRAINING MODEL

Perhaps the best known integrative approach to the training and supervision of counselors is that developed by Robert Carkhuff and associates (Carkhuff, 1969a, b; Carkhuff & Truax, 1965; Truax, Carkhuff, & Douds, 1964). Carkhuff's model is based on his theory of the helping process and the instrumental dimensions therein (Berenson & Carkhuff, 1967; Carkhuff & Berenson, 1967; Carkhuff, 1969a). Very briefly, Carkhuff's helping process may be described as having two principal phases—a downward or inward phase of exploring one's self and concerns with consequent increased awareness, and an upward or outward phase of emergent directionality. During the downward phase the counselor offers a psychologically facilitative relationship that enables the client to explore self and problems and activate personal resources. The important counselor-offered facilitative conditions at this phase of the helping process are empathic understanding, positive regard, personally relevant concreteness, genuineness, and counselor self-disclosure. As the helpee delves deeper in self exploration and receives higher levels of facilitative conditions, the counselor promotes a transition to phase two by offering the action-oriented helping conditions of confrontation and immediacy. These action-oriented conditions encourage helpee directionality and the resolution of concerns through constructive action.

Focus and Goals

The focus of Carkhuff's integrative approach to supervisory training is the facilitative interpersonal dimensions of empathy and respect, the facilitative and action-oriented dimensions of concreteness, genuineness, and self-disclosure, and the action-oriented dimensions of immediacy and confrontation. Goals of the Carkhuff approach are:

1. to enable counselors to offer effective levels of the facilitative and action-oriented conditions, and

2. to equip counselors with the skills of assisting helpees to construct and implement courses of action leading to constructive resolution of difficulties.

Methodology

Two of the most important aspects of Carkhuff's (1969a) supervisory methodology are the supervisor's level of therapeutic functioning and the integration of three learning modalities:

> Perhaps the most critical variable in effective counselor training is the level at which the [supervisor] is functioning on those dimensions related to constructive helper change (p. 152). . .Hopefully, the [supervisor] is not only functioning at high levels on these dimensions but is also attempting to impart learnings concerning these dimensions in a systematic manner, for only then will he integrate the critical sources of learning—the didactic, the experiential, and the modeling. (p. 153)

Throughout the Carkhuff model the supervisor offers psychologically facilitative conditions to supervisees (usually a group of eight to ten) while concurrently leading them through a three-stage program of integrative learning activities: *discrimination training, communication training,* and *training in developing effective courses of action.*

Discrimination Training. In discrimination training the counselor first learns to make gross discriminations between counseling which offers high levels and that offering low levels of the facilitative and action-oriented dimensions. Written exercises (choosing the best response) and listening to recorded counseling are typical gross discrimination activities. After gross discrimination has been mastered, the counselor receives training in individual discriminations. Concentrating on one dimension at a time and with supervisory assistance, the counselor learns to articulate dimensions, clarify their functions and effects, and assess their levels on a five-point rating scale through shaping exercises.

Communication Training. High levels of discrimination are a necessary but insufficient condition for high levels of communication, so communication training begins when discrimination is mastered. Focusing on each dimension singly, the counselor is supervised while responding to tape material and role playing. The goal is to reach a minimally helpful level of communication (level 3) rather than try initially for higher levels. Upon the attainment of at least minimally helpful communication levels the counselor is allowed to engage in single interviews with helpees. Although the counselor has not received training in the development of effective courses of action, the single interviews require only a facilitative interaction and do not constitute long term counseling or psychotherapy. The interviews are helpful to helpees, and extremely beneficial to counselors who can raise their levels of facilitative communication through supervised experience.

Training in Developing Effective Courses of Action. As the counselor gains single interview experience, training proceeds into the development of effective courses of action. The counselor is introduced to the skills of developing effective courses of action with the helpee, as well as receiving instruction and practice in "preferred modes of treatment" such as systematic desensitization. When these skills have been developed and demonstrated, the counselor is offered supervised experience in full-term counseling and/or psychotherapy with individuals and groups.

Integrated Learning Modes. The three-stage program of supervisory training activities continually integrates the experiential, didactic, and modeling learning modes. Only a brief overview of the Carkhuff Model has been presented, and Volume I of *Helping and Human Relations* (Carkhuff, 1969a) is the authorative source for a full description. In Volume I and Volume II of the same title (Carkhuff, 1969a) are presented a voluminous amount of empirical support for the Model and interesting case examples from counseling and supervision.

Forward Movement

At the heart of Carkhuff's theory of helpgiving and supervisory training are the well-known "facilitative conditions," three of which (empathy, respect, genuineness) Carkhuff has reassessed and further validated following their original presentation by Carl Rogers (1957). Since these conditions have been given a central position in counselor preparation, their role in supervision training will be reviewed.

A review of practicum research conducted by Hansen, Pound, Petro (1976) revealed that seventeen of twenty-five studies surveyed on supervision process and training examined some aspect of facilitative communication. Based on this research the investigators concluded that several supervision approaches are effective in teaching counselors to communicate facilitatively, and that supervision research also should investigate approaches for training other counselor skills. A second review of research on practicum supervision was conducted by Hansen, Robins, and Grimes (1982). This research was conducted between 1975 and 1980. The investigators did not find support for matching counselors and supervisors according to similar traits. Some support was found for modeling didactic, experimental methods, and peer supervision. Further the investigators found fewer research studies were published on supervision and the percentage of experimental designs decreased.

To complement the conclusions of Hanson, et al., (1982) it is recommended that supervisors give careful examination to the concept of empathy before assuming competence with the concept. As research on empathy and other facilitative conditions continues, the supervisor must translate this information into practice. Four such translations are the following:

1. Some research has contrasted that of Carkhuff (1969b) and has questioned the discriminate validity of facilitative conditions and like dimensions (Avery, D'Augelli, & Danish, 1976; Boyd & Pate, 1975; D'Augelli, Deyss, Gurney, Hershenberg & Sborofsky, 1974; Muehlberg, Drasgrow, & Pierce, 1969). Supervisors may want to treat these dimensions as overlapping to form a general facilitation factor. Training in general facilitative responding might be more efficient than giving separate attention and time to each dimension.

2. The influences that supervisors attribute to empathy should not overlook the possibility of accompanying variables (Bowman & Reeves, 1987; Brown & Smith,

1984; Gladstein & Feldstein, 1983; Kimberlin & Friesen, 1980; Perry, 1975; Peters, Cormier & Cormier, 1978; Pierce & Schauble, 1970; Pierce & Schauble, 1971). Dowling and Frantz (1975) have shown that the empathic counselor or supervisor is likely to be exerting a potent modeling influence, while Blane (1968), Brady, Rowe and Smouse (1976), Carlson (1971), Hosford and Barmann (1983), Kelly (1971) and Vitalo (1970) have shown that operant reinforcement also can exist within facilitative communication.

Responsibility in communicating facilitatively goes beyond the mere offering of a "minimally constructive level;" a certain level is not unquestionably beneficial—the effect depends upon how the communication influences the receiver. Modeling and reinforcement increase the possible effects of facilitative conditions.

For example, empathic responses to self deprecating helpee statements at a higher frequency than positive self reference may conceivably reinforce negative ideation. The counselor who models certain affective reactions to helpee problems, even though responding at a level 3 on facilitative conditions, may influence the helpee to imitate this reaction. In cases such as these an adept clinician should look beyond rated levels and deeper into the communication process.

3. Empathy rating is a supervisory activity where research has provided valuable information for practice. Melnick (1975) found that personal-social problems elicit more empathy from counselors than do vocational-educational concerns. Counseling in response to these two kinds of helpee problems may not be comparable on the empathy dimension.

Blass and Heck (1975) and Avery, D'Augelli, and Danish (1976) produced findings which suggest that a considerable amount of information about the helpee's phenomenological perspective is needed for accurate and valid empathy ratings. Supervisors probably need more than a "spot-check" of counselor performance in order to rate empathy competently. Further, Cicchetti and Ryan (1976) have warned that a rater can become attuned to a particular counselor's style and lose the ability to discriminate among the varying facilitation levels of that counselor's responses.

4. A training guideline for facilitative communication, drawn from the behavioral approach to supervision, has been supported by Gormally (1975) and Authier and Gustafson (1976). From their studies these researchers point out that effective supervision or training treatments teach counselors to discriminate among desirable and undesirable responses, and then to increase the former and decrease the latter. Three kinds of learning probably occur: learning to discriminate, learning to make new kinds of desirable responses and increasing the frequency of existing desirable responses, and unlearning undesirable response habits or decreasing the frequency of undesirable responses. Communication training may thus involve a restructuring of socially learned response patterns.

Forward movement in the supervisory treatment of core facilitative conditions demands that we improve our expertise. But supervision expertise also must be extended to other counselor skills lest counselor supervision becomes a narrow methodology.

A PSYCHOBEHAVIORAL APPROACH
TO COUNSELING SUPERVISION

Another integrative approach to counselor supervision was presented at the 1974 convention of the American Personnel and Guidance Association (Boyd, Nutter, & Overcash, 1974). Called a psychobehavioral approach, it is based upon the conclusions and practical outcomes of several years of integrative supervision experience in counseling practicum courses. Portions of a paper that accompanied the program presentation are reproduced here in a brief overview of psychobehavioral supervision.

Introduction

The psychobehavioral approach to counseling and psychotherapy (Woody, 1971) represents a conceptual rationale and technical frame of reference for the integration of methodology from the two broad dichotomies (London, 1964) of *insight counseling* and action-oriented or *behavioral counseling*. Insightists typically focus on helping their clients attain self-understanding or insight into their motives for behavior, while behavioral counselors focus directly on the client's maladaptive behavior and attempt to alter it toward more adaptive modes via the judicious use of psychological learning theory. The psychobehavioral stance posits that these two approaches have the potential for a *reciprocally beneficial* integration, and that the psychobehavioral counselor should practice a "technical eclecticism."

Counseling supervision seems to be another field where the psychobehavioral approach can be implemented efficaciously. The goals and methodology of supervision and counseling are quite similar, with the two major supervision approaches (i.e., psychotherapeutic/experiential and behavioral/didatic) being a corollary to the action-insight dichotomy of counseling. A psychobehavioral approach to supervision would thus integratively employ the methodology of both the psychotherapeutic and behavioral approaches.

Propositions

I. *The goals of psychotherapeutic and behavioral supervision are compatible and may be reciprocally beneficial.*

Psychotherapeutic supervision is directed at self awareness of inter- and intrapersonal dynamics as these are experienced in the counselor's relationships with the client and supervisor. The rationale for this awareness goal is that it will facilitate the counselor's personal adjustment, a prerequisite for competent counseling performance. Behavioral supervision is directed at the skills (behaviors) of counseling; it utilizes psychological learning theory to help the counselor learn desirable counseling skills and to extinguish or reduce counselor behavior which interferes with competent counseling.

Awareness of dynamics is a goal that is compatible with behavior change. Many theoreticians assert that dynamic awareness is a desirable process goal that facilitates behavior change. Moreover, when dynamics are operationally defined as covert sensory reactions to stimuli, and when they are identified as covert antecedents for overt counseling behavior, diagnosis in psychotherapeutic supervision merges with that in the behavioral approach.

II. *The methodology of psychotherapeutic and behavioral supervision can be integrated.*

Supervision activities of the psychotherapeutic approach consist of examining and discussing the dynamics which the counselor experiences in counseling and supervision. Emphasis is on discovering dynamics, finding their antecedents, and identifying their consequences (usually counselor behavior toward the client). The personalistic meanings which the counselor attributes to the stimuli encountered in counseling are explored.

The same kind of activity is involved in the behavioral assessment that should take place as the behavioral supervisor explores the counselor's undesirable counseling behavior. "Assessing the acquired meaning of stimuli is the core of social behavior assessment. . ." (Mischel, 1968, p. 190). Some activities in psychotherapeutic and behavioral supervision seem quite similar, but the intended effects of these activities are different. In the former, insight is the goal, and in the latter the gathering of data necessary for constructing behavioral change strategies is the goal. With only slight modification of technique, a supervision session could both impart insight and gather behavioral data. Following the exploration of covert dynamics a behavior change strategy could be employed.

III. *Psychobehavioral supervision is personalistic.*

An important characteristic of the psychobehavioral approach is its personalistic nature. Just as flexibility and versatility are essential ingredients for an effective psychotherapist (Lazarus, 1971), these also are necessary attributes for the psychobehavioral supervisor. The supervisor must practice a technical eclecticism, employing an integrative methodology, as well as choosing and implementing singular techniques from the psychotherapeutic and behavioral approaches at certain times. The characteristics of the counselor are a factor which should dictate methodology. The counselor should be offered a form of supervision which is uniquely tailored to the counselor's characteristics.

For example, supervision for an emotionally independent counselor would be different from that for a counselor with strong nurturance and the tendency to identify with client problems. The highly dogmatic counselor may require a different approach than the counselor who is open to experience. Counselors who avoid affect should have supervision to assist them with their avoidance while the affect voyeur must be assisted with the opposite problem.

IV. *During the psychobehavioral supervision process the counselor's learning needs change, thus dictating alterations in supervision methodology.*

Those supervision techniques and strategies that are appropriate in helping beginners face their first few counseling sessions may not be appropriate during the final stage of a semester- or year-long supervision process. Psychobehavioral supervision should be sensitive to the developmental changes of the counselor, and indeed should focus on such developmental tasks and stages as process goals (Bartlett, 1983; Bernard, 1979; Blocher, 1983; Brammer & Wassmer, 1977; Stoltenberg, 1981).

V. *Psychobehavioral supervision should facilitate and utilize the counselor's self-development ability.*

Two key factors in counseling supervision are instrumental, perhaps more than any other factors, in the success or failure of supervision. The supervisor's performance is one factor, and the manner in which the counselor reacts to supervision is the other. The supervisor is totally responsible for his or her performance, and is partially responsible for the counselor's reaction. This partial responsibility refers to the supervisor's elicitation and reinforcement of counselor self-development.

Posited here is that supervision should maximally facilitate and utilize the responsible self-development (Arnold, 1962; Goodyear & Bradley, 1983; Hart, 1982; Mueller & Kell, 1972; Patterson, 1983).

Methodology

The practice of psychobehavioral supervision, as described by Boyd, Nutter and Overcash (1974) has three identifiable stages. In each stage there is an effort to integrate the methodology of the psychotherapeutic and behavioral approaches to supervision in accordance with the changing needs of the supervisee. The techniques referred to the psychobehavioral supervision process (see Figure 5.1) are explained in Chapters 4 and 5 of this text.

Initial Stage. The initial stage of psychobehavioral supervision occurs at a time when counselors are preparing for and conducting their first few interviews. During the initial stage counselors are anxious and unsure of themselves. Advantageous methods from the psychotherapeutic approach are a self-development interview with the supervisor for an exploration of anxieties and expectations, interpersonal process recall focused on interpersonal dynamics, and experiential supervision focusing on intrapersonal dynamics. From the behavioral approach come self-appraisal techniques, global discrimination, much operant reinforcement from the supervisor, and the extra-supervisional use of modeling and structured exercises (micro-counseling) for the improvement of skills. The purpose of this initial stage is to reduce anxiety, establish a cooperative working relationship with the supervisee, and begin self-directed skill improvement.

Intermediate Stage. This stage encompasses the learning that a neophyte counselor gains during supervised practice (practicum course or in the field). Awareness of interpersonal dynamics has been acquired and initial anxieties have been overcome. The counselor may already have made skill improvements during the initial stage and may feel secure enough so that a more confrontive supervision treatment is possible. Techniques from the psychotherapeutic approach appropriate at this stage are interpersonal process recall focusing on

PSYCHOTHERAPEUTIC METHODOLOGY	BEHAVIORAL METHODOLOGY
Initial Stage	
Self-development interview before counseling practice begins: focus on relationship between supervisee's personality and the counselor's role, anxieties, expectancies, and so forth	Self appraisal of competencies before practice begins.
	Self appraisal of skill-behaviors in first few counseling sessions
Interpersonal Process Recall—focus on interpersonal dynamics	Global discrimination: showing the counselor effective vs. inappropriate skill behaviors
Within a counseling-like interaction assist the counselor to explore those intrapersonal dynamics of his/her first attempts at counseling	Extensive use of operant reinforcement, support, and encouragement
	Refer supervisee to modeling tapes, structured exercises, and so forth, for self improvement of skills
Intermediate Stage	
Interpersonal Process Recall—focus on interpersonal and intrapersonal dynamics	Supervisor helps the counselor become more discriminative in self appraisal
Within unstructured supervision sessions: examination of the dynamic patterns in counseling	Identification of skill deficiencies, set goals, construct strategies, begin a self-management plan, reinforce self-directedness
Therapeutic feedback from the supervisor regarding the dynamics in supervision	Active training within supervision sessions via role playing, modeling, shaping exercises, and so forth
Referral to counseling if appropriate	
Terminal Stage	
Assistance in using your experiencing as a therapeutic tool	Refinement of skills
Development of counselor's own style, less dependent on following guidelines	Emphasis on professional judgment: selecting and employing strategies
	Successful completion of self management projects

Figure 5.1. Psychobehavioral supervision process.

intrapersonal and interpersonal dynamics, the examination of dynamic patterns in counseling, therapeutic feedback from the supervisor regarding the dynamics of the supervisory sessions, and referral to counseling if the supervisee needs therapeutic assistance with problematic intrapersonal dynamics. Behavioral methodology includes a more discriminative evaluation of the counselor's performance, the identification of skill areas that need improvement, the initiation of self-managed behavioral strategies, and active training within supervision sessions via role playing, modeling, shaping, and so forth.

Terminal Stage. This psychobehavioral stage is reached when the counselor is functioning at a capable level and supervisory-training activities are not needed. The supervisor can be a consultant without ever leaving that stance for active training. The counselor is assisted in the psychotherapeutic technique of using experiencing as a therapeutic tool. The counselor's most comfortable style of counseling emerges and a perspective on future development is gained. Behaviorally, the supervisor assists the counselor in refining skill-behaviors, making professional judgments concerning diagnosis and strategies, and in completing self-managed behavioral adjustments.

Summary

The psychobehavioral approach to counselor supervision is more of a conceptual rationale and technical frame of reference than a verified approach. The propositions and guidelines of the approach have arisen from practitioners' inquiry and have not been researched formally. If research were to be directed at the psychobehavioral notion, it would target specific supervision situations rather than the entire approach. This is the crux of the psychobehavioral notion—that supervision must discover what methodology is most effective in what situations, and that the practitioner must practice a technical eclecticism in order to match the best technique with situations encountered (Cebik, 1985; Swensen, 1980). Swenson (1980) provided guidelines for helping the counselor select the most effective technique to meet the needs of the client.

PRACTICAL APPLICATION:
ILLUSTRATIVE CASES

Two case examples for integrative supervision are presented, the first applies an integrative approach to the supervision of group counseling. Case 1 is presented not only to demonstrate an integrative approach but also to illustrate that supervision methods can be adapted and applied to both administrative and clinical supervision and whatever skill-activity the counselor is attempting to practice, in this instance group counseling. The second case example is a lengthy session of counseling supervision which had a dramatically beneficial influence on the supervisee. The case demonstrates a variety of supervisory techniques employed within a rather intensive supervisory interaction.

Case 1*: An Integrative Approach To
The Supervision Of Group Counseling

Sally is a counselor in a high school of three thousand students located on the outskirts of a city of a quarter million people. She was employed as an English teacher when the school first opened and eight years later became a counselor, a position she has held for the past six years. Sally is in her mid-thirties and lives by herself in what she describes as a well-ordered life. She further describes herself as a happy person and one who thoroughly enjoys working with adolescents.

Sally is a dedicated professional counselor, active in the state guidance organization and a perpetual student, always taking courses and attending workshops to upgrade her counseling skills. She is recognized by her colleagues as an aggressive and innovative counselor.

Sally does a lot of group counseling with a variety of themes and goals like career decision making, living with parents, weight watchers, and self awareness. Sally describes her success with groups as good but lacking.

---

*This case was submitted by Dr. Richard Lear, Charlottesville, Virginia.

I do best when giving out information and am showing people how to run things, but I've never been able to get a group to, you know, really get together. Everything seems to go well when I talk and suggest different activities, but when I stop the group seems to stop.

By direct observation and listening to audio tape recordings of various groups the supervisor determined that Sally was attempting to facilitate groups predominently with a potpourri of techniques, exercises, and games without really having an understanding of timing and levels of group functioning. The resulting effect of Sally's leadership was to create an atmosphere of superficial acceptance and trust, one which lacked genuine cohesiveness, sharing and risk taking. Meaningful growth within the group membership was very low.

Further exploration with Sally revealed that, in actuality, Sally was using "technique" in an effort to form more humanized relationships with the members of the group and created an atmosphere of "doing to" rather than "exploring, experiencing, and sharing excitement, joy and a sense of caring."

Sally and her supervisor mutually determined that Sally needed to learn how to share the feelings and perceptions within herself and to understand that when these feelings are communicated, we fulfill ourselves and in turn give the members of a group the opportunity to fulfill themselves. Group supervision involved Sally's participation as a **member** of an unstructured group experience while concurrently cofacilitating a group with an experienced supervisor. Tape (video and audio) critique sessions were held immediately following the group sessions and in these the supervisor encouraged Sally through interpersonal process recall questions to explore her own feelings at various points of the group session. Emphasis also was placed on how she could better share her own feelings and perceptions with the members of the group.

As Sally developed more spontaneity within the group, her "experience" as a group member became rewarding and exciting. She became a group member in the affective sense, and progressed through the stages and crises which characterize group involvement. Following Sally's group membership experience she co-led a group with her supervisor who helped her develop the leadership skills necessary to facilitate the kind of group process she had experienced.

The results of supervision were gratifying. Sally learned to allow more time for the group to develop a working relationship by staying with the members at their various developmental stages and sharing her own feelings and perceptions as these were experienced. When Sally was adept in eliciting more self-exploratory behavior from group members, she was then supervised in the use of intervention strategies and techniques which helped the group members to do more in-depth exploration, try new behaviors, and develop a positive self perception.

Case 2: A Psychobehavioral Supervision Session

The following five excerpts were transcribed from an audio-recording of the fourth supervision session with a counseling-practicum student who was enrolled in a master's degree program in counseling. Collectively the five excerpts illustrate the psychotherapeutic approach to counselor supervision as the supervisor utilizes techniques from interpersonal process recall and experiential supervision, shifts to rational-emotive techniques for dealing with some of the counselor's ideational dynamics, and then closes the session with a behaviorally oriented role-playing exercise which combines modeling, skill practice, and social reward. The purpose of this integrative set of techniques is to help the counselor become aware of those dynamics which inhibited counseling progress, learn to control these dynamics, and replace inappropriate interview behavior with appropriate counseling skills.

At the time of this supervision session the counseling practicum was in mid-semester and the counselor (Bob) had conducted several interviews with other clients. In previous interviews Bob had demonstrated a congenial social manner, but this was accompanied by dominating verbal behavior, anxiety over counseling performance, and a lack of empathic communication. Within interviews Bob was so busy worrying about the "right thing to say" that he failed to listen attentively to the client.

Bob had a tendency to emotionally identify with clients, to experience sympathetic feelings for them, and to become frustrated when a solution to their concerns could not be found; all of these were causing him difficulty. Bob's frustration often changed to depression as he would blame himself for not being competent enough to solve client concerns.

In the interview which serves as the central topic for this supervision session, Bob encountered a client (Gail) whose sister had been killed five months earlier in an automobile accident. Coincidentally, Bob had also suffered the death of a loved one, his mother, six months before this interview. As Gail expressed grief over her sister's death, this stimulus evoked overwhelming feelings of grief within Bob. These feelings of grief, in addition to the previously mentioned dynamics of sympathy, frustration and depression, rendered Bob somewhat helpless in terms of proactive counseling performance.

First Excerpt

Supervisor (S)   Counselor (C)

S: *I'd like to do a certain kind of supervision with you today. . .and. . .the intent of the approach is to help you recall as much of the session as you can. The purpose of recalling is to help you examine some of your reactions, for example, as you mentioned to me earlier today, the reaction of identifying with the client.*

C: (laughing) *That's really unhealthy, isn't it?*

S: *No, I'm not saying that, in fact, I hope we can examine your thoughts and feelings without judging.*

C: *O.K. What do you want to do?*

S: *Well, let's just discuss some things in general, and then look at portions of the videotape.*

C: *O.K.*

S: *How do you feel you got along with Gail (the client)?*

C: *I thought it was really easy for her to talk. . .just because I've gone through some of that, I thought I said some things that were. . .said things for her, which she was experiencing. Like the dreams.*

S: *And it was easy to bring up stuff like that because of what you've gone through?*

C: *Yea, we've shared the same things, at least I thought we had and that she was feeling those things.*

S: *Un, huh* (nodding)

C: *The only thing I guess I really didn't like about it was . . . when I was thinking in those sessions . . . I felt that I had added too much of my own personal experience and therefore taken away some opportunities that she might have had to keep on talking.*

S: *Un, huh. . .felt like you got into talking about **your** experience.*

C: *Yes . . . more than I wanted to . . . not that mine was different, it's just that I felt like she would have talked more.*

Interpretation of the First Excerpt

The first excerpt demonstrates that the counselor had a superficial awareness of a troublesome dynamic pattern before supervision began. The counselor knew he had "identified" with the client, and gives a hint of self condemnation ("That's really unhealthy, isn't it?"). Given this state of awareness, the supervisor merely facilitated it with interpersonal process-recall questions, reflective responses, and directed supervision toward the goal of helping the counselor to more fully understand the counselor-client dynamic pattern.

Second Excerpt

S: *Let's take a look at this tape, and by the way, I'll handle the on-off button, but please signal me any* *time you feel something significant is happening between you and the client. Either something that was going on with her. . .or. . .a feeling, thought, or experience which you had that you felt was significant. . .O.K.?*

C: *O.K.*

A videotape excerpt was played in which the counselor began the counseling session by giving a five-minute monologue of personal information about himself.

S: *Did she ask you about. . .*

C: (Interrupting) *No, I did that purposely because Frank* (another supervisor) *observed last week's interview and said that I should be more self disclosing, so that's why I did it. . .I was uncomfortable doing it that way . . . except that I thought . . . well, here it is, five minutes of me. But I really withdrew from that other client.*

S: *How do you think this beginning affected the client?*

C: *I don't know. . .what her reaction was.*

S: *Let's see it.*

Interpretation of Second Excerpt

Video playback revealed to the counselor and supervisor that the personal monologue had not damaged the interview, but to speculate exactly how the client interpreted it was difficult. From the monologue incident both the counselor and the supervisor understood the fact that the counselor had been affected dramatically by the other supervisor's advice of the previous week, and had held a very definite objective (to disclose) in his mind that influenced his counseling behavior. This interpretation was made later in the session.

S: *You look as though you had this objective to disclose in your head and wanted so much to do it. . .because it was a way to improve your counseling. . .that you just blurted it out in the very beginning.*

C: *Yea, I guess so.* (downcast facial expression)

S: *No harm done! In fact, maybe this behavior is a good way to learn something about yourself. . .that when your needs are strong, in this case to improve performance by disclosing, they can propel you into acting in certain ways.*

Third Excerpt

The third excerpt occurred shortly after the second one, and the supervisor's goal continued to be dynamic understanding. However, the focal dynamics of this portion of the session became the counselor's perfectionistic demands, his performance mistakes, and a subsequent condemnation of himself. After viewing a videotaped segment of the interview in which the counselor had ignored the client's feelings and had launched into a treatise on his own grief reactions to parental loss, the tape was stopped at the insistence of the counselor, and the following dialogue ensued.

C: *That's. . .that's really bad. That's just really bad . . . That's just really bad!* (Voice escalates in loudness) (Laugh) *Turn it back on, oh, let's hope it gets better.*

S: *What are you reacting to?*

C: *I'm talking too much! That has nothing to do with. . .I don't want to do that!*

S: *Well, how did you get into it? What ticked off a reaction in you so that you started talking about your mother?*

C: *Probably thinking. . .that unless I explained a little bit more she wouldn't understand that I understood. But I went so far into my own thing. One week I withdraw and don't say anything about myself and the next week that's all I talk about. I just want to tell myself to shut up!*

S: *I think what you're looking for is a middle ground. . . where you're making disclosures and being genuine. . . enough to let the client know that you've had those same experiences and are really with it.*

C: *Yea, that's it. . .I know.*

S: *But keep the focus on him. . .if we can say there's a "boo boo" here it's that. . .where you maintain too much focus on yourself and not on her.*

C: *Can we stop looking at it* (the videotape). . .(nervous laugh). . .*I don't want to see the rest. Turn it off! That probably sums up the whole thing!*

S: *Bob, are you "awfulizing"* this thing now?*

C: *No, no. . .yes, I am. It is awful to me, I don't want to be like that!*

S: *O.K. That's why we want to look at it. Because if you can get in touch with some of the things which went through you emotionally, cognitively. . .during this counseling session. Those are variables which precipitated your keeping a focus on yourself.*

C: *O.K.* (very subdued tone, obviously upset)

S: *And it's not awful. . .*(noticing the counselor's emotion). . .*hmm??*

C: *Turn it on. . .*(the counselor is teary eyed)

(fifteen second silence)

S: What's going on now? (in a soft and warm tone)

C: *I see that as awful* (voice trembling). . .*it's not the way I want to be at all* (soft crying).

---

*Awfulizing is a term which is frequently used in the literature on rational-emotive therapy. It means a tendency to exaggerate the aversiveness of something or someone.

S: *The way you are is not the way you want to be.*

C: *The way I am in that tape is not the way I want to be in a counseling session.* (continued voice tremor) (long silence) *It's frustrating being at one end or the other. Not. . .not reaching the middle, not. . .One's as bad as the other. Two weeks ago it was that I wasn't involved and this one is bad on the other aspect. Why do I do that?*

S: *Sounds as though you're really frustrated because you go one way or the other.*

C: *Yea, I can't. . .I am!*

S: *I guess I can't agree with you that this is awful. . .let met tell you what I mean. Whenever you talk to someone about an emotional experience they're having, it sometimes taps the emotional things that you are working on—that are alive in your life. There's a great drawing out of your personal material, and it's very hard to deal with that. You know what I mean?*

C: *Uh, huh.*

S: *Ah. . .so that if somebody had said to me before your interview, hey, this client is going to talk to Bob about the death of her brother, I would have said, the chances are very great. . .that Bob is going to have a tough time dealing with that emotionally, because it's going to remind him of the pain he's gone through and is going through. . .*(counselor nods). . .*and I wouldn't have said, Bob is really going to do a lousy job with this client because he's such a lousy counselor and it's going to be awful! Because. . .if it had been me in there talking to a client who had a problem similar to mine, I would have found it difficult to deal with that. . .and I probably would have done some things which under other circumstances I wouldn't have done. I would have made boo-boos!*

C: ***You** wouldn't have. . .cause I don't see you that way at all.*

S: *You see me as perfect?*

C: *Almost. . .yea. You really have it under control I think.*

S: *Well, that's a nice compliment except that it's unrealistic* (laughing and smiling).

C: *I don't know that side of you, I just see you as extremely competent, that's all!*

S: *I think I am competent. . .but what I'm saying to you is that having emotional experiences like you had in this session. . .does not. . .it doesn't mean that you're not competent!*

C: *But not as effective as I could have been.*

S: *Probably not, yea. And that's not bad . . . that's realistic . . . whenever a client presents a problem that hooks your emotions one of the first things you must ask yourself is "can I handle it."*

(The supervisor continued by exposing Bob to several examples of counselors identifying with client problems and thereby losing their effectiveness.)

C: *Yea, I see what you mean.*

S: *But another thing that is happening to you today, in addition to this identification, is what I think you've been doing all semester. You find something you're doing which is not desirable, which you wish you had not done, and then you start awfulizing and putting yourself down. . .for not being perfect.*

C: *(Crying). . .but I want to be perfect.*

S: *Why. . .do you want to be perfect? I'm serious, that a good question, why do you want to be perfect? What will you have when you're perfect that you don't have now?*

C: *More self respect. . .(long silence).*

S: Maybe you should look at ways of getting more self respect, in ways other than being perfect. . .because that's a delusion. . . cause you're never going to be perfect.

C: No, so I won't be a counselor (still teary eyed). I'll be perfect in something else!

S: Is it difficult for you to have self respect and acceptance, as long as you're making boo-boos. . .in counseling or anything else?

C: Yes; counselors can't make mistakes because they are dealing with people's lives. They shouldn't leave people worse off after counseling.

S: You think that your client is now worse off?

C: No, but I don't want her to have all that information and feelings about me. If I lay out all that garbage she probably will. I won't be able to help her as much, she won't respect me. Does that make sense?

S: I think you are imposing your standards of perfection upon her. (counselor laughs) I think you're saying "she's not going to like or respect me because I wasn't a perfect counselor."

C: She probably won't know that I'm not a perfect counselor!

S: *That's right, good!* (counselor and supervisor laughing softly)

C: She probably won't know but I know. . .she won't know she got a raw deal.

S: Hold it! I thought we established about five minutes ago that she (the client) didn't have any bad reactions to this counseling session—that you really didn't leave her worse off than before and give her a raw deal.

C: I know.

S: O.K. so that's not an excuse to disturb yourself, right?

C: Yea, I guess.

S: Do you see how you just used it to upset yourself? But it's not a logical reason, so let's wipe it out!

C: (Laughing at himself) All right, I guess.

S: You really hate to give it up, don't you. Even though you know it's an irrational notion, not based on fact, you keep telling yourself you are a lousy counselor and person. In fact you try to make up reasons to support the nutty notion.

C: (Laughing) I guess I know she had a pretty good session.

S: So what's left to disturb yourself with. . .

C: Those little tiny imperfections.

S: Right, some boo-boos like focusing too much on yourself. And the reasons you did that were probably some encouragement last week from Frank, to disclose, and the fact that this client's problem tapped a problem which you are dealing with yourself.

C: But I would like to have more control than that!

S: That's why we're here in supervision. . .to help you work out this thing. . .but we can't do that until you stop awfulizing your mistakes and demanding a perfect performance.

C: O.K., O.K., turn it on.

S: Bob, before we look at more, can you tell me why this tape is not awful? I'm serious now, it's important for **you** to know why it's not awful, so give it a try.

C: *It's not awful because I can be expected to be somewhat emotionally involved since I am still going through that myself. It's not awful because the whole session turned out well, and that she liked me and I think respected me when she was finished. And it was helpful to her.*

Interpretation of the Third Excerpt

A great deal of rational emotive intervention was employed in this third segment because Bob began to engage in a self defeating pattern of intrapersonal ideational dynamics which he had exhibited in previous supervision sessions. Bob had made some performance mistakes (i.e., identified with the client and dominated the interview with self reference), then proceeded to unrealistically exaggerate their consequences and implications, and completed the sequence by depressing himself with self condemnatory ideation. Breaking up this intrapersonal dynamic pattern was necessary so that the counselor could regain "free attention," learn from mistakes, and develop appropriate skills.

For those unfamiliar with rational emotive technique, the supervisor's behavior may seem quite forceful, but such confrontation is often necessary if an individual is to break out of an illogical ideational set. The supervisor identified Bob's irrational ideas, vigorously disputed them, and then forced Bob to dispute them. Bob's ability to dispute his awfulizing was a positive sign indicating that he had gained an insight into his irrational thinking habit, and that he could overcome it. The sign proved to be valid as Bob immediately calmed down and ceased the awfulizing ideation.

Various psychotherapeutic techniques could have been used by the supervisor in response to Bob's emotional upset over his performance mistakes. The rational emotive technique was preferred because the supervisor had used it effectively in therapy, and because prior reflections and encouragement had not been sufficient to discourage Bob from his self disturbing dynamics.

Fourth Excerpt

Following the rational-emotive confrontation supervision returned to an examination of the dynamics which comprised the counselor's identification with the client's problem. As this fourth excerpt progresses the supervisor's techniques change. Initially, open leads and reflective responses were used to help the counselor understand the dynamics which constituted his emotional identification, then the supervisor slowly begins to focus on the counselor's skill-behavior and to encourage the counselor to explore alternative ways of responding to the client which would have been more appropriate. The supervisory approach gradually shifts from psychotherapeutic model to the behavioral model.

S: *What feelings did you have there* (referring to an incident on the videotape)?

C: *I was thinking that's just how it is, it feels that way, like it will never go away. People say your pain will pass but it doesn't.*

S: *What Gail said about her grief reminded you of yours?* (Counselor nods) *and you really got into your grief, felt it again?* (Counselor nods)

S: (Silence). . .*where was Gail while you were feeling your grief. . .what do you think was going on in her?*

C: (Silence). . .*I don't know. . .I guess she was listening to me talk about it.*

S: *Un hum. . .*

(Videotape segment was viewed.)

S: *What's going on here?*

C: *Just another of those places where. . .she mentioned fears about losing more loved ones. . .and I could recall doing exactly that. . .*

S: *How did you respond to her. . .I mean. . .as you thought about your having done that. . .what then did you say to Gail?*

C: *Well, there it is, you can see it!*

S: *What do you see?*

C: *I see myself talking about me everytime she pushes my button.*

S: *What would you rather have done?*

C: *Talked about her.*

S: *O.K., let's look at some places where your emotional button was pushed, and you focused on yourself, and let's find some better ways to have responded. O.K.?* (Counselor nods)

(Videotape segment was viewed.)

S: *Here's a good place. Was your button pushed here?*

C: *I guess.*

S: *You're recalling how little time you feel you spent with your mother, responding to what Gail said about not spending enough time with her sister.* (Counselor nods)

S: What would have been a better response?

C: *Oh. . .(silence). . .I don't know! What could I say?*

S: *To answer that, maybe we should identify what it is you should be trying to do in an initial interview. . . and then find a response which does those things.*

C: *I'm trying just to help her talk about her problem . . .I guess!* (Frustration evident in the counselor's voice)

S: *And let me add something to that. . .you are trying to communicate understanding while helping the client* explore her thoughts and feelings. . .does that sound right?

C: Yes, but how do you do all that. . .there's so much you're supposed to be doing!

S: It sounds like a lot, doesn't it? (Counselor nods) But it's far easier than you think, Bob. Let's take a simple verbal technique that we've talked about in seminar—the reflective response. If you had used one right here it would have communicated empathy and encouraged the client to further explore her concerns. That one little response would have done all that!

C: (The counselor is silent, attentive, yet with an exasperated facial expression. The supervisor interpreted it as indicative of the counselor's feelings of helplessness and incompetence.)

S: (Smiling). . .looks easier than it is I guess. . .can you think of a reflective response that would have fit here?

C: . . .ah. . .You're wishing you had spent more time with her.

S: Great. . .see how easy that was. (Both the supervisor and counselor are now laughing, at themselves and the struggle to solicit one reflective response from the counselor.) This is not the only one, we could make up lots of reflective responses, the crucial thing is just to communicate the deep perceptions, feelings, and attitudes you hear from the client.

C: Yes. . .and I really do understand what she's going through!

S: Right, you have a reservoir of empathic sensitivity that . . .well I'm sure few others have. . .because of your common experience. Let's look at some other points where you could use this strength by being empathic.

The counselor and supervisor examined several more segments where a reflective response and/or open-ended lead was constructed to replace inappropriate counselor responses. Appropriate counselor disclosures were also practiced. The counselor seemed to be gaining confidence and skill when suddenly he encountered a segment on the videotape which was discussing dreams about her deceased sister, dreams which were filled with hostility toward survivors of the car wreck which claimed here sister's life. Dynamics in the client exactly paralleled those in the counselor, and the supervisor sensed an emotional impasse but didn't understand it. As a method of better understanding the counselor's dynamics, helping the counselor to understand himself, and demonstrating effective counselor responding, the supervisor entered role playing with the counselor.

Fifth Excerpt

S: *Bob, why don't you play the role of the client, and I'll be the counselor, O.K.? And we'll see what turns up, and at least you can see one way of dealing with dreams.*

C: *O.K. I'm the client. . .ah. . .I sometimes have a dream about the wreck, and the guy who was driving the car is standing there. . .*

S: *He wasn't harmed?*

C: *No, and he's standing there. . .and I just want to scream at him. . .*

S: *What would you like to say to him. . .*

C: (Interrupting) *that he shouldn't be here, that it isn't fair. . .I just almost want to hit him.*

S: *It seems so unjust that he wasn't hurt. . .that you lost your sister and there he stands; it's like he's responsible for her death and. . .*

C: (Obvious tension in the counselor, fists clenched, jaw muscles prominent from clenched teeth) *Yes, I want to hurt him but know it won't do any good.*

S: *Nothing you could do to him would bring her back, or even take away your pain.*

C: (The counselor's head is drooped, hands hanging loosely.)

Interpretation. The role-playing exercise has thus far helped Bob gain a personal insight about his own anger. Vicariously, he has been therapeutically affected. While this is certainly desirable because it promotes a needed dynamic change in Bob (i.e., to resolve attitudes and feelings about his mother's death), it does not teach the counseling skills which Bob must acquire for an improved performance. In the next few minutes of this excerpt the supervisor attempts to bring closure to the therapeutic experience and move on to skill building, showing Bob that effective counseling skills promote the kind of insight he has just experienced.

S: (Supervisor leaves role playing and reenters his own role) *Bob, how do you feel about the way I've responded?*

C: *I think you're right, that it doesn't do any good to be angry.*

S: *You've found this out for yourself. . .when your mother died?*

C: *Yes, and today it fell into place.*

S: *How did it fall into place?*

C: *Cause of what you said. I was. . .almost hated my father because he had not treated mother well. . .but there's no use. . .*

S: *Bob, let me take you away from. . .your own feeling . . . look at all I've said to you. . just a few reflections. . . but they helped you look at yourself and learn something.*

C: *Yea. . .*

S: *I didn't do much work at all. . .just listened to what was going on in you and put it into words. . .and if we had gone further I probably would have used some leads, and even some RET things if there were some irrational ideas uncovered.*

C: *O.K.*

S: *Let's switch roles, I'm the client and you are the counselor. O.K., slow and easy. . .O.K. . .*(Supervisor now enters the client's role for the role-play exercise). *I have these dreams about the driver of the car in which my sister was killed and they're really upsetting.*

C: *What are the dreams like?*

S: *Oh. . .I see the wrecked car and the driver is standing there looking at it. . .and I just want to walk up and start beating on him.*

C: *What are some of the things you'd like to say to him?*

S: *You shouldn't be here, it's not fair that you're here. . . Look what you did to my sister. . .I just want to destroy him. . .hurt him. . .*

C: *Doctor, I. . .I don't know how to explain this. . .*(The counselor is stumped and leaves the role playing to seek help from the supervisor.)

S: *What could you say just reflectively. . .you're trying to help me* (the client) *understand what's going on inside. . .*

C: *Ah. . .O.K. . .*Reentry to role playing). . .*You really resent the fact that he's alive. . .that your sister died and it doesn't seem fair to you. . .*

S: (Back in the client role) *Yea, yea, I guess that's what it is. . .You really feel like I want to destroy him. . .but. . . but even if I did that it doesn't seem like it would help. . .*

C: (Leaving role playing, Bob again seeks guidance) *I guess my next rambling thought is what would your brother want you to do.*

S: *O.K., that's a thought-provoking question, but let's not try to give the client an answer, Bob, just reflect, O.K., just help the client explore. . .try reflecting what I just said. . .I'll say it again* (Reentry to client role) *I just feel like really destroying him, punishing him in the worst way. . .but it wouldn't make things any better.*

C: *It wouldn't do you any good. . .it's futile. . .to seek revenge.*

S: (Leaving role playing to reward the counselor) *See!? All you have to do is reflect that stuff because when I heard you say it's futile to seek revenge that sums it up perfectly. Inside I'm saying yes, that's just the way it is.*

C: *Yea. . .I see. . .it's just hard for me to only reflect and not jump in with a solution.*

S: *There's much more you can do than just reflect, you can offer leads, share your perceptions, and open up alternatives—but you can do all of this in a manner which does not remove responsibility from the client. You can do this without offering solutions. Let's try it. . . I'm the client and you respond flexibly with leads and responses.*

S: (As client) *I've got all this anger toward the driver, and I want to hurt him but even if I did. . .vengeance would be pointless. . .and I'm just stuck here with all these lousy feelings, there isn't anything I can do.*

C: *So, you're really confused and wondering what to do with the feelings you have.*

S: *Yes, there's nothing I can do. . .*

C: *Maybe you should allow yourself some time to be confused.*

S: *What do you mean?*

C: (Laughing because the supervisor as client is pressing for an answer) *Maybe it's all right to be angry and hurt, natural.*

S: *Yea, but how can I be sure of that and how long will will it take?*

C: (Silence, then the supervisor prompts the counselor to reflect . . . *seems like forever getting over some things.*

S: *Bob, that's great, you're really with me!!*

C: (In an exuberant tone) *Yea, Oh I just never think of these things!! I think of solutions.*

S: *What you did here that was so good was to give me several reflections, accurate ones, and then when you thought I was demanding that my grief go away, you offered a thought about allowing myself to have it. Then when I pushed you for answers you couldn't give, that no one could give, you went back to reflecting my frustration. That was good counseling, quite appropriate for a first interview.*

C: *Yea, I can't believe it.*

S: *It really helped me. All you did was really listen and reflect, you weren't responsible for coming up with quick solutions. You did share a constructive thought, but not a solution.*

C: *I don't like the responsibility of finding solutions. . . this is so much easier. . .and better.*

Epilogue

This particular supervision session was the turning point in the laboratory practicum for Bob. Before this session he had been plagued with an excessive amount of performance anxiety, a lack of confidence, and an inability to use basic counseling skills such as empathic responding, open-ended leads, and genuine sharing responses. After this fourth supervision session Bob's performance improved remarkably as he continued to counsel with Gail in a second interview. He was much more empathic than in any previous interviews, his verbosity was significantly reduced, and appropriate reflections and leads were numerous. Gail's exploration of her grief and fears about death was enhanced and reached a depth of self disclosure which is normally not present in a second interview. She continued counseling with Bob for a total of four interviews.

Bob completed the laboratory practicum course in a satisfactory manner and made rapid skill improvements during the last half of the semester. Counseling became enjoyable activity for him, one that brought him a sense of competence. Personally, Bob made great strides in reestablishing a relationship with his father which had deteriorated since his mother's death.

The psychobehavioral approach to supervision was probably a more efficacious treatment for Bob than either a strictly psychotherapeutic or behavioral approach. Psychotherapeutic supervisory techniques were successful in helping Bob break up the blockade of intrapersonal dynamics which prohibited his skill improvement, but the therapeutic treatment was obviously insufficient to produce effective counseling skill-behavior as evidenced by Bob's initial struggle within the role-playing exercises to perform fundamental listening and responding skills. Yet, through the learning paradigm of role playing (and in the absence of his usual prohibitive dynamics) Bob began to replace inappropriate social behaviors with approved counseling skills, and this transformation continued throughout the semester.

REFERENCES

Arnold, D.L. (1962). Counselor education as responsible self development. *Counselor Education and Supervision, 1,* 185-192.

Authier, J., & Gustafson, K. (1976). Application of supervised and nonsupervised microcounseling paradigms in the training of registered and licensed practical nurses. *Journal of Consulting and Clinical Psychology, 12,* 63-68.

Avery, A.W., D'Augelli, A.R., & Danish, S.J. (1976). An empirical investigation of the construct validity of empathic understanding ratings. *Counselor Education and Supervision, 15*(3), 177-183.

Bartlett, W.E. (1983). A multidimensional framework for the analysis of supervision of counseling. *The Counseling Psychologist, 11,* 9-19.

Berenson, B.G., & Carkhuff, R.R. (1967). *Sources of gain in counseling and psychotherapy.* New York: Holt, Rinehart and Winston.

Bernard, J.M. (1979). Supervision training: A discrimination model. *Counselor Education and Supervision, 19,* 60-68.

Blane, S.M. (1968). Immediate effect of supervisory experiences on counselor candidates. *Counselor Education and Supervision, 8,* 39-44.

Blass, C.D., & Heck, E.J. (1975). Accuracy of accurate empathy ratings. *Journal of Counseling Psychology, 22*(3), 243-246.

Blocher, D.H. (1983). Toward a cognitive developmental approach to counseling supervision. *The Counseling Psychology, 11,* 27-35.

Bowman, J.T., & Reeves, T.G. (1987). Moral development and empathy in counseling. *Counselor Education and Supervision, 26,* 293-299.

Boyd, J.D., Nutter, J., & Overcash, S. (1974). A psychobehavioral approach to counseling supervision. Program and paper presented at the American Personnel and Guidance Association Convention, New Orleans, Louisiana.

Boyd, J.D, & Pate, R.H. (1975). An analysis of counselor verbal response scale scores. JSAS: *Catalogue of Selected Documents in Psychology, 5,* 198.

Brady, D., Rowe, W., & Smouse, A.D. (1976) Facilitative level and verbal conditioning: A replication. *Journal of Counseling Psychology, 23*(1), 78-80.

Brammer, L.M., & Wassmer, A.C. (1977). Supervision in counseling and psychotherapy. In D.J. Kurpius, R.D. Baker & I.D. Thomas (Eds.), *Supervision of applied training.* Westport, CT: Greenwood Press.

Brown, P.D., & Smith, H.D. (1984). All inclusive conceptualization as a dimension of trainee empathic responding. *Counselor Education and Supervision, 23,* 341-346.

Carlson, K.W. (1971). Reinforcement of empathy: An operant paradigm for the training of counselors. Unpublished dissertation, Northern Illinois University.

Cebik, R.J. (1985). Ego development theory and its implications for supervision. *Counselor Education and Supervision, 24,* 226-234.

Carkhuff, R.R. (1969a). *Helping and Human Relations, Volume I.* New York: Holt, Rinehart and Winston.

Carkhuff, R.R. (1969b). *Helping and Human Relations, Volume II.* New York: Holt, Rinehart and Winston.

Carkhuff, R.R., & Berenson, B.G. (1967). *Beyond counseling and psychotherapy.* New York: Holt, Rinehart and Winston.

Carkhuff, R.R., & Truax, C.B. (1965). Training in counseling and psychotherapy: An evaluation of an integrated didactic and experimental approach. *Journal of Consulting Psychology, 29,* 333-336.

Cicchetti, D.V., & Ryan, E.R. (1976). A reply to Beutler et. al.'s study: Some sources of variance in accurate empathy ratings. *Journal of Consulting and Clinical Psychology, 44*(5), 858-861.

D'Augelli, A.R., Deyss, C.S., Guerney, B.G., Jr., Hershenberg, B., & Sborofsky, S.L. (1974). Interpersonal skill training for dating couples: An evaluation of an educational mental health service. *Journal of Counseling Psychology, 21*(5), 385-389.

Dowling, T.H., & Frantz, T.T. (1975). The influence of facilitative relationship on imitative learning. *Journal of Counseling Psychology, 22*(4), 259-263.

Gladstein, G.A., & Feldstein, J.C. (1983). Using film to increase counselor empathic experiences. *Counselor Education and Supervision, 23,* 125-132.

Goodyear, R.K., & Bradley, F.O. (1983). Theories of Counselor Supervision: Points of convergence and divergence. *The Counseling Psychologist, 11,* 59-69.

Gormally, J. (1975). A behavioral analysis of structured skills training. *Journal of Counseling Psychology, 22*(5), 458-460.

Hansen, J.C., Pound, R., & Petro, C. (1976). Review of research on practicum supervision. *Counselor Education and Supervision, 16*(2), 107-116.

Hansen, J.C., Robins, T.H., & Grimes, J. (1982). Review of research on practicum supervision. *Counselor Education and Supervision, 22,* 15-24.

Hart, G.M. (1982). *The process of clinical supervision.* Baltimore, MD.: University Park Press.

Hosford, R.E., & Barmann, B. (1983). A social learning approach to counselor supervision. *The Counseling Psychologist, 11,* 51-58.

Kelley, J.D. (1971). Reinforcement in micro-counseling. *Journal of Counseling Psychology, 18,* 268-272.

Kimberlin, C.L., & Friesen, D.D. (1980). Sex and conceptual level empathic responses to ambivalent affect. *Counselor Education and Supervision, 19,* 252-259.

Lazarus, A. (1971). *Behavior therapy and beyond.* New York: McGraw Hill.

London, P. (1964). *The modes and morals of psychotherapy.* New York: Holt, Rinehart and Winston.

Melnick, R.R. (1975). Counseling responses as a function of method of problem presentation and type of problem. *Journal of Counseling Psychology, 22*(2), 108-112.

Mischel, W. (1968). *Personality and assessment.* New York: John Wiley and Sons.

Muehlberg, N., Drasgow, T., & Pierce, R. (1969). A factor analysis of therapeutically facilitative conditions. *Journal of Clinical Psychology, 25*(1), 93-95.

Mueller, W.J., & Kell, B.L. (1972). *Coping with conflict: Supervising counselors and psychotherapists.* New York: Appleton-Century-Crofts.

Patterson, C.H. (1983). A client centered approach to supervision. *The Counseling Psychologist, 11,* 21-27.

Perry, M. (1975). Modeling and instructions in training for counselor empathy. *Journal of Counseling Psychology, 22,* 173-179.

Peters, G., Cormier, L., & Cormier, W. (1978). Effects of modeling, rehearsal, feedback and remediation on acquisition of a counseling strategy. *Journal of Counseling Psychology, 26,* 74-80.

Pierce, R.M., & Schauble, P.G. (1970). Graduate training of facilitative counselors: The effects of individual supervision. *Journal of Counseling Psychology, 17,* 210-215.

Pierce, R.M., & Schauble, P.G. (1971). Toward the development of facilitative counselors: The effects of practicum instruction and individual supervision. *Counselor Education and Supervision, 11,* 83-89.

Rogers, C.R. (1957). The necessary and sufficient conditions of therapeutic personality change. *Journal of Consulting Psychology, 21,* 95-103.

Stoltenberg, C. (1981). Approaching supervision from a developmental perspective: The counselor complexity model. *Journal of Counseling Psychology, 28,* 59-65.

Swensen, C. (1980). Ego development and general model for counseling and psychotherapy. *Personnel and Guidance Journal, 58,* 382-389.

Truax, C.B., Carkhuff, R.R., and Dowds, J. (1964). Toward an integration of the didactic and experiential approaches in counseling and psychotherapy. *Journal of Counseling Psychology, 11,* 240-247.

Vitalo, R.L. (1970). Effects of facilitative interpersonal functioning in a conditioning paradigm. *Journal of Counseling Psychology, 17,* 141-144.

Woody, R.H. (1971). *Psychobehavioral counseling and therapy.* New York: Appleton-Century-Crofts.

CHAPTER 6

SYSTEMS MODEL
OF SUPERVISION

Systems technology has had an auspicious debut in counseling and guidance during the last decade. The systems approach has been proposed as an accountable one for counselor education (Bernstein & LeComte, 1976; Canada & Lynch, 1975; Falvey 1987; Lewis & Lewis, 1983; Horan, 1972; Saylor, 1976; Thoresen, 1969; Winborn, Hinds, & Stewart, 1971) and the programatic delivery of helping services (Blocher, Dustin, & Dugan, 1971; Hosford & Ryan, 1970; Ryan & Zeran, 1972; Schmuck & Miles, 1971; Shaw, 1973). The ACES Committee on Counselor Effectiveness (ACES, 1969) has recommended that supervisors be trained in systems techniques.

The systems approach to counselor supervision is defined here as the application of systems technology to the supervisory function. The skills involved are in the form of thought processes, and the approach itself is a thinking mode: "a way of organizing and conceptualizing a phenomenon that will lead to the realization of specified goals" (Blocker, Dustin, & Dugan, 1971, p. 28). The systems approach is:

a disciplined way of analyzing as precisely as possible an existing situation by determining the nature of the elements which combine and relate to make the situation what it is, establishing the interrelationships among the elements, and synthesizing a new whole to provide means of optimizing system outcomes. (Ryan & Zeran, 1972, p. 13)

In no way is the suggestion made that any of the approaches presented in this book are sufficient individually for the supervisory function, and this is true for the systems approach. However in one place the systems approach particularly is applicable and valuable, and this is in the planning and management of a program of services. The supervisor can use systems techniques (Austin, 1978; Austin, 1981; Beck & Hillmar, 1986; Brett, 1984; Harper, 1986) in the operation of a supervision program and when supervising the planning and management of a helping-services program.

FOCUS AND GOALS

In the psychotherapeutic, behavioral and integrative approaches to supervision the focus is directly on the counselor and the supervisor's performance. A distinguishing feature of the systems approach is that the counselor and his/her performance are only a part of a larger and more encompassing conceptualization termed a *system*. Supervision focus in on the system which is defined as:

> . . .an integrated and related set of components (subsystems) organized for the purpose of obtaining a specific objective. (Horan, 1972, pp. 162-163)

> . . .the orderly organization of parts to make a whole in such a manner that each part is related to every other part, so a change in one part of the whole affects every other part, with each part and the totality of all parts functioning to produce specified outcomes. (Ryan & Zeran, 1972, p. 13)

The system of primary focus in counselor supervision is the program of helping services which the counselor is responsible for delivering. However, the supervisor must recognize that helping service programs are not isolated systems, they are usually subsystems (components) of larger systems. The school counseling program is a clear example; it is a component of the school's educational program, which itself is a subsystem of the supporting society. Counseling goals reflect and contribute to school system goals which reflect and contribute to society's objectives. The systems approach places all contingent systems in perspective.

By focusing on the "big picture," the systems approach sets a direction for the accomplishment of goals which are desperately needed for the accountability of helping-service programs. **Demonstrated effectiveness** is one of these goals. The counselor and supervisor must be able to demonstrate the effectiveness of their programs in attaining specified objectives. **Efficiency** is another goal of the systems approach gained by harmonious coordination of program components, and the utilization of team members based on a realistic division of labor and their special competencies.

A third goal of the systems approach, as applied through counselor supervision, is to **elicit the creative, innovative, and problem-solving potentials of the counselor and supervisor.** The systems approach enables an individual to understand and deal with complex problems. A "systems thinker" is challenged by difficult situations and responds with professional assertiveness.

As summarized by Blocher, Dustin, and Dugan (1971), a systems approach

> Offers us a way of focusing on the larger—picture the total environment that impinges upon any single individual or group. It enables us to identify the key variables and factors at work within a total process. In doing this, it enables us to specify the outputs or outcomes that we expect or desire from a given process and to conceptualize the needed inputs or interventions that will be needed to produce those ends.(p.3)

METHODOLOGY

Consistent with the supervisor role model presented in Chapter 1, the assumption is made that the supervisor will be in a consultative stance when implementing systems methodology. In this stance the supervisor is not the administrator or director for a program of helping services, but instead is a consulting supervisor to counselors, head counselors, program directors, and administrators. From the consultative stance the supervisor will collaborate with counselors and supervise the use of systems methodology as counselors develop, manage, and evaluate programs, and as they serve as system consultants to other system personnel. Also, the supervisor will employ systems techniques when planning and managing the supervision program. The skills and techniques of systems analysis, synthesis, flowchart modeling, writing performance objectives, simulation, and systems technology information are basic to the systems approach.

System Analysis

The skill of system analysis is a conceptual one (Abels & Murphy, 1981; Celotta, 1979; Gimmestad, 1976; Hosford & Ryan, 1970; Rimmer, 1981). It is the skill of identifying and visualizing systems and the components and operations of the system. The system analyst can pinpoint problems, and the macro-conceptualization of a system enables him/her to see the environment in which the problem exists and the elements in that environment which have a relationship to and influence on the problem. System analysis is thus a diagnostic breakdown skill.

A supervisor employs system analysis on a daily basis. If problems arise within the helping-service program (system), the supervisor can track them down with system analysis. Maintenance of the program should include a routine system analysis—an evaluative look at the entire operation. Additionally, the supervisor will continually be called upon to use **the system analysis skill when assisting counselors in managing their own activities and specific system components (e.g., testing program, college counseling) for which they are responsible.**

When a supervisor performs a system analysis on a program of helping services, many separate analysis tasks are performed, each having underlying evaluative questions that are answered by the information gained through investigation. For illustration a number of these basic analysis tasks are offered in the following:

Basic System Analysis Tasks

Task 1: Identify the target system (helping-service program) to be analyzed, and any larger systems of which it is a part.

This task provides the supervisor-analyst with a picture of the target system and its environmental context. After only one analysis task the analyst begins to identify some of the environmental forces which impinge upon the target system.

Task 2: Identify the needs of the population served, and the needs of any larger systems which the target system serves.

A helping-service program always directs its efforts toward client-population needs as well as needs of parent systems (e.g., community agency, school system, society, district, or state).

Task 3: Identify the goals of the target system.

Goals of a target system ordinarily reflect the needs of the population or larger system(s) which it serves.

Task 4: Analyze the congruency between goals of the target system, and the needs of the population and larger system(s) served.

Sources of discrepancy, which necessitate a change in target system goals, are as follows:

a. Goals of the target system may not reflect the needs of the population and larger systems served.

b. Goals of the target system may be deficient, not encompassing some important population and/or larger system needs.

c. Goals of the target system may not be realistic, encompassing too many population and/or larger system needs.

Task 5: Identify the helping services and functions which are performed by the target system.

a. Are services and functions absent from the program that could be effectively employed to reach system goals?

b. Is the program capable of performing existing services and functions—does it have the necessary personnel, skills, time, materials, and so forth?

c. Are the existing services and functions of the system the most effective and efficient methods for accomplishing system goals?

Task 6: Identify and assess the degree of coordination among the system's components (services or functions) and personnel.

a. Does overlap and inefficiency occur.

b. Does sufficient communication exist among system personnel so that each is aware of how his/her efforts relate to those of other personnel and to program goals?

Task 7: Identify the evaluative methods by which the target system determines if it is reaching its goals.

a. Are these evaluations valid?

b. Do these evaluations cover all system goals?

Task 8: Identify the methods by which the target system remains "open", (i.e., receptive to and solicitous of a continuing stream of information from the population and larger system(s) served).

a. Are the existing methods actually used?

b. Are so few methods present that the target system is somewhat closed?

c. Do too many methods exist; or, does the system fail to discriminate among incoming data, becoming hypersensitive to it?

Task 9:   Identify the processes by which the target system changes as a result of making use of incoming information from the population and larger system(s) served, and from system evaluations.

An open and effective system is sensitive to its environment, and adapts to changing conditions therein. A closed system of helping services which does not adapt will quickly become outdated and will be seeking to meet needs and accomplish goals which are irrelevant.

Synthesis

Contrasting the breakdown skill of analysis is the "putting-together" skill of synthesis. Synthesis is the establishment of relationships between previously unrelated parts, and the combining of these parts into a new whole. Ryan and Zeran (1972, p. 14) have equated synthesis with innovation.

Analysis and synthesis are back-to-back skills, and they represent an orderly process for creating a new system or improving an existing system, as opposed to a trial-and-error or intuitive approach (Hosford & Ryan, 1970). Information gained from the nine analysis tasks mentioned earlier could lead to the following synthesis actions:

1. Reorganization and/or establishment of a comprehensive and realistic set of system goals which are congruent with and a reflection of the needs of the population and larger system(s) served.

2. Reorganization and/or establishment of a comprehensive and realistic set of helping services which would effectively and efficiently reach system goals, and the establishment of functional communication channels among personnel and system components so that interchange leads to moment-by-moment coordination and system unity.

3. Reorganization and/or establishment of evaluation methods by which the system can assess the

effectiveness of its helping services by determining if goals are being accomplished.

4. Reorganization and/or establishment of a "change function" within the system. This function would consist of methods for receiving and processing information from the environment and from system evaluations (see item 3), and then changing the system where needed in order to keep it effective and in congruence with environmental conditions.

Flowchart Modeling

Analysis and synthesis is aided by the drawing of graphic models to depict systems, system components, and the relationship among components. A graphic form makes information and abstract concepts more understandable, and the process flow is analoguous to a road map—prescribing a systematic routing toward system goals (Hosford & Ryan, 1970). Figure 6.1 is a flowchart model constructed by Hosford and Ryan (1970, p. 226) for the development of counseling and guidance programs.

In figure 6.1 numbers 1.0 to 10.0 are identifiers referring to sub-systems within the total model, and smaller numbers indicate the functions within each subsystem. The symbol (⟶) is a signal path between functions indicating the flow of action, information, and objects. Each function element can produce feedback Ⓕ , output that feeds back to another function and has an effect on it.

The construction of a model requires extensive effort, usually the product of a supervised team effort. Persons unfamiliar with models may be confused by such figures and a narrative description should accompany them. A description of Figure 6.1 is presented later in the practical application section of this Chapter.

Writing Performance Objectives

The writing of performance objectives is a system-approach skill which is crucial to the accountability of any helping-

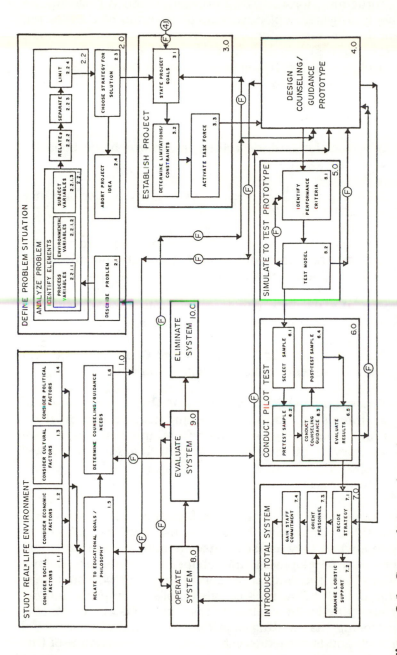

Figure 6.1. Counseling and guidance program development system model (Hosford & Ryan, 1970, p. 226). Reprinted with permission from American Personnel and Guidance Association, Copyright 1970.

services program (Horan, 1972; Thoresen, 1969). A performance objective is a system objective stated in terms of the desired behavior of the target population (school students, clientele, counselor-trainees). Three criteria to meet when writing performance objectives are the following (Hosford & Ryan, 1970):

1. the objective should state the outcome in terms of behavior that the target individual will demonstrate,

2. the conditions are described under which the behavior will occur, and

3. an acceptable level (extent or degree) of performance should be specified.

Well written performance objectives are pertinent to broader program goals; they are realistically attainable and are measurable. These quality criteria are evident in the following performance objective from a school counseling program. The objective is the type for which a counseling program could assume responsibility and be held accountable.

> **School Counseling Program Broad Goal:** Informed and realistic career decisions by school students.

> **Performance Objective:** Following the administration of an interest and aptitude test, and participation in three group counseling sessions where the test results are interpreted and discussed, each ninth grade student will choose three career areas for later study in career education class.

The system-skill of writing performance objectives (Beck, Hillmar, 1986; Granwold, 1978; Slavin, 1985) is needed by supervisors when they assist counselors and program directors with program development and change. If counselors do not themselves have the skill, an in-service training workshop may be required, with follow-up supervision of skill implementation. Numerous pitfalls in training and supervision exist, the foremost being that writing objectives becomes an obsessional end in itself and is carried to extremes. A classic example of this pitfall is the teacher who sought the author's praise for a list on one hundred and fifty behavioral objectives that were established for an elementary grade curriculum. Such a large number of objectives rarely serves a useful function; actual evaluation of them is not feasible nor can one do justice to that many, therefore accountability for their accomplishment would be impossible. Exhaustive lists are usually an attempt to state every suspected behavioral influence of the professional upon the target population.

A different approach to writing behavioral objectives is to view them as useful tools to serve the helping service program. Instead of writing grandiose objectives, supervisors can remain with basics which are realistic for their particular helping-service programs. As a program gains maturity and basic objectives are met, the old objectives can be replaced with more sophisticated ones. This pragmatic view is reflected in the following illustrative list of Supervision Goals and Objectives which comprises the core of a year-long supervision program. The objectives relate to a supervisory program serving a number of small helping-service programs, each one staffed by three or four counselors and a program director.

Illustration of
Supervision Goals and Objectives

Broad Supervision Goal: An Accountable Helping-Service Program

> **Performance Objective:** The counselor, in collaboration with the counselor staff, program director, and supervisor, and through group meetings and individual assignments, will plan the helping service program each year. The plan will reflect the past year's evaluation results and other evaluative data offered by the staff regarding program relevance and accountability.

> **Performance Objective:** With supervisory assistance, the counselor will be responsible for monitoring a particular function, service, or designated area of the helping-service program and will report on its operation to the program

director and counselor staff in several regularly scheduled program management meetings.

Performance Objective: The counselor will utilize the supervisor's assistance in conducting a yearly evaluation of that function, service, or designated area of the helping service for which he/she has monitoring responsibility, and will present an evaluative report to the program director and to the counselor staff within program evaluation meetings.

Performance Objective: The program director will meet with the supervisor at regularly scheduled times for consultative assistance regarding program administration, management, and evaluation.

Broad Supervision Goal: Accountable Counselor Services and Activities

Performance Objective: Following the yearly establishment of the helping-service program by the staff, the counselor, in consultation with the supervisor, will prepare a personal plan of activities for that year which coincides with the program and contributes to it.

Performance Objective: The counselor will consult with the program director and supervisor during the year when professional problems block the satisfactory implementation of his/her planned activities, and will meet with the supervisor twice yearly to review progress on the activity plan.

Performance Objective: The counselor will prepare an evaluation of his/her activity program at year's end, review it with the supervisor, and based upon the evaluation will make recommendations for next year's activity program.

Broad Supervision Goal: Self-Directed Competency Development

> **Performance Objective:** In consultation with the supervisor, and using the supervisor's assistance to a mutually agreed upon degree, each year the counselor will select and engage in a series of competency development activities and summarize these learning experiences in a report to the supervisor and program director.

> **Performance Objective:** As part of the counselor's competency development program he/she will select and engage in at least one skill-training experience each year (outside the in-service program), and will share the experience with colleagues during a regularly scheduled staff session.

> **Performance Objective:** Each year the counselor will demonstrate to the supervisor, through an approved pre-post assessment procedure, the acquisition or improvement of one skill-behavior or skill-activity.

> **Performance Objective:** As part of the counselor's competency development program, he/she will participate with the staff, program director, and supervisor in planning an in-service training program, and with supervisory assistance will prepare and conduct at least one in-service training session during the year.

Broad Supervision Goal: Counselor Personal Adjustment

> **Performance Objective:** The counselor will utilize the supervisor for confidential discussions of personal life concerns and issues which may influence the counselor's performance of his/her professional duties.

Performance Objective: The counselor will confidentially discuss professional problems with the supervisor which arise from inter-personal conflict with staff members or clientele.

Broad Supervision Goal: Professional Orientation and Development

Performance Objective: Counselors in their first year of practice will meet frequently and regularly with the supervisor during the first month in their position, and monthly thereafter during the year, for supervisory assistance in adjusting to a new position, preparing an activity plan, and establishing a professional identity and role.

Performance Objective: Newly employed but experienced counselors will frequently and regularly meet with the supervisor during the first week in their position, and bi-monthly thereafter during the year, for supervisory assistance in adjusting to a new position and preparing and implementing an activity plan.

Performance Objective: Within regularly scheduled staff meetings the counselor will be informed of and encouraged to participate in professional development activities (e.g., professional organizations, conferences, legislative lobbying, and so forth).

It is worth noting that the performance objectives in the foregoing list are *immediate objectives,* i.e., performance behaviors that are demonstrated in the present. The supervisor has considerable control over the elicitation of these behaviors and therefore can be held accountable for them.

Another type of objective which is important, but for which the supervisor cannot accept total responsibility because he/she does not have the necessary controls, is the *ultimate performance objective.* An ultimate performance objective is that ideal which hopefully will be produced by immediate performance objectives. For example, one immediate performance objective under the broad goal of self-directed competency development is: "each year, the counselor will demonstrate to the supervisor, through an approved pre-post assessment procedure, the acquisition or improvement of one skill-behavior or skill-activity." This immediate performance objective hopefully will lead to the ultimate objective of a master counselor who consistently functions at facilitative levels of empathy, respect, and honesty, and who demonstrates mastery in consultation skills, counseling skills, and program management. Obviously this ultimate objective is highly desirable and it produces a strong motivational striving, but the supervisor does not have the omnipotent powers to guarantee its attainment. Therefore, the recommendation is that the supervisor base his/her accountability only upon those objectives which can be realistically produced, and that the supervisor relegate ultimate objectives to the realm of covert ideals. Whereas the supervisor needs ideals for which to strive, basing accountability upon them would be self-defeating.

Another characteristic of the foregoing illustrative list of Supervision Goals and Objectives is that it may deceive the reader into thinking that the accomplishment of such fundamental things does not require a full-time professional who has been specially trained in supervision methodology, and that the objectives could probably be accomplished without a supervisory function. The supervisor, who translates complex systems and their operations into understandable concepts via system techniques such as performance objectives and flow-charting, must be prepared to correct deceptions and oversight.

Simulation

The technique of simulation is employed to test a newly created system and can be used also when analyzing an existing system to determine weaknesses. Simulation consists of the verbal and mental exercise of applying the system to a host of expected situations and running a variety of inputs through the system to check on practicality and to check whether or not operations would be smooth and results predictable.

Simulation is one of several system techniques which is employed by the supervisor to accomplish performance objectives regarding the planning of a helping-services program or to prepare an activity plan for an individual counselor. In the former case the supervisor meets with a staff of counselors and together they apply the newly developed or revised program to situations that are likely to occur in the future. Each component and operation of the system is exercised and evaluated.

A similar simulation meeting with an individual counselor is scheduled to check out his/her activity plan to be sure it is realistic and likely to reach intended goals and objectives. An enjoyable method for conducting such a simulation conference is to create a game-like atmosphere in which the supervisor offers difficult situations for the counselor to simulate through the activity plan. The counselor is challenged to create the most effective plan possible, one that could accountably process any input situation, and then to "problem solve" and adapt system operations to unusual input situations offered by the supervisor.

Systems Technology Information

Systems technology is foreign territory for most counselor supervisors, but a solid foundation of knowledge about systems is a prerequisite for the supervisor who becomes a "consultant-expert" when working with counselors on a systems project. References throughout this presentation on the systems approach are excellent informational sources, and they give a more thorough treatment to systems information than is possible in this Chapter. Several additional sources by systems authorities are recommended:

Burns, D.P. (1969). Behavioral objectives: A selected bibliography. *Education Technology, 9,* 57-58.

Celotta, B. (1979). The systems approach: A technique for establishing counseling and guidance programs. *Personnel and Guidance Journal, 57,* 412-414.

Falvey, J. (1987). *Handbook of administrative supervision.* Washington, D.C.: American Association for Counseling and Development.

Kennedy, D.A. (1976). Some impressions of competency-based training programs. *Counselor Education and Supervision, 15*(4), 244-250.

Krumboltz, J.D. (1966). Stating the goals of counseling. *California Personnel and Guidance Association Monograph*, No.1.

Lewis, J.A., & Lewis, M.D. (1983). *Management of human service programs.* Monterey, CA: Brooks/Cole.

Personnel and Guidance Journal (special issue). (1970). Technology in guidance, 28(3).

Rimmer, S. (1981). A systems approach model for counselor education program development and redefinition. *Counselor Education and Supervision, 21,* 7-16.

Ryan, T.A. (1969). Systems techniques for programs of counseling and counselor education. *Educational Technology, 9,* 7-17.

Silvern, L.C. (1968). Systems approach—What is it? *Educational Technology, 8,* 5-6.

Silvern, L.C. (1968). *Systems engineering of education I: Evolution of systems thinking in education.* Los Angeles: Education and Training Consultants Co.

Windle, C. (Ed.). (1984). *Program performance measurement: Demons, technology and dangers.* Baltimore, MD: Department of Health and Human Services.

THE SYSTEMS APPROACH: EMPIRICAL SUPPORT

The systems approach is an empirical method (Rimmer, 1981; Thoresen, 1969) and each application provides evidence of effectiveness. Evaluation is a definitive element of a system. Objectives are stated in behavioral terms so that the success of the system is actually observable, and ongoing system evaluation is conducted through the cybernetic concept or feedback (see Figure 6.1). Feedback is the information flow by which the components of a system influence and are influenced by each other. "The critical feature of feedback is information flow that alters (controls) the component receiving it. Information flow that does not have the capability of producing change is not fedback" (Thoresen, 1969, p.8).

The effectiveness of a system thus is known to its creators; ineffectiveness is antithetical to the systems approach. A more difficult empirical question is comparative effectiveness—is the systems approach better than other methods of doing things?

This may be a moot question, because systems methodology is not an all-or-none entity. Any program or methodological approach will implement something akin to systems techniques; an effort without any systemization is erratic behavior. A more realistic issue for counselors and supervisors is whether a **deliberately concerted** application of systems methodology can improve existing programs.

Studies of organizational development in industry and school systems, reviewed by Schmuck and Miles (1971), provide considerable support for the improvement of existing organizations through the infusion of systems technology (including the training of personnel). Complementing research evidence are objective reports of successful applications of systems technology in guidance programs (*Personnel & Guidance Journal,* 1970, 28, pp.31-34) and counselor education (Horan, 1972). Thus, available evidence suggests that the systems approach to program planning and management leads to accountable results. The systems approach is not a panacea, **but its principles and methodology bring about efficient and effective programmatic efforts.**

SYSTEMS APPLICATION IN COUNSELOR SUPERVISION

A supervisor will find that the application of "systems thinking" permeates daily activities. One major application whould be the systems design of a supervision program. Another application is in the development, management, and evaluation of a program of helping services. Celotta (1979), Hosford and Ryan (1970) and Rimmer (1981) applied the systems approach to the development of counseling programs. Hosford and Ryan (1970) constructed a systems model (See Figure 6.1) for program development which is applicable to the development of any helping-services program. The model's components represent the steps that a supervisor and team of counselors would follow; the narrative description by Hosford and Ryan is reprinted in the next section of this Chapter as a guide to supervisors who want to lead a group of counselors in the systematic development of a helping-service program. Figure 6.1 should be consulted as the description of the ten functions are read. The ten functions are as follows:

Study real-life environment (1.0)
Define problem situation (2.0)
Establish project (3.0)
Design counseling/guidance program prototype (4.0)
Simulate to test program prototype (5.0)
Pilot-test model (6.0)
Introduce system (7.0)
Operate system (8.0)
Evaluate system (9.0)
Eliminate system (10.0)

SYSTEMATIC DEVELOPMENT OF A HELPING-SERVICE PROGRAM

Study Real-Life Environment (1.0)

A counseling system cannot function effectively apart from the real-life environment of which it is a part. In 1.0 the focus is on this real-life environment. In 1.1., 1.2, 1.3, and 1.4 some of the dynamic conditions which combine to make up the real-life environment are considered. Inclusion of these social, cultural, economic, and political factors as dynamic conditions in the environment carries an implicit mandate (1.5) for awareness of the value structure and the immediate and long-range goals of the total educational enterprise in which the counseling program is to function. In considering these real-life environment factors, assessment of need for counseling is explicated (1.6). In this subsystem the relevance of counseling to the changing conditions of the real world is achieved.

Define Problem Situation (2.0)

This function serves the purpose of elucidating the need for counseling identified in 1.6. The general description of the problem situation (2.1) is followed by analysis of the problem (2.2). Analysis involves identification of elements (2.2.1) including process variables, environmental variables, and subject variables; determining relationships among these elements (2.2.2.); separating the elements (2.2.3); and limiting elements (2.2.4). Analysis of the problem should result in a decision (2.3) as to whether or not the situation is one that calls for developing a counseling program (3.0) or would one left to some other avenue of endeavor, in which case the program idea is aborted (2.4).

Establish Project (3.0)

Assuming the decision is reached that a counseling program is in order, the parameters of the program must be defined. This calls for stating the mission goal (3.1) determining limitations and constraints (3.2), and activating a task force to develop the program (3.3.). Clarity in stating the mission goals is of paramount importance. The need for launching an all-out counseling program will be non-existent particularly if the program purpose is vaguely defined. If at the outset the outcomes are not clearly intended, the chance of determining if or when the program goals have been realized is impossible.

Design Counseling and
Guidance Program Prototype (4.0)

Figure 6.2 is an expansion of Design Counseling/Guidance Program Prototype (4.0) subsystem in Figure 6.1. In this function three tasks are implemented at the outset: assess resources (4.1), study student population (4.2), and process data from the environment (4.3).

Assessing resources involves identifying available personnel, time, finances, and facilities. The assessment of resources, study of student population, and data from the environment lead to definition of alternative strategies and determination of priorities (4.4). Once resources have been determined, goals may need to be redefined. This is shown in Figure 6.2 through the use of a feedback loop from assess resources (4.1) to state project goals (3.1).

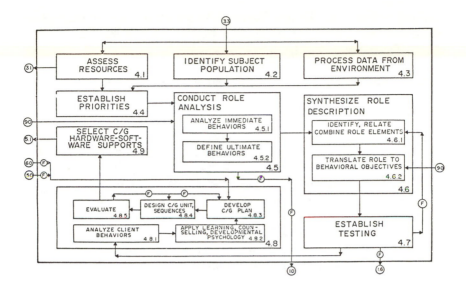

Figure 6.2. Design counseling/guidance program prototype. A detail design of space 4.0 with same title in Figure 6.1 (Hosford & Ryan, 1970, p. 227). Reprinted with permission from American Personal and Guidance Association, Copyright 1970.

Broadly stated, program outcomes set up in 3.0 must be defined in terms of immediate and ultimate subject behaviors; this is accomplished through role-analysis (4.5). "Role" is simply that behavior necessary for effective functioning within a social group. In the counseling context, for example, we assume that a person should be able to demonstrate self-actualizing behaviors, achieve economic efficiency, perform civic responsibilities, and be socially productive in the community, as well as demonstrating facilitating behavior in the counseling situation. The role description achieved in 4.6 as a result of synthesizing those behaviors identified in role analysis should result in a definition of the behavioral objectives (4.6.2) of the counseling program. These behaviors should be stated in terms of knowledge, skills, and attitudes required for fully functioning in the community. In addition, the behaviors should elaborate intended levels of achievement and describe exact conditions under which client behaviors will be demonstrated. The signal path from role analysis (4.5) back to study of real-life environment (1.0) indicates that the definition of role takes place in relation to the real-life environment from which the person has come and to which he/she will return.

Processing of data (4.3) involves continuing data collection, analysis, and interpretation to keep role-analysis in tune with the real world. This serves the purpose of keeping the system dynamic and makes possible the maintenance of harmony between the system and the environment.

Testing (4.7) of the subject group identified in 4.2 will determine the extent to which the target population—in this case the students—possesses the immediate and ultimate behaviors described in role definition (4.5); and on the basis of this information we can make any necessary redefinition of the counseling program needs (1.6). An important activity is to use criterion-based tests to measure subject behaviors against program objectives. The program which is expected to produce the client behavioral outcomes is put together in 4.8. In this subsystem analysis of client behaviors (4.8.1) and the relation of this information to experience and knowledge from learning psychology, counseling psychology, and developmental psychology (4.8.2) is necessary. Objects, information, and actions which mediate interaction between individuals in the subject group and the counseling process variables must be identified and synthesized in a counseling plan (4.8.3). This plan serves the purpose of guiding and directing construction of specific counseling experiences and environments and development of counseling units and sequences (4.8.4). The plan is checked against the real-life environment to insure optimum transfer from the counseling setting to the real world. The plan developed (4.8.3) results in development of specific counseling units and sequences will be supported by hardware and software (4.9) which are identified, evaluated, selected, and combined to make for effective and efficient counseling.

In making the counseling units, the human counselor is included as one of the media elements, together with other machine, audio, and video adjuncts. Creation of the counseling units involves comparing alternative strategies in terms of costs and benefits. The counseling units and sequences make up the program. Each sequence and unit, as well as the total program, must be evaluated (4.8.5) and then revised as needed. This continuing evaluation and revision is shown by the signal paths between 4.8.3, 4.8.4, and 4.8.5.

Simulate To Test Program Prototype (5.0)

Before the counseling program is implemented, simulation to test the program should be carried out either with the computer or by verbal walk-through so that necessary repairs can be made before the program is launched. As the model is simulated one could find that costs could make initiation of a full-blown program in the real-world impractical, without changes in the design. Possibly a comparison of alternatives will point up particular combinations to maximize the counseling program operation in terms of goal achievement.

Pilot Test The Model (6.0)

An initial try-out of the newly designed counseling program units and sequences should be made on a trial-run basis involving only a limited number from the subject population. If results from a pilot test of sequences and units indicate these elements are effective, then the total program should be subjected to a field test. This will be followed by further refining and modification before total implementation. The field test serves the important function of permitting collection and analysis of performance data and comparison of these data against program objectives. Evaluation carried out as part of field testing should determine the extent to which the system satisfies criteria of effectiveness.

Introduce the System (7.0)

The results of evaluation during field testing of the counseling program determine when, how, and for whom the total system will be established. Specification for staffing, facilities, equipment and community involvement to implement the plan designed (4.8.3) can be drawn up. Such specifications must be subjected to check and possible modification on basis of data gathered through simulation and field testing. Checking and revising are indicated by the feedback signals from 5.0 and 6.0 to 4.8.3 (Figure 6.1).

Many systems fail because of ill-conceived or inadequate plans for initiation of the model. To specify staff, facilities, equipment, and community resource requirement is not enough. Some provision must be made to decide on a strategy for launching the system (7.1). This is accomplished by arranging logistic support (7.2) to the new program. Personnel should be thoroughly trained not only in the use of the new media, methods, techniques, and materials utilized in the sequences and units of counseling but also in the behaviors required for implementing new roles which they may fulfill. A concerted effort must be made to see that counsleing system operators are committed to the new program (7.4) before the system becomes operational (8.0).

System Operation (8.0),
Evaluation (9.0),
and Elimination (10.0)

This discussion has been concerned primarily with development of a counseling system. Therefore, evaluate system (9.0) and eliminate system (10.0) (Figure 5.1) will be discussed only in relation to program development.

The results of the subsystem, introduce system (7.0), lead directly to system operation (8.0). Here is where the model is put into operation, with a full complement of logistical support, inclusion of client population of counseling units and se-quences. System evaluation (9.0) has the effect of looking at ways in which the target group is able to perform in the real-life world. The focus in 9.0 is on the behaviors of the clients after their return to the larger community. Are they adjusting to demands of society? Are they achieving economic efficiency, civic responsibility, self-actualization?

Our society changes rapidly, with conditions undergoing constant change. Only by feedback from client performance in the real world to system goals, design, and operation can the system be validated. An essential is for continuous evaluation to be built into the total system model. This is shown as a feedback signal from evaluation (9.0) to determining needs (1.6), which has the effect of checking the program against real-life world demands.

In evaluation, the system products are tested against criteria formulated in 4.6 when behavioral objectives of counseling were defined. This appears as feedback in the signal path from 9.0 (evaluation) to 4.6 (developing behavioral objectives).

Effectiveness of a counseling system should never be taken for granted. A constant checking operation should be maintained (9.0), and whenever an indication occurs that any unit or sequence is not serving the purpose for which it was intended, re-examination of the item should be made. As a general rule, piecemeal patching-up of weak or malfunctioning systems is not desirable; a better procedure is to analyze the total system.

In presenting this generalized model, the intent has been to provide a means for producing a model for counseling program development. The use of this generalized model for designing and evaluating counseling programs can lead to several benefits to those with vested interest in achieving effective, efficient programs.

Communication within the profession and between the profession and others involved in counseling can be facilitated. The obligation for accountability can be satisfied. Weaknesses, gaps, missing links in a system working against wholeness, strong interrelationships, compatibility, and optimization can be emphasized. Increased creativity and innovation can be achieved. Improvements in the total system, strengthening of functions, and tightening of interrelationships among functions can be realized through the provision for continuing evaluation in light of previously defined behavioral objectives.

SUMMARY

The systems approach to counselor supervision has been defined as the application of systems technology to the supervision function via a conceptualizing/problem-solving process which leads to the attainment of specified goals. Operationally, systems thinking takes the form of techniques such as analysis, synthesis, flowcharting, etc. which are employed by supervisors as they establish their own supervision programs, and as they teach these techniques to supervisees and oversee subsequent implementation.

Counselors and supervisors are known for their work with people, and indeed nearly all helping services depend upon the practitioner's interpersonal competence. But the goals and objectives toward which these interpersonal competencies are directed cannot be reached through uncoordinated helping efforts. The work of professional helpers must be systematically planned, managed, and evaluated in order to be *accountable,* and the systems approach can lead supervisors and counselors toward this accountability.

REFERENCES

Association for Counselor Education and Supervision, Committee on Counselor Effectiveness. (1969). Commitment to Action in Supervision: Report of a National Survey of Counselor Supervision.

Abels, P., & Murphy, M. (1981). *Administration in the human services: A normative systems approach.* Englewood Cliffs, NJ: Prentice-Hall.

Austin, M. (1978). *Management simulations for mental health and human service administration.* New York: Haworth Press.

Austin, M. (1981). *Supervisory management for human services.* Englewood Cliffs, NJ: Prentice-Hall.

Beck, A. & Hillmar, E. (1986). *Positive management practices.* San Francisco, Ca: Jossey-Bass.

Brett, J. (1984). Managing organizational conflict. *Professional Psychology: Research and Practice, 15,* 664-678.

Bernstein, B.L., & LeComte, C. (1976). An integrative competence based counselor education model. *Counselor Education and Supervision, 16*(1), 26-36.

Blocher, D.H., Dustin, E.R., & Dugan, W. E. (1971). *Guidance Systems.* New York: Ronald Press.

Burns, D.P. (1969). Behavioral objectives: A selected bibliography. *Educational Technology, 9,* 57-58.

Canada, R.M. & Lynch, M.L. (1975). Systems techniques applied to teaching listening skills. *Counselor Education and Supervision, 15*(1), 40-47.

Celotta, B. (1979). The systems approach: A technique for establishing counseling and guidance programs. *Personnel and Guidance Journal, 57,* 412-414.

Falvey, J. (1987). *Handbook of administrative supervision.* Washington, D.C.: Association for Counselor Education and Supervision.

Gimmestad, M. (1976). A systems approach to curriculum revision. *Counselor Education and Supervision, 16,* 156-158.

Granwold, D. (1878). Supervision by objectives. *Administration in Social Work, 2,* 199-209.

Harper, S. (1986). Adding purpose to performance reviews. *Training and Development Journal, 40,* 53-56.

Horan, J. J. (1972). Behavioral goals in systematic counselor education. *Counselor Education and Supervision, 11,* 162-170.

Hosford, R. E. & Ryan, T. A. (1970). Systems design in the development of counseling and guidance programs. *Personnel and Guidance Journal, 49,* 221-230.

Kennedy, D.A. (1976). Some impressions of competency-based training programs. *Counselor Education and Supervision, 15*(4), 224-250.

Krumboltz, J. D. (1966). Stating the goals of counseling. *California Personnel and Guidance Association Monograph,* No. I.

Lewis, J., & Lewis, M. (1983). *Management of human service programs.* Monterey, CA: Brooks/Cole.

Personnel and Guidance Journal (special issue). (1970). Technology in guidance, 28(3).

Rimmer, S. (1981). A systems approach model for counselor education program development and redefinition. *Counselor Education and Supervision, 21,* 7-16.

Ryan, T.A. (1969). Systems techniques for programs of counseling and counselor education. *Educational Technology, 9,* 7-17.

Ryan, T. A., & Zeran, F. R. (1972). *Organization and Administration of Guidance Services.* Danville, IL: Interstate Printer and Publishers.

Saylor, R. H. (1976). Managing competency-based preparation of school counselors. *Counselor Education and Supervision, 152*(3), 195-199.

Schmuck, R.A., & Miles, M. B. (1971). *Organizational development in schools.* Palo Alto, CA: National Press.

Shaw, M. D. (1973). *School guidance systems.* Boston: Houghton Mifflin.

Silvern, L.C. (1968). Systems approach-what is it? *Educational Technology, 8,* 5-6.

Silvern, L.C. (1968). *Systems engineering of education I: Evolution of systems thinking in education.* Los Angeles: Education and Training Consultants Company.

Slavin, S. (Ed.). (1985). *Social administration. The management of the social services, Volume I and II.* New York: Haworth Press.

Thoresen, C.E. (1969). The systems approach and counselor education: Basic features and implications. *Counselor Education and Supervision, 9,* 3-18.

Winborn, B. B., Hinds, W.C., & Stewart, N. (1971). Instructional objectives for the professional preparation of counselors. *Counselor Education and Supervision, 10*(2), 133-137.

CHAPTER 7

PERSON-PROCESS MODEL OF SUPERVISION: A DEVELOPMENTAL APPROACH

Michael D'Andrea, Ed.D.

This chapter will present a new approach to the process of supervision called the Person-Process Model (PPM). The model represents a developmental perspective and is based on three fundamental premises. First, the process of supervision is viewed as a complex, multifaceted experience. Second, the process undergoes a set of distinct transitions which may be conceptualized in three distinguishable stages. The PPM emphasizes numerous characteristics associated with each stage and provides guidelines for supervisors to consider as they orchestrate the supervisory process in such a manner as to enhance the professional development of their trainees.

The third fundamental premise rests in the presupposition that the effectiveness of supervision largely depends upon the tailoring of specific supervisory techniques to meet the developmental needs of the supervisee. This premise is called "meeting supervisees on their own turf." Further, this model stresses the importance of promoting facilitative conditions that best compliment the supervisee's level of development in order to create an optimal learning experience.

The "Person-Process Model of Supervision" does not provide discussion of a phase in supervision commonly referred to as the "termination" or "closing" stage. The author points out that rather than interpreting this as an omission in the model, it is an intended commission reflecting an important philosophical principle. Drawing from a new perspective emerging from management theory (The Stone Center, 1987) combined with major advancements in the field of female psychology (Gilligan, 1982), the PPM approach is guided by a realization that as the process of supervision effectively progresses, supervisees and supervisors move from a preoccupation with "achievement" (skill development) to an "affiliative" orientation. This affiliative orientation is based on an increasing sense of professional and personal "connection" between supervisors and supervisees resulting from the genuine commitment and mutual respect manifested throughout the process of supervision.

SUPERVISION

All of life could be said to be like going to school. Each day we are afforded new experiences and bits of information which over time may help us to simultaneously learn about ourselves, others, and our surroundings. Oftentimes, this sort of learning empowers a person to make changes in the way one thinks, feels, and even acts. For this sort of life-long learning to occur, however, the individual needs experiences that appropriately challenge and stimulate his/her interest and attention.

The workplace can easily be thought of as an avenue in which this sort of "continuing life education" is available daily as workers and supervisors have numerous opportunities to learn about themselves, others, and better ways of doing things. Regardless of whether a person is employed in an organization or provides clinical services in a therapeutic setting, the work environment often provides new challenges and demands to which he/she must respond. The manner in which one responds to such challenges largely determines an individual's overall effectiveness, productivity, and personal satisfaction in a work setting.

With this in mind, the suggestion is that the primary function of supervision is to stimulate increased effectiveness, productivity, and satisfaction through an expansion in the supervisee's knowledge and skill-base. If we view supervision as a special type of educational experience in which the supervisor is identified as the primary person responsible for assisting the supervisee to think and act in a more confident and competent manner, the need for systematic and comprehensive approach to the process becomes clearly apparent. While the method of supervision varies among supervisors, several factors are common to the process of supervision in most organizational and clinical settings. Kurpius and Baker (1977) listed four important factors which constitute the basis of successful supervision in most settings. These factors call upon the supervisor to

1. have a clear conceptualization of the supervision process,

2. logically and consistently implement a supervisory strategy,

3. maintain an appropriate level of control in the process, and

4. demonstrate conscientious management of the supervision sessions.

Generally supervision is basically used to help people acquire specific skills and develop competencies regardless of the work setting. However, to classify all supervision under the rubric of "developmental supervision" would not be correct. The following section distinguishes supervision that may generally nurture professional and/or personal growth from a more deliberate set of strategies that constitute a "developmental model for supervision."

DEVELOPMENTAL SUPERVISION

A supervisory relationship is indeed a special relationship. Fundamentally, it involves the matching of a presumably competent professional with a lesser experienced and knowledgeable person for the primary purpose of expanding the latter's skill, knowledge-base, and overall work performance. The supervisor is responsible for providing regularly scheduled, structured supervisory sessions that include the implementation of a variety of training, education, and consultation services in order to enhance the supervisee's level of professional competency and effectiveness (Corey, Corey, & Callanan, 1988).

Beyond professional competency building, another unique aspect of the supervision process is its potential propensity to enhance the personal growth of both the supervisor and the supervisee. In fact, both can be affected by the interpersonal exchanges and information gained through the process of supervision in such a way as to develop new self insights and increased awareness of others and the world around them. This may, in turn, lead to specific changes in the way one acts and the choices one makes. Thus, by integrating newly acquired insights in the context of one's life, the original purpose of supervision (i.e., professional competency building) may additionally stimulate positive changes in other dimensions of the supervisor and/or supervisee's lives (i.e., personal development).

Case Study: Tom

For example, let's take the case of Tom, an experienced supervisor employed by a large "for profit" organization. Tom is a highly competent and conscientious supervisor. He takes his professional responsibilities very seriously and genuinely feels obligated to do as good a job as he can supervising other employees. As a supervisor, Tom has always felt his primary focus should be directed towards supervisees' skills and their ability to achieve designated organizational goals.

On several occasions, Tom's supervisees misinterpreted his emphasis on goal achievement as being reflective of a cold, uncaring, and emotionally detached person. Tom started receiving this sort of feedback as a result of a new supervision evaluation component initiated by the organization.

Although genuinely surprised by the feedback, Tom recognized that was not the type of professional image he wanted to project. After thinking about it more, Tom began to see how his enthusiasm and satisfaction with his job was leading him to spend more time at work and less time with his family. He wondered if some of his family members also were feeling a sense of detachment from him.

As a result of these thoughts and insights, which were initiated as a result of the feedback he received from the process of supervision, Tom was able to take stock of himself. He began to modify some specific behaviors that clearly were not consistent with the way he intended others to view him. Consequently, Tom's professional and personal development were positively affected by the insights he gained and the changes he began to make both in supervision and with his family.

The Case Study of Tom was presented to demonstrate how a person can be influenced by supervision in even unintended ways. It should not, however, be mistaken for "developmental supervision" which represents a succinct and systematic approach to the process of supervision. **Developmental supervision is defined as a dynamic process that occurs over time in which supervisees acquire new professional behaviors and cognitions.** Developmental supervision also involves a series of active interactions between the supervisor and the supervisee in which the focus and quality of the interactions undergo a set of predictable changes (Hart, 1982).

A developmental framework for supervision incorporates three separate but interrelated human dimensions into a unified process. These dimensions include consideration of the supervisee's

attitudes and motivation,
skill level, and
knowledge base.

This type of supervision directs much attention to the changes these dimensions undergo as both the supervisory process and the supervisee proceed through a set of identifiable stages. According to Hart (1982), the reactions of supervisees to the goals they have attempted to accomplish and the expressed desire to formulate higher standards often represent a transition in the process of supervision.

While numerous efforts are currently being made to promote developmental models as the zeitgeist for contemporary supervision, Holloway (1987) stressed that more in-depth examination of the basic assumptions and underlying principles of such models are sorely needed. In addition, Worthington (1987) lobbied for better descriptions of the specific factors that contribute to a transition from one stage to another in the process of developmental supervision.

The following is a description of a comprehensive supervisory paradigm that addresses the shortcomings of previously stated models. This paradigm is called the "Person Process Model of Supervision" (PPM). It consists of two separate components, each with its own set of characteristics, stages, and transitional factors.

COMPONENT 1: UNDERSTANDING THE PERSONAL MEANING MAKING SYSTEM OF THE SUPERVISEE

The first component of the PPM model focuses on the supervisee as a person and more specifically, how and why supervisees differ from each other. Realizing that individuals may interpret and react to the same experiences differently is not shocking. For those of us who have supervised people, we often note that supervisees will react very differently to the same style of supervision coming from the same supervisor. As one supervisor recently said, "I don't understand it. I know I'm saying the same thing to my supervisees, but some of them react so differently to what I have to say!" In reality, supervisees, who are at different developmental levels, do learn different things from the same set of supervisory experiences and react differently to the same supervisor. The obvious question is, "Why does this occur?"

The tremendous strides made in the areas of developmental and adult psychology in the recent years (Erickson, 1977; Kohlberg & Turiel, 1971; Loevinger, 1976; Perry, 1970; Selman, 1974) help to answer this question. Perhaps these strides can be summed up briefly by saying that individuals at different stages of psychological maturity approach, interpret, and react to reality differently (Magana, Whiteley, & Nelson, 1980; Perry, 1970; Sprinthall & Collins, 1984).

Based upon research, individuals clearly pass through a definite sequence of psychological stages as they develop and mature. Each stage provides the person with a qualitatively different set of glasses through which he/she views life's experiences and consequently, makes meaning out of them. The different developmental lens through which we see the world leads individuals to make different interpretations and react differently to a common experience. The increase of knowledge in the area of developmental psychology may be particularly helpful to those supervisors who have experienced tremendous differences in their success with various supervisees and have not fully understood why.

Loevinger's (1976) work in the area of ego development offers supervisors a rich description of the sequence of psychological stages that constitute an individual's personal development. Figure 7.1 provides an overview of various stages of psychological and professional development as well as some of the major characteristics that are particularly relevant in the process of supervision.

The first component of the PPM, entitled "Understanding the Personal Meaning Making System of the Supervisee", uses Loevinger's (1976) theory in an effort to facilitate the supervisor's ability to

1. assess the supervisee's level of personal and professional development,

2. develop an effective supervision strategy, and

Corresponding Levels of Professional Development	Loevinger's Stages	Major Characteristics	Effective Supervisory Techniques/Methods
Preconformist Level	Impulsive Stage Self-Protective Stage	thinks in simple and concrete terms (unable to understand abstract and complex responsibilities) marginal problem-solving ability insensitive to others (thoughts and feelings) highly impulsive (very likely to act upon one's feelings without considering consequences) manipulative and exploitive of others . . . easily frustrated and angered by others experiences difficulty in following rules dominating personality in dealing with others not a good team member	one-to-one supervision preferred expectations presented in concrete terms with clearly defined consequences for violation of policies presented throughout early phases of supervision reward behaviors that conform to company regulations teach decision making skills written supervision contracts

Figure 7.1. Stages of psychological/professional development and matching supervisory techniques.

Figure 7.1. Continued.

Corresponding Levels of Professional Development	Loevinger's Stages	Major Characteristics	Effective Supervisory Techniques/Methods
Conformist Level	Conformist Stage	pleasing social personality	group supervision
		tries to be genuinely helpful and cooperative	verbal feedback by supervisors
		better able to understand consequences of their behavior than preconformist	role playing
			activities involving teamwork
		more sensitive to others	less structure than preconformist but supervisors viewed as expert/teacher
		likes to be a "team-player"	
		concerned with what others think about them; how they look to others (reputation, prestige oriented)	
		seeks acceptance and validation from others (supervisors, peers)	
		more open and less defensive to criticism	
		conforms to rules and procedures conscientiously	

Figure 7.1. Continued.

Corresponding Levels of Professional Development	Loevinger's Stages	Major Characteristics	Effective Supervisory Techniques/Methods
Self-Aware/Postconformist Level	Conscientious Stage Autonomous Stage	intellectually mature	shift towards greater consultation and collaboration
		understands others' perspectives accurately	provides opportunities for greater responsibility, creativity, and self-initiation
		developed empathic understanding of others	leadership training
		can more accurately evaluate self	peer supervision
		utilizes criticism for skill development	
		higher expectation of supervision as a growth producing experience	
		achievement-oriented with attention toward quality of work completed	
		places high regard on fairness in relationships	
		creative and self-initiating	

3. implement an effective supervisory method that is tailored to meet supervisee's specific developmental needs.

This first component consists of three distinct levels. They include:

Levels	Loevinger's Stages
1. Preconformist Level	Impulsive Stage Self Protective Stage
2. Conformist Level	Conformist Stage
3. Self-Aware Level/ Postconformist Level	Conscientious Stage Autonomous Stage

The field of supervision is clearly beginning to be influenced by gains in new knowledge in the area of adult development (Fowler, 1981; Gilligan, 1982; Kegan, 1982; Loevinger, 1976; Perry, 1970) and the charting of normal changes that normally occur during the adult life span (Cebik, 1985). The work of Gould (1972, 1978), Kegan (1982), and Levinson, Darrow, Klein, Levinson and McKee (1978) suggest that adult development occurs in a somewhat predictable set of stages. The nature of these developmental stages/levels is such that they represent qualitative transformations in the way a person thinks, feels, and acts towards life experiences (D'Andrea, 1984). As individuals move from one stage or level of development to the next they are better able to

1. express their own professional goals and expectations of supervision,

2. understand others more effectively,

3. interpret events (especially complex organizational and/or clinical events) more accurately,

4. synthesize their experiences more completely, and

5. respond to such experiences more competently (Bartunek, Gordon, & Weathersby, 1983).

In the PPM model of supervision are described three levels of professional development in which most supervisees can be identified. Utilization of this component as a guide in assessing supervisee's level of performance can be especially helpful to supervisors in at least two ways. First, it provides the supervisor with a clearer understanding of the supervisee as a person. Second, it provides a framework from which a supervisor can plan specific strategies that will systematically facilitate the supervisee's professional growth. What follows is a discussion of three levels of professional development in which most supervisees can be identified. Characteristics of each level are described as well as a discussion of specific supervision techniques and methods that best fit supervisees at each level.

Preconformist Level

The preconformist level represents an immature phase of adult development. As a result of the extensive training and selection process usually associated with clinical supervisees, supervisors working in a clinical setting will rarely encounter persons who are operating from this developmental level (Swensen, 1980). However, the likelihood is that administrative supervisors periodically will find themselves supervising individuals at the preconformist level. In either case, persons at this level of professional development are likely to present multiple problems in the work setting because of major limitations inherent in their psychological disposition, cognitive/intellectual capacities, and general repertoire of skills.

The preconformist level coincides with the impulsive and self-protective stages of Loevinger's (1976) developmental model. Persons at this level think very simply and concretely. Thus, the presentation of complex responsibilities, expectations, and goals in supervision are frequently beyond the preconformist level supervisee's comprehensive ability.

A person at the preconformist level is distinguishable from individuals at higher levels in that he/she often demonstrates much difficulty understanding a supervisor's directions and an organization's policies. Their ability to solve problems (Piaget, 1950) and interact with others in a sensitive, mature, and professional manner also is notably limited (Selman, 1974).

The preconformist's motivation to follow directions and go along with organizational rules is qualitatively different than a person at a higher level. Rather than following rules and policies because of fundamental reasonableness or rightness, the preconformist level worker is primarily motivated to go along with the rules when his/her compliance results in an immediate personal advantage. This reflects a kind of "what's in it for me" attitude that often becomes manifested in different ways during the process of supervision.

The lack of sophisticated cognitive/problem-solving abilities tremendously limits the preconformist level supervisee's capacity to understand the relative effectiveness and/or ineffectiveness of his/her actions. For example, supervisors will observe trainees at this level identifying something they do as being "bad" only if they are "caught" by someone in authority and directly experience some sort of negative outcome (i.e., disciplinary action/write-up, suspension). Interestingly the supervisee, who is at the preconformist level will frequently blame others for something going wrong rather than assessing his/her own contribution or responsibility for the occurrence of a specific problem.

Another outstanding characteristic of this level is the tendency to have a dominating and rather insensitive interpersonal style. This often leads others to view the preconformist as a "quick talker" because of his/her manipulative interpersonal style. While supervisees at this level are observed to distort situations in their verbal reporting, supervisors often note that those same supervisees lack a sense of guilt or shame in misleading and manipulating others.

A potential strength for persons functioning at this developmental level rests in a very competitive spirit that is manifested at work. Unfortunately, however, this competitive drive often inhibits the individual's interest and ability to work cooperatively as part of a team with others. As a result, the type of work ethic that is reflected by a person at the preconformist level is typified by the statement, "I'll only do what others do." Since preconformist persons generally view life in competitive terms, they often project a "It's a dog eat dog" attitude in the way they act and the things they might say during conversations in the process of supervision. This competitive orientation combined with a characteristically marginal level of impulse control frequently breeds understandable problems at the workplace. The following Case Study of David is provided to review a supervisor's assessment and method of working with a preconformist level client.

Case Study: David

David is a nineteen year old client employee who is at a large recreational resort. His job responsibilities involve running one of many concession stands where customers may purchase a variety of refreshments. David's counselor's attention has been called to problems David has been having with doing his job. Several of his co-workers complained that he was frequently late for work and took numerous unauthorized breaks during the work day. This often caused undo stress for those persons assigned to work with David. In addition, two customers reported incidents in which they felt that David was "rude" in his interactions with them.

These reports matched some of the counselor's own impressions. For example, the counselor noted that David acted impulsively during weekly group counseling sessions, frequently speaking out of turn and diverting the nature of the group discussion with inappropriate statements and gestures. When other clients tried to provide constructive criticism about his behavior, David would either laugh it off or aggressively respond by blaming someone else for the incident. In short, David was described as unreliable, uncooperative, and always prepared to give a reason for his ineffective performance. **This case was presented by David's counselor to his clinical supervisor for a case review.**

Based upon these observations, the supervisor helped the counselor to assess David as functioning at the preconformist level. As a result of this assessment, numerous alterations were immediately made. First, David's counselor met with David's job supervisor who indicated that David would be required to meet weekly for individual counseling sessions in addition to the group sessions. During the initial individual session, the counselor explained the "ground rules," being very direct in terms of the purpose and expectation of the weekly meetings. In addition, the counselor explained that David's work performance was not meeting agency expectations and unless he was able to make specific changes he probably would not be working there for a long period of time.

While the counselor was direct in his assessment, he also communicated a sense of genuine interest and support by telling David he wanted to work together in assisting him to learn new skills and ways of dealing with other people. At the conclusion of their initial session, the counselor set up a regularly scheduled 30 minute time period that the two of them would meet to discuss David's progress each week. The counselor also scheduled weekly sessions with supervisor.

Over the next three weeks, David and his counselor worked to identify specific behaviors that were considered to be ineffective. Similarly David's counselor met with his clinical supervisor. In the course of these discussions, the supervisor pointed out potential consequences of David's behavior (a dissatisfied customer, specific disciplinary action, etc.) as well as suggesting new ways of acting in different situations (skill development).

Both David and his counselor found that writing a contract during their second session together was helpful. The contract specified those behaviors most disruptive at the current time and listed respective alternative strategies that David agreed to implement. This contract was modified throughout the course of future counseling sessions and was used as a means of assessing David's progress with the counselor's supervisor.

While David did experience a few minor conflictual incidents with co-workers during the following two months, his overall work performance improved significantly. He was consistently punctual and did not take any work breaks except for those standard times established by company policy. He demonstrated more interest and appropriate participation during the group sessions which several other workers noticed and commented their appreciation.

Although much supervisory time and energy were invested in this particular individual, the results reflected a "win-win" situation for both the company and David. The company benefited from a more productive worker who was better able to conform to its policies and expectations. David gained new skills and competence in his adaptation to the work environment. David's counselor, through direct supervision, gained from the insights gleaned from the supervision sessions.

As a result of his experience David was better able to consistently demonstrate such basic employment competencies as being punctual, cooperative, and courteous to co-workers and customers. In many ways, the process of supervision could clearly be considered a growth-producing experience for David and his counselor.

From a practical point of view, unless the supervisee at the preconformist level matures psychologically and develops more effective communication and job-related skills, the prognosis for successful and satisfying employment experiences is poor. Supervisors working with supervisees at this level may want to review the following guidelines in an attempt to provide more effective supervision services in order to facilitate supervisees' development to a higher level of functioning.

Be Clear. Supervisors are encouraged to keep in mind that individuals at the preconformist level require clearly defined job assignments. Since their level of intellectual functioning is underdeveloped, they are unable to handle complex expectations. Clearly, supervisees at this level of development are inappropriate in a clinical setting. Consequently, assisting such persons to reassess career plans and goals might be an important though uncomfortable approach the supervisor may consider in clinical supervision with individuals at this level.

Provide Structure. The supervisor must provide guidance in establishing a well-structured set of job-related responsibilities. Consequences for not fulfilling these responsibilities must clearly be defined in order to establish a basic understanding of the positive and negative ramifications of the supervisee's actions.

Provide One-to-One Supervision. Since the preconformist level supervisee will often manipulate and disrupt group interactions, one-to-one supervision is strongly recommended. Supervisors will find a one-to-one approach to be less distracting and more effective in clarifying goals and reconfirming expectations.

Establish Meeting Times and Agenda for Each. Obviously, the preconformist supervisee will require a certain type of approach by the supervisor in order to be successful. Establishing regularly scheduled supervision sessions with a preestablished agenda may help to maximize the supervisor's efforts and minimize frustration that results in the process of supervising persons at this level.

Conformist Level

Supervisors, in either administrative or clinical settings, will often find many of their supervisees demonstrating characteristics that fall into the conformist level. Persons at this level seem to be "qualitatively" different than those at the preconformist level. For example, the supervisee at this level of development projects a pleasing social personality which underlies a general tendency to be helpful and cooperative. Contrary to the preconformist level, individuals at the conformist level possess the capacity to better understand the consequences of their actions both for themselves and others. Such persons are more sensitive to others and can participate as a team member much more effectively than workers at the preconformist level.

An important motivational factor for supervisees at the conformist level is rooted in a strong desire to gain acceptance and personal validation for their work efforts both by their supervisor and peers. They are genuinely concerned about what others (i.e., peers and supervisors) think of them. Therefore, they are much more receptive to act upon criticisms and recommendations made by a supervisor and co-workers in a more professionally diligent manner than preconformist level supervisees.

Persons at the conformist level place strong emphasis on following rules and procedures of the organization. This particular characteristic, however, can be both a blessing and a curse. Certainly, conformity to the operating procedures of a company provides both the supervisor and supervisee with a sense of predictability and confidence that the job will get done. Strict conformity, however, may sometimes immobilize the conformist level supervisee from greater professional effectiveness as a result of stifling her/his sensitivity and creativity to unexpected situations or events. An example of this sort of "developmental liability" is discussed later in the chapter in a case study involving individuals at multiple levels of professional development.

While financial reward is a prime motivational factor for preconformist level supervisees, the conformist level supervisee is a little different. Although money is an obvious motivating thread for workers at all levels of development, verbal feedback also represents a potent means of facilitating changes with supervisees at the conformist level. Most supervisors normally use this sort of feedback naturally with their supervisees by praising successful accomplishment of expectations and encouraging alterations of other less effective aspects of their work performance. However, the PPM approach to supervision suggests that unless supervisees are functioning at the conformist level or above, this technique, in itself, is relatively ineffective. Simply stated, not until an individual has matured to the conformist level is that person genuinely concerned about his/her work performance and reputation becoming strong motivational factors in one's professional development. These concerns in turn, stimulate the supervisee's receptivity to feedback and his/her willingness to make corrective changes as a result of the supervision process.

Use of group supervision techniques are particularly helpful with supervisees at the conformist level. Their professional development is often greatly enhanced by participating in cooperative ventures that emphasize teamwork. Access to peers dealing with similar supervisory issues and observation of other "role-models" (i.e., persons who are professionally somewhat more advanced in terms of their knowledge and skills) provide the conformist level supervisee with concrete "blueprints" for professional development in a supportive, non-threatening atmosphere. This latter point (i.e., the use of role models in group supervision) represents an innovative method known as "pacing" the supervisee (D'Andrea, 1984). In this instance, persons utilize stimulating and provocative experiences through their interactions with others to propel their own professional effectiveness by increasing their learning.

Self-Aware/Postconformist Level

Many supervisors in both administrative and/or clinical settings will readily recognize the personality profile of supervisees functioning at the self-aware/postconformist level. Persons at this level reflect much greater cognitive complexity both in the way they approach their work experiences and solve problems that arise in either an organization or clinical setting. This sort of cognitive complexity is the direct result of having matured intellectually and leads to an expansion in the supervisee's ability to perceive situations from different angles. As a result of acquiring this developmental characteristic, postconformist level supervisees are better equipped psychologically and behaviorally to

1. understand situations from different perspectives,

2. consider several approaches or solutions to a particular problem,

3. more accurately assess the consequences of the choices they make in given situations, and

4. more effectively evaluate the outcome of their actions.

This latter point is a particular strength of persons involved in the process of supervision. Supervisees at the postconformist level are much better able to make self-evaluated judgements of their work performance and accept constructive criticism from supervisors in a much less threatening manner than persons at either the preconformist or conformist levels (Cebik, 1985).

The uniquely different style about the self-aware/postconformist level supervisee is readily identified by the astute supervisor in other ways. For instance, supervisees at this level often tend to carry an agenda into the supervision experience that is more complex and advanced than those at the preconformist or conformist levels. This is commonly observed in supervisees' expressed concern over the quality of their performance within the organization or as a result of their interactions with clients. While supervisees at the two lower levels are primarily motivated by extrinsic factors (money, supervisor's feedback/evaluation, etc.), individuals at the postconformist level place greater emphasis upon achieving self-established standards. **In addition, supervisees at this level demonstrate an inclination to strive for an "ideal" performance which reflects a conscious sense of pride in their work.**

Personal gratification for the postconformist supervisee is frequently based upon the successful achievement of his/her goals as well as those established by the organization. This rather intense achievement drive is fortified by a sophisticated sense of personal obligation towards one's clients and/or the organization that is notably absent among supervisees at lower developmental levels. Consequently, the behavior of the self-aware/postconformist level supervisee is often guided by a driving force to "do no less than my best".

Unlike persons at the earlier stages, the postconformist persons are preoccupied with a sense of purpose in life that becomes reflected in their job performance. In general, they view themselves as fairly competent persons who are capable of making constructive contributions through their work. They accept the premise that they are capable of learning, growing, and developing in new ways and, therefore, are apt to approach the process of supervision in a more positive and less threatening manner than preconformist and/or conformist level supervisees.

The process of supervision is generally enhanced when it is taken to the self-aware/postconformist level because of the inherent value individuals place upon relationships. Supervisees at this level are particularly receptive to relationships that encourage mutuality and reciprocity. From this, the supervisor is well-advised to promote a climate in which the worker feels that his/her input is not only heard but valued, respected, and, at times, is a stimulus for the enhancement of the supervisor's own professional growth. The self-aware level person is also noticeably different from the supervisee at the preceding levels in that he/she demonstrates greater sensitivity and understanding of other persons' (i.e., supervisor's, clients', customer's) point of view as well as being more competent in communicating thoughts and feelings clearly with them.

Supervisors working with persons at this level will usually find them to be highly conscientious and dependable. The work ethic associated with persons at this level is considerably different than that manifested at the preconformist or conformist levels and may be characterized by statements such as "I'll try to do what's best for the client (or the setting)" and "I'll do whatever the job demands". As noted earlier, the self-aware supervisee is more concerned with "how well" (the quality) the work was done rather than focusing on "how much" (the quantity) work was done. Upon reviewing these characteristics, one easily can understand that supervisors would feel confident about allowing workers at this developmental level to assume greater amounts of responsibility over longer periods of time than they would with supervisees functioning at either the preconformist of conformist level (D'Andrea, 1987).

In addition to the recommendations previously mentioned, supervisors can implement additional techniques to enhance the effectiveness of the supervision process with the self-aware/postconformist level supervisee. Briefly stated they are

1. provide situations for the supervisee to initiate responsibility, creativity, and personal initiative;

2. create opportunities that permit greater achievement of self-directed goals; and

3. utilize collaborative efforts with the supervisee in reassessing goals and objectives throughout the process of supervision.

The following case study examines a supervisor's approach to a difficult supervision dilemma involving persons at both the conformist and self-aware/postconformist levels. As will be noted, this supervisor was working directly with an individual assessed at the conformist level (Ms. Bates). A majority of the nursing students with whom Ms. Bates interacted were seen to be functioning at or moving towards the self-aware/postconformist level of development. As a result, some interesting but not surprising conflicts emerged necessitating the involvement of a third party mediator. Below is a review of the case study, a discussion of the supervisor's plan of action and a brief report of the results of the process of supervision.

Case Study: Ms. Bates

Several nursing students at a large university training facility approached the head of their department concerning their supervisor, Ms. Bates. She was a registered nurse who had supervised nursing students for the past twenty-one years at the same university. The students all agreed Ms. Bates was usually helpful and cooperative but her strict adherence to the "rules and procedures" of the university were sometimes unrealistic and resented by students. Although they had approached her concerning this matter, she reacted defensively and stated that it was an inappropriate issue to be raised by the students. She concluded that there were "proper channels" students could use to voice their concerns specifically referring to the department head. The head of the department, in fact, was Ms. Bates' supervisor. Having supervised her for several years, she was aware of Ms. Bates' tendency to be somewhat rigid in terms of her strict adherence to rules and regulations. **While Ms. Bates may not have been the most popular nursing supervisor, the department head readily agreed** that she was clearly one of the most competent and reliable.

In her next supervision session, the department head raised the students' concerns and immediately met with defensive resistance from Ms. Bates. When explained that part of her responsibility was to understand reasonable explanations by students who did not exactly follow regulations, she responded by saying, "If I started accepting excuses from one student, they all would have excuses when they did something wrong. After all, that's what rules are for, to help things run smoothly and I think it's my job to enforce them."

In the course of the supervisory session, the department head turned to a discussion of Ms. Bates' reputation as a highly competent and respected nurse supervisor. From this discussion, Ms. Bates grew less resistant to her supervisor's feedback and acknowledged her willingness to learn ways of improving her overall effectiveness. They both agreed on reviewing new techniques that she might choose to implement in future situations with her students. Although reluctant at first, she became more open to role-playing realistic dilemmas with her supervisor as a means of thinking about various approaches to a variety of problems that might arise with the students.

The department head also provided follow-up services with the students by meeting with them weekly for three sessions. During these meetings, she briefly presented her assessment of the situation, reaffirming both the legitimacy of the students' concerns and Ms. Bates' perspective as their supervisor. Then she presented a developmental analysis of the problem, emphasizing the notion that people at different levels of development react and expect different things from a given experience. Interestingly, this developmental approach led many of the students to raise questions not only about their interactions with Ms. Bates but with other patients, doctors, and students as well.

The department head was particularly impressed with her interactions with the students. She noted that they were able to conceptualize the developmental framework and its implications for working with others in ways that even exceeded Ms. Bates' understanding. It was obvious that the students were genuinely concerned with the services they provided to their patients, the commitment they made to their work, and steps they were taking to improve their relationship with Ms. Bates.

As a result of these interactions, the department head concluded that one of the dynamics underlying the problem was a mismatch between a supervisor, who was at the conformist level, and her self-aware/postconformist level supervisees. This sort of "developmental mismatch" frequently occurs and undoubtably leads to a host of interpersonal conflicts in the process of supervision.

The department head later revealed that she didn't think Ms. Bates' made significant changes in her supervisory style with the students. However, she noted that Ms. Bates did show a tendency to be more patient and less rigid in her demand for strict adherence to regulations in a few situations where students' circumstances warranted reasonable consideration. Perhaps of greater significance, however, were the changes she noted in the students' attitude toward Ms. Bates. They appeared more tolerant of her supervision and accepting of her perspective. As one student remarked, "I think we understand her point of view better now and that seems to help us accept the situation."

Certainly not all of the problems raised by this situation were resolved as a result of this supervisory approach. Nonetheless, the students and Ms. Bates made it through the semester without further demise in their working relationship.

COMPONENT 2:
STAGES OF SUPERVISION

The second component of the PPM model focuses attention upon the supervision process and refers to three distinguishable stages that are marked by distinct characteristics and tasks. Much of the description of these stages comes from the work of Hess (1987) and parallels numerous features in the developmental schemata introduced by Erikson (1963). In Figure 7.2 are presented listings of stages of supervision and a description of major milestones associated with each stage.

Research in the fields of administrative and clinical supervision supports the notion of supervision stages (Carifio & Hess, 1987; Fleming, 1953; Hess, 1987; McElhose, 1973; Nelson, 1978) although some researchers differ in their conceptualizations of these stages. Through the work of Hart (1982), there emerges a synthesizing of several basic assumptions about the stages and the underlying process of supervision. These key assumptions are summarized as follows:

1. Both the supervisor and supervisee proceed through supervision as a unit with each person responsible for the stage of supervision attained and the rate of speed at which more advanced stages are reached.

2. Supervision is a dialectical process between the supervisor and supervisee in which each influences the other. As a result of this interactive process, both persons are subject to changes as the nature of the interaction proceeds.

3. An open discussion of the expectations and goals of supervision is of critical importance at the inception of the process.

4. After supervisees gain increased knowledge and confidence in their performance, their goals for supervision change. Therefore, an appropriate procedure is for the supervisor to facilitate a periodic reassessment of goals and objectives throughout the process of supervision.

Stages	Major Milestones
Inception Stage	establish a general sense of confidence and trust towards supervision and one's supervisor
	supervisee gets "rooted" into the work-setting
	adapts to a "student-teacher" relationship with one's supervisor
	begins to assess goals and expectations of supervision
Exploratory Stage	development of a broader base of professional skills and competencies
	acquisition of a professional sense of autonomy and self direction
	learning "new ways of operating" in terms of relating to others and resolving conflicts
Consolidation and Mutuality Stage	development of a more clearly defined professional identity
	learning a more sophisticated and effective leadership style
	utilize "facilitative conditions" to realize one's creative potential
	shift in supervisory relationship from "student-to-teacher" to "colleague-to-colleague" collaboration
	manifestation of "higher-order" competencies

Figure 7.2. Stages of supervision and major milestones.

5. In general, most supervisors believe that supervisees enter supervision in a dependent position and are capable of proceeding through a series of sometimes difficult but usually successful clinical and/or organizational experiences with the help of a supportive supervisor.

6. As supervisees advance, they become less defensive and more open to challenging supervisory techniques. However, frequently beginning supervisees resist feedback that is critical of their work especially if the feedback is incompatible with their own assessment of their performance on the job.

7. **A set of developmental tasks are specific to each stage of supervision. They represent essential objectives that supervisors should address so as to facilitate movement towards the next developmental stage. They include**

   a. climate-building

   b. goal identification, and

   c. evaluation of supervisee progress.

Inception Stage

The initial stage in the process of supervision is call the *inception stage.* The importance of this stage should not be minimized since first impressions created in the earliest supervisory meetings are often long-lasting. This stage is a relatively short phase encompassing as few as one or two sessions. However, it is an important period to review because of the type of anxieties, concerns, and needs commonly observed to emerge at this time.

One of the most important functions of the inception stage is to establish a relationship based on mutual trust between the supervisor and his/her supervisees. According to Erikson (1963), the development of a sense of trust is rooted in the "quality" of one's relationship with important others. At the inception stage, therefore, one of the supervisor's primary tasks is to communicate his/her belief that the process of supervision can be an exciting, challenging, and growth producing experience for the supervisee. This can be reinforced by expressing confidence in the trainee's ability to learn new skills as a result of actively participating in the process of supervision. Since supervisors are expected to set the tone of the process during the initial meeting, supervisees' sense of professional trust is **stimulated when their supervisor presents her/himself in a friendly, open, yet direct demeanor.**

Appropriate expectations associated with this supervision stage are similar to those described in Ard's (1973) preceptorship stage. Ard (1973) concluded that supervisees look for concrete information and guidance at this stage. The need to get "rooted" into the flow of the organization is immediately obvious. At this point, the administrative or clinical supervisor can be most helpful by providing a general orientation of the organization including clarification of policies as well as **encouraging initial discussion of specific professional goals and expectations.**

The supervisor may often find him/herself providing more didactic instruction during this phase of supervision. This is understandable and appropriate especially with supervisees who lack previous supervision experiences. In fact, inexperienced supervisees comfortably welcome the role of "pupil/ learner" (Gaoni & Neumann, 1974) as they try to put together

1. What is expected of them, and

2. What they expect from the supervision process (Yogen, 1982).

Delaney (1972) offered several general guidelines a supervisor may want to keep in mind in an effort to facilitate a positive and constructive supervisory relationship at this stage:

1. **Be sensitive to the supervisee's anxieties! A moderate level of supervisee uneasiness is normal at this stage of supervision. It is commonly associated with general feelings of insecurity and dependency that e-merge from being placed in an unfamiliar setting**

accompanied with new demands and expectations. However, in order to begin to transform their sense of dependency and anxiety into more constructive feelings of autonomy and confidence, supervisors are encouraged to provide clarity in their orientation and project a sense of professional support during the inception stage.

2. Clearly express basic parameters for supervision so as to create a sense of trust and confidence. Supervisors are cautioned, however, to discuss explicit organizational and/or clinical expectations without overwhelming supervisees with excessive amounts of information and directives.

3. Let the supervisee know what he/she can reasonably expect from you. Discuss the specific times and frequency of supervision sessions. If you use individual and/or group supervision techniques, discuss some of the differences in these approaches with the supervisee during the inception stage.

4. Provide opportunity for the supervisee to ask questions and get clarification of any points that may be unclear.

5. Be sure to come to an agreement on the time and place where the next supervision meeting will occur.

Exploratory Stage

Following the inception stage, a distinctly different phase emerges in the process of supervision accompanied by its own unique developmental characteristics and tasks. A noticeably more complex period occurs as the types of challenges placed upon both the supervisor and supervisees increase and change. **One of the most commonly observed tasks associated with the exploratory stage involves the supervisee's desire to develop a sense of autonomy and self-direction in his/her work.**

At this supervisory stage, supervisees really begin to dig into the work at hand. It is a time when delivery of specific organizational services and/or clinical techniques are assessed and discussed. During the exploratory stage, supervisees normally demonstrate a sense of self-direction that is shaped by their clinical experiences and organizational responsibilities. In Erikson's (1963) analysis of the development of autonomy and self-direction, he stressed that an individual is greatly influenced by the type of supervision, guidance, and support one receives from others as he/she attempts to master new skills that meet the demands of his/her environment.

While supervisees are driven to demonstrate their competencies as a result of acquiring new skills at this stage, they normally experience a heightened sense of insecurity that is rooted in what Hogan (1964) called a "dependency-autonomy" conflict. This conflict is based in the supervisees' desire to gain more freedom to "show their stuff" in meeting challenges of their work while alternately feeling anxious about their own ability to succeed. As a result, heightened feelings of anxiety and uncertainty with supervisees at the exploratory stage is often observed. In order to assist them with their professional development during this extended supervision phase, supervisors are encouraged to

1. continue to be supportive and sensitive to the supervisee's changing needs as the process of supervision unfolds;

2. give well-defined, concrete examples of alternative ways of working when corrective assistance is warranted;

3. address their ambivalence (the dependency-autonomy conflict) when appropriate; and

4. discuss and clarify specific goals and expectations for supervision.

Supervisors need to keep in mind, however, that preconformist, conformist and self-aware/postconformist level supervisees are likely to react differently to the various tasks associated with the exploratory stage. For example, postconformist level supervisees demonstrate a greater sense of obligation and responsibility in the way they act in an organization and/or with their clients than supervisees at either the conformist or preconformist levels. Simple responsibilities such as adapting to an appropriate dress code, maintaining accurate record keeping, and communicating in a professional manner are all skills postconformist level supervisees are quick to learn. In contrast, preconformist level supervisees frequently reveal deficiencies in their interactive style with other employees, their ability to accurately complete organizational forms, maintain records, and even in the way they physically present themselves (appearance, dress code) within the work setting.

Acknowledging that the primary task of the exploratory stage is to facilitate new ways of operating (skill development) in order to assist supervisees to become more autonomous, confident, and effective professionals requires supervisors to carefully consider matching specific supervision techniques with supervisees at different levels of development (Cebik, 1985). This fundamental guideline is of particular importance as supervisors are expected to assist supervisees learn new skills tailored to meet the specific tasks of the organization and/or the counseling process during the exploratory stage.

The key to learning a new skill, however, rests with an individual's desire or motivational level. Clearly, an unpredictable and boring environment is not conducive for optimal learning for most people. All people, however, are not motivated by the same learning conditions. The challenge for supervisors at the exploratory stage is to assess the particular supervisory techniques that "best" motivate superviees to learn new professional skills that promote greater professional confidence and autonomy.

The supervisee at the self-aware level, may be less motivated and perhaps even frustrated by supervisors who maintain a highly structured, instructional supervisory approach during the exploratory stage. Greater skill development is likely to result when self-aware level supervisees are incorporated more fully in the process of supervision as the supervisor consciously seeks to engage them through collaborative and consultative techniques. While postconformist level supervisees tend to work well in team or group supervision settings, they frequently demonstrate a preference to have opportunities available in which they can independently demonstrate their own initiative and talents. Consequently, supervisors are encouraged to provide less structure and greater leeway for supervisees at this exploratory stage.

Conformist level supervisees, on the other hand, will predictably experience heightened anxiety as a result of the ambiguity created if supervisors reduce the structure of supervision too quickly. This heightened anxiety may hinder the conformist level supervisee's motivation for supervision and lessen his/her capacity for learning new skills. Therefore, a more gradual reduction of the initial structure of supervision is an important consideration in assisting this type of supervisee to develop new skills, confidence, and autonomy as a professional.

The conformist level supervisee is notably more receptive to group supervision that is conducted in a supportive manner. Team-building, role-playing, and conflict resolution techniques are helpful supervisory approaches that generally result in promoting the motivation and acquisition of skills among conformist level supervisees during the exploratory stage.

In contrast, preconformist level supervisees often tend to demonstrate greater motivation to learn concrete organizational skills during the exploratory stage when supervisors maintain a highly structured atmosphere. Consistent clarification of explicitly stated goals and expectations supported by a clearly defined evaluation component are key factors for effective **supervision with persons at the preconformist level. Supervisors often will find themselves reiterating these techniques for preconformist level supervisees throughout the process of supervision.**

A major theme running throughout the developmental model reviewed in this chapter is that supervision is a highly complex process which varies from supervisee to supervisee depending on his/her developmental level. Most will move from the inception stage to the exploratory stage without tremendous difficulty. The tasks, goals, and expectations become more complex and challenging, however, for both the supervisee and supervisor during the exploratory stage.

Three fundamental criteria are associated with exploratory stage which determine the degree of success accomplished during this phase of supervision. A helpful procedure is to translate these criteria into specific evaluative questions which administrative and/or clinical supervisors can implement in assessing the impact of supervision up to this point. Some of these questions are as follows:

1. How well has the supervisee adapted to the organization/clinical setting in terms of promoting the overall policies and mission of the agency, institution, or school?

2. **Has the process of supervision facilitated the learning of new skills and knowledge that has enhanced the overall effectiveness of the supervisee to meet organizational/ clinical challenges in a constructive manner?**

    a. Specifically, what are the new skills manifested by supervisees as a result of the learning process?

    b. In what ways has the utilization of these skills promoted productive outcome within the organization and/or the process of counseling clients?

3. Has the supervisee developed greater self-awareness as a result of gaining personal insights throughout the process of supervision?

    a. What are some of these insights?

    b. How have these insights affected the supervisee in terms of his/her work performance or counseling style?

    c. How have these insights affected the supervisee in other more general ways?

Many preconformist and conformist level supervisees remain at the exploratory stage even to the end of the formal supervisory relationship. However, supervisors will often observe many conformist and self-aware level supervisees moving to a third stage of supervision. This phase is referred to as the consolidation and mutuality stage.

Consolidation and Mutuality Stage

At this stage, supervisors notice that the "hierarchical distance" (Hogan, 1964) in the supervisor-supervisee relationship is safely reduced to the point where they more frequently act as "consultants" and "collaborators" with their supervisees. Supervisees at this stage have demonstrated their competencies as a result of learning numerous skills during the exploratory stage. This sort of professional development is usually accompanied by increasing confidence and trust between supervisors and supervisees as well as within supervisees themselves. From this maturational process emerges a new set of developmental tasks uniquely connected with the consolidation and mutuality stage.

One of the major tasks associated with this stage involves the consolidation of a well-verbalized and integrated sense of one's professional identity. An individual's sense of "identity" is a potent guiding force that, when developed to a higher level of awareness, promotes greater personal competence in life (Erikson, 1963). Since one's "professional life" encompasses a significant portion of a person's daily experience, the suggestion is that a positively integrated identity leads to a further enhancement of the supervisee's overall organizational and/or clinical performance.

During the first two stages of supervision, supervisees are appropriately preoccupied with becoming oriented and adaptive to the diverse demands of their organizational/clinical settings. At the third stage of supervision, a stronger drive to integrate a maturing professional identity is commonly observed. Certainly, identity formation is an on-going process in which we are constantly more or less aware. However, at the consolidation and mutuality stage supervisees are developmentally "receptive" and "ready" for a new set of supervisory experiences specifically designed to help them synthesize and consolidate their learning in a more professionally meaningful manner.

Supervisors can facilitate entry to this stage in a number of ways. First, the supervisor may gradually initiate a different behavior pattern in the supervisory relationship. Supervisors may find it helpful to shift their supervisory style from an instructional (teacher-student) mode of operating to a more interdependent, collaborative, colleague-colleague relationship. This sort of shift in the process of supervision provides the type of "facilitative condition" (Littrell, Lee-Borden, & Lorenz, 1979) that better fits the needs of the developing supervisee at the third stage of supervision.

Besides enhancing skill development during the exploratory stage, the assumption is that supervisors are equally concerned about modeling a high level of empathy, regard, genuiness, and concreteness in their interactions with supervisees. Research shows that when supervisors provide these conditions in supervision, they tend to stimulate the realization of supervisees' own potential for empathy, regard, genuiness, and concreteness (Maslow, 1968; Pierce & Schauble, 1970, 1971a, 1971b). Thus, a supervision process that simultaneously stimulates supervisees' skill development, empathy, regard, genuiness, and concreteness lays the bedrock for their own conscious formation of a positive professional identity during the consolidation and mutuality stage.

Kolb and Pry (1975) and Wethersby (1980) detailed other ways in which supervisors can promote specific "facilitative conditions" that assist supervisees to consolidate their professional identity and gain a greater sense of mutuality with their supervisors. When implemented in the process of supervision, these techniques and guidelines ultimately create a more complex learning environment for both supervisors and supervisees. These "facilitative" techniques and guidelines are as follows:

1. Supervisors may initiate more complex analyses of specific situations supported by frequent referral to personal experiences and self-disclosure during supervisory sessions.

2. Supervisors can encourage supervisees to take advantage of unique organizational and/or clinical opportunities that compliment an observed drive for self-initiated action during the third stage of supervision.

3. Successful passage through the consolidation and mutuality stage challenges supervisors to be particularly sensitive to nurturing an interpersonal climate that allows for greater interdependence, risk-taking, and supervisee self-disclosure.

4. The unique tasks associated with this stage require supervisors to provide time for supervisees to verbally reflect upon the meaning of their organizational and/or clinical contributions in either individual or group supervision settings. These personal and professional de-briefing sessions naturally encourage a more highly individualized analysis of various events supervisees have experienced.

By consciously promoting these conditions in the process of supervision, supervisors create a pace-setting venue that encourages the development of abstract, higher-order competencies. Theorists have noted that these "higher-order competencies" become manifested by an increase in supervisees'

1. ethical reasoning regarding various professional dilemmas;

2. capacity for introspection, complex self-awareness, and self-criticism;

3. ability to understand interpersonal dynamics more accurately and thoroughly; and

4. greater comprehension of the impact of their work within an organization, and upon their clients' lives (Bartunek, Gordon, & Weathersby, 1983).

At the consolidation and mutuality stage, supervisors are pressed to assist supervisees in developing greater appreciation of their own unique leadership and creative potential. Clearly, many of today's supervisees will ultimately be tomorrow's leaders in mental health agencies, institutions of education, and industry. Thus, this supervisory stage provides a valuable opportunity to assist supervisees to constructively consolidate their experiences into a more conscious and effective leadership style.

Effective leadership training goes hand in hand with an unleashing of the supervisee's creative potential. While some supervisors might argue whether the development of supervisees' creativity is an important dimension of supervision, the Person-Process Model considers it to be a hallmark of ultimate supervisory success. Further, the suggestion is that a lack of interest in this developmental task may be more a reflection of a supervisor's own resistance to creative action in organizational and/or clinical settings rather than an unimportant dimension of the total supervisory experience itself.

Arieti (1976) pointed out that creativity is one of the major channels by which a person learns to realize his/her human potential and become more fully functioning in one's personal and professional endeavors. Enhancing supervisee creativity does not simply mean allowing a person to exercise his/her originality in an unlimited manner. Creative action obviously imposes restrictions. Consequently, supervisors are encouraged to support supervisees' creative potential during the third stage of supervision by assisting them to find ways to introduce innovative strategies in a manner that other people will understand, accept, and appreciate.

Promoting supervisees' creativity during the consolidation and mutuality stage does not imply that supervisors would or should totally abandon supervisory techniques which are directive and critical of the supervisee's professional performance. On the contrary, researchers assert that supervisors who balance facilitative conditions with feedback that is direct and critical receive high effectiveness ratings by their supervisees (Blumberg & Amidon, 1965; Blumberg, 1968). For persons involved in clinical supervision, they should note that clients tend to report greater therapeutic gains with supervisees trained by super-visors combining a facilitative and critical approach in the process of supervision (Oratio, 1977).

The increasing sense of professional mutuality that emerges between supervisors and supervisees during the third stage of supervision is accompanied by new supervisory options and challenges. For example at this stage, supervisors may consider introducing a peer supervision component into the process. By offering supervisees the opportunity to function as peer supervisors with other less experienced supervisees concretizes the supervisor's respect and confidence in the supervisee. It also extends a unique experience for supervisees to further develop their own leadership capacities and creativity by accepting more challenging administrative and/or clinical responsibilities.

TERMINATION

While readily understood that a formal termination of the supervision relationship is inevitable, effective developmental supervision often results in an on-going bond between many supervisees and their supervisors. This phenomenon is achieved as a result of the special nature of the supervisory relationship in which supervisors and supervisees strive to successfully accomplish the various tasks associated with the three stages of the process.

Rather than viewing a termination phase marking an end to a unique interpersonal relationship, the Person-Process Model suggests that the connection developed through supervision may continue into the future at a higher level of collegial collaboration. This phenomenon has been discussed by D'Andrea and Reynolds (1987) who observed the emergence of numerous "informal networks" constituted by former supervisors and supervisees. These networks are commonly sustained long after the formal supervisory relationship has ended. A dual purpose is frequently served through these on-going connections as valued input is exchanged and emphatic support for one's work is available when needed. Therefore, instead of turning to a discussion of the termination of supervision, the PPM model of supervision encourages supervisors and supervisees to extend the benefits of supervision by periodically drawing upon the best attributes of each other in order to expand their professional/personal horizons long after the formal supervisory relationship ends.

CONCLUSION

In conclusion, the Person-Process Model of Supervision has been presented to stimulate a new way of thinking about the process and the person in supervision. Hopefully, it will be used as a set of blueprints for facilitating a greater understanding of the supervision process as well as building a more effective atmosphere that assists supervisees and supervisors to become more successful in their professional and personal endeavors.

REFERENCES

Ard, B.N. (1973). Providing clinical supervision for marriage counselors: A model for supervisor and supervisee. *The Family Coordinator, 22,* 1973, 91-97.

Arieti, S. (1976). *Creativity: The magic synthesis.* New York: Basic Books.

Bartunek, J.M., Gordon, J.R., & Weathersby, R.P. (1983). Developing "complicated" understanding in administrators. *Academy of Management Review, 8*(2), 277-284.

Blumberg, A. (1968). Supervisory behavior and interpersonal relations. *Educational Administration Quarterly, 4,* 34-45.

Blumberg, A., & Amidon, E. (1965). Teacher perceptions of supervisor-teacher interaction. *Administrator's Notebook, 14,* 1-8.

Carifio, M.S., & Hess, A.K. (1987). Who is the ideal supervisor? *Professional Psychology: Research and Practice, 18*(3), 244-250.

Cebik, R.J. (1985). Ego development theory and its implications for supervision. *Counselor Education and Supervision, 24*(3), 173-281.

Corey, G., Corey, M.S., & Callanan, P. (1988). *Issues and ethics in the helping professions.* Pacific Grove, CA: Brooks/Cole.

D'Andrea, M. (1984). The counselor as pacer: A model for the revitalization of the counseling profession. *Counseling and Human Development, 16*(6), 1-15.

D'Andrea, M. (1987). Managing teenagers: A guide for supervisors. Unpublished manuscript from the Institute for Human Development. Nashville, TN.

D'Andrea, M., & Reynolds, M. (1987). Notes on the developmental approach to supervision. Unpublished paper. The Institute for Human Development. Nashville, TN.

Delaney, D.J. (1972). A behavioral model for the practicum supervision of counselor candidates. *Counselor Education and Supervision, 12,* 46-50.

Erickson, V.L. (1977). Beyond Cinderella: Ego maturity and attitudes toward the rights and roles of women. *The Counseling Psychologist, 7*(1), 83-88.

Erikson, E.H. (1963). *Childhood and society* (2nd ed.). New York: W. W. Norton.

Fleming, J. (1953). The role of supervision in psychiatric training. *Bulletin of the Menninger Clinic, 17,* 157-169.

Fowler, J. (1981). *Stages of faith: The psychology of human development and the quest for meaning.* New York: Harper and Row.

Gaoni, B., & Newmann, M. (1974). Supervision from the point of view of the supervisee. *American Journal of Psychotherapy, 23,* 108-114.

Gilligan, C. (1982). *In a different voice: Psychological theory and women's development.* Cambridge, MA: Harvard University Press.

Gould, R. (1972). The phases of adult life: A study in developmental psychology. *The American Journal of Psychiatry, 129*(5), 33-43.

Gould, R. (1978). *Transformations.* New York: Simon and Schuster.

Hart, G.M. (1982). *The process of clinical supervision.* Baltimore, MD: University Park Press.

Hess, A.K. (1987). Psychotherapy supervision: Stages of supervisee and supervisor development. *Professional psychology. Research and Practice, 18*(3), 251-255.

Hogan, R.A. (1964). Issues and approaches in supervision. *Psychotherapy: Theory, Research and Practice, 1,* 139-141.

Holloway, E.L. (1987). Developmental models of supervision: Is it development? *Professional Psychology: Research and Practice, 18*(3), 209-216.

Kegan, R. (1982). *The evolving self: Problem and process in human development.* Cambridge, MA: Harvard University Press.

Kohlberg, L., & Turiel, E. (1971). Moral development and moral education. In G.S. Lesser (Ed.), *Psychology and educational practice.* Chicago, IL: Scott, Foresman.

Kolb, D.A., & Pry, R. (1975). Towards an applied theory of experiential learning. In C. Cooper (Ed.), *Theories of group processes* (pp. 33-58). New York: John Wiley.

Kurpius, D.J., & Baker, R.D. (1977). The supervisory process: Analysis and synthesis. In D.J. Kurpius, R.D. Baker, & I.D. Thomas (Eds.). *Supervision of applied training: A comparative review.* Westport, CT: Greenwood Press.

Levinson, D., Darrow, D., Klein, E., Levinson, M., & McKee, B. (1978). *The season's of a man's life.* New York: Ballantine Books.

Littrell, J.M.. Lee-Borden, N., & Lorenz, J. (1979). A developmental framework for counseling supervision. *Counselor Education and Supervision, 19,* 129-136.

Loevinger, J. (1976). *Ego development: Conceptions and theories.* San Francisco, CA: Jossey-Bass.

Magana, H., Whiteley, J.M., & Nelson, K.H. (1980). Sequencing of experiences in psychological interventions: Relationships among locus of control, moral reasoning and ego development. In V.L. Erickson & J.M. Whiteley (Eds.), *Developmental counseling and teaching.* Monterey, CA: Brooks/Cole.

Maslow, A. (1968). *Toward a psychology of being.* New York: Van Nostrand.

McElhose, R.T., (1973). *Supervisor—supervisee complimentarity and relational distance as related to supervisor experience level.* Unpublished doctoral dissertation, Michigan State University.

Nelson, G. (1978). Psychotherapy supervision from the trainee's point of view: A survey of preferences. *Professional Psychology, 9,* 539-550.

Oratio, A.R. (1977). *Supervision in speech pathology: A handbook for supervisors and clinicians.* Baltimore, MD: University Park Press.

Perry, W.G., Jr. (1970). *Forms of intellectual and ethical development in the college years.* New York: Holt, Rinehart and Winston.

Piaget, J. (1950). *The psychology of intelligence.* London: Routledge & Kegan.

Pierce, R.M., & Schauble, P.G. (1970). Graduate training of facilitative counselors: The effects of individual supervision. *Journal of Counseling Psychology, 17,* 210-215.

Pierce, R.M. & Schauble, P.G. (1971a). Follow-up study of the effects of individual supervision in graduate school training. *Journal of Counseling Psychology, 18,* 186-187 (a).

Pierce, R.M., & Schauble, P.G. (1971b). Toward the development of facilitative counselors: The effects of practicum instruction and individual supervision. *Counselor Education and Supervision, 11,* 83-89.

Selman, R.L. (1974). Toward a structural developmental analysis of interpersonal relationship concepts: Research with normal and disturbed preadolescent boys. In A. Pick (Ed.), *X annual Minnesota symposium on child psychology.* Minneapolis: University of Minnesota Press.

Sprinthall, N.A., & Collins, W.A. (1984). *Adolescent psychology: A developmental approach.* New York: Random House.

Swensen, C.H. (1980). Ego development and a general model for counseling and psychotherapy. *Personnel and Guidance Journal, 58,* 382-388.

The Stone Center (1987). Work in progress: For developmental services and studies at Wellesley college. Symposium conducted at Wellesley College, Wellesley, MA.

Wethersby, R.P. (1980). Ego development. In A.W. Chickering & Associates (Eds.), *The modern American college* (pp. 51-75). San Francisco: CA: Josey-Bass.

Worthington, E.L. Jr. (1987). Changes in supervision as counselors and supervisors gain experience: A review. *Professional Psychology: Research and Practice, 18*(3), 189-208.

Yogen, S. (1982). An eclectic model of supervision for beginning psychotherapy students. *Professional Psychology, 13*, 236-243.

PART III
APPROACHES,
PREPARATIONS, and
PRACTICES

CHAPTER 8

DIFFERENTIAL SUPERVISION: ROLES, FUNCTIONS, AND ACTIVITIES

Ruth C. Meredith, Ed.D.

Loretta Bradley, Ph.D.

In this chapter are described roles supervisors assume, functions they effect, and activities they assign as they assist supervisees who are working toward professional and personal goals. The term "differential supervision" refers to the efforts by the supervisor to match supervisor role, function, and activity tasks to the developmental level of the supervisees. The beginning part of the chapter provides a brief description of supervisor roles and functions, and the levels of developmental supervision. The remainder of the chapter is devoted to activities appropriate to the developmental level of the supervisee. Case illustrations and assessment scales have been added to clarify concepts. Unless specifically stated, differential supervision activities apply to both the clinical supervision of counselors employed in social service and/or mental health agencies.

SUPERVISORY ROLES AND FUNCTIONS

Supervision is a fundamental component of training programs for psychologists, counselors, and social workers, as well as a monitoring process (Kadushin, 1985) for professionals new to the field (Ellis & Dell, 1986; Reising & Daniels, 1983). New professionals and those in preparation need feedback regarding their performance. Close monitoring protects client welfare and indicates supervisee growth. Supervisors, in attempting to meet the variable needs of their supervisees, have approached the supervisory task from a variety of roles. Boyd (1978) described the supervisor from the perspective of a trainer/instructor, counselor, consultant, and evaluator. Hess (1980) defined multiple roles of psychotherapy supervision as those of a lecturer to convey global schemes, techniques, and generate enthusiasm; a teacher of specified content and skills; a case reviewer to explore ways of thinking and relating to cases; a monitor to ensure at least minimal levels of acceptable service; a therapist to nurture growth; and collegial peer to give support and provide a different view.

Evidence of the supervisor's role and function has been shown in several studies (Ellis & Dell, 1986; Stenack & Dye, 1982). Based on Bernard's (1979) model of supervision. Stenack and Dye used counseling faculty and doctoral students to rate a series of supervisory behaviors as appropriate to either teacher, counselor, or consultant roles. The results indicated that both counseling faculty and doctoral students made a rather clear distinction between teacher and counselor role behaviors, but the consultant role behaviors overlapped the other two roles. In Figure 8.1 are shown the focus, intention, specific activities, and central issues associated with the supervisor roles of teacher, counselor, or consultant.

Ellis and Dell (1986) also explored Bernard's (1979) model of supervision. In this study, supervisors and supervisees rated nine supervisory tasks based on a matrix of supervisor role of

(Continued on p. 305)

ROLE 1: TEACHER

A. Focus of the interaction is on the supervisee as a counselor.

B. Intention or goal of the supervisor is to instruct.

C. Specific activities in the teacher role include
    1. evaluate observed counseling session interactions;
    2. identify appropriate interventions;
    3. teach, demonstrate, and/or model intervention techniques;
    4. explain the rationale behind specific strategies and/or interventions; and
    5. interpret significant events in the counseling session.

D. In order to describe the appropriate style or method of delivery for the teacher role, the concept of overt control of the interaction can best be utilized. In most supervision sessions, especially in situations where a close supervision relationship has not yet been established, overt control of the interaction rests with supervisor. In the case of the teacher role, the supervisor also retains overt control of the interaction. The teacher-supervisor remains in charge, determines the direction of interaction, and functions as advisor/expert.

ROLE 2: COUNSELOR

A. Focus of the interaction is on the supervisee as a person.

B. Intention or goal of the supervisor is to facilitate supervisee self-growth as a counselor.

C. Specific activities involved in the counselor role include
    1. explore supervisee feelings during the counseling and/or supervision session,
    2. explore supervisee feelings concerning specific techniques and/or interventions,

Figure 8.1. Description of three supervisor roles.

Figure 8.1. Continued.

---

   3. facilitate supervisee self-exploration of confidences and/or worries in the counseling session,
   4. help the supervisee define personal competencies and areas for growth, and
   5. provide opportunities for supervisees to process their own affect and/or defenses.

D. The counselor-supervisor functions in much the same capacity as a counselor with a client. The same counseling skills are involved. The major difference between a counselor-supervisor and a counselor is that the goal of the supervision process is related to supervisee functioning as a counselor. The supervisee does not become a client. Within the limitations of counseling specific situations, however, the counselor-supervisor does utilize many of the counseling behaviors.

ROLE 3: CONSULTANT

A. Focus of the interaction is on the client of the supervisee.

B. Intention or goal of the supervisor is to generate data.

C. Specific activities involved in the consultant role include

   1. provide alternative interventions and/or conceptualizations for supervisee use;
   2. encourage supervisee brainstorming of strategies and/or interventions;
   3. encourage supervisee discussion of client problems, motivations, etc.;
   4. solicit and attempt to satisfy supervisee needs during the supervision session; and
   5. allow the supervisee to structure the supervision session.

D. The appropriate style or method of delivery for the consultant role can best be described by referring to the concept of overt control of the interaction introduced in

Figure 8.1. Continued.

Role 2. In the consultant role, the supervisor allows the supervisee to exert overt control of the interaction. The consultant-supervisor provides alternatives and options instead of answers as in the teacher role. The consultant-supervisor also encourages supervisee choice and responsibility.

Note: From "Behavioral descriptions of counseling supervision roles" by R.J. Stenack and H.A. Dye, 1982, *Counselor Education and Supervision, 21,* p. 302. Copyright 1982 by *Counselor Education and Supervision.* Reprinted by permission.

teacher, counselor, and consultant according to three supervisor functions of process, conceptualization, and personalization. In Figure 8.2 is provided a definition for each of the nine tasks.

Supervisees participating in the study were asked to rate the nine tasks as similar vs. dissimilar. Supervisors were asked to describe the roles, using a set of bi-polar attributes (examples: cognitive, emotional, supportive, behavioral) to indicate their criteria in making role comparisons. Study results showed that the process and conceptualization functions were perceived as anchoring opposite ends of the behavioral attribute, and the consultant role was contrasted to the combined roles of teacher/counselor. The personalization function and the teacher role were contrasted, with the former being strongly supported by the emotional attribute, and the latter strongly supported by the cognitive attribute.

The Ellis and Dell (1986) study offers empirical evidence in support of Bernard's (1979) model and the conclusions by Stenack and Dye (1982). Both studies point to an awareness of the structure of supervision by those who teach supervision and those who are "in the field." Apparently instructors, students, supervisors and supervisees perceive distinct roles that the supervisor may assume. Further, the supervisor's role choice must be selected in order to elicit specific behaviors from the supervisee.

Stimulus	Definition
Teacher-process	Demonstrates or describes specific interpersonal, treatment, or intervention techniques and skills
Counselor-process	Helps supervisees determine what hinders or facilitates their executing interventions with a specific client; focuses on reducing inhibitions, encouraging experimentation within counseling sessions, or both
Consultant-process	Works with supervisor to explore different uses of an intervention and jointly practices them; focuses on mutual learning of interventions and skills
Teacher-conceptualization	Demonstrates or describes one or more ways to classify, organize, and understand client's behavior, thoughts, and problems
Counselor-conceptualization	Helps supervisees understand how their stereotypes, conceptualizations, and unresolved issues affect the counseling session and provides alternative perspectives
Consultant-conceptualization	Works with supervisees to mutually explore issues and implications of theories, models and alternative conceptualization to counseling.
Teacher-personalization	Demonstrates or describes the potential importance of supervisee's affect and ways of recognizing and using one's own affect during counseling
Counselor-personalization	Helps supervisee work through personal issues or feelings associated with counseling sessions

Figure 8.2. Nine supervisor roles: Stimuli and Definitions

Figure 8.2. Continued.

Stimulus	Definition
Consultant-personalization	Works with supervisee to explore mutually personal concerns relevant to counseling

Note: From "Dimensionality of supervisors' roles: Supervisors' perceptions of supervision" by M.V. Ellis and D.M. Dell, 1986, *Journal of Counseling Psychology, 33*, p. 284. Copyright 1986 by *Journal of Counseling Psychology*. Reprinted by permission .

As supervisors become aware of the rich and varied repertoire of supervisor roles and functions, they look for ways to effect a "best possible fit" of supervisory behavior to supervisee need. One of the most profitable means of accomplishing this purpose is to identify the level of professional development of the supervisee. "Developmental Supervision" is the process of evolving stages of supervisee growth. For a more complete explanation of developmental supervision, the reader is referred to Chapter 7 in this book. This chapter will focus on recent research efforts which validate the process and stress an understanding of the supervisee's developmental level as the key ingredient in influencing the supervisor's choice of role or function.

RESEARCH SUPPORTING
DEVELOPMENTAL SUPERVISION

In developmental supervision, the term "developmental" implies a dynamic process that occurs over time in which supervisees acquire professional and personal behaviors and cognitions that necessitate new reactions to, new goals for, and new expectations of supervisors (Hart, 1982). A number of studies provide empirical evidence of developmental models of supervision (Cross & Brown, 1983; Friedlander & Snyder, 1983; McNeill, Stoltenberg, & Pierce, 1985; Rabinowitz, Heppner, &

Roehlke, 1986; Wiley & Ray, 1986). Reising and Daniels (1983) concluded that counselor training, as a developmental process arising from changing trainee characteristics and needs, has been historically and extensively addressed by Eckstein and Wallerstein (1972), Hogan (1964), and Mueller and Kell (1972). Hogan's (1964) four-level model depicted trainees as struggling from the status of anxious novice toward that of autonomous peer. **Level 1** characteristics showed the supervisee as dependent on the supervisor for support and the profession as a model. Supervisees were highly motivated to apply what had been taught, but remained insecure regarding their abilities and uninsightful about the effect their personal behavior had on client or supervisor. At **Level 2,** the supervisee's growing self-awareness created dependency/autonomy struggles with the supervisor and fluctuating motivation toward the profession. **Level 3** supervisees were "masters of the trade," possessing increased self-confidence, stable motivation and commitment to the profession. **Level 4** supervisees had evolved to a "seasoned artist," a therapist with personal autonomy adequate to independent practice. Hogan (1964) stated that supervision needs to be appropriate to the developmental level of the supervisee and proposed more advanced supervisory methods evolving as the supervisee progressed.

Related research efforts have shown support for the developmental model of supervision that accounts for changes over time in supervisee perceptions and complimentary supervisor activities (Grater, 1985; Hart, 1982; Loganbill, Hardy, & Delworth, 1982; Stoltenberg, 1981; Stoltenberg & Delworth, 1987). In Figure 8.3 is illustrated Stoltenberg's (1981) counselor-complexity model, with four discrete levels of supervisee development, and the supervision environment which supports that development.

A structure for developmental supervision has been substantiated in empirical studies (Cross & Brown, 1983; Friedlander & Snyder, 1983; McNeill, Stoltenberg, & Pierce, 1985; Reising & Daniels, 1983; Wiley & Ray, 1986). Practicum supervisees preferred supervisors high in task orientation, as opposed to intern supervisees who ranked as high factors such traits as attractive and interpersonally sensitive (Friedlander & Snyder, 1983). The time, structure, and method of supervision

Counselor Level	Counselor Characteristics	Optimal Environments
1	Dependent on supervisor: Imitative, neurosis bound, lacking in self-awareness, categorical thinking with knowledge of theories and skills, but minimal experience	Encourage autonomy within normative structure. Supervisor uses instruction, support, awareness training, and exemplification; structure is needed
2	Dependency-autonomy conflict; increasing self-awareness; fluctuating motivation, striving for independence, becoming more self-assertive and less imitative	Highly autonomous with low normative structure. Supervisor uses support, ambivalence clarification, exemplification, with less instruction; less structure is necessary
3	Conditional dependency: Personal counselor identity is developing with increased insight, more consistent motivation, increased empathy and more differentiated interpersonal orientation	Autonomous with structure provided by the counselor. Supervisor treats counselor as a peer, with more sharing, mutual exemplification and confrontation
4	Master Counselor: Adequate self and other awareness, insightful of own strengths and weaknesses, willfully interdependent with others, and has integrated standards of the profession with personal counselor identity	Counselor can function adequately in most environments. Supervision now becomes collegial, if continued

Note: From "Approaching supervision from a developmental perspective: The counselor-complexity model" by C. Stoltenberg, 1981. *Journal of Counseling Psychology, 28,* p. 60. Copyright 1981 by *Journal of Counseling Psychology.* Reprinted by permission.

Figure 8.3. Expected characteristics and appropriate environments.

was rated highly by inexperienced supervisees, while experienced supervisees gave higher rankings to support and rapport (Cross & Brown, 1983). Supervisors tended to match their activities to the level of supervisee development (Wiley & Ray, 1986), and higher experience supervisees reported greater self-awareness, autonomy, acquisition of counseling skills, and theory understanding than did supervisees at lower experience levels (McNeill, Stoltenberg, & Pierce, 1985). Reising and Daniels (1983) suggested a complex rather than simple stage developmental model of supervision. Their study used 141 premasters, masters, interns, and Ph.D. level students who responded to two sets of questions, one regarding supervisee growth, and the other involved supervisee preferences for supervision. Study results supported Hogan's (1964) model for counselor development, but not necessarily the supervisory recommendations. For beginning counselors-in-training, factors of anxiety, dependence, and skills focus were highly rated. As the supervisees grew toward professionalism, independence and self-confidence were ranked higher. However, except for skills training and respectful confrontation, supervisory preferences were seen as desirable at all levels of supervisory development. The authors suggested that a simple stage model was inadequate to describe the complex interplay of counselor need, growth, and supervisory interventions. "Counselor development appears to be a complex rather than simple process" (Reising & Daniels, 1983, p. 239).

Emerging from the research exploration is a strong support for a complex model of developmental supervision, marked by definitive stages which evolve through supervisor-supervisee interactive responses to stage demands. The inexperienced, anxious supervisee struggling with the counselor role gives way to the accomplished counselor grappling with the strengths and limits of professionalism. The accompanying supervisory behaviors ranged from didactic to consultatory, with supervisors at various times assuming roles of teacher, model, counselor, and peer.

While the process of developmental supervision may be affected by situation, personality, or interactional variables (Holloway & Wampold, 1983; Ward, Friedlander, Schoen, & Klein, 1985; Worthington & Stern, 1985) the process provides a good indicator of supervisory behavior. With knowledge of the supervisee's experience and training, the supervisor may differentiate supervisory activities.

DIFFERENTIAL SUPERVISION ACTIVITIES

Differential supervision proposes stage related supervisory activities that directly support supervisee needs at the beginning, intermediate, and advanced levels of supervision. The levels are basically equivalent to students in pre-practicum or beginning practicum (beginning level), late-practicum or advanced practicum (intermediate level), or internship/Ph.D. student (advanced). The extent and intensity of the supervisor's role and function at each level is dependent upon the supervisee's ability to assume responsibility for and accomplish tasks associated with each stage. Beginning level issues are assessment, goal setting, direct teaching, modeling and demonstrating support, and encouragement in establishing a good relationship. Intermediate level supervision issues deal with supervisor-supervisee conflict, and the development of the supervisee's personal counseling style. Advanced level supervision supports the supervisee's developing commitment to the profession.

BEGINNING LEVEL SUPERVISION

The beginning level supervisee approaches supervision with anxiety undergirded with a high motivation to succeed (Hill, Charles, & Reed, 1981; Miars, Tracey, Ray, Cornfield, O'Farrell, & Gelso, 1983). Part of the anxiety stems from the realization that the supervisee must now "produce." The supervisee is forced by the demands of supervision toward internal and external growth (Sansbury, 1982). Externally, he or she must develop good counseling skills and a general approach for structuring client interviews which will lead toward accomplishment of the client's goals. Concurrently, the demands of internal goals, such as developing a feeling that one really "is" a counselor, or learning to use the legitimate authority of the supervisor, further increases the supervisee's apprehension. As with any person faced with a new situation which threatens esteem and confidence, the supervisee responds with dependence upon the supervisor (tell me how), doing what is known (relying on theory), asking for example (show me how), and reliance on structure (there must be a way) (Borders & Leddick, 1987). The following case study illustrates the supervisee dilemma.

Case Study: Mary Jane

The original incident occurred in a beginning supervision class, where the supervisor had invited class members to verbalize some of their feelings about taping client sessions. One supervisee's practicum placement made taping difficult, and her frustration heightened as she described how the refusal of her "best" clients to permit taping made it impossible for her to be evaluated fairly. She was asked if she would agree to tape a discussion between her and the supervisor concerning the "unfairness" and taping fear issues. She consented, and the last part of the tape appears as follows. Comments to this point concerned the nature of her clients, difficulties in securing permission to tape, the poor technical quality of the tapes she did turn in, and her own "rigid" performance on them.

Note—SR is used for Supervisor and SE for Supervisee

SR: *So what would happen? What's the worst thing that could happen about the tapes? . . . (no response) . . . What is the thing that is absolutely "the end?"*

SE: *Just that it would be embarrassing.*

SR: *To whom?*

SE: *. . . to . . . to be..to think I have come this far, and made the grades that I have gotten, done the things that I have done in the counseling (program) requirements, and then not be able to demonstrate them on tape. . .have an instructor hear how clumsy. . .I got to thinking "maybe I have chosen the wrong field if I can't even handle this."*

SR: *You said "gotten the grades I have gotten" . . . What grades have you gotten?*

SE: *All "A's" except one "B" in a requirement and one "B" in an elective.*

SR: *So you really have been a top student.*

SE: *Yes. I like to do my best.*

SR: *So now you have "got to be" a top counselor.*

SE: *No. I just like to think I can do it. It's just that I turn into this different person. I start **thinking** what's right and wrong. I am more conscious of myself as well as watching my client's nervousness.*

SR: *When does the client show a lot of nervousness?*

SE: *In the hesitancy and verbal process that I have to go through to even get the tape on. I have to go through a form and that still doesn't satisfy them (relates story of refused permission by a client who became uneasy over consent forms and procedures).*

SR: *So that gets the "hyper" up. Is there any way you can reconstruct this process to prevent this?*

SE: *I wonder. I am open to suggestion. I have done something different each time I have approached someone. So far, three were successful and three weren't. I got the tape recorder on three times. I've tried a different approach. . to be more relaxed. . each time.*

SR: *So you have a success rate of 50%.*

SE: *Yes, but they were crummy! I'm embarrassed to turn them in.*

SR: *What makes them crummy?*

SE: *The sound on two. I am really afraid you will not hear them. . .you know. . .the recording.*

SR: *OK, so we have a problem with numbers. Half said yes and half said no. And we have a problem with technique, using the tape recorder. And then we have a problem using counseling skills. I would like to go to that if it's ok with you. I get the feeling that you think you should demonstrate right now everything you think you have learned. . .my question is "how much practice have you had in counseling?"*

SE: *As far as using skills I have learned. . .as far as thinking of them as specific skills, like reflecting, uh. . .none. . .up until now. . .in terms of specific skills, I think the reason I chose counseling is because they **were** there in some form. Maybe I don't say "this, this, or this," but people do seek me out, you know. . .I just felt helpful, and could make them feel a little bit better about themselves. . .so now is the time I **am** looking at techniques. . ."this, this, and this."*

SR: *Do you think that skills and techniques will verify this quality you have that makes people seek you out?*

SE: *I am not sure what you are asking.*

SR: *I'm not sure either. I'm feeling for something, and I get the feeling that you think that because you can demonstrate responding, probing, any kind of counseling lead, that that justifies your ability which brought you into the profession.*

SE: *Let me see. I feel like now I will be looked at, through you, to see if I am demonstrating these skills. I am conscientious, you know it's on my mind a lot, getting them in there, making sure I am doing it right. Is that what you are asking?*

SR: *Sort of. What I'm getting at is what do you do when your client comes in, sits down in front of you, and this person is really hurting. . .*

SE: *Well. . .this happened yesterday. I. . .uh. . .said. . . what's the problem?. . .what's going on?. . .She just rocked. . . she was crying. . .she kept stopping. . .long pauses. . .and then I didn't. . .I wasn't. . .you know. . .it just kept coming* **naturally. It wasn't like I was thinking "pause, you're supposed to wait!"**

SR: *Uh-huh. Yeah.*

SE: *And when the tape's on, I am thinking those things in my mind. That's the difference. With that client, it just came naturally. I paused naturally. I gave her time. When she started, I wouldn't interrupt, I would let her come on out with it, and when I felt like she needed encouragement, I gave her encouragement. I probed; I did all those things* **without thinking.**

SR: *Does that ever happen to you on tape?*

SE: *I don't know, I hope so.*

SR: *You say you have never practiced counseling before?*

SE: *No, just role-playing in classes, what everybody else does. Looking at the terminology and reflecting back on it. I probably have thousands of times, whenever you talk to people, share with them, give feedback on some things, but as far as counseling, no, I haven't.*

SR: *If you gave yourself a mark on a scale of one to ten as a counselor right now, where would you put yourself?*

SE: *. . .(long pause). . .that's hard. . .to rate yourself . . .five.*

SR: *Five. OK. And given this semester's 14 weeks left for practicing, how much growth do you expect to show?*

SE: *I would hope. . .I would hope to reach an 8 or 9 (begins to laugh as supervisor jokes "maybe a 10?"). I don't think anybody can be perfect. . . but I would hope to grow that much.*

SR: *What do you think your instructor would want you to show, the one who is going to listen to all these tapes?*

SE: *That's what I don't know. . .I don't know what the instructor really expects. . .I know by this, this and this being done, but what she is looking for I am not sure.*

SR: *Do you think the instructor might want to see growth, progress? Do you expect to be an 8, 9, or 10 when you finish 14 weeks of practicum?*

SE: *I would like to be.*

SR: *Think about your expectations. Are you setting impossibly high expectations for yourself?*

SE: *I may want to get it done in a semester when it takes years and years of experience to select skills wisely. I am putting it in a small time frame when it may take years.*

This exchange points to the need for a more careful preparation for supervision by both parties. Had the supervisee been more familiar with the counseling process and related skills, she would not have judged herself so harshly, nor would she have been so ignorant of her basically sound counseling approach. The supervisor could have alleviated anxiety even more so by clarifying the exact parameters of "counselor growth." Beginning level supervision calls for such specificity.

The following paragraphs describe in detail these specific activities which establish a sound structure for beginning level supervision: (1) Pre-assessment, (2) setting up the initial supervisory session, (3) goal setting, and (4) skills training and interventions.

Pre-Assessment: The Supervisor

Prior to beginning supervision, the supervisor should anticipate the task by considering the modality of supervision, emphasis within supervision, range of focus, style of supervision, type of role to take with the supervisee, handling of formal evaluations, and accommodating to one's own personal and professional limitations as supervisor (Styczynski, 1980). The supervisor can facilitate preparation for the supervisor's role by reviewing previous supervisory training and experiences, along with a candid assessment of supervision-related knowledge and skills (Borders & Leddick, 1987). A resume format, listing the supervisor's experiences in the teacher, counselor, consultant role (Boyd, 1978), would enable the supervisor to formulate the parameters of his or her approach. In Figure 8.4 is shown an example of such a format. Additionally, the supervisor's self-assessment of supervision-related knowledge and skills, as detailed in Figure 8.5, provides a means of identifying strengths upon which to capitalize, and weaknesses to overcome. Knowledge gained from the resume and self-assessment will enable the supervisor to establish a profile of probable supervisory style, in which the preferred role, supervisee type, counseling orientation, intervention strategies, and expectations for supervision will become evident (Borders & Leddick, 1987, p. 6).

Prior to the first supervision meeting, the supervisor should use both formal and informal measures to assess the supervisee's counseling skills (Borders & Leddick, 1987). Supervisor and supervisee may evaluate audiotaped counseling sessions previously conducted by the supervisee; or the supervisor may wish to observe the supervisee in an actual counseling session with a client. Feedback on the supervisee's counseling skills can be provided by use of observational instruments completed by both supervisor and supervisee. The *Interview Record Form*, shown in Figure 8.6 is a supervisee self-report of his or her perceptions of the counseling session. Use of this interview form will enable the supervisor to discern the supervisee's ability to determine counseling skills and to conceptualize client problems. The supervisee's self-report can be compared to the supervisor's evaluation of the same counseling session. Figure 8.7, the *Interview Feedback Sheet*, may be used by the supervisor to show how he or she rated basic counseling skills demonstrated by the supervisee. A less subjective means of assessment can be provided through use of the *Inventory of Counseling Behaviors* (ICB), (Dustin, Engen, & Shymansky,

(Continued on p. 325)

Supervision-Related Skills and Knowledge

Name _____ Date _____

Teacher

Date

Position, setting, students
Descriptive statement of knowledge and skills

Counselor

Date

Position, setting, clients
Descriptive statement of knowledge and skills

Consultant

Date

**Position, setting, clients
Descriptive statement of knowledge and skills**

Researcher

Date

Descriptive statement of knowledge and skills

Supervisor

Date

Position, setting, supervisees
Descriptive statement of knowledge and skills

Supervisee

Date   Setting   Supervisor

Mode of supervision

Individual and/or Group

Interventions (e.g., audiotapes, IPR, casenotes)

Supervisor's counseling orientation

Supervisor's supervision style, including relationship/interpersonal

---

Note: From *Handbook of Counseling Supervision* (p. 8) by L.D. Borders and G.R. Leddick, 1987. Alexandria, Virginia: American Association of Counseling and Development. Copyright 1987 by The American Association of Counseling and Development. Reprinted by permission.

Figure 8.4. Resume format for a self-assessment of knowledge and skills developed in previous supervision-related roles and experiences.

Teaching Skills	Needs Development			Expertise	
Ability to identify learning needs of supervisee	1	2	3	4	5
Ability to identify learning style of supervisee	1	2	3	4	5
Ability to write learning goals and objectives	1	2	3	4	5
Ability to devise instructional strategies to accommodate needs and learning style of supervisee	1	2	3	4	5
Ability to present material in a didactic manner	1	2	3	4	5
Ability to present material in an experiential manner (e.g., demonstrate, model)	1	2	3	4	5
Ability to explain the rationale for an intervention	1	2	3	4	5
Ability to evaluate supervisee's learning	1	2	3	4	5
Comfort in authority role	1	2	3	4	5
Ability to give constructive feedback to supervisee	1	2	3	4	5
Other _____	1	2	3	4	5
Counseling Skills					
Ability to establish rapport, a working relationship with supervisee	1	2	3	4	5
Facilitative skills (e.g., warmth, primary empathy, genuineness, concreteness, etc.)	1	2	3	4	5

Figure 8.5. Assessment of supervision-related knowledge and skills

Figure 8.5. Continued.

Counseling Skills (Con't)	Needs Development			Expertise	
Challenging skills (e.g., self-disclosure, advanced empathy, confrontation, immediacy, etc.)	1	2	3	4	5
Ability to facilitate supervisee self-exploration of strengths, limitations, and concerns about counseling skills	1	2	3	4	5
Ability to help supervisee explore feelings about client, purposes of counseling, counseling interventions	1	2	3	4	5
Ability to help supervisee explore feelings about supervision	1	2	3	4	5
Ability to conduct intake sessions	1	2	3	4	5
Ability to conduct closure sessions	1	2	3	4	5
Ability to make referrals	1	2	3	4	5
Knowledge of interpersonal dynamics	1	2	3	4	5
Knowledge of counseling theories	1	2	3	4	5
Expertise in counseling techniques (specify) _____	1	2	3	4	5
Expertise with particular clients and issues (e.g., suicide, career)	1	2	3	4	5
Ability to identify themes, patterns of behavior	1	2	3	4	5
Ability to model counseling skills	1	2	3	4	5
Ability to respond with flexibility	1	2	3	4	5
Ability to integrate data about supervisee into comprehensive "case conceptualization"	1	2	3	4	5
Other _____	1	2	3	4	5

Figure 8.5. Continued.

Consultation Skills	Needs Development			Expertise	
Ability to objectively assess problem situation	1	2	3	4	5
Ability to provide alternative interventions and/or conceptualizations of problem/client	1	2	3	4	5
Ability to facilitate supervisee brainstorming of alternatives, options, solutions	1	2	3	4	5
Ability to encourage supervisee to make own choice, take responsibility for decisions concerning client and counseling	1	2	3	4	5

Note: From *Handbook of Counselor Supervision* (p. 9) by L.D. Borders and G.R. Leddick, 1987. Alexandria, Virginia: American Association of Counseling and Development. Copyright 1987 by the American Association of Counseling and Development. Reprinted by permission.

Confidential

Identifying Data

Supervisee Name _____   Interview Number ___

Client Name _____   Time _____

Date _____

    I.   **Goals for Session:**

   II.   **Course of Interview** [Include (A) Brief notes on what transpired behaviorally, what client and counselor said, how client acted; (B) Interpretations of content of session, what counselor thought was going on and how this effects progress]:

       A.

       B.

  III.   **Counselor's Reaction to Session:**

  IV.   **Plans for Ensuing Sessions** (homework, long and short term goals):

   V.   **What Counselor Would Have Done Differently:**

Figure 8.6. Interview Record Form.

Supervisee's Name	Date of Observation

Client's Name

Supervisory Evaluation   ( ) Meets Minimum Competency Skill Levels

( ) Does Not Meet Minimum Competency Skill Levels

On the activities listed below use the following Rating Scale:

Rating Scale

1	2	3	4	5

| Poor | | Acceptable | | Excellent |

Note: The above scale is to be applied to the following statements. A rating below **3** does not meet minimum standards.

_____   1. Supervisee greets client in friendly, warm manner and opens the session with appropriate amount of structure.

_____   2. Supervisee encourages client to tell his/her story by being accepting, interested, and allowing client to set own pace and determine initial directions.

_____   3. Supervisee timing appropriate in that he/she does not rush client, allows for silences, etc.

_____   4. Supervisee employs open-ended responses as means of encouraging client to talk.

Figure 8.7. Interview Feedback Sheet.

Figure 8.7. Continued.

_____ 5. Supervisee tracks client statements accurately— does not lead or lag behind.

_____ 6. Supervisee responses accurately reflect both the content and the affect of the client's message.

_____ 7. Supervisee allows client to lead by feeding back and clarifying client messages rather than sending his/her own messages.

_____ 8. Supervisee uses responses effectively in controlling the direction of the counseling session.

_____ 9. Supervisee communicates warmth, caring and regard through voice, tone, etc.

_____ 10. Supervisee closes the session appropriately.

Comments:

Supervisor _____ Date _____

1982). The ICB is used to record counts of specifically described counseling skills and facilitative behaviors observed during stated time intervals. Figure 8.8 shows a list of behaviors recorded in the ICB; a more complete description of the ICB behaviors appears in Figure 8.9. Use of the ICB can help supervisees obtain a more objective view of their counseling behavior. Additionally, a comparison of the supervisee's objective and subjective reports on counseling skills and client problems, (*Interview Record Form*, Figure 8.6), along with the supervisor's *Interview Feedback Sheet* (Figure 8.7) can facilitate understanding of the difference between how the supervisee talks about his or her actions and how the supervisee really behaves with his or her clients (Worthington & Roehlke, 1979). Assessing the supervisee's counseling skill level will lead to the establishment of counseling goals for the supervisee , and the use of observation and feedback forms will aid in goal attainment evaluation. Additional measures of assessment for supervisors and supervisees can be found in Borders and Leddick (1987), Boyd (1978), Hart (1982) and Stoltenberg and Delworth (1987).

Initial Supervisory Session

The first session between supervisor and supervisee is singularly important in that it establishes the parameters of supervision and sets the tone for the working relationship. How the supervisor can achieve the difficult task of building rapport and establishing a supportive relationship within the context of the teacher-evaluator has been examined by researchers (Worthington, 1984; Worthington & Roehlke, 1979) looking at supervisees' perceptions of good supervision. Beginning supervisees rated supervision better when "new counseling behaviors were taught directly within a supportive relationship," when the supervisor "blends direct teaching with good relationship enhancement skills," and when they enact relationships that are "somewhat structured and informative, but are also pleasant and personal" (Worthington & Roehlke, 1979, p. 71).

Accordingly, the goals of the initial supervisory session are to establish clear expectations about the structure of supervision and the nature of the supervisory relationship.

(Continued on p. 330)

Code	Title	
A	Approval/Praise	Positive evaluation, "Good"
C	Silence	No one talking during interval
D	Disapproval	Negative evaluation
E	Encourager	Non-evaluative, non-sentences, "hm-hm"
F	Accurate Feeling	Reflection of client that is acknowledged
G	Inaccurate Feeling	Inaccurate or corrected by client
H	Self-disclosure	Information about counselor, "I" statement
I	Interpretation	Counselor opinion about client
J	Topic Jumping	New topic by counselor
L	Listen	Client talking in interval
O	Perception Check	Question about feelings
P	Paraphrase	Repeats client question.
Q	Question	Any definite question
R	Interrupt	Cuts off client
S	Summary	Rephrase of earlier client statement
T	Propose Action	Tells client to do one thing
U	Unclassifiable	Unable to fit into any category
V	Should	Should or ought statement
W	Propose Client Alternatives	Tell client to carry out more than one activity
X	Explanation	Giving factual information
/	Slash	Interruption of interview

Note: From "The ICB: A Tool for counselor supervision" by R.E. Dustin, H.B. Engen, and J.A. Shymansky, 1982. *Counselor Education and Supervision.* Reprinted by permission.

Figure 8.8. Inventory of counselor behaviors (ICB): list of behaviors recorded.

The Inventory of Counselor Behaviors (ICB):
Code, Title, Definition, and Examples

E. Richard Dustin
James A. Shymansky
Harold B. Engen

Code	Title	Definition and Examples
Q	Question	Any definite question. **Must** have a question word (e.g., what, who, when, where, have you . . ., are you . . ., do you . . .) "How are you doing in physics?"
E	Encourager	Simple acceptance, non-evaluative, non-sentences. "Who," "huh, huh," "hm." Must be followed by client response.
C	Silence	No one talking during interval.
L	Listen	Counselor quiet while client talks.
A	Approval/Praise	Positive evaluation of client and/or action. "Good." "That was a nice thing to do." Does not include an "I" statement
U	Unclassifiable	Rater unable to fit item into any other category of classification. Examples: mumble; both persons talking at the same time; incomplete response.
/	Slash	Used to indicate when counselor is out of office, on phone, or any break in the tape. Must hear something.

Figure 8.9. The inventory of counselor behaviors (ICB): code, titles, definition, and examples.

Figure 8.9. Continued.

Code	Title	Definition and Examples
W	Propose Client Alternative	Suggests or directly tells client to do **more than one** thing. Counselor gives client more than one choice. "You can stay in school or you can drop out."
V	Shoulds	Any should or ought statement "You should marry the brother." ("V" overrides "T" if "should" is included.)
R	Interrupts	Cuts off or breaks into client's statement. "I want to . . ." (counselor) "I'm sure you can handle that yourself." (A subtle and difficult rating.)
J	Topic Jump	Moves toward new topic without reference to client's content. (**Not** a question; **Not** self-disclosure) "I'm really mad at my Lit. teacher." (Counselor "I want to talk about your ACT score.")
P	Paraphrase	Repeats/rephrases immediately what the client has said; **No** feeling involved. "I haven't been to math all week." (counselor) "You cut math."
S	Summary	Rephrasing/repeating and/or clarifying what was said **earlier.** "Earlier today you said . . ." "Last time we met you said you wanted help making a study schedule. I suggested a couple. You were to choose one."
I	Interpretation	Identifies patterns, meanings, causes, and/or results of client's behavior. Is the opinion of the counselor. "You got drunk, I think, because you knew it would make your wife mad."

Figure 8.9. Continued.

Code	Title	Definition and Examples
F	Accurate Feeling Restatement	Restatement or reiteration of client's feelings. **Must** be accurate and acknowledged by client. "Even though you love him, you still get mad at him and this confuses you." (client) "Yes, that's it." or "Yes, somewhat."
G	Inaccurate Feeling	Same as "F" except inaccurate or **not** acknowledged, or if the client "corrects" the counselor.
O	Perception Check	Question about feelings. "Are you mad?" "How are you feeling?" "Does that confuse you?"
H	Self-disclosure	Information about counselor (self), past or present. Opinions or feelings of counselor using an "I" statement. "I really get upset when clients don't keep appointments." "When I was in school, I had similar problems."

Pertinent factors related to the structure of supervision are the frequency and length of supervisory meetings, structure of the meetings, number and type of clients in supervisee's caseload, client presentations made (i.e., audio or video tapes, observations) group supervision requirements, and field site requirements. The supervisory relationship focuses on the establishment of the supervisee's counseling goals, means of formal and informal evaluation, and legal and ethical issues involving client confidentiality and problems inherent in the supervisor's contradictory roles of counselor-evaluator to the supervisee. Figure 8.10, *Checklist for the Initial Supervision Session,* contains a list of topics important to the initial supervision session.

The establishment of a supportive relationship is an equally important goal of the initial supervisory session (Hart, 1982; Hess, 1980; Stoltenberg & Delworth, 1987) but one that would not likely be completely accomplished during the first supervisory session. Rather, a supportive supervisor-supervisee relationship unfolds throughout the length of supervision and is reinforced by positively perceived supervisor behavior. Supervisees reportedly value supervisors who call them by name, use humor in the supervisory session, allow observations, share counseling experiences, help the supervisee develop strengths and a personal counseling style, and lead the supervisee to realize that developing new skills is an awkward process (Worthington & Roehlke, 1979).

Goal Setting

In preparing for goal setting, the supervisor may find that the novice supervisee lacks knowledge of basic principles for setting attainable goals (Martin, Hiebert, & Marx, 1981), such as (1) identifying a specific observable goal, (2) knowledge of action steps necessary to reach a goal, and (3) ways to recognize goal attainment. Additionally, the goals for supervision may be viewed differently. The supervisor's goal-setting agenda may be oriented toward the supervisee gaining independence, while the supervisee may be content to focus on skill development.

Successful goal-setting is an interactive process in which both parties focus on selecting and defining goals (Cormier &

Checklist for the Initial Supervision Session

I. Introducing Supervisor and Supervisee

    A. Supervisee describes personal counseling background

        1. Types of counseling experiences

        2. Settings of experiences

        3. Influences of experiences on present counseling orientation

        4. Reasons for interest in becoming a counselor

        5. Motivation for present training in counseling

    B. Supervisor's reciprocal description of background

        1. Relates to experience of supervisee

        2. Demonstrates qualifications for being in supervisory role

II. Presentation of specific requirements and meeting times

    A. Time required on site

    B. Taping requirements

        1. Releases required

        2. Number of tapes required

        3. Tape reviews to be throughout the semester (evenly spaced)

        4. Variety of tapes (different clients, different phases)

        5. Tape write-up to accompany each tape (format presented)

    C. Evaluation

        1. Acknowledgement of supervisee's fears concerning evaluation

Figure 8.10. Checklist for the initial supervision session.

Figure 8.10. Continued.

    2. Presentation of possible evaluation criteria and methods

    3. Supervisee's feedback on evaluation criteria and methods

    4. Agreement on type of evaluation to be used

    5. Definition of relationship between on-site supervisor and intermediate or regional supervisor

    6. Policy for dealing with perceived inter-supervisor disagreement

  D. Site visits

    1. To be done with supervisee

    2. For gaining further understanding of site structure

    3. Meeting with on-site supervisor

III. Describing anticipated structure and process of supervision sessions

  A. Teaching mode in beginning, moving toward consultation

  B. Review tapes and/or explore process issues of site

  C. Supervisee to explore issues concerning personal development

  D. Make plans for possible group supervision

  E. Resource materials from supervisor may be requested or assigned

  F. Exploration of supervisee's expectations of supervision

  G. Planning for next supervision session

    1. Time scheduling

    2. Arrangements for getting tape and write-up to supervisor before next session

  H. Discuss ethical/professional concerns

Cormier, 1985). In selecting skill and personal growth goals for beginning level supervision, the supervisor and supervisee can successfully identify mutual goals through (1) discussing positive expectations of supervision, (2) selecting several skill development and personal growth areas to develop as goals, (3) describing ways in which the supervisee will change in working toward these goals, (4) establishing the level to which the change is to occur, (5) identifying the sequence of intermediate action steps, and (7) reviewing progress (Cormier & Cormier, 1985, p. 220). An example of this type of goal setting is presented in Figure 8.11, *Supervisee Goals.* This sequence was used to promote skill development and personal growth goals of the supervisee who was the subject of the Case Study of Mary Jane presented earlier in this chapter.

The supervisor must remember that the supervisee may need to break down even intermediate steps into their component parts in order to facilitate his or her understanding of the required behavior necessary to achieve the goal. In Figure 8.12, *Effective Goal Setting,* is illustrated this point, showing Hackney's (1976) goal-setting exercise (quoted in Borders & Leddick, 1987). Information pertaining to Figures 8.11 and 8.12 appeared in descriptive form in its original context. In this instance, tables have been used for further clarification.

After a thorough discussion of goals which will occur over several sessions, early in supervision, the supervisor and supervisee can establish mutual goals relating to the supervisee's understanding of the structure of supervision, demonstration of counseling skills, application of a personal counseling theoretical approach, and evaluation of the counseling profession. A pattern for monitoring goals should be set early in supervision, with an awareness by both supervisor and supervisee that new goals will be selected to replace those accomplished.

Skills Training and Interventions

The manner in which the supervisor "delivers" supervision in the area of skills training with appropriate interventions is a function of supervisee learning goals, style, and experience level in interaction with the learning goals and the theoretical

Goals

Skill Goal: To utilize basic counseling skills while counseling clients

Personal Growth Goal: to increase knowledge of emotionally ill persons

Criteria for Supervisee Change

Skills are used naturally and appropriately as observed in critique of audio/video taped counseling sessions

Feeling comfortable around emotionally ill persons is demonstrated in the calm, caring and forthright manner in which supervisee speaks to them

Level of Change

All basic skills taught in practicum will be appropriately used by supervisee in counseling client

Supervisee will learn definition, causes, prognosis of emotional illnesses associated with her clients; impact on individual and family

Intermediate Steps

Read about, observe, role-play skills; obtain feedback from peers and supervisor; use skill with client, get feedback from supervisor

Read articles, attend professional meetings, organizations or self-help group meetings on emotional illness; interview family members, recovered persons

Obstances to Progress

Time, fear of failure

Time

Resources

Supervisor, peer feedback, client responses, commitment

Field supervisor, community organizations, commitment

Progress Review

Weekly throughout training, successful counseling with client

After each intermediate step, check supervisee's awareness of expansiveness and limitations in working with emotionally ill client

Figure 8.11. Supervisee goals.

Goal	Focus on affect: Respond to affective content of client statement.
Action Step:	Each time I hear an emotion word in client's statement, I will respond with a statement that reflects that feeling.
Evidence:	Upon analysis of audio or video tape, I will have responded to 80% of the emotion words stated by the client.

Note: Based on Hackney's (1976) goal setting exercise as quoted in Borders and Leddick (1987).

Figure 8.12. Effective goal setting.

orientation of the supervisor. Historically, the content of supervision has been tied to counseling theory (Bartlett, 1983; Holloway & Hosford, 1983) with supervisors conceptualizing supervision in terms of their counseling orientation. Supervision approaches and techniques evolved from therapeutic techniques described in psychoanalytic (Eckstein & Wallerstein, 1972; Mueller & Kell, 1972), client-centered (Patterson, 1983), rational-emotive (Wessler & Ellis, 1983), behavioral (Linehan, 1980), and social learning (Hosford & Barmann, 1983) counseling theories. In consideration of the developmental level of the supervisee, who at the beginning stage of supervision has been described as dependent, imitative, a categorical thinker lacking insight (Borders & Leddick, 1987), supervisors may find didactic skills training and task-oriented interventions most helpful with supervisees.

The following paragraphs describe how specific interventions of self-reports, micro-training, modeling and role-playing, live observations, live supervision, interpersonal process recall (Kagan, 1975, 1980), and anxiety management may be used by the supervisor at the beginning level of supervision.

Self-reports call for the supervisee to analyze his or her counseling behavior, usually by describing the counselor/client interaction that occurred during audio or video taped counseling sessions with the client. The supervisee may give a verbal report or use a form similar to the one shown in Figure 8.6, *Interview Record Form*. In preparing the report, the supervisee should focus on (1) how the counseling session began and ended; (2) counseling skills appropriate to the beginning, middle, or end of the session; (3) significant responses and interventions related to client issues; (4) sections portraying counselor confusion or client resistance, and (5) discrepancies between verbal and non-verbal behavior of counselor or client. The self-report is useful in determining the supervisee's conceptualization abilities, but its effectiveness is limited by the supervisee's natural tendency to present strengths and ignore weaknesses.

Microtraining describes the specific one-at-a-time teaching of separate, identifiable beginning or advanced counseling skills (Forsyth & Ivey, 1980; Ivey, 1971, 1980; Ivey & Authier, 1978). A recent manuscript (Richardson & Bradley, 1984) adapted this approach to supervision. The training sequence includes lectures with written handouts describing the skill; role-playing or modeling by supervisee and/or supervisor to demonstrate the skill; feedback from supervision group members or by self-observation of audio or video tapes; and remediation where supervisees role-play or interview each other, evaluate their interaction, and conduct a second, more effective interview making a conscious effort to correct mistakes. In the role as supervisor, we have observed beginning level supervisees experiencing difficulty in practicing isolated skills. They complained that concentrating on skills "feels awkward," "makes me too self-conscious," "interferes with counseling." The Case Study of Mary Jane appearing earlier in this chapter illustrates some of the complaints. A sequence we follow is to introduce the skill in group supervision with lecture and handouts. The presentation of separate skills proceeds from low influencing skills of attending, encouraging, reflection of content, feeling, meaning; to moderately influencing skills of focusing and questions; and finally to the highly influencing skills of providing information and giving directives, examining consequences, and confrontation (Ivey, 1980). Supervisees then practice skills in triads; two role-playing and one observing to give feedback. Supervisees gain further experience by critiquing counseling tapes and a volunteer counseling role-play between supervisor and a supervisee. Invariably, during their critiques, supervisees center their discussion on "the counseling issue," or "the problem solution." They must be guided in looking for specific skills related to the counseling process.

Modeling and role-playing are natural complements to skills teaching. Realistic modeling or role-play, with supervisor or supervisees exchanging roles, allows the supervisee to experience the client's frame of reference, enact different client responses, replay confusing incidents, rehearse alternative responses, observe modeling of interventions, and experience the effects of his/her own behavior. An example of role-playing can be seen in the following vignette taken from an actual single supervision seminar discussion. One supervisee was overwhelmed at the number of tasks she had to do, how unmanageable her life had become, and the fact that she had not the slightest job prospect after her upcoming graduation. A man volunteered to role-play her counselor, and the two performed a scenario where he rather perfunctorily led her through time management. The feedback from the group suggested that the "counselor" had overlooked the "client's" main source of discontent—no job prospects. A second man volunteered to be the "counselor," and in this session the "counselor" confronted the "client" with the many "things" she was doing instead of looking for a job. Somewhat defensively, the "client" responded that she was unsure about any job that would require her to leave home. At this point, the role-play was stopped and the discussion was lively. A third role-play was suggested between a woman playing the supervisee's mother and the supervisee playing herself. The "mother" appeared angry and resentful over the "daughter's" possible departure, and the "daughter" appeared fearful yet adamant about leaving. At the supervisor's suggestion, the mother reversed her position and became positive and supportive, eliciting hesitancy and tears from the "daughter!" The judicious use of role-play displayed counseling style and conflicting client motivation in a way not possible by lecture.

Live observations are methods of immediate intensity. They provide an urgency to the counseling dynamic that is somewhat lacking in the time-removed observation of audio or video taped counseling supervision. Through live supervision, with the supervisor observing the supervisee and client through a one-way mirror, the effect of the supervisee's body language becomes apparent. At the end of the session, the supervisee will know immediately how his or her eye movements; body posture; and hand, arm, or leg placement affected the "flow" between counselor and client. Likewise, the supervisor should look for instances of facilitative behavior during live observation, such as: How was the session opened? Did the supervisee encourage the client to thoroughly explore the issues? Were the related thoughts, feelings, and behaviors of the client identified? Was the "problem" stated and owned by the client? Were problem-solving goals mutually agreed to? How did the session end? Figure 8.13, *Live Observation Form,* can be used by the supervisor to briefly chart the counseling dynamics. Note that specific skills are not observed in this session. Since live observation is more difficult to arrange, the supervisor should utilize the opportunity to look for that which it best provides, a chance to see how the supervisee uses self as a counselor.

Supervisee _____ Date _____

Client _____ Total time of
observation _____

Non-Verbal Behavior   Supervisee   Client

Eye Movement:

Body Posture:

Arms, Legs:

Hands, Feet:

Position Change:

Supervisee Facilitative Statements During Counseling

Beginning part: opening statements? encouraging comments? Key focus?

Middle part: summaries? clarifying comments? problem identification?

Ending part: action steps? homework? further counseling? closing remarks?

Figure 8.13. Live Observation Form.

Live supervision, even rarer than live observation, provides a means by which the supervisor may directly intervene during the supervisee's session with the client. Using either an intercom device with a "bug-in-the-ear" (Baum & Lane, 1976; Boylston & Tuma, 1972) or having the supervisee briefly leave the session, the supervisor may redirect the counseling process with behaviorally concise directions (Borders & Leddick, 1987). Directing the supervisee to "respond to the client's remark about her mother" or "confront the client about his ambivalence toward his job" will enable the supervisee to see the effect of focus. What the counselor chooses to focus on will often influence the direction of the counseling session.

Interpersonal Process Recall, IPR (Kagan, 1975, 1980; Kagan & Krathwohl, 1967) utilizes playback exposure (audio or video recordings) augmented by assistance from a recall supervisor who utilizes inductive reasoning to direct the supervisee's attention to the intrapersonal and interpersonal dynamics of the client/counselor interaction (Boyd, 1978).

The following questions, taken from the work of Dandy (1971), illustrate those which might be used to lead the supervisee toward self-confrontation:

1. What do you think he/she was trying to say?

2. What do you think he/she was feeling at this point?

3 Can you pick up on any clues from his/her nonverbal behavior?

4. What was running through your mind when he/she said that?

5. Can you recall some of the feelings you were having then?

6. Did anything prevent you from sharing some of your feelings and concerns about the person?

7. If you had another chance, would you like to have said something different?

8. What kind of risk would have occurred if you had said what you really wanted to say?

9. **What kind of person do you want him/her to see you as?**

10. What do you think his/her perceptions are of you?

The insecurity and anxiety of the beginning level supervisee may limit the early use of IPR. For example, in the role-play vignette described earlier in this chapter, the supervisee acting as the first "counselor" could not think of alternative actions or feelings with which to describe his "client." However, continued use of the IPR will enhance the supervisee's growing ability to conceptualize client issues.

Anxiety management through a rational-emotive approach has been suggested as a means for helping supervisees manage anxiety. The following sequence initially described by Dodge (1982) shows the steps in the process:

1. Identification of supervisee behaviors related to anxiety avoidance, such as discussing tangential issues, rationalizations, showing anger and aggression, making judgmental statements of blaming others, and using anxiety as a defense, e.g., "I can't do it, I'm too nervous."

2. Recognition by the supervisee of the cognitive patterns undergirding approval and performance demands, such as "I must be a perfect counselor, if not, I'm a failure," or, "I must have my supervisor's approval; if I don't get it, that's just more evidence I'm not a good counselor."

3. Challenging and disputing identified irrational beliefs with questions such as "How awful will it really be if I don't get what I want?" "Where is the evidence that I must always be competent?"

4. Constructing more rational and logical thoughts relating to anxiety or anger. Examples may be "Yes, I want to be a competent counselor, but there are times I need and want assistance from others. This is not a weakness in me"; or "Why should she act the way I want her to? Just

because her style is different from mine doesn't make her an ineffective supervisor."

5. The last step occurs when the supervisee is willing to take a behavioral risk which would prove that the logical arguments are sound. For example, the reader may recall the Case Study of Mary Jane presented earlier in this chapter. The supervisee's last statement. . ." I may want to get it (skills) done in a semester when it takes years of experience to select skills wisely" showed her efforts to construct more rational thoughts (Step 4). Eventually, she did present her tapes to the supervision group for critique and feedback.

INTERMEDIATE LEVEL SUPERVISION

The more experienced supervisee, in moving toward autonomy, is described as showing "fluctuating motivation, striving for independence, becoming more self-assertive and less imitative" (Stoltenberg, 1981, p. 60). By this time, the supervisee has a grasp of basic counseling skills and interventions that have been successful with some clients. However, at this stage, the supervisee struggles to cope with strengths and weaknesses and the limitations of the counseling experience. An increased awareness of the client's frame of reference results in an over-identification with the client. Additionally, this submersion within the client's issues may result in the supervisee's inability to "move" the client, especially if the client objects or resists interventions prescribed in accordance to a theoretical model of counseling. This feeling of "stuckness" elicits a transference/counter-transference situation between the supervisee and the client, which in turn is superimposed on the supervisor/supervisee relationship. The supervisee may become so focused on the client as to be ineffective in counseling, and thus doubt the efficacy of counseling itself. The key supervisee issues at this time are disruption, ambivalence, and instability—a trying time for both supervisor and supervisee (Stoltenberg & Delworth, 1987).

Case Study: Wilma

The following transcript of a case study well demonstrates the intermediate level supervisee. This supervisee was a master's level student who had already completed one practicum. In this second field placement, Wilma's counseling client was an older woman, terminally ill, who had enjoyed a prestigious professional career. As our supervision progressed, it became apparent to the supervisor that the supervisee had several troubling issues. She resisted any constructive feedback regarding her skills as a counselor even though her counseling behavior was adequate for her experience. What soon became evident was that she had not reviewed her counseling tapes prior to the supervisory sessions, nor was she responsive to either praise or criticism from the supervisor. After hearing a taped counseling session where she appeared to be in deep emotional distress over the client's condition, the supervisor felt that the supervisee had become too emotionally involved with her client.

Up to the point where this transcript begins, the supervisee had related that she did not like taping her counseling sessions because "her client had had enough" and that she resented being "criticized" for her behavior when she was trying to be so "open" to the demands of relating to her client, dealing with her training program, and handling herself as a counselor.

Note—SR is used for Supervisor and SE for Supervisee

SE: *I guess it was something you said earlier, I feel things very deeply, it doesn't matter whether they are positive things or negative things, I just feel them deeper, and, if it's something that's negative, something that I have to work through, you can rationalize it, uh, you can say, well, it's a lot of crap anyway. You got all kinds of defenses, I use as many defenses as I possibly can just because I feel I am extremely sensitive, and yet, I don't know, I don't. . .I sense in this whole program, when you are working so much with. . .when you are working so much with the affective domain with other people. . .you know, I think that. . .uh. . . in trying to get them in touch with their feelings. . .*

*when you are so tough with your feelings. . .you
know what I mean. . . .*

SR: *People shouldn't put you down, then, while your
feelings are so exposed?*

SE: *Yeah, that's part of it.*

SR: *That's part of it. What's the rest of it?*

SE: *I think the rest of it is you have to. . .uh. . .that
kind of toughening up process that I need to do as
opposed to the softening up process that so many
other people have to do. It's just as difficult and,
you know, in terms of criticism, when you get
criticism and, as you said, when you are opened
up, I think it's difficult to. . .well, you're opened up
and you are trying to take in and get things to
form part of yourself, let it become a part of
yourself and let it become a behavior, to me that's
more exposure rather than closing up, and I feel
like a kind of a door, like a sliding door that's
supposed to be moving back and forth, and often
when criticism comes, I don't take it on the
intellectual level. I take it on the affective level
because that's when. . .*

SR: *Criticism came while the door was open for you?*

SE: *Right.*

SR: *And it just went right to the heart?*

SE: *Right.*

SR: *Yeah. What you said was really a beautiful
interpretation, more like an analogy, an opening
door and a closing door. You yourself need to
toughen up as well as remain soft. I think the use
of skills will help you identify the very things you
are trying to get a handle on. And that's what's so
hard, that's what's really difficult.*

SE: *Right.*

SR: *So you've got to have your own opening and closing mechanisms going all the time.*

SE: *Right. And that's what I find so hard in this program, because I've gotta open myself up and change myself all around and yet, I experience often and, what you said earlier, I have to close the door again sometimes with a client, so that I can open it again, because I can't leave it open all the time because everybody's problems go right to my heart. See what I mean?*

SR: *That's what I felt when you cried and cried with your client, you know, at the end. That's when I wanted you to toughen up, and close the door, pull in your counseling skills and get working with her on some directionality. At that point, you couldn't. When I want you to open up is to know yourself. Say "Where am I? How do I feel about this, and how do I feel about working with old people? How do I feel about death? How do I feel about the whole program?" and experience your own emotionality.*

SE: *Right.*

SR: *Because until you are comfortable with your own emotionality, you can't be very comfortable with your client's.*

SE: *Well, that's right, that's right. I know my own emotionality is. . . . this is the toughest thing I have to learn in this whole program. These skills are just peanuts compared to. . . .*

SR: *They are just a vehicle to get to where you want to go, but they are very important.*

SE: *Yeah, they are important, I realize that, and that is what I am working on, but in terms of working* on the emotions, those are the worst. (Sighs, sobs, blows nose.) *I think that has had a lot to do with. . . open and closed. . .when I walk in the door to talk to you, I'm open, I know how to work the mechanism to open up and close up. I know how that works, I know that much about myself, but I open it up, and then I go away, and then I close up, usually at the end of the session, I'm thinking what I need to do is close up sooner. I don't know, you might. . .*

SR: *I would suggest that you, after the end of each counseling session that you have with your client, you play your tape through and write out what you are thinking and feeling, I think at that . . .as soon as possible. At that time you haven't closed it off, you are ready to interpret and. . .*

SE: *Well that's what I tried to do in that second session, like the feelings I had in the second session, when you said, you know, listening to the second tape, well, I did start to listen to the second tape. I wrote down how I was feeling from that, and I went on in terms of that, and kept on going in terms of that, the second tape, you know, what transpired, what I was coming out with, and I got to that point and I just couldn't put through any more ideas, any more thoughts* (deep sigh, shows SR several pages of notes). *I was trying to in terms of how I felt and how other people would feel.*

SR: *I like your sentence here "You cannot lose anything from the experience except your own fears." I kinda hope that that is what's gonna happen to you in practicum.*

SE: *Oh, it will, it will.*

SR: *You're pretty sure about that, huh?*

SE: *Yep.*

SR: *You don't look it.* (both laugh) *Right now your behavior is not saying it.*

SE: *Oh yeah, I know. But again, you know, the door is open at the moment. But, I started out with all the fears. I came out of there going. . .My God!*

SR: *It's a scary feeling.*

SE: *How scary can you get, you know. Sitting there looking at somebody who's gonna die.*

SR: *Who may not be able to get up again. All that medication that you have to take; thinking that if you can hold out for just a few minutes, that aspirin will relieve the constant pain in your head.*

SE: *And if that aspirin doesn't help. That's part of the things that were coming through with this lady; the aspirin doesn't help. . .nothing's getting better. . .*

SR: *And she's going to die.*

SE: *And. . .she's gonna die.*

SR: *Is that where you are in this fear? That no matter how well you do and how much you have going for you at one time that eventually you are going to die?*

SE: *Well. . .I haven't figured that out yet. I think dying, to me has got a lot to do with what happens to the other people in your life.*

SR: *The people who are left?*

SE: *Right.*

SR: *Like what? Give me an example.*

SE: (long pause) *Well, the people that are left behind.*

SR: *OK. Like when your sister died. Who was left behind?*

SE: *Oh, there are a lot of people. I am a good example. My parents.*

SR: *Yeah. Your parents.*

SE: *My parents. My surviving sister. My oldest sister's death affected a number of people. The same thing with my father-in-law. The same thing with my client's husband.*

SR: *How did your sister's death affect you?* (long pause, SE: sighs)

SE: *How did it affect me? That's difficult to answer.*

SR: *How did it affect you as a child? What do you remember about the feeling as a child?*

SE: (sighs) *Well, my sister was, well she was like my mother, she was. . .my mother had never had a lot of time for me because she was busy always having to do things for my oldest sister, so that sister always had the time, and when she died, I was completely alone. That was it! My mother went out to work she couldn't stand to stay home anymore. My father went back to work. Neither of them could stand to talk about her. My. . .uh. . . other sister got pregnant and moved out of the house, and that was it.*

SR: *So it sounds like you lost your sister and your mother at the same time.*

SE: *Right.*

SR: *After never having had a mother.*

SE: *Right, right.*

SR: *That's a bad place to be at what? Fourteen? Fourteen years old?*

SE: *And then my parents, after a period of time, all of a sudden discovered. . .I call it discovered for that's as close as I can get; they discovered me you know.*

SR: *Well, there's my daughter!*

SE: *Right. What does she want? What does she think? What does she want to do with her life? Who is this person? I don't know this person? And all of a sudden they turned around and they said "OK, give me a synposis of what you are like kid! I got time for you, I got ten minutes! You know, what is your life like?" Yeah, that's. . . .*

SR: *There's a lot of resentment there. . .because they didn't pay attention to you sooner?*

SE: *I don't think there's resentment there as there is resentment for death. And that's part of this death thing, and I know it's stupid because you can't go around mad at the person who dies. . .who's responsible for their death. . .you should be annoyed at that person for dying. . .(sobs) but. . . those are the things I'm trying to work through.*

SR: *It's hard to own up to those feelings, feeling angry at the person dying, and angry at your mother, too, and angry at your father, angry at your sister—of all times for her to get pregnant—*

SE: *Right.*

SR: *There wasn't any time for anybody to pay any attention to you, until they finally turned around and said "Oh my goodness, here she is! We haven't said much to her so hello!" and you said "Where have you all been in the last 14 years?"*

SE: *Right. That's exactly. . . .*

SR: *I see you, sorta, trying to make up for that by being a really top-notch person which you are, intellectually, physically, mentally, energy-wise, goal-wise, achievement-wise. (Yes.) As if you affirmed yourself.*

SE: *Yes. There's a lot of feelings like, "If I were a better person maybe they would accept me or. . .more like my sister who died, maybe they would accept me because they loved her". . .I think two years ago, maybe a year and a half ago, I've been working on this a long time, this isn't something I have been working on since I started talking about death, it's something that's been driving me, for, 30 years. . .*

SR: *Quite a driver!*

SE: *I went through some assertiveness training and I was able at that point to go, and my mother said "why aren't we close?" and I was able to say "well, one reason we're not close, we've never been close, first of all. As a child you were never close to me, or I was never close to you, that wasn't the relationship we developed. "Well, I said to her "as a child, I was very afraid of you.". . .just scared stiff. I would practice in my bedroom four or five times, rehearse the lines I was going to say to her before I went down and said them—to my mother. This is what I was like as a kid, because I would have to say them in such a way that first of all she would listen to me, and second of all, that she would understand. I used to do that all the time; go up and practice, go over it, how am I going to say it? And that's how I grew up as a child; I would go and talk to my sister and I could work out all kinds of things and well, she'd go talk to my mom about them. But, like she was always an interpreter. It wasn't my older sister, it was my second sister who was an interpreter.*

SR: Which one died?

SE: The oldest.

SR: The oldest. So you were really third down the line.

SE: Oh yeah. I'm the youngest, the baby.

SR: Your middle sister was an interpreter for you.

SE: Oh yeah. Then she took off. . .the little devil!

SR: Left you in the lurch, huh! You lost your interpreter?

SE: Yeah, My mother is a very powerful. . .The way I
would interpret her is a very. . .you know. . .has a
lot to do about feelings about people. . .as a child
part of the fear was the fact that she was such a
strong personality. She is also very emotional, but
her emotions usually came out as anger. When
she is throwing all the silverware at you. . .let me
out of here! You know, when you walk in a room
and you didn't do anything and all of a sudden
you get belted with wooden spoons. . .you go, well,
guess I'll get down the road, and then you think—
no, guess I'd better not, then she'll get. . .

SR: I've got some feelings I want to check out with
you. One is that you said you resented death
more than you resented your parents' treatment.

SE: Yeah.

SR: I just want to suggest to you that it's easy to say "I
resent death." Death is something inanimate out
there instead of risking the fear of facing your
parents and saying "I resent the way you treated
me." You have a right to say that because, from
the sound of it, you were treated crummily, all
unaware on their part; I'm sure they didn't single
you out. . .it would take a great deal of

assertiveness to say to them "I resent the way you treated me." The second thing is. . .

SE: *Well, I got to the point where I could say that. . . you know. . .The thing I want to say to my mother the most was the fact that I was afraid of her. She scared me to death.*

SR: *I should think so, and that would have something to do with your running away from emotion. And also, when you said, "I had to practice what I said to my mother," I felt your intense dislike of doing that, and I related that to your intense dislike of using skills here, saying, "These don't amount to a hill of beans because I'm just practicing again to be what I want to be."*

SE: *That's right. Yeah. That has a lot to do with it. Because I had stopped practicing, and here I am not practicing again; what do I have to say? Yeah . . .that has a lot to do with it.*

The supervisor's task in this instance was to help the supervisee come to terms with her own emotions, with her relationship with her client, and with her reaction to the authority represented by the supervisor and/or program demands. However, issues relevant to this level are not always in the conscious awareness of the supervisee. The supervisor has to proceed with care and caution, acting in the role of counselor. An appropriate procedure at this point is to address personal issues related to the supervisee's counseling effectiveness, as in this case example where the supervisor explored the supervisee's fearful childhood feelings which were eventually tied to her present resistance to counseling.

Several studies have shown appropriate supervisor behaviors for middle level supervision (Allen, Szollos, & Williams, 1986; Reising & Daniels, 1983; Zucker & Worthington, 1986). Supervisees highly regard supervisors who display respectful, appropriate confrontation, and who emphasize personal growth issues over the teaching of technical skills. In reference to

Sansbury's (1982) description of the supervisee's external and internal pressure to expand, activities at this level dealing with external expansion could focus on developing new therapeutic techniques or interventions, improving conceptualizations of client dynamics, and modifying theory based on experience (Hulse & Jennings, 1984; Loganbill & Stoltenberg, 1983; Swensen, 1968). Internal expansion would be affected by the supervisee's developing sense of competence, in understanding the reciprocal nature of the counseling relationship, and in establishing limits of responsibility and involvement with clients. Due to the increased self-awareness of the more experienced supervisee, interventions of *Interpersonal Process Recall*, modeling, and/or role-playing will be more effectively utilized by the supervisee to develop insight regarding personal and/or client issues. Additionally the cognitive, behavioral interventions, case conceptualizations, and parallel processes described in the following paragraphs will prove doubly useful in providing a means by which the supervisor can work through supervisee issues, and can in turn be used by supervisees in working with their clients.

Parallel process refers to the several levels of conflict within supervision. Supervisees doubt their counseling effectiveness and may think something is wrong with their personality. They both want feedback and try to avoid it (Borders & Leddick, 1987), thus setting up conflict with their supervisor. Opposing forces of desire for and resistance to change are also experienced by the supervisee in the therapeutic relationship with his/her client. This mirroring of conflict within the supervisor/supervisee/client relationship is called parallel process, and is the basic tool by which the supervisee learns to be therapeutic (Eckstein & Wallerstein, 1972).

Mueller and Kell (1972) described a similar process, "parallel re-enactment," based on "impasse" in the supervisee-client relationship. *Impasse* is a disagreement that both parties believe to be unsolvable due to (1) ambivalence by the client resulting in resistance, (2) adequacy concerns by the supervisee resulting in retreat from the client, and (3) inappropriate identification with the client (I have the same problem, how can I help?), resulting in immobilization. Parallel impasse in the supervisor-supervisee relationship becomes a source of growth as the supervisor models how to respond therapeutically to conflict. A greater awareness of the dynamics underlying personal conflict about change sharpens the supervisee's understanding the client's conflicts. At the same time, the working through of conflict in the relationship with the supervisor provides a means for the supervisee to help the client deal with conflict (Russell, Crimmings, & Lent, 1984). However, instruction techniques are an insufficient supervisory intervention to these issues. The supervisory relationship itself becomes the vehicle for learning (Eckstein & Wallerstein, 1972).

The degree to which parallel process conflict can be resolved is determined in part by the supervisee, or by issues that keep occurring in the supervisee-client relationship. "Specified interventions" are not indicated, but the literature suggests ways to deal with conflicting relationships between the supervisor/supervisee (Bauman, 1972; Cutheil, 1977; Hess, 1986; Moskowitz & Rupert, 1983; Mueller & Kell, 1972; Yager & Beck, 1985).

Risk-taking or anxiety avoidance may be overcome through exposure to appropriate supervisee behavior by pre-viewing audio/video tapes of preceding "generations" of super-visees (Yager & Beck, 1985).

Authority and intimacy issues may be handled through use of nondefensive interpretation and confrontation. Indirect approaches such as generalizations, ignoring, role-playing, and listening to audiotapes together may prove beneficial (Kadu-shin, 1985; Mueller & Kell, 1972).

Avoidance of issues such as sexuality, evaluation, or authority conflicts must be addressed. The supervisor can increase his or her willingness to deal with these issues through consultation, or, as exemplified in parallel process, explore these issues with the supervisee. The means chosen are not as important as the supervisor's willingness to act. Issues avoided in the supervision session will likewise be avoided in the supervisee/client sessions (Aldrich & Hess, 1983).

Cognitive-behavioral interventions may be used with the supervisee to provide a learning experience transferable to the supervisee client counseling process. An example of this is shown in a multiple-base single-case research design suggested by Holahan and Galassi (1986) and used to evaluate the effectiveness of an intervention. The sequence is as follows:

1. Supervisee showed little use of skills previously mastered in pre-practicum (open questions and reflection).

2. Baseline data (on questioning) were collected from three audiotapes prior to intervention.

3. Supervisee presented with data and taught to self-monitor questioning, using Hill's (1978) criteria. In subsequent supervisory sessions, supervisor praised increased use of open-ended questions.

4. Supervisee self-monitoring stopped, but continued data collection by supervisor and independent rater showed continued use of open-ended questions by supervisee.

5. Same process for increased use of reflective statements was successfully utilized during subsequent supervisory sessions.

Various formats and procedures designed to help supervisees formulate client treatment plans are very useful at this level of supervision. Presser and Pfost (1985) devised a format for casenotes that includes observation and inferences about the client, counselor, and client-counselor interaction, and details progress and future plans. Hill and O'Grady's (1985) coding system of 19 intentions (i.e., support, challenges, reinforcers to change) of counselor interventions helps supervisees identify their intentions, become aware of their motivations, and examine their interventions. Kurpius, Benjamin, and Morran (1985) developed a similar system for a systematic cognitive self-instruction strategy to form a clinical hypothesis about a client.

Case conceptualization formats (Berven, 1985; Stoltenberg, 1981) have been used successfully in helping supervisees synthesize the cognitive, behavioral, emotional, and interpersonal aspects of the client's issues. Figure 8.14, *Case Conceptualization Format* (Loganbill & Stoltenberg, 1983), has been successfully used to help supervisees organize data, clarify relationships among factors, and develop intervention strategies for clients.

Case Conceptualization Format

1. Identifying Data: This section will include all relevant demographic information.

   a. age
   b. sex
   c. race
   d. marital status
   e. university classification

   f. living situation
   g. manner of dress
   h. physical appearance
   i. general self-presentation

2. Presenting Problem: This section should include a listing of the problem areas, from the client's perspective, noting particularly the client's view of their order of importance. Suggested items to focus upon include the following:

   a. Was there a precipitating set of circumstances?
   b. How long has the problem(s) persisted?
   c. Has this problem occurred before? What were the circumstances at the time?

3. Relevant History: This section will vary in comprehensiveness according to depth and length of treatment, and will vary in focus according to theoretical orientation and specific nature of the problem(s).

4. Interpersonal Style: This section should include a description of the client's orientation toward others in his/her environment and should include two sections:

   a. Is there an overall posture he/she takes toward others? What is the nature of his/her typical relationships? Karen Horney's conceptualization may be useful here:

      1) Moving toward (dependency, submission)
      2) Moving against (aggressive, dominance)
      3) Moving away (withdrawal)

      Is there a tendency toward one or the other polarity of dominance vs. submission, love vs. hate?

   b. How is the client's interpersonal stance manifested specifically within the therapeutic dyad? What is the client's interpersonal orientation toward the counselor?

Figure 8.14. Case Conceptualization Format.

Figure 8.14. Continued

5. Environmental Factors: This section should include:

   a. Elements in the environment which function as stressors to the client. Both those centrally related to the problem and more peripheral stresses.

   b. Elements in the environment which function as support for the client: friends, family, living accommodations, recreational activities, financial situation

6. Personality Dynamics

   a. Cognitive Factors: This section will include any data relevant to thinking and mental processes such as

      1) intelligence
      2) mental alertness
      3) persistance of negative cognitions
      4) positive cognitions
      5) nature and content of fantasy life
      6) level of insight—client's "psychological mindedness" or ability to be aware and observant of changes in feeling state and behavior and client's ability to place his/her behavior in some interpretive scheme and to consider hypotheses about his/her own and other's behavior
      7) **capacity for judgment—client's ability to make decisions and carry out the practical affairs of daily living**

   b. Emotional Factors

      1) typical or most common emotional states
      2) mood during interview
      3) appropriateness of affect
      4) range of emotions the client has the capacity to display
      5) cyclical aspects of the client's emotional life

   c. Behavioral Factors

      1) psychosomatic symptoms
      2) other physical related symptoms
      3) existence of persistent habits or mannerisms

Figure 8.14. Continued

4) sexual functioning
5) eating patterns
6) sleeping patterns

7. Counselor's Conceptualization of the Problem: This section will include a summary of the counselor's view of the problem. Include only the most central and core dynamics of the client's personality and note in particular the inter-relationships between the major dynamics. What are the common themes? What ties it all together? This is a synthesis of all the above data and the essence of the conceptualization.

A Systematic approach to formulate clinical hypotheses has been developed by Holloway and Wolleat (1980) in the form of a *Clinical Assessment Questionnaire* (CAQ). Tasks outlined in the CAQ are used to assess (1) behavioral inferences, (2) time frames used in understanding the client, (3) categories used to support conclusions (i.e., client's verbal and non-verbal behavior, counselor-client relationship), (4) facts and categories which support conclusions (client family, history, attitudes, goals), and (5) number of divergent questions asked by the counselors. Following the tasks outlined in the CAQ, the counselor-supervisee poses two client hypotheses and indicates additional information he or she would like to have.

Group supervision provides a rich source of learning for group members. Patterson (1983) described a group seminar format as "students being supervised meet in two two-hour seminar sessions per week devoted to discussion of philosophy, theory, and practice as well as professional ethics, special problems. . ." (p. 22). Group process in group supervision can facilitate supervisee exploration, openness, and responsibility, and is an ideal vehicle to promote risk-taking (Sansbury, 1982). As with individual supervision, group supervision goes through a series of stages which reflect the issues supervisees confront in their professional development. In light of the necessary and sufficient conditions which promote developmental stage growth, Stoltenberg and Delworth (1987) stated that the best "developmental mix" for group supervision contains beginning and intermediate level supervisees together with some more advanced students. These authors suggested group discussion about the developmental needs of supervisees, in that each group receives validation in this manner. Stoltenberg and Delworth's (1987) *Supervisee Levels Questionnaire*, Figure 8.15, may be utilized to identify levels of supervisee functioning. Even though it is still in the experimental stage, the questionnaire is useful in identifying supervisee characteristics at different levels of supervision.

ADVANCED LEVEL SUPERVISION

The supervisee at the advanced level of supervision has transcended the fluctuations typical of middle level supervision. Motivation to the profession is relatively stable; motivational doubts are expressed as concerns relating to "how the perceived counselor/therapist role will fit into the counselor's professional and personal identity" (Stoltenberg & Delworth, 1987). The maturity at this level will enable the supervisee to appreciate the wide diversity of client motivation and the variable strengths and weaknesses of both self and supervisor without becoming overwhelmed.

While the middle level supervisee might have "lost self in client concerns," the advanced level supervisee can be closely empathetic to the client's world and yet maintain enough objectivity to process the interaction. This deeper level awareness also expands to the supervisee's own heightened sense of the use of self in therapy. With a greater understanding of self and client, the supervisee will feel free to employ appropriate theoretical approaches and interventions in accordance with his/her level of competence. Additionally, he/she may now feel "released to learn." For example, the supervisee trained in client-centered therapy may want to learn cognitive-behavioral approaches. Typically, the advanced supervisee feels comfortable with that which is effective. Usually they have had experience in a number of interventions and, therefore, show flexibility in adapting interventions according to client need. They seek to become familiar with the client's culture. The supervisee's confidence and competence in

(Continued on p. 366)

Supervisee Levels Questionnaire—Revised
(November, 1987)

In terms of your own *current* behavior, please answer the items below according to the following scale as explained previously.

1: NEVER   4: HALF OF THE TIME

2: RARELY   5: OFTEN

3: SOMETIMES   6: MOST OF THE TIME

                             7: ALWAYS

1. Within supervisory and counseling/therapy relationships, I am sensitive to my *own* dynamics

   NEVER   ALWAYS

   1   2   3   4   5   6   7

2. I feel genuinely relaxed and comfortable in my counseling/therapy sessions.

   NEVER   ALWAYS

   1   2   3   4   5   6   7

3. I find myself using the same specific techniques in most of my therapy sessions.

   NEVER   ALWAYS

   1   2   3   4   5   6   7

4. I am able to critique counseling tapes and gain insights with minimum help from my supervisor.

   NEVER   ALWAYS

   1   2   3   4   5   6   7

5. I am able to be spontaneous in counseling/therapy, yet my behavior is relevant.

   NEVER   ALWAYS

   1   2   3   4   5   6   7

Figure 8.15. Supervisee Levels Questionnaire—Revised.

Figure 8.15. Continued.

6. I lack self confidence in establishing counseling relationships with diverse client types.

    NEVER   ALWAYS

    1   2   3   4   5   6   7

7. I find it difficult to express my thoughts and feelings clearly in counseling/therapy.

    NEVER   ALWAYS

    1   2   3   4   5   6   7

8. My verbal behavior in counseling/therapy is pretty much the same with most clients.

    NEVER   ALWAYS

    1   2   3   4   5   6   7

9. I am able to apply a consistent personalized rationale of human behavior in working with my clients.

    NEVER   ALWAYS

    1   2   3   4   5   6   7

10. I tend to get confused when things don't go according to plan and lack confidence in my ability to handle the unexpectd.

    NEVER   ALWAYS

    1   2   3   4   5   6   7

11. I find myself intellectualizing about my client's problems without being in touch with their feeling states.

    NEVER   ALWAYS

    1   2   3   4   5   6   7

12. The overall quality of my work fluctuates; on some days I do well, on other days, I do poorly.

    NEVER   ALWAYS

    1   2   3   4   5   6   7

Figure 8.15. Continued.

13. I depend upon my supervisor considerably in figuring out how to deal with my clients.

    NEVER   ALWAYS

    1   2   3   4   5   6   7

14. I find myself working with my clients as I think my supervisor, or some other counselor/therapist I know of, would.

    NEVER   ALWAYS

    1   2   3   4   5   6   7

15. During counseling/therapy sessions, I am able to focus completely upon my client.

    NEVER   ALWAYS

    1   2   3   4   5   6   7

16. I feel comfortable in confronting my clients.

    NEVER   ALWAYS

    1   2   3   4   5   6   7

17. Much of the time in counseling/therapy, I find myself thinking about my next response, instead of fitting my intervention into the overall picture.

    NEVER   ALWAYS

    1   2   3   4   5   6   7

18. My motivation fluctuates from day to day.

    NEVER   ALWAYS

    1   2   3   4   5   6   7

19. I feel most comfortable when my supervisor takes control of what we do in supervision.

    NEVER   ALWAYS

    1   2   3   4   5   6   7

20. At times, I wish my supervisor could be in the counseling/therapy session to lend a hand.

    NEVER   ALWAYS

    1   2   3   4   5   6   7

21. I find myself focusing less on learning new techniques and approaches to counseling/therapy and thinking more about my general professional development.

    NEVER   ALWAYS

    1   2   3   4   5   6   7

Figure 8.15. Continued.

---

22. During counseling/therapy sessions, I find it difficult to concentrate because of my concern with my own performance.

    NEVER   ALWAYS

    1   2   3   4   5   6   7

23. In describing clients and/or viewing videotapes, I am very concerned about my supervisor's evaluation of my performance.

    NEVER   ALWAYS

    1   2   3   4   5   6   7

24. Because there is so much to learn, I am highly motivated to use my supervisor as an educational resource.

    NEVER   ALWAYS

    1   2   3   4   5   6   7

25. Although at times I really want advice/feedback from my supervisor, at other times I really want to do things my own way.

    NEVER   ALWAYS

    1   2   3   4   5   6   7

26. In counseling/therapy sessions, I am very concerned about my clients' evaluation of my skills.

    NEVER   ALWAYS

    1   2   3   4   5   6   7

27. The more I learn, the more impressed I am with the counseling process.

    NEVER   ALWAYS

    1   2   3   4   5   6   7

28. Sometimes my supervisor is too structured and too directive with me.

    NEVER   ALWAYS

    1   2   3   4   5   6   7

29. **Sometimes the client's situation seems so hopeless, I just don't know what to do.**

    NEVER   ALWAYS

    1   2   3   4   5   6   7

30. It is important that my supervisor allow me to make my own mistakes.

    NEVER   ALWAYS

    1   2   3   4   5   6   7

Figure 8.15. Continued.

31. I find myself becoming so in touch with my clients' emotions that I find it difficult to regain my objectivity.

NEVER ALWAYS

1 2 3 4 5 6 7

32. Given my current state of professional development, I believe I know when I need consultation from my supervisor and when I don't.

NEVER ALWAYS

1 2 3 4 5 6 7

33. Sometimes I question how suited I am to be a counselor/therapist.

NEVER ALWAYS

1 2 3 4 5 6 7

34. I find myself becoming so in touch with my clients' emotions that I find it difficult to help them see alternatives.

NEVER ALWAYS

1 2 3 4 5 6 7

35. Regarding counseling/therapy, I view my supervisor as a teacher/mentor.

NEVER ALWAYS

1 2 3 4 5 6 7

36. Sometimes I feel that counseling/therapy is so complex, I will never be able to learn it all.

NEVER ALWAYS

1 2 3 4 5 6 7

37. **I find myself more inclined to think about how to help clients solve their problems than to empathize with how they feel.**

NEVER ALWAYS

1 2 3 4 5 6 7

38. I believe I know my strengths and weaknesses as a counselor sufficiently well to understand my professional potential and limitations.

NEVER ALWAYS

1 2 3 4 5 6 7

39. Regarding counseling/therapy, I view my supervisor as a peer/colleague.

NEVER ALWAYS

1 2 3 4 5 6 7

Figure 8.15. Continued.

40. I think I know myself well and am able to integrate that into my therapeutic style.

   NEVER   ALWAYS

   1   2   3   4   5   6   7

41. I find I am able to understand my clients' view of the world, yet help them objectively evaluate alternatives.

   NEVER   ALWAYS

   1   2   3   4   5   6   7

42. At my current level of professional development, my confidence in my abilities is such that my desire to do counseling/therapy doesn't change much from day to day.

   NEVER   ALWAYS

   1   2   3   4   5   6   7

43. I find I am able to empathize with my clients' feeling states, but still help them focus on problem resolution.

   NEVER   ALWAYS

   1   2   3   4   5   6   7

44. I am able to adequately assess my interpersonal impact on clients and use that knowledge therapeutically.

   NEVER   ALWAYS

   1   2   3   4   5   6   7

45. I am adequately able to assess the client's interpersonal impact on me and use that therapeutically.

   NEVER   ALWAYS

   1   2   3   4   5   6   7

46. I believe I exhibit a consistent professional objectivity, and ability to work within my role as a counselor without undue overinvolvement with my clients.

   NEVER   ALWAYS

   1   2   3   4   5   6   7

47. **I believe I exhibit a consistent professional objectivity, and ability to work within my role as a counselor without excessive distance from my clients.**

   NEVER   ALWAYS

   1   2   3   4   5   6   7

Figure 8.15. Continued.

Scoring Key (preliminary)

Subscales

Self and Other Awareness

1, 2, 3*, 5, 7*, 8*, 9, 11*, 15, 16, 17*, 21, 22*, 23*, 26*, 31*, 34*, 37, 41, 43, 44, 45, 46, 47

Motivation

12*, 13*, 18*, 20*, 24*, 27*, 29*, 33*, 36*, 38, 40, 42

Dependence—Autonomy

4, 6*, 10*, 13, 14, 19*, 20, 25, 28, 30, 32, 35*, 39

* Indicates reverse scoring

The subscales are based on three developmental structures identified in the Integrated Developmental Model described in Stoltenberg, C.D., & Delworth, U. (1987). *Supervising Counselors and Therapists: A Developmental Approach.* Jossey-Bass: San Francisco.

counseling enables him/her to alter counseling activities without losing faith in the client or in the efficacy of counseling.

Supervision at this level emanates from the position of peers who respect the unique contribution each brings to the relationship. Supervisees welcome supervisors who share personal examples of counseling behaviors, yet allow the supervisee the freedom to act on the information as he/she sees fit. Typically, the supervisor acts as consultant to supervisees working in some counseling program or agency where they may be completing their practicum or internship. Caplan's (1970) concept of mental health consultation provides a model which illustrates specific organizational or client concerns that may be the focus of consultation (Dustin & Blocher, 1984). The following descriptions show the client, consultative, and program-centered focus of consultation.

In *client-centered case consultation,* the goal of consultation is to assist the consultee in finding effective treatment for the client. The supervisee has realized that not every client is responsive and mature enough to seek help without feeling threatened.The supervisee is therefore open to suggestions or shared experiences from the supervisor that may re-direct the course of therapy with the client.

Consultee-centered case consultation focuses directly on the supervisee's difficulties within the work situation. The supervisee experienced some lack of understanding, will, objectivity, or confidence in dealing with clients served by that particular agency.

In *consultee-centered administrative consultation,* the supervisee seeks assistance for difficulties in carrying out administrative policies. In some cases, the supervisee disagreed with the treatment accorded clients. Disagreements may have occurred within staff relationships or in the process of program planning.

In the last area, *program-centered administrative consultation,* the supervisee, as representative of the a-gency, sought consultation about some aspect of program management, staff development, or policy implementation. The consultant worked with the supervisee to develop plans affecting various aspects of the program's operations. An example of the peer relationship-consultant role supervision at the advanced level is shown in the Case Study of Alice.

Case Study: Alice

The first author supervised Alice while she completed a community counseling degree. She had a varied educational career, having been a student in other programs before selecting counseling. At the time of this report, Alice was a director of a local community mental health project. The purpose of the project was to provide a "community club" for recovering mental health patients, a place where the recovering patients could plan and implement their social, recreational, and volunteer community projects. Supervision with Alice was mutually beneficial for supervisor and supervisee, as well as for the less experienced supervisees who participated in group supervision seminars. Individual sessions with Alice focused on such pertinent personal issues as (1) exploring psychodrama as an intervention to teach her clients socially accepted interaction, (2) discussing her relationship with the field supervisor, whom Alice felt "didn't understand" her clients or the program, (3) critiquing a program about her project that Alice was preparing for a national meeting, and (4) compiling a list of community activities in which her clients might participate. In group seminars, the exchange of information about persons recovering from mental illness, or grant writing efforts to secure funds for this project, proved enlightening to all participants. As this case study illustrates, the successful implementation of advanced level supervision enhanced the skills of supervisor and supervisee, and focused on the benefits of collegial relationships within the profession.

TERMINATION OF SUPERVISION

The feelings of supervisees at the end of supervision are a factor of his/her level of development. Supervisees at the earliest stage may be reluctant to separate from the security of a guide or mentor, and will quickly seek to establish a new bond (Mueller & Kell, 1972). Supervisees at the middle level of supervision, if their supervisory relationship was positive, will not easily separate allegiance from the relationship. Advanced supervisees accept the supervisory separation as inevitable, much like the parting of old friends (Stoltenberg & Delworth, 1987). Female supervisees, having a tendency to bond to the relationship, may have difficulty in separating from their supervisor. Male supervisees, focusing on the task rather than the relationship, may suppress the effects of separation.

SUMMARY

In summary, this chapter presented differential supervision as an on-going process effected by the supervisor in working with supervisees at various levels of experience. Supervisory roles of teacher, counselor, consultant, and evaluator have been examined within the functions of process, conceptualization, and personalization. The concept of developmental supervision, with its developmental stages related to supervisee growth, has been presented as a complex interaction of supervisee need and supervisor responses, compounded by the experience level of the supervisee.

In this chapter was described the supervisee at beginning, intermediate, and advanced levels of supervision. Studies and numerous activities appropriate to the supervisee's developmental level were presented. Explanatory tables were used to demonstrate concepts. Clarifying examples from actual supervision experiences were related to the cognitive concepts presented.

In essence, this chapter was written to help clinical and administrative supervisors prepare for supervision. The activities were suggested as a means to help supervisees explore the parameters of each developmental level. However, what must be understood is that the supervisee's fullest realization of developmental levels is not dependent upon the length of time in supervision nor on the implementation of stage-related activities. In the context of developmental sequences, personality variables of supervisor and supervisee (cognition, motivation, energy) interact with environmental opportunities (location, facilities, clients) to effect assimilation and accommodation at each stage.

REFERENCES

Aldrich, L., & Hess, A.K. (1983, March). *Parallel process: Its prevalence, content and resolution in counseling and psychotherapy supervision.* Paper presented at the meeting of the Southern Psychological Association, Atlanta, GA.

Allen, G.J., Szollos, S.J., & Williams, B.E. (1986). Doctoral students' comparative evaluations of best and worst psychotherapy supervision. *Professional Psychology: Research and practice, 17,* 91-99.

Bartlett, W.E. (1983). A multidimensional framework for the analysis of supervision of counseling. *The Counseling Psychologist, 11*(1), 9-17.

Baum, D., & Lane, J. (1976). An application of "bug-in-the-ear" communication for training psychometrists. *Counselor Education and Supervision, 15,* 309-310.

Bauman, W.F. (1972). Games counselor trainees play: Dealing with trainee resistance. *Counselor Education and Supervision, 11,* 253-256.

Bernard, J.M. (1979). Supervision training: A discrimination model. *Counselor Education and Supervision, 19,* 60-68.

Berven, N.L. (1985). Reliability and validity of standardized case management simulations. *Journal of Counseling Psychology, 32,* 397-409.

Borders, L.D., & Leddick, G.R. (1987). *Handbook of counseling supervision.* Alexandria, VA: American Association of Counseling and Development.

Boyd, J. (1978). *Counselor supervision.* Muncie, IN: Accelerated Development.

Boylston, W., & Tuma, J. (1972). Training mental health professionals through the use of a "bug-in-the-ear." *American Journal of Psychiatry, 129,* 124-127.

Caplan, G. (1970). *The Theory and practice of mental health consultation.* New York: Basic Books.

Cormier, W.H., & Cormier, L.S. (1985). *Interviewing strategies for helpers* (2nd ed). Monterey, CA: Brooks/Cole.

Cross, D.G., & Brown, D. (1983). Counselor supervision as a function of trainee experience: Analysis of specific behaviors. *Counselor Education and Supervision, 22,* 333-341.

Cutheil, T.G. (1977). Ideology as resistance: A supervisory challenge. *Psychiatric Quarterly, 49,* 88-96.

Dandy, R.F. (1971). *A model for the training of undergraduate residence hall assistants as paraprofessional counselors using videotape playback techniques and interpersonal process recall.* Unpublished doctoral dissertation, University of Michigan.

Dodge, J. (1982). Reducing supervisor anxiety: A cognitive-behavioral approach. *Counselor Education and Supervision, 22,* 55-60.

Dustin, D., & Blocher, D.H. (1984). Theories and models of consultation. In S. Brown & R. Lent (Eds), *Handbook of counseling psychology,* (pp. 751-784). New York: Wiley.

Dustin, R.E., Engen, H.B., & Shymansky, J.A. (1982). The ICB: A tool for counseling supervision. *Counselor Education and Supervision, 22,* 70-75.

Eckstein, R., & Wallerstein, R.S. (1972). *The teaching and learning of psychotherapy* (2nd ed). New York: International Universities Press.

Ellis, M.V., & Dell, D.M. (1986). Dimensionality of supervision roles: Supervisees' perceptions of supervision. *Journal of Counseling Psychology, 33,* 282-291.

Forsyth, D.R., & Ivey, A.E. (1980). Microtraining: An approach to differential supervision. In A.K. Hess (Ed.) *Psychotherapy supervision: Theory, research, and practice* (pp. 242-261). New York: Wiley.

Friedlander, M.L., & Synder, J. (1983). Trainees expectations for the supervisory process: Testing a developmental model. *Counselor Education and Supervision, 22,* 342-348.

Grater, H.A. (1985). Stages of psychotherapy: From therapy skills to skilled therapist. *Professional Psychology: Research and Practice, 16,* 605-610.

Hackney, H. (1976). *Practicum manual.* Unpublished manuscript, Purdue University, West Lafayette, IN.

Hart, G.M. (1982). *The process of clinical supervision.* Baltimore: University Park Press.

Hess, A.K. (1980). Training models and the nature of psychotherapy supervision. In A.K. Hess (d.), *Psychotherapy supervision: Theory, research, and practice* (pp 15-25). New York: Wiley.

Hess, A.K. (1986). Growth in supervision: Stages of supervisee and supervisor development. *The Clinical Supervisor, 4,* 51-67.

Hill, C.E. (1978). Development of a counselor verbal response category system. *Journal of Counseling Psychology, 25,* 461-468.

Hill, C.E., Charles, D., & Reed, K.G. (1981). A longitudinal analysis of changes in counseling skills during doctoral training in counseling psychology. *Journal of Counseling Psychology, 28,* 428-436.

Hill, C.E., & O'Grady, R.E. (1985). List of therapist intentions illustrated in a case study and with therapists of varying theoretical orientations. *Journal of Counseling Psychology, 32,* 3-22.

Hogan, R.A. (1964). Issues and approaches in supervision. *Psychotherapy, Research and Practice, 1*(3), 139-141.

Holahan, W., & Galassi, J.P. (1986), Toward accountability in supervision: A single case illustration. *Counselor Education and Supervision, 25,* 166-173.

Holloway, E., & Hosford, R.E. (1983). Toward developing a prescriptive technology of counselor supervision. *The Counseling Psychologist, 11*(1), 73-77.

Holloway, E., & Wampold, B.E. (1983). Patterns of verbal behavior and judgments of satisfaction in the supervision interview. *Journal of Counseling Psychology, 30,* 227-234.

Holloway, E., & Wolleat, D.L. (1980). Relationship of counselor conceptual level to clinical hypothesis formation. *Journal of Counseling Psychology, 27,* 539-545.

Hosford, R.E., & Barmann, B. (1983). A social learning approach to counselor supervision. *The Counseling Psychologist, 11*(1), 51-58.

Hulse, D., & Jennings, M.L. (1984). Toward comprehensive case conceptualization in counseling: A visual integrative technique. *Professional Psychology, 15,* 251-259.

Ivey, A.E. (1971). *Microcounseling: Innovations in interview training.* Springfield, IL: Thomas.

Ivey, A.E., (1980). *Counseling and psychotherapy: Skills, training and practice.* Englewood Cliffs, NJ: Prentice-Hall.

Ivey, A.E., & Authier, J. (1978). *Microcounseling: Innovations in interviewing, counseling, psychotherapy, and psychoeducation* (2nd ed.). Springfield, IL: Thomas.

Kadushin, A. (1985). *Supervision in social work* (2nd ed.). New York: Columbia University Press.

Kagan, N. (1975). *Interpersonal process recall: A method of influencing human interaction.* East Lansing, MI: Michigan State University.

Kagan, N. (1980). Influencing human interaction: Eighteen years with IPR. In A.K. Hess (Ed.), *Psychotherapy supervision: Theory, research, and practice* (pp. 262-283). New York: Wiley.

Kagan, N. & Krathwohl, D.R. (1967). *Studies of human interaction: Interpersonal process recall simulated by videotape.* East Lansing, MI: Michigan State University.

Kurpius, D.J., Benjamin, D., & Morran, D.K. (1985). Effects of teaching a cognitive strategy on counselor trainee internal dialogue and clinical hypothesis formulation. *Journal of Counseling Psychology, 32,* 263-271.

Linehan, M.M. (1980). Supervision or behavior therapy. In A.K. Hess (Ed.), *Psychotherapy supervison: Theory, research & practice.* New York: Wiley.

Loganbill, C., Hardy, E., & Delworth, U. (1982). Supervision: A conceptual model. *The Counseling Psychologist, 10*(1), 3-42.

Loganbill, C., & Stoltenberg, C. (1983). The case conceptualization format: A training device for practicum. *Counselor Education and Supervision, 22,* 235-241.

Martin, J., Hiebert, B.A., & Marx, R. (1981). Instructional supervision in counselor training. *Counselor Education and Supervision, 20,* 193-202.

McNeill, B.W., Stoltenberg, C.D., & Pierce, R.A. (1985). Supervisees' perceptions of their development: A test of the counselor complexity model. *Journal of Counseling Psychology, 32,* 630-633.

Miars, R.D., Tracey, T.J., Ray, P.B., Cornfield, J.L., O'Farrell, M., & Gelso, C.J. (1983). Variation in supervision process across trainee experience levels. *Journal of Counseling Psychology, 30,* 403-412.

Moskowitz, S.A., & Rupert, P.A. (1983). Conflict resolution in the supervisory relationship. *Professional Psychology, 24,* 632-641.

Mueller, W.J., & Kell, B.L. (1972). *Coping with conflict: Supervising counselors and psychotherapists.* New York: Appleton-Century-Croft.

Patterson, C.H. (1983). A client-centered approach to supervision. *The Counseling Psychologist, 11*(1), 21-25.

Presser, N.R., & Pfost, K.S. (1985). a format for individual psychotherapy session roles. *Professional Psychology: Research and Practice, 16,* 11-16.

Rabinowitz, F.E., Heppner, P.P., & Roehlke, H.J. (1986). Description study of process and outcome variables of supervision over time. *Journal of Counseling Psychology, 33,* 292-300.

Reising, G.N., & Daniels, M.H. (1983). A study of Hogan's model of counselor development and supervision. *Journal of Counseling Psychology, 30,* 235-244.

Richardson, B., & Bradley, L. (1984). Microsupervision: A skill development model for training clinical supervisors. *The Clinical Supervisor, 2,* 43-54.

Russell, R.K., Crimmings, A.M., & Lent, R.W. (1984). Counselor training and supervision: Theory and research. In S.K. Brown & R.W. Lent (Eds.), *Handbook of counseling psychology* (pp. 625-681). New York: Wiley.

Sansbury, D.L. (1982). Developmental supervision from a skills perspective. *The Counseling Psychologist, 10*(1), 53-57.

Stenack, R.J., & Dye, H.A. (1982). Behavioral descriptions of counseling supervision roles. *Counselor Education and Supervision, 21,* 295-304.

Stoltenberg, C. (1981). Approaching supervision from a developmental perspective: The counselor-complexity model. *Journal of Counseling Psychology, 28,* 59-65.

Stoltenberg, C.S., & Delworth, U. (1987). *Supervising counselors and therapists: A developmental approach.* San Francisco: Jossey-Bass.

Styczynski, L.E. (1980). The transition from supervisee to supervisor. In A.K. Hess (Ed.), *Psychotherapy supervision: Theory, research, and practice* (pp. 29-40). New York: Wiley.

Swensen, C.H. (1968). *An approach to case conceptualization.* Boston: Houghton-Mifflin.

Ward, G.W., Friedlander, M.L., Schoen, L.G., & Klein, J.G. (1985). Strategic self-preservation in supervision. *Journal of Counseling Psychology, 32,* 111-118.

Wessler, R.L. & Ellis, A. (1983). Supervision in counseling: Rational-emotive therapy. *The Counseling Psychologist, 11*(1), 43-39.

Wiley, M.O., & Ray, P.M. (1986). Counseling supervision by developmental level. *Journal of Counseling Psychology, 33,* 439-445.

Worthington, E.L., Jr. (1984). Empirical investigation of supervision of counselors as they gain experience. *Journal of Counseling Psychology, 31,* 63-75.

Worthington, E.L., Jr., & Roehlke, H.J. (1979). Effective supervision as perceived by beginning counselors in training. *Journal of Counseling Psychology, 26,* 64-73.

Worthington, E.L., Jr., & Stern, A. (1985). Effects of supervisor and supervisee degree level and gender on the supervisory relationship. *Journal of Counseling Psychology, 32,* 252-262.

Yager, G.G., & Beck, T.D. (1985). Beginning practicum: it only hurt until I laughed! *Counselor Education and Supervision, 25,* 149-157.

Zucker, P.J., & Worthington, E.L. (1986). Supervision of interns and postdoctoral applicants for licensure in university counseling centers. *Journal of Counseling Psychology, 33,* 87-89.

CHAPTER 9

EXPERIENTIAL SUPERVISION: CASE ILLUSTRATIONS

Julius Seeman, Ph.D.

In this chapter is discussed the process of counseling supervision conducted within an experiential framework. The first part of the chapter sets forth underlying theory and practice of experiential supervision. The second part of the chapter illustrates the process through transcripts of verbatim audiotaped passages of supervision, together with explanatory comments.

EXPERIENTIAL THEORY

Experiential supervision is based on the assumption that the task of becoming a professional counselor is a basic developmental task involving the whole person. The task in fact involves nothing less than the development of a professional concept of self. As such it is a subset of the broader phenomenon of personal development, and many of the principles relevant to this broader phenomenon are applicable to the development required in becoming a competent counselor. Thus a general model of personal development can inform us of some ways that we can facilitate the development of an effective professional self.

A model that I have found useful is a human systems model. Angyal (1941) has defined a system with the term **unitas multiplex**—that is, a system has multiple components or subsystems, all of which are linked and interdependent such that an underlying unity exists to a system, no matter how complex the system is. No single part is isolated or independent, but all are held together through related function and joined by a communication system. I cannot emphasize too strongly the role of communication in effective system function. The human system has an exquisitely intricate matrix of communication processes, including electrochemical modalities at the micro level, joining individual cells and cell clusters. At progressively more molar levels there are neuromuscular processes of communication, perceptual communication, cognitive communication, and finally, at the most molar level, interpersonal communication.

Within the foregoing framework, an effectively functioning person has effective communication resources, with maximal access to his or her organismic signals. A free-flowing awareness of self and situation occurs, an awareness based on openness to experience and a high capacity to receive and process information. Carl Rogers (1961, 1963) has described the fully functioning person thus:

> He is more able to live fully and with each and all of his feelings and reactions. He makes increasing use of all his organic equipment to sense, as accurately as possible, the existential situation within and without. He makes use of all the information his nervous system can supply, using it in awareness...(1961, p. 191)

Norbert Wiener (1954) has similarly emphasized the central role of communication in his description of cybernetics. Indeed, the very definition of cybernetics is that it is the science of communication and control. Wiener described in detail the ways in which communication serves the purpose of organismic regulation and adaptation, and specifically included recursive communication, or feedback, in his description. The value of feedback is that it supplies ongoing information to the organism such that appropriate regulation is possible. The centrality of this information yield is emphasized by Wiener. His assertion concerning effective functioning is that "To live effectively is to live with adequate information" (p. 27).

EXPERIENTIAL SUPERVISION

The foregoing human-system model has decisive implications both for general learning and development, and for
learning to become a counselor. Specifically, the model suggests
that if we can foster and facilitate a person's awareness of self,
an openness to the person's ongoing immediate experiencing
process, and a capacity for communicating this awareness, we
are by that token enhancing the person's capacity to become, in
Rogers' terms, a more fully functioning person.

This capacity to develop a fully functioning "professional
self" is precisely what experiential supervision is designed to
foster. It does so by paying attention to the supervisee's ongoing
process of immediate experiencing in ways that illuminate this
process for both supervisee and supervisor. A decided quality of
presentness and immediacy exists in the process, and a very
close attention occurs to the ways in which the supervisee
communicates both within self and with the counselee. For the
communication process is what activates learning and carries
the burden of counseling.

What I have described so far conveys the general principles
of growth and development, but it does not yet differentiate
supervision as a specific task. The foregoing description could
just as well hold for counseling itself as a process, and so the
goals specific to supervision (i.e., the learning/teaching task
specific to becoming a counselor) must enter into this
description. Here too, human-system theory has some guidance
to offer, for the theory recognizes the multiple behavioral
subsystems through which persons learn. For our purposes the
cognitive subsystem offers another avenue to learning. We as
humans have the capacity to conceptualize what we are doing,
and to form generalizations that provide structures for learning.
The experiential supervisor whether in an administrative or
clinical setting, does not neglect this resource, but determines
ways in which this resource may be used as part of the
experiencing process. In brief, we can say that when concepts
connect with the supervisee's direct experience, and indeed
when they grow out of the experience, conceptualization has its
firmest basis. To put the matter another way, cognitive
processes—the direct transmission of information or opinions

by the supervisor—are likely to be most useful and effective when they are joined to the supervisee's immediate experiencing of the moment.

The foregoing process formulations have a direct bearing on "where the action is" in the supervisor-supervisee dialogue. Specifically, when I am supervising, the only person present with me is the supervisee, and so that is the only person to whom I can relate then and there. The client is not present, and I cannot relate to her or him. Yet so often the focus of a typical supervisor-supervisee dialogue is on the client, and much of the dialogue consists of a narrative or story about the client. In experiential supervision the action takes place between the supervisor and supervisee, and the narrative about the client is only a vehicle for entry into the livingness of the supervisee. Thus the client-focused narrative is brief, and it is incidental to the heart of the supervision process.

CASE ILLUSTRATIONS

The case illustrations that follow represent vignettes of experiential supervision. In order to make these passages most meaningful I have added my own commentary, highlighting either the thoughts that prompted my response at the time or some theory-oriented appraisal of the interchange. In any case, all of the commentary is designed to illuminate the supervision process.

An explanatory word about the case illustrations is in order. Two sets of illustrations are given. Both sets arise from my professional task. The first illustration comes from a course entitled *Practicum in Counseling.* The supervisee, Rhonda, is a student in the course, and I supervise her practicum experience.

The second set of illustrations arise from another course that I teach, entitled *Supervision of Counseling.* Students in this course are advanced doctoral students in a counselor education program. They have completed practica and internships and are now learning the theory and practice of counseling supervision. In order for them to gain hands-on supervision experience, each student in the course is assigned to the supervision of a more junior student. My task as course instructor is to supervise the supervision experience of students in this advanced doctoral course.

Case Illustration: Rhonda

In this passage, the counselor (Rhonda) is a practicum student. As is true for many of our students, she is an employee in a human service agency, and that is her practicum site. The agency has a policy of short term help, with a major responsibility for foster placement.

The counselor had seen this client a few years earlier, and the client has returned for additional help at this time because she is upset by an unstable family situation. The counselor feels drawn toward this service need, but also feels constrained by the agency's policy of short-term help and wishes to find a way to terminate counseling.

In this passage, Rhonda is the counselor and her responses are labeled Co and my responses as supervisor are labeled Sr. The counselor is talking about her dilemma with respect to terminating the counseling process.

Sr 1: *How did you feel about bringing up the question of ending?*

Co 1: *I brought it up near the end of the interview. I felt like the client who brings up something ten minutes before the end of the hour.*

Sr 2: *Did you feel ambivalent about bringing it up? How was it for you?*

Co 2: *I felt—Let's see, how did I feel? I felt somewhat cautious. She is particularly hooked with me as a person, and her issues aren't painful enough for her to continue with somebody else. She puts more value on me than on the counseling.*

Sr 3: *That's all part of the issue for you, isn't it?*

Co 3: *Right. I need an ending point with Betty (the client). I said to her "we need to figure out how to best use this month and next month." I can see taking that much time. She said that she felt sad about the idea of ending. I said to her "My concern is that you'll feel rejected. That's not my intent. I'm not rejecting you."*

Sr 4: *I'm imagining, first of all, that it was hard for you to bring it up.*

Co 4: *Yes, yes it was, and I said to her "This is hard for me, because I'm aware that you have some strong feelings, and I also have feelings about— how do we end this thing?" I also said "That doesn't mean that I'm never available to you ever again" and I thought to myself, "Are you trying to soften this too much by saying that I can still be available?" I don't know how to . . . (Pause).*

Sr 5: *It was really very hard for you to cut it definitely off, wasn't it? It was too hard to. . .*

Co 5: *Say I'm not seeing you.*

Sr 6: *And so there's still a process going on with you and her. It's still in the works (Co: that's right) as far as how that's going to go with you and her.*

Co 6: *Yes. . .Do you have any guidance for me in furthering our process?*

Sr 7: *Let me center that in terms of what kinds of uncertainty you feel.*

Co 7: *Yes. I guess I—the fact that I would—How can I say I want to be available to you without being—I mean, I can see myself being available if there was a crisis, a kind of one-shot thing,* *but I don't want to get back into an ongoing counseling relationship. I wouldn't mind being a resource to her if I could define it differently.*

Sr 8: *And I do hear you defining it.*

Co 8: *Maybe I am defining it. But I don't know how I would communicate it to her.*

Sr 9: *There's some lingering mixed feelings for you in this Rhonda, isn't there? It really makes it hard for you to be that definite.*

Co 9: *Um hum. I think it's because I feel in part responsible for her confusion about how she will view me. I've extended myself in ways that might be confusing. I felt that counseling didn't take place just in the confines of an office, so we also met over coffee, and I feel some responsibility about that.*

Sr 10: *So are you saying, "I had a part in the relationship that developed, and I have some responsibility about that, (Co: Yes, that's right) so I want to be awfully sure not to hurt her." One question that you have is, how can you deal with your feeling of responsibility, isn't that where it is?*

Co 10: *Um hm. I think, by talking about it and giving it a lot of thought. Facing it.*

Sr 11: *I wonder if you have some qualms like "Hey, I didn't handle this quite right."*

Co 11: *Um hum. I feel two ways about that. It wouldn't have worked if I had tried to be just the conventional counselor. And then the other part is, I didn't handle this quite right. There's a part of me that thinks that.*

Sr 12: *So we still come out with, how can you deal with the situation and still be OK with yourself? Is that a germane question?*

Co 12: *Yes, I think it's that, as well as keeping Betty's welfare in mind. I want to do right by her as well as doing right by myself professionally and personally. I felt tremendous relief last week when you said "So you've got the remainder of the calendar year (2 months) to work with her."*

Sr 13: *So you're saying "I can live with that and I like that" (Co: Yeah, yeah)—Are you saying that's OK?*

Co 13: *Yeah, I can give her time and still set a limit. I feel better.*

Sr 14: *That's as much as you can do and you're saying, furthermore, "That's as much as I should do professionally." So we still have another point: You said, "I don't want to cut her off altogether."*

Co 14: *Um! Yeah.*

Sr 15: *You said Um like "Hey, wait a minute." That's an issue for you, isn't it?"*

Co 15: *Yes. I don't want to cut, I can't, no, I don't want to cut her off. That's true; that is a true statement. I just get anxious, because I feel her just wanting to reel me back in.*

Sr 16: *There is a feeling of vulnerability on your part like "I'm letting myself open."*

Co 16: *Yes, but I can deal with that.*

Sr 17: *What you're saying is "That's not going to be easy. It'll test me professionally, but I'm just going to do it." What you want to do, it seems, is to leave the door open for an emergency, but only that. The way to say that clearly to Betty is to be clear in your own mind as to what you want, and what you're willing to do.*

Co 17: *I feel a sigh of relief coming out. That's OK; I feel fine about that.*

Comments on Case of Rhonda

As can be deducted from the typescript, my energy as supervisor was focused on Rhonda's conflicted feelings about terminating the counseling process, and on helping her to explore and clarify her feelings. As I saw it, what was at stake here was Rhonda's professional concept of self. She felt a need to comply with the agency's limitations, but she also wanted to serve two other goals: she wanted to end the experience with personal and professional integrity, and she also wanted to maintain a limited lifeline for the client in the event of emergency. In short Rhonda was trying to evolve and act upon the mature professional self-concept.

One function that I think the supervisory conference carried out clearly was to help Rhonda retain ultimate responsibility for her own continued professional development, and for the evolution of her own professional self-concept. While the conference in general was conducted in a way compatible with that purpose, I think one point in the conference particularly highlights that emphasis. I am referring here to Co6, where Rhonda requests my guidance in resolving her relational dilemma with the client. I see moments like this as critical choice points, moments when I need to discern the underlying message. I want to indicate how experiential theory deals with this issue, but first I want to say what this experiential moment is not. Counselors early in their training are often taught about procedures that are "right" and procedures that are "wrong." One procedure sometimes labeled as "wrong" is the procedure of answering questions. Thus when beginning counselors are confronted with questions they experience discomfort and try to learn avoidance strategies.

In my view, experiential theory frames the issue quite differently, in ways that obviate the whole question of avoidance and that permit supervisor or counselor to maintain her or his own sense of personal congruence. Experiential theory seeks to discern what the person is experiencing, where the person's energy and livingness are at that moment, and to respond in terms of that energy. It is entirely possible in supervision that the supervisee is raising a point of information, or is grappling with an intellectual issue. If so, that is the place I would like to be and a factual answer may suffice. But it is also the case that supervisees may express all kinds of experiential messages in the form of questions, and I do not wish to be misled by the grammatical form of the message. I would prefer to discern the experience. Thus, in the case of Co6, I heard Rhonda's beseeching tone, her cry for help, as though the relational dilemma was straining her personal resources. The theory provides my structure at that moment: the task is to stay with the experiencing process and to help explore and deepen the process. In my judgment, that is what took place after Co6. Her next response (Co7) is a halting, groping, confused expression that nevertheless includes with remarkable completeness just what she wants the relationship to be, and in Sr8 I let her know that that is what I heard.

One final point to be discussed in connection with The Case of Rhonda has to do with the boundaries of the experiential process in supervision. I have already indicated that one major goal in experiential supervision is to foster the development of the counselor's concept of professional self. The guideline that helps determine the boundary of relevance is the term "professional self" as distinguished from personal self. While this distinction can get fuzzy at times, we can nevertheless be guided by the contextual modifier "professional" and concentrate on the supervisee-as-counselor. This contextual boundary may momentarily (and appropriately) connect with the personal self in the service of clarifying the professional self-definition, and I would not want to be doctrinaire about disregarding such connections. Nevertheless, I wish also to establish the clear principle that I am not the supervisee's personal counselor. To take that role would lead to a morass of conflicting functions where "unconditional positive regard" would be on a collision course with the necessary and legitimate function of evaluation for which I am responsible as a supervisor. But it is also the case that within the boundaries of professional self-exploration I do not wish to inhibit or set limits to depth of exploration. As exemplified in the typescript, Rhonda is confronting some fundamental issues of professional conduct and values, and that is as it should be.

As Rhonda's supervisor, I see the level of clarification that she reached in this passage as a beginning and not an end. Much unfinished relational work needs to be done in the time that remains, and both Rhonda and I will need to track that process with care. In particular, I will want to keep paying attention to any internal sense of ambivalence that Rhonda might feel about herself as counselor in this counseling relationship. One cognitive task that fits for me in this connection is to help Rhonda distinguish between guilt and regret, and to see which one fits most for her. If it is guilt, we may have more work to do. If it is regret—why not?

Addendum

In my subsequent meeting with Rhonda, we worked on firming up the plan that she had for the termination process. In the meeting, it became evident that Rhonda's sense of professional self was firmly enough established to help her dispel any lingering guilt and to accept clearly the necessity of termination. Rhonda also recognized and accepted the fact that she could not resolve in any fundamental sense the client's affectional attachment to Rhonda, but needed to deal with it on the basis of reality based limitations.

Case Illustration: Helen

Passage 2 consists of three excerpts, recorded in successive conferences between the supervisee (Se) and me (Sr). The supervisee, Helen, is a student in the Supervision of Counseling course that I teach. She supervises a student in practicum, and is required to tape record a number of her supervisory conferences so that she and I have a basis for studying the communication that occurs. Thus, three levels of taping are involved in this total process. *Level One* is the taped record of the practicum student's counseling with the client. *Level Two* is the record of the same practicum student's conferences with the student supervisor, where the Level One tapes are studied. *Level Three* is the record that appears in this case illustration, the conferences between the student supervisor and me. We use the Level Two tapes to study the work of the student supervisor.

The excerpts that are included in this case portray aspects of the student supervisor's development as a counseling supervisor. From the perspective of this developmental process, two points become evident. We note, first, that the student and I are working on the development of Helen's professional concept of self as supervisor. As we see this process evolve, we note also that these professional issues are inextricably bound to her concept of self as a person—to her need to "play it safe" and avoid risks, her issues with assertiveness, and her positive motivation to be a competent professional person.

My basic stance in this process is to stay attuned to the experiential data that the supervisee brings out as we talk, and to facilitate the process through my own communications to her. At the same time, I am ready to challenge the supervisee with realities of my own when I see them as useful, and to offer cognitive stimulation and information where I believe that it is useful.

Excerpt 1

Se 1: *Did you want me to start with the tape?*

Sr 1: *I want you to do whatever is appropriate in your judgment.*

Se 2: *I guess I'd just as soon play a little bit of the tape, to give us something to take off from.*

Sr 2: *Sure.*

Se 3: *I don't have any particular issues, other than wondering—you know, when I read about the supervisory relationship, it's more ideal than I see our relationship.*

Sr 3: *I wonder, do you think you're getting less of a supervisory experience?*

Se 4: *No, it's just different.*

Sr 4: *So it isn't that you're feeling that you're getting less of it, but something is different. Is that OK* *with you, or is there some sense in which you're wanting to see something else happen?*

Se 5: *We're comfortable in the relationship, but I might not be able to demonstrate—or to deal with some kinds of issues.*

Sr 5: *It sounds like you're saying either that there are some things you just can't learn or some things that you won't be able to demonstrate to me.*

Se 6: *Yes, that's it. I think I can learn about them, but maybe not demonstrate to you. (Pause) I'd like for us to listen to a part of the tape where some relationship issues come up.* (Se. plays a tape segment and explains the relationship issues that she perceives developing in the counselor-client interaction.)

Sr 6: *That tells me where the counselor and client are in the relationship. I'm interested in where you are with Joan (the counselor-supervisee) around that issue.*

Se 7: *What I'm doing is seeing that Joan's feelings are making her hesitant. Yet I don't want to push it too much. I'm letting Joan talk and go where she wants to, and then, if it comes back, I would maybe pick it up.*

Sr 7: *But you're not sure? I'm getting the message "I'm aware of this but I'm not seeing a need to intervene at this time."*

Se 8: *Yes, that's on target. Part of my style, I guess, is that I like the person to—it's their journey, and so I don't want to be too directive. I might see things that I thought were important but I would like to kind of do it naturally. I might have to wait until it kind of fits it. As I see myself developing a style, that's part of it.*

Sr 8: It seems to me that you're saying "I'd feel pushy if I were to come in. I don't feel any need to intervene at this point because I'm not getting a signal from my supervisee."

Se 9: Yes.

Sr 9: So you don't want to intrude.

Se 10: If I have an underlying feeling that there's something to be dealt with—but so far we haven't come up with too many of those.

Sr 10: (Stops the tape). *I notice that in this passage a lot of the conversation is an anecdotal narrative report of what's going on between Joan and her client.*

Se 11: Yes (stated emphatically).

Sr 11: When you say yes like that, what are you saying?

Se 12: I noticed. I was thinking the same thing.

Sr 12: Now, you say that a little abashedly.

Se 13: Maybe a little. It's like when I listen to the tape later I think: "Well, that really went on for a long time—too long." Obviously she needs to present some, but maybe I need to intervene and not let her go on that long. I feel that I have some responsibility in there as to the direction. This is one of the things I have problems with, knowing just how and when to intervene. Because sometimes Joan will say something, and immediately it's like a little flag, and I think, "Hmm, what do you mean by that?" But I didn't get in fast enough, and she's off to something else. How do you deal with that sort of thing?

Sr 13: *I wonder if you're presenting a general issue here, (Se: Yes, I am) which is something like "I'm uncertain how assertively I should intervene, and I have some real questions about how and when to intervene." There's real uncertainty on your part.*

Se 14: *Yes.*

Sr 14: *How do you play that out? What are some of your thoughts about that?*

Se 15: *Well, it goes back to what you were saying about the anecdotal part. Sometimes it keeps us away from issues and I'm thinking "How do I refocus?" That's it! "How do I refocus sometimes?" I don't want to just barge in on somebody who's doing some thinking, but yet sometimes I think "Well, this is going too far afield. It isn't getting us anywhere".*

Sr 15: *So you get the sense of your letting it go, but the other part of that seems to be "But I'm reluctant to come in. Sometimes I feel like I'm interrupting."*

Se 16: *I'm getting more ideas of how to do it, but— how do I do it in a nice manner to not make the person think that I'm cutting them off? Yet I don't want to avoid productive talk about it.*

Sr 16: *OK, well, that's a real question: how can you do that? I see us talking about two things here. We're not only talking about your attitude here; we're also talking about technology. You have the attitude of not wanting to be intrusive—*

Se 17: *Yes. When I see clients at the Counseling Center, sometimes they're in real pain, and they just value having someone really listen.*

Sr 17: *But I see a real issue here, friend (Se: What?) Joan's not a client in pain. Who is she?*

Se 18: *She's a capable counselor.*

Sr 18: *OK. There's quite a difference (Se: Yes). So now we're saying, there's a difference between counseling a client and working with a capable counselor.*

Se 19: *There is, there's a big difference there.*

Sr 19: *So you say, "Yes, I think it's really good when I'm counseling a person who is vulnerable and in pain." But now—and this is me talking—we don't have that situation (Se: Exactly); we have a different situation, and the question is, does it call for anything different?*

Se 20: *I think it does call for something different, but this role is new to me and so, even though I'm getting ideas, I haven't been able to integrate getting into it and feeling confident in what I'm doing.*

Sr 20: *Yes, I'm aware of the uncertainty that you're talking about, and one place where it comes in is in the question "What kind of risk behavior are you willing to engage in?" (Se: That's right). Is there another way to formulate that issue (Se: No) or is that OK?*

Se 21: *I think that's a lot on target, because Joan is not a vulnerable client, she's very self-assured and she can take it. So I have a good place—I don't have to tiptoe around Joan.*

Sr 21: *Are you saying "I don't need to be afraid to take some risks here"? (Se: Yes). So here's a chance for you to try out and to venture, and you and I will have a chance to check it out.*

Commentary on Excerpt 1

Several points stand out for me in the foregoing excerpt. From the standpoint of the supervisee, it becomes clear that her inexperience weighs heavily upon her and makes her cautious in responding to her counselor-supervisee. She begins to see the lost opportunities that result from her caution and entertains the possibility of intervening more assertively. She is beginning to evolve her professional self-definition.

In the foregoing excerpt what is evident is that on my part a noticeable absence of instruction by me has occurred as to how the supervisee should behave. Such absence is no happenstance. My view is that the primary learning task for the student is not only to evolve her own professional self-concept but also, as part of this task, to develop her own theory of counseling and supervision. Experiential theory is compatible with this goal in its emphasis upon the illumination of the supervisee's own phenomenology.

But all this is not to say that I have adopted a laissez-faire structure: by no means. For example, in Sr6 and Sr10 I am setting standards of communication that limit external narration and emphasize self-relevant exploration. In addition, confrontation and challenge, as in Sr17, are part of our process.

Excerpt 2

Two different tapes are involved in this excerpt. The first very brief segment comes from the tape of supervision between Joan (Co, the counselor) and Helen (Ss, the student supervisor). The rest of the excerpt reverts to the conference between the student supervisor and me.

Tape of Counselor (Co) and Student Supervisor (Ss)

Co 1: *There's some acknowledgement of the emotional problem by the client. But I wonder if there's other stuff that I should be doing.*

Ss 1: She sounds like a complex person, and you can't deal with all of the issues, all at once.

Tape of Student Supervisor (Se) and me (Sr)

Sr 1: Are you experiencing or perceiving some request to you from the counselor?

Se 1: Well, I did a little bit when she said, "I wonder if there's something else I should be doing?" I didn't like the response that I made. What I think was going on with me was that I tried to turn it back to her, rather than just say, "Well, you should be doing this or doing that".

Sr 2: Ok, you didn't want to do that. How would you characterize what you did do?

Se 2: I deflected the question.

Sr 3: Was that one of the things you wanted to do?

Se 3: I did, kind of,

Sr 4: The other thing that I caught was a note of reassurance from you to Joan.

Se 4: Yes, that was there.

Sr 5: Let's get back to Joan's comment "I wonder. . ." etc. You were saying that you didn't want to use that as a cue to give her advice. OK, but she may be raising an issue that's real for her. Did you catch anything more in that "I wonder" response? What's going on in that response?

Se 5: Well, it might be that "I don't feel that I'm doing enough for the client."

Sr 6. Yes, it may be "I have some doubt" or "I have some uncertainty."

Se 6: *Or "you sound unsure." Well, not unsure.*

Sr 7: *Yes, it's not quite that, is it? (Pause) I want to go back to your comment "I deflected her question."*

Se 7: *I wanted to get away from making a direct answer, and also I wanted to reassure her.*

Sr 8: *OK, that's what you chose to do. There's one other thing that you could do. When she says "I wonder if I'm doing all I can" she's tangling with an issue that's real for her, and it's possible to go deeper. I would say to the counselor, "You're raising a question. Check that out and let's see what's in that question for you." There's no need to respond by giving her advice, and there's also no need to sidestep the issue—*

Se 8: *That's right. At the time I said to myself, "Well, jeez, this isn't exactly what I want to be doing." It's like, this thing is going on within me and I'm saying, "Well, how am I going to do this?" I want to step back, but then the moment is gone. I need to do something that's a holding pattern.*

Sr 9: *I see. You were buying time. Did you feel some pressure there?*

Se 9: *Yes, a little bit of pressure not to answer directly. But I also missed what was going on with her.*

Sr 10: *Looking back now, can you see something that you'd rather be doing?*

Se 10: *It would be not choosing that avoidance type of response, and staying with that question of hers. It's a perfect opportunity to get into her feeling, which I missed.*

Sr 11: *It was hard for you, at that instant, to be there.*

Se 11: *Yes. I'm getting better at getting the messages, but I still have a long way to go, to be really there on the spot. And I have to ask myself, "Are you afraid of something? Are you afraid of dealing with feelings?" I don't think I am, but I'm not sure.*

Sr 12: *Are you saying, "I want to be thinking about this?"*

Se 12: *Yes. I'm not sure if it's fear or if it's a lack of knowledge about how to do it.*

Sr 13: *That's where practice and experience come in. There's one little clue for me. If I feel myself avoiding something, I ask, "What's going on here in me?" Because I don't want to do that. And I realize that you felt discomfort and a bit sneaky about avoiding the issue.*

Se 13: *If I make a leap and it's a bad leap, I'm afraid I'll be stuck in the middle of nowhere. But I don't see any point in being afraid of that; it just holds me back.*

Commentary on Excerpt 2

I see two elements that characterize this excerpt. One element centers on the work that we were doing to help the supervisee comprehend more deeply what she was experiencing during her supervisory session. Specifically, she became aware of her discomfort and dissatisfaction with her response to her counselor-supervisee, and was able with my help to pinpoint the source of her discomfort as avoidance behavior. As the experiential issues became clearer in ways that helped her define goals for new behavior, the second element came into play, namely, a more cognitively oriented discussion of alternative and more satisfying ways of responding. Here I could **bring to bear my own experience by suggesting (in Sr. 8, Sr 13) technical procedures that could meet her goals.**

The way that experiential theory assists in situations of this kind is that the theory makes us sensitive to an appropriate sequence in the respective use of experiential and cognitive modes of response. The theory specifies that cognitive strategies are most relevant when psychological readiness to learn and use the strategies has been enhanced by an experiential understanding of the issues. Such understanding internalizes the issues and enhances ownership of the issues by the learner.

Excerpt 3

(Listening to tape of conference between the counselor and student-supervisor—Level 2 tape)

Se 1: I'm trying to see where this is going, so I'm not responding to any of it. I wonder about that.

Sr 1: When you say "I wonder about that," tell me what you mean. What's that wonderment made of?

Se 2: If I'm not responding I'm passing over some promising areas.

Sr 2: So you're asking if you're missing some opportunities.

Se 3: Yes. I'm still being plagued by my continual questioning about how and when do I get to that. I'm always afraid that I might derail her. Also, I'm afraid that I won't know what to do if I open up something. I could bring it in the here and now.

Sr 3: That may be a major way to do it. Also, giving yourself permission to stumble around a bit as you do that might also help you.

Se 4: Yes, I'm stopping myself. That's the bottom line, you might say. I'm afraid to open things up and then not know what to do with it.

Sr 4: *Here's my thought on that—there's a process that goes on all the time, and that is, listening to the person and staying with her. It may turn out that there's nothing new to do, but to stay in the present.*

Se 5: *So if we just keep on interacting, there's nothing new to be afraid of.*

Sr 5: *Yes, it's always in the present.*

Se 6: *I like that idea. I think, as you said, it's a matter of giving myself permission, because I'm never going to do it unless I make that step. I wasn't able to stay in the present with Rhonda and I missed that chance. So the thing for me to do is to get in there with her. That's my assignment for the next time.*

Later that afternoon

The supervisee and I chanced to meet in the hall that afternoon. She said that the morning's meeting (above) helped her to integrate feeling and action and that she was eager to try more active procedures. She said, "I want to get going. I can hardly wait."

Commentary

The three excerpts reveal that a major developmental task with the supervisee was to help her get successively closer to the feelings that kept her from responding to the counselor with whom she was working. Once these feelings became clear, we were ready for both cognitive and relational steps: the cognitive steps pinpointed the actions that she could take, and the relational step in this instance was for me to help empower and support some new procedures in the face of her anxiety about them. This latter relational step may remain prominent until the supervisee's experience helps her achieve personal internal empowerment and confidence.

CONCLUDING COMMENTS ON EXPERIENTIAL SUPERVISION

In the proceeding passages we have seen experiential supervision at close range. The theoretical framework that structures this task postulates that growth in competence comes about as we enhance awareness and help the person get in touch with and utilize her or his own experiential data. This is the fundamental procedure in experiential supervision, and this is what we saw in action.

The foregoing processes represent the seedbed of learning, but more needs to be done. Supervision also involves skill learning, and in this respect more cognitively oriented instruction is useful, along with relational processes that empower and support the supervisee. What we have, then is a combination in which the experiential exploration helps the supervisee maintain ownership of his or her own experiences and discoveries, and frees the person to accept and try out new ideas without needing to imitate blindly the style of the supervisor. We then create a situation in which the supervisee can grow in competence and also maintain her or his own selfhood. These tasks are fundamental learning tasks oriented toward the goal of professional self-development.

REFERENCES

Angyal, A. (1941). *Foundations for a science of personality.* New York: The Commonwealth Fund.

Rogers, C.R. (1961). *On becoming a person.* New York: Houghton Mifflin.

Rogers, C.R. (1963). The concept of the fully functioning person. *Psychotherapy: Theory, Research, and Practice, 1,* 17-26.

Wiener, N. (1954). *The human use of human beings.* New York: Avon Books.

CHAPTER 10

GROUP SUPERVISION

Richard L. Hayes, Ed.D.

In a book devoted entirely to the issue of supervision, some may question the need for a separate chapter on group supervision. Clearly, many of the skills and methods used within a group setting are no different than those used by all counselors and supervisors in whatever setting. The same may be said of the general knowledge and skills that any counselor brings to the tasks of helping. Yet the supervision of counselors in a group is not the same as supervising them individually, any more than group counseling is merely the counseling of individuals in a group. Moreover, the supervision of counselors learning group facilitation skills is not the same as the supervision of a group of counselors.

TOWARD A DEFINITION

At least four distinct but overlapping forms of supervision may properly be called group supervision. As Holloway and Johnston (1985) noted in their review of the literature, the applications of group supervision have included

> (a) group supervision of trainees in a practicum setting who are learning individual counseling skills, (b) group supervision of trainees learning pre-practicum interviewing skills, (c) leaderless groups in which trainees provide peer supervision in group format, and (d) group supervision of trainees in a practicum setting focusing on learning group facilitation skills. (p. 333)

More to the point, however, is the important distinction that group supervision takes place in a group and, as such, "the members see themselves and are seen by others as psychologically interdependent and interactive in pursuit of a shared goal" (Dagley, Gazda, & Pistone, 1986, p. 131). The essential task for the group supervisor, therefore, is to facilitate the development of a productive work group as preparatory to effective supervision. What should be the shared goals of supervision? What leadership style is most appropriate for the realization of these goals? What balance of approaches is most productive? What role should evaluation play in the various components of group supervision? These questions must be addressed by group supervisor (see Holloway & Johnston, 1985).

BENEFITS OF GROUP SUPERVISION

Beyond the obvious and much touted use of groups to reduce supervisory time, the real benefits to be realized in group supervision are from the unique contributions groups have to make to the personal and professional development of supervisees. Drawing upon the work of Dagley, Gazda, and Pistone (1986) and Kaul and Bednar (1978), who have enumerated the unique learning opportunities to be found in group as opposed to individual counseling, the following advantages can be found for group as opposed to individual supervision:

1. Group supervision offers each supervisee the opportunity to reality-test self-perceptions.

2. Through group interactions, distorted perceptions and false assumptions of self and others may become more apparent and lose their value.

3. Group supervision may provide a sense of psychological safety to support the elimination of self-defeating behaviors.

4. Group supervision provides an opportunity to interact in real-life situations, thus providing supervisees with chances to try out new behaviors in a safe environment.

5. Responses of others, especially one's peers, can help supervisees to appreciate the universality of some personal concerns.

6. Group supervision enables supervisees to increase their abilities to give and to solicit appropriate self-disclosures and feedback, thus enhancing opportunities to function as both helpers and helpees.

7. Interaction with others in a group can enhance one's empathy and social interest.

8. Groups of some duration offer supervisees opportunities to make systematic progress toward personal changes, receiving reinforcement for changes.

9. Group supervision exposes supervisees to alternative modes of helping, which can help supervisees to develop deeper understandings and acceptance of different counseling styles.

10. Consistent feedback from others in group supervision can enhance the supervisee's accuracy of perception and communication.

Although "the field of counselor training is at a rudimentary level of explaining and understanding group supervision" (Holloway & Johnston, 1985, p. 338), much is known about the specifics of group process and of its potential contributions to the enhancement of interpersonal effectiveness (Yalom, 1985). To understand the nature of group supervision, therefore, one must understand the nature of groups themselves. As will be presented in the pages to follow, group supervision may be described by three dimensions: type, dynamics, and development.

TYPES OF GROUPS

Groups are commonly classified on the basis of such shared properties as number of members, duration, function, membership characteristics, setting, level of prevention, leadership, goals, and so forth. These classifications refer to the focus or content of the group and generally may be said to describe characteristics of the group that are known prior to its first meeting. As such, these dimensions are generally under the control of the supervisor and may be manipulated in the formation of the group.

These characteristics describe separate but interacting elements of the group. The number of supervisees anticipated to be in the group, for instance, will affect the formation of the group along other dimensions. The greater the number of members, the greater will be the demands on the setting to provide sufficient seating and privacy for the members. Further, increased numbers will change the nature of the supervision if everyone is to be provided an opportunity to speak and to share his or her concerns during the session. In addition, opportunities for each member to give and receive feedback may demand that the group meet longer or that interactions are held to certain previously agreed upon limits. How one decides whether and to what extent to involve each member depends in part upon the purposes of supervision and its level of prevention.

Member characteristics such as level of experience and expertise or diversity of work or practicum sites, for example, will affect the level and focus of supervision. Experienced supervisees employed in a community agency are more likely to possess wider variability of experiences and expertise than will be found among pre-practicum students taking their first course as part of a master's program. How one responds to these differences depends upon and is influenced reciprocally by the general goals of the supervisory group.

As noted above, these variables are known to some extent prior to the initial meeting of the group and are, therefore, more predictable and subject to greater control. Within academic settings, for example, the admissions process, combined with the structure of prerequisites within the curriculum, tend to control the selection and progression of supervisees on the basis of previous knowledge and level of mastery of relevant skills. In community agencies, hospitals, or clinics, however, staff members come and go more irregularly, and typically present a more heterogeneous mixture of professionals. How the group is structured initially depends upon the supervisor's sensitivity to and knowledge of these dimensions of the group. As noted repeatedly, however, how members may be involved best in the development of a significant group supervision experience is related to the shared goals of the group itself.

Supervisory Goals

A review of the group supervision literature yields a general consensus on four components of group supervision and training that meet distinct but overlapping supervisory goals (Coche, 1977; Shapiro, 1978; Tauber, 1978; Yalom, 1985). These goals may include the mastery of theoretical concepts, skill development, personal growth, or the integration of the supervisee's skills, knowledge, and attitudes as effective counseling tools.

The first of these goals is met most characteristically through some academic component of the supervisee's training and is not a major goal of supervision. Nonetheless, the supervisor may require selected readings on general issues of concern to supervisees or may suggest readings relevant to the concerns of specific students.

Skill development is the most frequent goal for supervision and should be focused upon the identification and skillful handling of recurrent clinical situations. Yalom (1985) cautions, however, that it is a mistake

> to allow the group to move into a supervisory format where members describe problems they encounter in their therapeutic work with patients: such discussion should be the province of the [individual] supervisory hour. Whenever a group is engaged in discourse that can be held equally well in another formal setting, I believe that it is failing to use its unique properties and full potential. (p. 529)

Moreover, when the supervisees are engaged in group work, skill development should be focused on issues that have a high relevance for the development of group as opposed to individual skills.

In response to calls for more humanistic and experiential training practices (see Holloway & Johnston, 1985) to promote personal growth, counselor educators in the 1960s began to incorporate interpersonal process groups into their training programs. Despite methodological difficulties in proving the efficacy of such approaches in improving supervisees' functioning, "group supervision still retains, however, some of the early emphasis on the facilitator role in supervision" (Holloway & Johnston, 1985, p. 335). Although group supervision can and should be therapeutic, individual therapeutic change is a secondary consideration to the primary goals of training, which are "the intensive group experience, the expression and integration of affect, [and] the recognition of here-and-now process" (Yalom, 1985, p. 527).

Skill integration may be the most important goal of supervision. Group supervision, specifically, presents a unique training opportunity by providing a context for such integration. The experience within a group of situations illustrative of actual psychodynamic as well as group dynamic issues helps supervisees to make important connections between their academic knowledge and clinical practice. Supervisees learn "when to trust [their] intuition, how to use data from within, when to self-disclose and to what extent, when to push, and when to back off" (Coche, 1977. p. 237).

To the four goals of mastery, skill development, personal growth, and integration, evaluation may be added. Although inclusion in the group is based in part on previous performance, supervision often serves the purpose of ongoing evaluation. Beyond the ethical issues raised by the dual role of supervisor-evaluator (see Reisman, 1985; Yalom, 1985) are the very real problems that arise when supervisees are asked to self-disclose personally and professionally relevant material to persons in a position to evaluate them. Despite the supervisor's best efforts to model openness, self-disclosure, and the professional limitations of assuring complete confidentiality, supervisees remain reluctant to self-disclose, especially in front of their peers and their supervisor at the same time.

Faced with the dilemma to administer or supervise, Yalom (1985) believed that "the group becomes a far more effective vehicle for personal growth and for training if led by a leader outside the institution who will play no role in the [supervisee] evaluation" (p. 527). Barring this possibility, supervisors are advised to make clear the extent to which self-disclosure will become part of any evaluation and what the penalties are likely to be, if any, for failing to participate.

In summary, the important thing to note is that the characteristics that differentiate one group from another interact to create unique training conditions. Differences in the group's characteristics require that adjustments be made to maximize the training opportunities to be found within each group. The interaction of member-related and goal-related characteristics creates the essential dynamic of the group and accounts for its success and uniqueness as a training medium. How the group supervisor can best exploit the learning opportunities presented by each group is a function of the group's dynamics, the second dimension of group supervision.

GROUP DYNAMICS

Despite their characterization by the rather static dimensions of size, membership, duration, and the like, groups have a dynamic quality to them. As Knowles and Knowles (1959) noted, a group "is always moving, doing something, changing, becoming, interacting, and reacting" (p. 12). Just as the group's characteristics interact to place limits upon one another, so too the events that act themselves out in the group interact with one another and with the various dimensions of the group itself. The struggle by group members to balance the forces associated with accomplishing goal-related tasks and building a shared community creates the group's dynamics. According to Lakin (1976), eight core group processes occur in all types of experiential groups regardless of the quality of the members or the leader. These processes are described in pages to follow.

Cohesiveness

A unique characteristic of groups and one which, perhaps more than any other, contributes to the sense of "we-ness" members experience in more successful groups is cohesion. The development of a shared frame of reference helps to bind members to common goals as well as one another. The more stable structure that results helps members to tolerate greater diversity of opinion within the group and to withstand threats to group solidarity from without (Lakin, 1976). Whatever the goals of the group, therefore, the group supervisor should attempt to establish and maintain group cohesion, especially early in group's history.

Norms

Norms refer to behavior that is "expected" of others in the group. They act as guidelines for acceptable behavior in the group and are associated with certain rewards and punishments. Because norms may arise within the group as shared expectations, whether implicit or explicit, group members may not be consciously aware of the influence of group norms on their behavior in the group.

The task of the supervisor is to help group members to identify norms that may be operating within the group and to help members to examine their relevance for the group's activity. Because norms play such an important role in helping to socialize members into the group (Lakin & Carson, 1966), supervisors should take an active role in modeling appropriate behaviors such as responding empathically, showing genuine concern and respect for others, or confronting out of caring. Such behaviors, especially early in the group's life, can be important in setting the tone for a productive supervisory group. Of course, the supervisor is cautioned not to be too directive in setting norms for the group. Supervisees are more likely to be committed to norms in which they have had a hand in their development (Hayes, 1980).

Validation and Feedback

One of the important outcomes of participation in a group is the opportunity for members to test their perceptions and improve their communications with others. Group supervision provides supervisees the opportunity to receive validation for their own ideas in the company of their peers. As Jacobs (cited in Gazda, 1984, p. 57) and Stockton and Morran (1982) have cautioned, however, positive feedback, whether or not it is followed by negative feedback, is more effective than negative feedback in influencing members to change their behavior, especially in early sessions. Consequently, supervisors are advised to limit feedback in early sessions to the description of desirable behaviors and to emphasize that feedback is only the perception of the giver.

Emotional Immediacy

The increased awareness of feelings, especially as generated within the here-and-now context of the group, is an important part of group work. Nonetheless, the expression of all feelings or even of some feelings fully is not necessarily in the best interests of either the group or its members (see Giges & Rosenfeld, cited in Gazda, 1984, p. 58). Although full expression can and often does help the one with the feelings, members react with feelings of their own, and if expressed, generate feelings in other members in reaction. Sorting through the maze of feelings created in even the briefest exchange, can lead to chaos. To reduce the potential for such breakdowns in communication, the supervisor is advised to limit such exchanges to either the full expression of feelings or to the clarification of ideas. Further, the supervisor should push members to make explicit connections to the group's goals for supervision and to norms operating within the group.

Problem Solving

If one considers a problem as the difference between how things are and how they ought to be, then a group provides recurrent opportunities for problem solving as members test their own perceptions and ideals against those of other group members (Wasik & Fishbein, 1982). Group supervision not only provides opportunities for problem solving, but it should require the active participation of all members in assuming responsibility for the productivity of the group. Acting in the context of group-effected problem-solving processes places responsibility upon supervisees for their own conduct, both in and outside the group. Further, the full exploration of alternatives by the group is likely to lead to a more effective solution than one offered by single members or even the leader (see Johnson & Johnson, 1975; Slavin, 1983).

Leadership

As used here, leadership refers to a dynamic function of the group wherein members' activities are directed to the satis-faction of group goals. Therefore, leadership is viewed as more a function of the group than it is a role occupied by a single member. As the needs of the group change, the demands placed upon its members will change. Although the supervisor may begin as the leader of the group, supervisees may be called upon periodically as the group's needs demand.

In Turquet's (1974) words, leadership requires "appraisal" rather than "discharge." The supervisor acts not so much to direct the group as to create a climate in which the group finds its own direction. The supervisees' efforts should be evaluated in relation to the group's efforts rather than by comparison with the efforts of the supervisor.

Reflecting upon the goals for group supervision, one can deduce that each of the five goals can be expanded to include leadership development. Mastery of concepts relative to leadership theory should be included in the more academic dimensions of group supervision. In addition, supervisees should be given opportunities to develop skills in leading their supervisory group as preparation for leading other, "less receptive" groups of their own. Practice in leading their peers will provide supervisees with the opportunity to exert their power and influence under somewhat controlled conditions.

Accepting that a group presents a microcosm of society, replete with a wide variety of personal and interpersonal problems, group supervision offers a unique opportunity for integrating theoretical concepts with practical problems. As a result, "the need for a wide variety of expertise will allow all group members the opportunity to exercise their influence at one time or another. Those who seek to dominate or to be dominated should emerge, and these life-styles will then be grist for the group mill" (Gazda, 1984, p. 59).

Finally, the possibility of evaluation gives rise to important considerations about the nature and extent of one's influence over the group process and the nature of the supervisor's authority. Just as the counselor's effectiveness is measured ultimately by the client's success in meeting his or her own goals, so too supervisees must learn that their success lies in meeting their own goals relative to standards previously agreed upon.

Self-disclosure

The person who enters a group is faced with a dilemma: how to become a part of the group's collective identity and at the same time preserve one's individual identity. Self-disclosure needs come into conflict as members seek affirmation for the resolution of past struggles, on the one hand, while fearing the disapproval that can come with confessing one's weaknesses on the other (see Lakin & Carson, 1966).

Group supervision poses the problem, as noted earlier, of subjecting oneself to the potential criticism of one's peers in an effort to gain the approval of one's supervisor, and vice versa. Complicating the situation for the supervisor is the realization that supervisees may have different levels of need satisfaction (see Stockton & Morran, 1982; Thibault & Kelley, 1959). Group supervision offers supervisees a vivid demonstration of the differential needs of persons to self-disclose and can serve as an important object lesson in the need to respect clients' rights to self-disclose in their own ways.

Roles

One of the great benefits of participation in a group is the opportunity to try out different roles with different people. Indeed, the great benefit to group supervision is the possibility of testing a variety of roles in practice situations. For the supervisor, group work provides the opportunity to try on a variety of roles as well (see Stenack & Dye, 1982). In a study of group supervision behaviors, Savickas, Marquart, and Supinski (1986) found students judged the following role requirements to be most important for group supervisors: modeling target behaviors; teaching skills, techniques, and strategies; evaluating performance; and facilitating exploration, critical thought, and experimentation (p. 23). Clearly, the most important role of the supervisor may be in modeling the variety of behaviors necessary to respond to the demands posed by different supervisees experiencing different problems.

DEVELOPMENT

Counselors and counselor educators have long recognized the important relationship that exists between counseling and human development. As early as the 1940s, Robert Mathewson (1962) was among the first to argue that development should be the essential principle in organizing and implementing programs of guidance and counseling. Surprisingly, counselor educators and supervisors have been slow to apply the known principles of human development to the supervisory process, especially group supervision.

The work that has been done has tended to focus on the supervisee's stage of learning in becoming a counselor (see Holloway & Johnston, 1985), although studies have reported the application of a developmental framework to group supervision (Sansbury, 1982; Wilbur, Roberts-Wilbur, Hart, & Betz, 1986; Yogev, 1982). With the possible exceptions of Bernier (1980), Blocher (1983), and Tennyson & Strom, (1986), whose approaches may be considered structural, models of developmental supervision have tended to rely on either behavioral or maturational approaches to development (see Hayes, 1986). The effect has been to build models around the supervisee's level of mastery of selected skills in a sequence of progressively more difficult behaviors (see, for example, Delaney, 1972; Forsyth & Ivey, 1980; Grater, 1985; Hill, Charles, & Reed, 1981; Hosford & Barmann, 1983; Ponterotto & Zander, 1984; Richardson & Bradley, 1984; Schmidt, 1979; Strosahl & Jacobson, 1986) and/or around a sequence of preferred professional activities (see, for example, Heppner & Roehlke 1984; Hess, 1986; Miars, Tracey, Ray, Cornfield, O'Farrell, & Gelso, 1983; Moskowitz, 1981).

To date, I am unaware of any report that describes a group supervision model that accounts for the relationship between the supervisee's level of mastery of relevant counseling behaviors, the sequence of concerns in group development, and the cognitive, ego, and moral development of the supervisee over the course of training. The limitations of the present chapter make a complete proposal impossible, but enough is known about counseling, supervision, and human development to offer a skeletal hypothesis about what a comprehensive program of developmental group supervision might include.

Level of Mastery

Ivey (1988) has identified four levels of mastery of interviewing skills that can be used to structure a training program:

Level 1: Identification. You will be able to identify the skill and the impact of the skill on the client.

Level 2: Basic mastery. You will be able to use the skill in the role-played interview.

Level 3: Active mastery. You will be able to use the skill with specific impact on the client.

Level 4: Teaching mastery. You will be able to teach the skill to clients and other trainees. (p. 340)

By referring to Carkhuff (1983); Combs and Avila (1985); Egan (1982); Gazda, Asbury, Balzer, Childers, and Walters (1984); or Ivey (1988), for examples, the experienced counselor educator or supervisor can identify specific counseling skills to be developed.

As for group counseling skills, the Association for Specialists in Group Work (1983) has identified the minimum core of group leader (cognitive and applied) competencies and Gazda (1984, pp. 376-379) has reproduced an extensive list of competencies and performance criteria for group counseling. Because space does not permit a detailed presentation of these competencies here, the interested reader is encouraged to consult the original sources. Certainly the supervisor interested in conducting group supervision should be familiar with and competent to at least these prescribed levels prior to initiating group supervision.

Sequence of Activities

Whatever the model (psychoanalytic, humanistic-existential, social learning, TA/Gestalt, eclectic) or setting (administrative, clinical) of supervision chosen, the supervisor must also choose a modality by which to apply the model. Different modalities have different effects on supervisees and make different demands on the skills of both the supervisees and the supervisor.

In general, Hart (1982) has suggested that the supervision "begin at the least complex level and proceed gradually to more complex levels. When applied to modality, this rule suggests that supervisors begin with individual supervision and later add group and/or peer supervision" (p. 204). Within the context of group supervision, this rule suggests that group supervision represents a median level of supervision that presumes prior experience and demonstrated mastery in individual supervision **and that is preparatory to peer supervision. Certainly, any program of supervision might include various patterns of** individual, group, and peer supervision that respond to the changing needs of the supervisees and the demand characteristics of the training site (time, staff, availability of space, etc.).

As Savickas, Marquart, and Supinski (1986) suggested, "level of training may be a more important variable in research on effective group supervision than is type of student" (p. 24). In a survey of experienced group psychotherapy supervisors, Dies (1980) found that the preferred sequence of training activities should begin with an academic component and then move progressively through an observational component, an experiential component, and conclude with supervision of actual practice.

In a related study, Dies (1974) found that experienced group therapists rated twelve different training experiences from most to least helpful as follows:

1. Co-therapy experience with a qualified therapist.

2. Discussion of your own therapy tapes with a supervisor.

3. Supervised experience in individual therapy.

4. Co-therapy experience with a peer, followed by sessions with a supervisor.

5. Attendance at group psychotherapy workshops.

6. Attendance at T-group training workshops.

7. Participation as a patient in a therapy group.

8. Discussion of films or videotapes produced by experts.

9. Careful analysis and discussion of audiotapes produced by experts.

10. Serving as a recorder-observer in a group.

11. Didactic seminars (theory, research, case study).

12. **Learning by doing, self-taught (practice, reading). (Dies, 1980, p. 340)**

In its *Professional Standards for Group Counseling* (ASGW, 1983), the Association for Specialists in Group Work recommended the following types of supervised experience (the minimum number of clock hours recommended for graduation from a master's level program appear in parentheses):

1. Critique of group tapes (5).

2. Observing group counseling (live or media presentation) (5).

3. Participating as a member in a group (15).

4. Leading a group with a partner and receiving critical feedback from a supervisor (15).

5. Practicum: Leading a group alone, with critical self-analysis of performance; supervisor feedback on tape; and self-analysis (15).

6. Fieldwork of Internship: Practice as a group leader with on-the-job supervision (25).

Although these standards actually exceed the standards currently in force for counselor education programs accredited by the Council for the Accreditation of Counseling and Related Educational Programs (CACREP), they are considered to be minimal standards for practitioners and do not constitute more advanced standards that might be appropriate for supervisors of group counseling supervisees.

Notably, these recommended experiences refer to a sequence of activities that is appropriate from the perspective of the individual supervisee. On the group level, supervisees are not only engaged in a sequence appropriate to their own professional development but are members of a supervisory group that can be described by its own developmental sequence.

Research (Bonney, 1976; Gibbard, Hartman & Mann, 1974; Mills, 1964; Tuckman & Jensen, 1977; Yalom, 1985) has suggested that although each group is unique, effective small groups follow a generalizable pattern from initiation to termination. This pattern is formed by a sequence of overlapping stages that are characterized by a set of focal concerns that rise and fall in importance as the group moves toward maturity. Although the particular names and boundaries of these stages vary from description to description, a fair synopsis of this research would provide a sequence similar to the one that follows:

Forming: A stage of testing and encounter during which members attempt to find out who the members are and how they will relate to one another. There is a concern for individual needs, where security and safety are important elements.

Storming: A stage of intragroup conflict, emotional expression, and role-modeling. Primary concerns are focused on the nature of legitimate authority, the role of the leader, and the proper balance between task and process variables.

Norming: A stage of group cohesion through the development of social sanctions. Members are engaged in identifying and evaluating group norms, in establishing acceptable roles within the group, and in redefining group and individual goals.

Performing: A stage of role-relatedness and production during which members come to terms with the realities of this group, its work, and the members' roles relative to the tasks to be accomplished.

Mourning: A stage of separation, assessment, and evaluation during which members must deal with the termination of this group experience, the consolidation of any personal gains, and the transition to a life after the group.

The supervisor who is aware of these different stages recognizes that different tasks must be performed relative to the stage-related needs of the group. During the *forming stage,* for instance, the supervisor is advised to provide a greater degree of structure and direction in helping supervisees establish personal goals for supervision and in modeling group-appropriate behaviors. To move the group into the *storming stage,* supervisors need to challenge supervisees to examine their reasons for being in the group and to take greater responsibility for their behavior.

Movement into the *norming stage* is facilitated by helping the group to identify norms already operating within the group and to encourage an analysis of their effectiveness relative to accomplishing individual and group goals. Of course, the general goals for the supervisory group remain, and it is during the *performing stage* that supervisees are encouraged to get down to the actual work of the group. Finally, if the group has been at all effective, members will be reluctant to end the experience and/or will attempt to ascribe any success to some uniqueness in the group or its members. During this *mourning stage,* the supervisor should help members to confront this denial process directly and to facilitate the important work of "letting go" of the group experience, recognizing both the losses and opportunities to be gained from termination. The interested reader is encouraged to consult Corey (1985), Hayes (1980), and Stanford (1977) for more detailed descriptions of stage-related group leader behaviors.

Psychological Development

The existence of universal stages of psychological development provides the supervisor with a theoretical framework for supervision, the purpose of which is to stimulate supervisees to higher levels of development. The most extensive application of group counseling to individual development can be found in Gazda's (1984) synthesis of interview group counseling and life-skills training models with a developmental tasks concept of human development.

Drawing upon the work of various developmental theorists, Gazda has attempted to create a comprehensive guide for group counseling with all age levels and with various populations across seven domains: (1) psychosocial, (2) vocational, (3) physical-sexual, (4) cognitive, (5) moral, (6) ego, and (7) affective. Although his presentation is focused primarily on populations other than healthy adults, his chapter on "Group Counseling for the Adolescent and Adult" does provide some insight into a possible model for group supervision. He fails to provide the necessary connections, however, between stage-related tasks to be accomplished for each group member and specific leader behaviors. Promising models do exist, however, that may be adapted for use with adults in group supervision.

The work of Blocher (1983) and Tennyson and Strom (1986) mentioned above reported attempts to integrate structural developmental interventions into counselor supervision. In addition, the work of Kohlberg, Kauffman, Scharf, and Hickey (1974) with adults in correctional facilities, Swensen's (1980) work investigating the match between counselor and client developmental levels and counselor effectiveness, Young-Eisendrath's (1985) analysis of authority issues in counseling, Knefelkamp and Slepitza's (1976) work in career development, and the work of Thies-Sprinthall (1984) and Thompson (1982) with teachers suggest that developmental interventions with adults in groups can be an effective stimulant to ego, moral, and ethical development.

Nonetheless, a unified model integrating adult development theory with specific group leadership practices is still unavailable.

CONCLUSION

Despite its shaky beginnings and the inflated claims of earlier proponents, group work continues to promise unique opportunities for training in counseling. Its wide acceptance in counselor supervision is tempered by the recognition that a systematic analysis of the process of group supervision has yet to be reported. Nonetheless, supervisors and counselor educators in search of ways to improve their supervision are faced with numerous excellent proposals. Until the necessary program of systematic research reveals the connections between group supervision and counselor effectiveness, supervisors are well-advised to take heed of the suggestions for practice offered in the studies cited here. And above all, become involved in the systematic examination of your own and others' behavior both as a member and as a leader of supervised groups.

REFERENCES

Association for Specialists in Group Work. (1983). *ASGW professional standards for group counseling.* Alexandria, VA: Author.

Bernier, J.E. (1980). Training and supervising counselors: Lessons learned from deliberate psychological education. *Personnel and Guidance Journal, 59,* 15-20.

Blocher, D. (1983). Toward a cognitive developmental approach to counseling supervision. *Counseling Psychologist, 11,* 9-18.

Bonney, W.C. (1976). Group Counseling and developmental processes. In G.M. Gazda (Ed.), *Theories and methods of group counseling in the schools* (2nd ed., pp. 313-342). Springfield, IL: Charles C. Thomas.

Carkhuff, R.R. (1983). *The art of helping* (5th ed.). Amherst, MA: Human Resource Development Press.

Coche, E. (1977). Training of group therapists. In F. Kaslow (Ed.), *Supervision, consultation, and staff training in the helping professions* (pp. 235-253). San Francisco: Jossey-Bass.

Combs, A.W., & Avila, D.L. (1985). *Helping relationships: Basic concepts for the helping professions* (3rd ed.). Boston: Allyn and Bacon.

Corey, G. (1985). *Theory and practice of group counseling* (2nd ed.). Monterey, CA: Brooks/Cole.

Dagley, J., Gazda, G., & Pistone, C. (1986). Groups. In M. Lewis, R. Hayes, & J. Lewis (Eds.), *An introduction to the counseling profession* (pp. 130-166). Itasca, IL: F.E. Peacock.

Delaney, D.J. (1972). A behavioral model for the practicum supervision of counselor candidates. *Counselor Education and Supervision, 12,* 46-50.

Dies, R. (1974). Attitudes toward the training of group psychotherapists: Some interprofessional and experience-associated differences. *Small Group Behavior, 5,* 65-79.

Dies, R. (1980). Group psychotherapy: Training and supervision. In A.K. Hess (Ed.), *Psychotherapy Supervision* (pp. 337-366). New York: Wiley.

Egan, G. (1982). *The skilled helper* (2nd ed.). Monterey, CA: Brooks/Cole.

Forsyth, D., & Ivey, A. (1980). Microtraining: An approach to differential supervision. In A.K. Hess (Ed.), *Psychotherapy supervision: Theory, research and practice* (pp. 242-261). New York: Wiley.

Gazda, G. (1984). *Group counseling: A developmental approach* (3rd. ed.). Boston: Allyn and Bacon.

Gazda, G., Asbury, F., Balzer, F., Childers, W., & Walters, R. (1984). *Human relations development: A manual for educators* (3rd ed.). Boston: Allyn and Bacon.

Gibbard, G., Hartman, J., & Mann, R. (Eds.). (1974). *Analysis of groups.* San Francisco: Jossey-Bass.

Grater, H.A. (1985). Stages in psychotherapy supervision: From therapy skills to skilled therapist. *Professional Psychology, 16,* 605-610.

Hart, G.M. (1982). *The process of clinical supervision.* Baltimore: University Park Press.

Hayes, R. (1980). *The democratic classroom: A program in moral education for adolescents.* Unpublished doctoral dissertation, Boston University.

Hayes, R. (1986). Human growth and development. In M. Lewis, R. Hayes, & J. Lewis (Eds.), *An introduction to the counseling profession* (pp. 36-95). Itasca, IL: F.E. Peacock.

Heppner, P., & Roehlke, H. (1984). Differences among supervisees at different levels of training: Implications for a developmental model of supervision. *Journal of Counseling Psychology, 31,* 76-90.

Hess, A.K. (1986). Growth in supervision: Stages of supervisee and supervisor development. *The Clinical Supervisor, 4*(1-2), 51-67.

Hill, C.E., Charles, D., & Reed, K.G. (1981). A longitudinal analysis of changes in counseling skills during training in counseling psychology. *Journal of Counseling Psychology, 28,* 428-436.

Hosford, R., & Barmann, B. (1983). A social learning approach to counselor supervision. *The Counseling Psychologist, 11*(1), 51-58.

Holloway, E., & Johnston, R. (1985). Group supervision: Widely practiced but poorly understood. *Counselor Education and Supervision, 24,* 332-340.

Ivey, A.E. (1988). *Intentional interviewing and counseling: Facilitating client development* (2nd ed.). Pacific Grove, CA: Brooks/Cole.

Johnson, D.W., & Johnson, R.T. (1975). *Learning together and alone: Cooperation, competition, and individualization.* Englewood Cliffs, NJ: Prentice-Hall.

Kaul. T., & Bednar, R. (1978). Conceptualizing group research: A preliminary analysis. *Small Group Behavior, 9,* 173-191.

Knefelkamp, L., & Slepitza, R. (1976). A cognitive-developmental model of career development: An adaptation of the Perry scheme. *The Counseling Psychologist, 6,* 53-58.

Knowles, M., & Knowles, H. (1959). *Introduction to group dynamics.* New York: Association Press.

Kohlberg, L., Kauffman, K., Scharf, P., & Hickey, J. (1974). *The just community approach to corrections: A manual (Part I).* Cambridge, MA: Moral Education Research Foundation.

Lakin, M. (1976). The human relations training laboratory: A special case of the experiential group. In M. Rosenbaum & A. Snadowsky (Eds.), *The intensive group experience.* New York: The Free Press.

Lakin, M., & Carson, R. (1966). A therapeutic vehicle in search of a theory of therapy. *Journal of Applied Behavioral Science, 2,* 27-40.

Mathewson, R. (1962). *Guidance policy and practice* (rev. ed.). New York: Harper & Row.

Miars, R., Tracey, P., Ray, P., Cornfield, J., O'Farrell, M., & Gelso, C. (1983). Variation in supervision process across trainee experience levels. *Journal of Counseling Psychology, 30,* 403-412.

Mills, T.M. (1964). *Group transformation: An analysis of a learning group.* Englewood Cliffs, NJ: Prentice-Hall.

Moskowitz, S.A. (1981). A developmental model for the supervision of psychotherapy: The effect of level experience on trainees' views of ideal supervision (Doctoral dissertation, Loyola University, 1981). *Dissertation abstracts International, 42,* 1184B-1185B. (University Microfilms No. 8119985).

Ponterotto, J., & Zander, T. (1984). A multimodal approach to counselor supervision. *Counselor Education and Supervision, 24,* 40-50.

Reisman, B. (1985). Conflict between teaching a group class and being an ethical counselor. *Michigan Personnel and Guidance Journal, 16*(2), 35-39.

Richardson, B.K., & Bradley, L.J. (1984). Microsupervision: A skill development model for training clinical supervisors. *The Clinical Supervisor, 2*(3), 43-54.

Sansbury, D. (1982). Developmental supervision from a skills perspective. *Counseling Psychologist, 10,* 53-58.

Savickas, M., Marquart, C., & Supinski, C. (1986). Effective supervision in groups. *Counselor Education and Supervision, 26,* 17-25.

Schmidt, J.P. (1979). Psychotherapy Supervision: A cognitive-behavioral model. *Professional Psychology, 10*(1), 278-284.

Shapiro, J. (1978). *Methods of group psychotherapy and encounter.* Itasca, IL: F.E. Peacock.

Slavin, R.E. (1983). *Cooperative learning.* New York: Longman.

Stanford, G. (1977). *Developing effective classroom groups.* New York: Hart.

Stenack, R.J., & Dye, H.A. (1982). Behavioral descriptions of counseling supervision roles. *Counselor Education and Supervision, 21,* 295-304.

Stockton, R., & Morran, D.K. (1982). Review and perspective of critical dimensions of therapeutic small group research. In G. Gazda (Ed.), *Basic approaches to group psychotherapy and group counseling* (3rd ed.). Springfield, IL: Charles C. Thomas.

Strosahl, K., & Jacobson, N.S. (1986). Training and supervision of behavior therapists. *The Clinical Supervisor, 4*(1-2), 183-206.

Swensen, C. (1980). Ego development and a general model for counseling and psychotherapy. *Personnel and Guidance Journal, 58,* 382-388.

Tauber, L. (1978). Choice point analysis-formulation, strategy, intervention, and result in group process therapy, and supervision. International *Journal of Group Psychotherapy, 28,* 163-184.

Tennyson, W.W., & Strom, S.M. (1986). Beyond professional standards: Developing responsibleness. *Journal of Counseling and Development, 64,* 298-302.

Thibault, J., & Kelley, H. (1959). *The social psychology of groups.* New York: Wiley.

Thies-Sprinthall, L. (1984). Promoting the developmental growth of supervising teachers: Theory, research, programs, and implications. *Journal of Teacher Education, 35,* 53-60.

Thompson, L. (1982). *Training elementary school teachers to create a democratic classroom.* Unpublished doctoral dissertation, Boston University.

Tuckman, B., & Jensen, M. (1977). Stages of small group development revisited. *Group and Organizational Studies, 2,* 419-427.

Turquet, P. (1974). Leadership: The individual and the group. In G. Gibbard, J. Hartman, & R. Mann (Eds.), *Analysis of groups* (pp. 349-371). San Francisco: Jossey-Bass.

Wasik, B.H., & Fishbein, J.E. (1982). Problem solving: A model for supervision in professional psychology. *Professional Psychology, 13,* 559-564.

Wilbur, M., Roberts-Wilbur, J., Hart, G., & Betz, R. (1986). Structured group supervision: Integrating supervision models and group modalities. Unpublished manuscript.

Yalom, I. (1985). *The theory and practice of group psychotherapy* (3rd ed.). New York: Basic Books.

Yogev, S. (1982). An eclectic model of supervision: A developmental sequence for beginning psychotherapy students. *Professional Psychology, 13*, 236-243.

Young-Eisendrath, P. (1985, January). Making use of human development theories in counseling. *Counseling and Human Development, 17*, 1-12.

CHAPTER 11

ETHICAL PRINCIPLES IN SUPERVISION

Loretta J. Bradley, Ph.D.

Over the last decade, ethical issues in counseling have received increased attention. As the concept of client as consumer has evolved, the number of books and manuscripts on ethical issues have multiplied. *According to Webster's Third New International Dictionary* (Gove, 1981) ethics is the discipline dealing with what is good and bad or right and wrong; the principles of conduct governing an individual or profession (p. 780). One of the beliefs of every professional organization is that its members must perform their professional duties according to an established code of ethics. Without an established code, a group of people with similar interests cannot actually be considered a professional organization (Allen, 1986).

One of the earliest codes, the Hippocratic Oath, was established for the medical profession. In more recent times, various professions have established codes of ethics that guide their professional behaviors. Some of the organizations establishing codes for counselors and psychological practitioners are the American Association for Counseling and Development (AACD) formerly the American Personnel and Guidance Association, American

Association for Marriage and Family Therapy (AAMFT), American Psychological Association (APA), National Academy of Certified Clinical Mental Health Counselors (NACCMHC), and the National Association for Social Workers (NASW). Additionally speciality guidelines have been prepared for specific types of practitioners. Examples include those guidelines of the National Association of Social Workers for the private practice of clinical social work; the APA for clinical psychology, counseling psychology, industrial and organizational psychology, and school psychology; the American Psychiatric Association; and the Association for Specialists in Group Work (Corey, Corey & Callanan, 1984, p. 147).

The professional organization for counselors, now titled the American Association for Counseling and Development (AACD), was established in 1952 as the American Personnel and Guidance Association. The following year Donald Super established an Ethical Practices Committee to develop a code of ethics. After studying the APA Code of Ethics, a Proposed Code of Ethics for APGA was formulated in 1959. This code entitled *Ethical Standards* was adopted in 1961 with revisions occurring in 1974, 1981, and 1988. Since the adoption of the *Ethical Standards*, six divisions of AACD have designed their own ethical codes.

Van Hoose and Kottler (1978) cited three major reasons why ethical codes exist: ethical codes allow professions to govern and regulate themselves rather than to risk governmental regulations, ethical codes protect the profession from internal struggling and bickering, and ethical codes protect the practitioner from public malpractice suits providing the practitioner has behaved in accordance with standards judged acceptable by the profession. Despite their many assets, Alexander (1976) and Talbutt (1981) alert counselors that AACD's *Ethical Standards* have major limitations. One limitation involves conflicts within the standards and another involves ethical and legal issues not covered by the *Ethical Standards*. The authors quoted from Sections A and B of the AACD *Ethical Standards* which state:

Section A: General

2. The member has a responsibility both to the individual who is served and to the institution within which the service is

performed to maintain high standards of professional conduct. The member strives to maintain the highest levels of professional services offered to the individuals to be served. The member also strives to assist the agency, organization, or institution in providing the highest caliber of professional services.

Section B: Counseling Relationship

1. The member's primary obligation is to respect the integrity and promote the welfare of the client(s), whether the client(s) is (are) assisted individually or in a group relationship.

4. When the client's condition indicates that there is clear and imminent danger to the client or others, the member must take reasonable personal action or inform responsible authorities.

5. Records of the counseling relationship, including interview notes, test data, correspondence, tape recordings, and other documents, are to be considered professional information for use in counseling and they should not be considered a part of the records of the institution or agency in which the counselor is employed unless specified by state statute or regulation. (AACD Ethical Standards, 1981)

The *Ethical Standards* could place the counselor in a dilemma in that on the one hand they state the counselor's primary obligation is to the client (Section B-1) and on the other hand they state the member has a responsibility both to the individual who is served and to the institution where service is performed (Section A-2). In some instances the needs of the client and the institution or agency served conflict, and thus the counselor must decide where his/her responsibility lies. The counselor's decision may be in conflict with one of two powerful forces—the client whose rights need to be protected and the institution or agency for which the counselor works. In a study of how do counselors resolve ethical dilemmas, Hayman and Covert (1986) reported that 93% of the counselors in their study relied on common sense. Fewer than one-third used published professional guidelines.

Although the American Association for Counseling and Development (AACD) has published an ethics code for standards of ethical behavior between counselor and client, specific guidelines for ethical behavior between a supervisor and supervisee have not been established by AACD. To date only one group, the North Atlantic Regional Association for Counselor Education and Supervision (NARACES) has developed standards for educators and supervisors, although the American Association for Counselor Education and Supervision (ACES) has established a committee to develop guidelines for supervisors. Given the importance of the supervisory process on the development of a competent counselor, an examination of ethical issues in relation to counselor supervision seems warranted. Except for a few recent publications (Bernard, 1987; Borders & Leddick, 1987; Cormier & Bernard, 1982; Falvey, 1987; Goodyear & Sinnet, 1982; Newman, 1981; Stadler, 1986; Upchurch, 1985), the literature has virtually ignored the importance of ethical issues confronting supervisors. Yet supervision is perhaps the most important component in the development of a competent practitioner because within the context of supervision, trainees begin to develop a sense of professional identity and to examine their own beliefs and attitudes regarding clients and therapy (Corey, Corey, & Callanan, 1984, p. 219).

This chapter addresses ethical issues often encountered by counselor supervisors in both administrative and clinical settings. Additionally, legal aspects of supervision will be discussed in conjunction with its impact on ethical issues. Using an outline similar to the one described by DePauw (1986), ethical issues in counselor supervision will be discussed in two major categories. These include (1) the pre-supervision considerations, and (2) supervision considerations.

PRE-SUPERVISION CONSIDERATIONS

Most supervisors are employed in settings in which they provide direct services to supervisees. In the area of counselor supervision, this usually includes a college or university faculty member supervising students enrolled in practicum or internship classes or a doctorate level counseling student supervising a masters level counseling student enrolled in a practicum or internship class. In the area of administrative supervision, the administrative supervisor supervises counselors employed at his/her setting or assigns others to perform the supervisory process. Regardless of setting, critical issues occur which the supervisor must acknowledge and formulate a plan before entering the supervision process. Some of the issues are more integral to the supervisor's role and others are more integral to the counselor's role. Regardless of whether the issue has a direct or indirect involvement, all do have an influence on the supervisory process.

Skills

A fundamental issue that any supervisor must ask is "What are my qualifications for supervision? Do I have the skills, training and interest to engage in the supervision process?" In the AACD *Ethical Standards* (1988) is stated that members must define and describe the parameters and levels of professional competency. One means for self-assessment of supervision skills and knowledge is to construct a supervision resume similar to that described by Borders and Leddick (1987).

Although much attention has been devoted to counselor supervision in the last decade, several counselor preparation departments do not offer training in supervision (Richardson & Bradley, 1986). Thus many supervisors are supervising without any formal supervision training. This statement is not meant to suggest that only supervisors with formal training are competent to supervise; instead it is meant to call attention to the fact that certain skills are necessary and indeed critical for effective supervision. Each supervisor has the ethical responsibility to be sure that he/she as well as others that he/she assigns to supervise have the supervision skills, experience, and training to supervise.

Models for the preparation of the role of supervisor are available. In the first chapter of this book was outlined the role of the supervisor while in Chapters 3 through 6 were provided a theory base for supervision. Other information on the preparation of supervisors may be found in books (Borders & Leddick 1987; Falvey, 1987; Hart, 1982; Hess, 1980; Kaslow, 1986; Mueller & Kell, 1972; Stoltenberg & Delworth, 1987), articles (Bartlett, 1983; Bernard, 1979; Loganbill, Hardy, & Delworth, 1982; Stenack & Dye, 1982), and special journal issues [*Journal of Counseling and Development,* 1986, Vol. *64* (5); *The Counseling Psychologist,* 1982, Vol. *10* (1); and *The Counseling Psychologist,* 1983, Vol. *11* (11)].

Client Welfare

Once the supervisor has determined that he/she has the skills to supervise, the supervisor must address other supervisory service provision issues. Consistent with the AACD *Ethical Standards* (1988), the welfare of the client must remain paramount. The primary ethical responsibility of the supervisor is to assure the welfare of the client. In congruence with ths responsibility, the supervisor must focus interventions for the purpose of facilitating learning for the supervisee (Loganbill, Hardy, & Delworth, 1982). In instances where the supervisory function and the welfare of the client may be in conflict, the supervisor must closely monitor the sessions to assure that the welfare of the client is maintained. In the case of beginning supervisees, this may involve the supervisee being unable to move at the speed at which the client is ready to move. In this instance, the training model that is best for the supervisee may not be the one that is best for the client. Supervisors must accept the responsibilty to continually monitor the progress of both client and supervisee. In instances where the supervisee is not performing at an acceptable level, the supervisor has the ethical responsibility to take action. In some instances, especially in clinical supervision, this can involve withdrawing the supervisee from counselor training. In administrative supervision, this can involve the termination of employment. In any case prior to entering into the supervisory process, the supervisor must be clear on the guidelines defining the ethical principle of competence as it relates to the client's welfare. Other issues (informed consent, confidentiality) relating to client welfare will be discussed later in this chapter.

Due Process

Due process refers to the counselor's right to be knowledgeable of training objectives, assessment procedures and evaluation criteria. Supervisors are responsible for informing their supervisees about their roles, expectations, goals, and criteria for evaluation at the beginning of supervision (Cormier & Bernard, 1982). Communication of supervision expectations are "a must" at the beginning of supervision. For the clinical supervisor, this clarification will provide the trainee with information about how to successfully complete the supervisory experience. For those supervisees enrolled in practicum and internship classes, this information will provide data at the outset on how to successfully complete the course requirements. For many supervisees engaged in administrative supervision, this information will provide a concrete means for the supervisee to understand how to retain his/her employment. A model of topics to be covered in the initial supervision session is provided by Bradley, Brian, and Richardson (1988). Basically this model provides an explicit means for the supervisor to cover such topics as when and how supervision will be conducted, who will be responsible for supervision, the supervisor's credentials to supervise, role expectations by supervisor and supervisee, client welfare, evaluation by supervisor, confidentiality, and termination issues.

The issue of evaluation is usually an area of critical concern for the supervisee in either clinical or administrative supervision. Past history in higher education has compounded the importance of assessment to the point that supervisees experience tremendous anxiety about when, where, and how evaluations will be conducted. Before the first supervision session, an important procedure is for the supervisor to determine how the supervisee's skills will be evaluated. This information should be conveyed to the supervisee at the initial supervision session. Consistent with AACD's *Ethical Standards* (1988), members must influence the development of the profession by continuous efforts to improve professional practices, teaching, services, and research. The supervisor must realize that the supervisee has a legal right to feedback throughout the supervision process. This means that feedback should be scheduled regularly rather than on occasion. Regular periodic feedback is important for the professional development of the supervisee. While some of the feedback will be oral, an important procedure is for the supervisor to provide formal, written feedback to the supervisee. The supervisor must keep a record of the feedback provided. In the case of negative feedback, even if given orally, a very important procedure is for the supervisor to record what, when, how, and why events occured in supervision, with the information maintained in a record known to both the supervisee and supervisor. Giving the supervisee negative feedback only at the termination of supervision is considered a violation of the supervisee's due process rights. Likewise in the case of an administrative supervisor attempting to terminate the supervisee, the supervisee's due process rights have been violated unless the supervisor has documented the negative feedback at various intervals and provided feedback on ways and means for the supervisee's performance to improve. Thus the administrative supervisor and the clinical supervisor are in legal violation unless they document the negative feedback and provide evidence that ways for improvement have been provided. A strong recommendation is for all evaluations (positive or negative) to be written and signed by the supervisor and supervisee. An example of a written form is provided in Figure 11.1.

Dual Relationship

Probably the area receiving the most publicity is that of the dual relationship. No doubt this publicity has stemmed from reported sexual contacts between supervisor and supervisee. Cormier and Bernard (1982) reported a survey of United States psychology training programs in which 10% of the students reported having had sexual contact with an instructor, of which 47% of the females and 86% of the males reported having had sex with a clinical supervisor. The AACD *Ethical Standards* (1988) are clear on the sexual contact issue when in Section B-14 was stated that "The member will avoid any type of sexual intimacies with clients. Sexual relationships with clients are unethical."

In the AACD *Ethical Standards* reference is made to a second type of dual relationship in Section B-13, "when the member has other relationships, particularly of an administrative, supervisory and/or evaluative nature with an individual seeking counseling services, the member must not serve as the counselor but should refer the individual to another professional." Yet authors have characterized the role of supervisor akin to that of counselor (Boyd, 1978; Hart, 1982) and especially akin to counselor in facilitating the growth of the supervisee (Mueller & Kell, 1972). Clearly instances do occur in which focusing on personal issues during supervision is appropriate especially when the issue impairs the supervisee's

Date _____

Professor _____   Practicum Student _____

On-Site
Supervisor _____   Practicum Setting _____

PRACTICUM EVALUATION FORM

In an attempt to evaluate the counseling practicum field experience of the above student, please complete this evaluation form and return it to my office. This report will be included in the overall evaluation of the student's progress as a counselor trainee along with various on-campus assessments. Thank you for your valuable assistance in providing this professional service to our program and for your continued support of our practicum students.

Please evaluate the student's performance on each of the following activities (where applicable):

	Poor	Good	Excellent	Comments
1. A. Individual Counseling	___	___	___	_____
B. Group Counseling	___	___	___	_____
C. Consultation	___	___	___	_____
D. Testing & Appraisal	___	___	___	_____
E. Relationships with Staff	___	___	___	_____
F. In-Service Training	___	___	___	_____
G. Staffings/Meetings	___	___	___	_____
H. Other (Explain)	___	___	___	_____
2. Overall Performance	___	___	___	_____
3. Potential as a future Counselor	___	___	___	_____

4. If you were in a position to add this person to your staff, would you feel comfortable employing him/her?

_____   _____
  Yes   No

Additional Comments: _____

_____

_____

I have had an opportunity to review this evaluation and am aware of its content.

_____   _____   _____   _____
Practicum Student   Date   Evaluator   Date

Figure 11.1. Practicum Evaluation Form.

ability to counsel with his/her client. For example, if the supervisor becomes aware that whenever the client mentions death and dying issues, the supervisee (counselor) seems to direct the client away from the issue, then the appropriate procedure is for the supervisor to explore the personal dynamics influencing the supervisee's behavior. Further, if the supervisor finds the supervisee has a number of unresolved issues involving death that in the supervisor's opinion will require extended counseling, then the supervisor should refer the supervisee to another counselor. If the supervisor engaged in an extended counseling relationship with the supervisee, this would constitute a dual relationship. In this instance, the supervisor must initiate action to remove the dual role. Failure to do so would result in unethical behavior by the supervisor.

Bernard (1987) cited a third illustration of the dual relationship. She wrote:

> Often persons working together who have a good deal in common become close personal friends. When the relationship makes objective assessment extremely difficult or impossible, a dual relationship has evolved. It is not always imperative to remove a supervisor in this case, but at the very least, outside consultation should be sought by the supervisor to affirm that his or her evaluation of the supervisee is accurate. (p. 53)

Employees (supervisees) generally get to know and may become friends with their administrative supervisor (boss) as do student counselors (supervisees) and faculty supervisors. Friendships with persons in the work environment are common. The point of caution becomes real when the relationship interferes with professional and objective clinical or administrative supervision. At this point a dual relationship exists, and action must be taken to eliminate the dual relationship. Dual relationships are not confined to the initial stage, but may arise at other stages of the supervisory relationship. Without doubt, the dual relationship can cause considerable legal liability. At the very heart of the issue is the welfare of the client. Clearly clients have every right to expect their counselor (supervisee) is receiving component supervision. Clearly the AACD Ethical Standards caution against dual relationships. Equally clear is that supervisors must maintain professional distance from their supervisees. Corey, Corey, and

Callanan (1984) provide a timely summary for this issue when they provide a conclusion by Wolman (1982) who contended that a good therapist must not become personally involved with patients, or get caught in the murky waters of counter-transference feelings. Seeing personal involvement as a gross violation of therapeutic ethics, Wolman (1982) offered excellent advice in the statement, "A good psychotherapist gets involved with the patient's case without getting involved with the patient's personality."

SUPERVISION CONSIDERATIONS

The supervisor should not enter into a supervisory relationship until he/she has addressed and resolved the issues outlined as pre-supervision considerations. After the pre-supervision issues have been resolved, the supervisor will be faced with supervision considerations that occur throughout the supervision process. Whether at the beginning, middle, or end of the supervision process there are a number of ongoing supervision issues that must be addressed. These include informed consent, confidentiality, privacy, privileged communication, and dangerousness.

Informed Consent

According to AACD's *Ethical Standards* (1988), a prospective client must be informed of any aspects of the counseling relationship that may affect his or her willingness to participate. By the very nature of the supervision process, the supervisor is involved in an indirect relationship with the client via the supervisee. The supervisor whether in an administrative or clinical supervision role has the responsibility to see that the client is informed of all aspects of the supervision process. For supervisees in training, this means the client must be informed that the counselor is in training and is being supervised. The nature of supervision must be discussed. For example, if tapes or live observations are required, then the client must be informed and allowed to give or withhold consent. In the case of administrative supervision, the client needs to know who at the agency will be supervising the counselor as well as how supervision will be handled. In essence the client must be informed about any aspects of the supervisory relationship that might affect the client's willingness to participate. Some agencies have limits on the number of sessions that clients may be seen. The administrative supervisor should make sure that the client is informed about this and other policies at the onset of counseling. The client should be reminded before the termination that the limited number of sessions have almost been met. The supervisor must make sure that referral is provided if the client needs to explore further issues. Although the informed consent approach may run the risk of hindering both the counseling relationship between client and counselor and the supervisory relationship between supervisee and supervisor, issues of informed consent must be covered at the beginning of the supervisory process.

Confidentiality

Confidentiality, privacy, and privileged communication are three terms that have caused confusion. While the three terms are related, researchers, (Herlihy and Sheeley, 1987; Shaw, 1969, 1970a, 1970b) have discussed succinct distinctions. Herlihy and Sheeley (1987) concluded that **confidentiality** is an ethical standard that protects clients from disclosure of information without their consent, whereas **privacy** is an evolving legal concept that recognizes individuals' rights to choose the time, circumstances, and extent to which they wish to share or withhold personal information. **Privileged communication,** a narrower concept, regulates privacy protection and confidentiality by protecting clients from having their confidential communications disclosed in court without their permission.

The ethics of confidentiality is grounded on the principle that the counseling relationship is an intense personal relationship operating on the premise that what clients reveal in the counseling process will be kept confidential. Certainly counseling is dependent on the client's trust to reveal personal information, and clients will not reveal this information if they perceive their discussions will not be kept private.

Siegel (1979) took an extreme position in which he argued that absolute confidentiality is necessary in a therapeutic relationship. He further posited that therapists must not break the client's confidentiality under any circumstances. Later

Siegel modified his view and concluded that while absolute confidentiality is needed, one cannot disobey the law. Other clinicians have questioned the premise that absolute confidentiality is necessary for an effective relationship (Corey, Corey, & Callanan, 1987; Denkowski & Denkowski, 1982). Denkowski and Denkowski (1982) cited reasons for limited and qualified confidentiality. Corey, Corey, and Callanan (1987) concluded that because confidentiality is not absolute, then a necessity is to determine under what circumstances it cannot be maintained.

In the AACD *Ethical Standards* (1988) in Section B is stated that:

2. The counseling relationship and information resulting therefrom must be kept confidential. In a group counseling setting, the counselor must set a norm of confidentiality regarding all group participants' disclosures.

4. When the client's condition indicates that there is clear and imminent danger to the client or others, the member must take reasonable personal action or inform responsible authorities. Consultation with other professionals must be used where possible. The assumption of responsibility for the client's(s') behavior must be taken only after careful deliberation. The client must be involved in the resumption of responsibility as quickly as possible.

The AACD *Ethical Standards* are clear in their statement that the counseling relationship must be kept confidential. Counselors who break confidentiality are not only at variance with the ethical guidelines but in addition they place themselves subject to a malpractice lawsuit. Additionally, professional material (records, interview notes, test data, correspondences, documents) deemed confidential cannot be released. If counselors release the confidential material, then the client's privacy has been invaded and he/she can sue the counselor. Neither should the professional materials be considered a part of the institution or agency in which the supervisor or counselor is employed unless specified by state statute or regulation. Sometimes agencies have trouble accepting the fact that records are not a part of the institution. The administrative and clinical supervisor has the ethical responsibility to see that records are kept confidential and only revealed to others with the expressed consent of the client. Although evaluation teams often request access to client files and clerical staff may need certain information for billing purposes, protecting the confidentiality of client records must be maintained and this is an important ethical responsibility of administrative supervisors (Falvey, 1987). As part of the confidentiality issue, the supervisor must be certain that the counselor has informed the client about confidential matters at the beginning of the counseling relationship before problem issues arise.

Although the AACD *Ethical Standards* are clear that the counseling relationship must be kept confidential, they are not so clear when confidentiality conflicts with the rights of others. Basically most ethical codes of professional organizations, including AACD and APA, have taken the position that confidentiality cannot be maintained when clear and imminent danger exists to the client or others. But the uncertainty enters because the ethical codes do not provide specific guidelines to determine under what situations that confidentiality cannot be maintained. This leaves the judgment to the professional of whether the case involves clear and imminent danger. Certainly in counseling sessions, the supervisor supervises counselors seeing clients who have had violent behaviors, attempted suicides, threatened to kill someone, etc. The question that the counselor and supervisor must address relates to whether the client poses a serious threat to self or others? Often this is not an easy question to answer. In fact this issue has been at the heart of many malpractice suits. Probably the most famous of the legal suits is the 1969 case of *Tarasoff vs. Board of Regents of the University of California.* The state supreme court held university psychotherapists liable for failure to warn an individual threatened by a client. In the Tarasoff case, Poddar who was an outpatient at the University of California Hospital informed his psychotherapist that he planned to kill Tatania Tarasoff when she returned from South America. The university therapist contacted the University of California Police and requested that Poddar be detained. Poddar was taken into custody, but he was released after he promised to stay away from Tatania Tarasoff. After Tatania returned from South America, Poddar went to her home and killed her. Tatania's parents sued the university regents, police, and doctors in the university hospital charging that the defendants negligently permitted Poddar to be released without notifying the parents that their daughter was in grave danger. The Superior Court of Alameda County ruled in favor of the defendants, the parents appealed. The Supreme Court of California reversed the judgment and ruled in favor of the parents because the defendants were negligent in their failure to warn. The court concluded that psychotherapists treating a dangerous client have the duty to warn threatened persons. The court stated "Public policy favoring protection of the confidential character of the patient-psychotherapist relationship must yield in instances in which disclosure is essential to avert danger to others; the protective privilege ends where the public peril begins" (Van Hoose & Kottler, 1978, p. 88). The issue in the Tarasoff case was the failure of the psychotherapist and his supervisor to warn the intended victim.

Clearly the Tarasoff case represents more than confidentiality. It is a clear illustration of a conflict that can occur between counseling practice and the law. Further it is an indicator that variations in the law make it difficult to know when one is in conflict with the duty to warn. To date, neither ethical codes nor the courts have clearly dealt with this issue. Although ethical codes speak of clear and imminent danger, the counselor is left to decide what constitutes clear and imminent danger. While guidelines are not explicit, supervisors are legally responsible for the welfare of the clients that their supervisees are counseling. Cormier and Bernard (1982) concluded that the most important legal doctrine applied to supervisor's responsibilities to clients is that of respondent superior.

Privacy

While confidentiality is an ethical standard, privacy is a legal concept. Supervisors must make sure their supervisees do not invade the privacy of their clients. Often in the desire to help, the supervisee will press for information that the client does not want to reveal. Supervisors must help supervisees realize that clients have the right to choose whether to reveal specific personal information; the client has the right to decide when, where, and how information, if any, will be revealed.

Privileged Communication

Privileged communication is a legal concept that refers to the client's right not to have his/her privileged communication used in court. The privilege belongs to the client not the counselor or supervisor. To protect the client's disclosures, many state governments have established laws and evidence codes. In a recent article, Herlihy and Sheeley (1987) presented findings regarding extant privileged communication statutes and rules of evidence in the 50 states and District of Columbia for selected helping professionals, psychologists, social workers, marriage and family therapists, counselors, school counselors, and licensed professional counselors. Additionally they reported exceptions to privilege specified by state laws.

In their study Herlihy and Sheeley (1987) found that although all 50 states and the District of Columbia certify school counseling practice, only 20 states have enacted privileged communication for the disclosure of school children's communications to their counselors. Of the 18 states who license professional counselors, 12 contain privileged communication provisions. Although the model for licensure advocated by the American Association for Counseling and Development advocates that the state licensure laws provide for privileged communication, only Alabama and Arkansas provide for the broad type of privilege recommended by AACD. Thus supervisors and counselors need to be aware that even in states where privileged communication laws exist, many exceptions are provided in the law. Supervisors must be aware of the law and be able to explain its ramifications to their supervisees. Certainly supervisees need to be aware that in the absence of privileged communications statutes, counselors can be required by the courts to reveal communications between counselor and client. For a more complete coverage on state law provisions, the reader is encouraged to review the manuscripts by Herlihy and Sheeley (1987) and Shaw (1969, 1970a, 1970b).

IMPLICATIONS

The more supervisors consider the ramifications of ethical issues raised in this chapter, the clearer becomes an understanding that ethical matters are not neatly defined. Faced with conflicting alternatives, ethical issues are problematic for clinical and administrative supervisors. Yet a mark of professionalism is to be able to simultaneously weigh these considerations and to make sound judgments which are in the best interest of both the client and others (Herlihy & Sheeley, 1987).

Given the existence of the potential for ethical issues to arise, what is the role of the administrative supervisor or clinical supervisor in training for ethics? The belief of the author is that supervisees must be given as much information as possible to help them make correct decisions when ethical dilemmas arise. The information about ethical issues can be presented in writing, at staff meetings, through an audiotape or videotape, or during supervision sessions. While a number of ways exist to disseminate the information, supervisors have the responsibility to try to prevent ethical violations. One way to reduce ethical violations is by training.

The author used a videotape containing twenty vignettes to provide ethical training. On the videotape, a supervisor and supervisee presented a 2 to 3 minute ethical dilemma. At the end of each vignette, supervisors in training were asked to identify the ethical dilemma, describe the solution to the dilemma, and state their rational for the solution. Examples of the dilemmas were client welfare, confidentiality, dual relationship, due process, informed consent, and imposing values on supervisees.

Before and after the ethical training via videotape, the supervisors in training were administered the *Ethical Discrimination Inventory*, Figure 11.2, (Baldick, 1980). Based upon the results obtained, formal ethical training helps supervisors discriminate between effective and ineffective solutions to ethical dilemmas. A study by Baldick (1980) found support for the efficacy of formal training in ethics. Baldick concluded that any training or exposure ethics results in more effective discrimination of ethical problems encountered in clinical practice and clinicians can be taught how to think in ethical terms and recognize ethical problems.

ETHICAL DISCRIMINATION INVENTORY

DIRECTIONS

1. Please fill out the enclosed information sheet as completely as possible.

2. This questionnaire consists of 12 ethical problem situations, in which you as a psychologist might find yourself. For each situation, please indicate in a two to five word phrase, the possible ethical problem or problems involved in each situation. (It is not intended for you to resolve the posed ethical dilemma, but to recognize what the problems or considerations are in each situation.) The example below illustrates the test procedure and indicates that more than one problem may be involved in each case.

Example: A graduate student in psychology is in the midst of his dissertation. He is mailing a questionnaire to two groups of licensed psychologists. Because it might interfere with his results he gives misleading reasons for their cooperation. In addition, he disguises a recently published questionnaire as his own in an effort to evaluate professional reaction to student efforts.

The three ethical problems are:

1. Inappropriate publication credit.

2. Misuse of research subjects.

3. Supervision and student status.

Please identify the problem(s) associated with the 12 ethical dilemmas listed below.

---

1. A client informs his therapist that he plans to murder his girlfriend due to her unfaithfulness to him. He is extremely angry. The therapist later contacts both the girl and the local authorities explaining the situation.

Figure 11.2. Ethical Discrimination Inventory

Figure 11.2. Continued.

2. While running a weekend encounter group, where the rule is that "each member is totally responsible for himself and what he does," the therapist has sexual intercourse with one of the group members. This is described as a "deeply moving and releasing experience" for both of them, and was healthy and therapeutic since it was thoroughly shared with other group members."

3. A psychologist serving a small city was consulted by the local high school guidance counselor and asked if he would "look over" M.M.P.I. profiles of certain students from time to time and write a "rough" interpretation so that the counselor can help the students better understand themselves.

4. As a professional psychologist you receive an announcement from a licensed colleague inviting you to a nude marathon weekend. The literature states that "the effectiveness of the nude marathon has been proven . . . unquestionably superior to clothed marathons in fostering self-actualization."

5. During a cross-country flight, the passenger sitting next to a psychologist begins to unfold his many troubles. The psychologist feels he can help the passenger so he encourages him to talk, and is able to make several interpretations and interventions. When they reach their destination the passenger says, "I don't know whether I feel better or worse after talking with you." Then they go their separate ways.

Figure 11.2. Continued.

6. A mother of a teenage son consults with a psychologist about the conflicts that she is confronting at home and further arranges for her son to see the therapist the following week. The day following his appointment the mother comes into the office to pay her bill and asks, "What did he say to you?"

7. A claustrophobic patient contracts with a therapist to be treated by a flooding technique, involving continued exposure to the conditioned stimulus until extinction. The therapist carefully explains the procedure and its theoretical justifications. Accordingly, the patient is placed in a confined space with avoidance blocked by locking the door. After a time, she panics and pleads with the therapist to be released. He refuses, based on the fact that his panic must be overcome in order for extinction to take place.

8. A psychologist has been counseling with a young married female for about a year. Her husband becomes quite psychologically dysfunctional and is a suicide risk. He is hospitalized and treated by a local psychiatrist and his staff. In the course of his treatment the psychologist working with the husband meets with the wife, discusses her therapy and suggests she terminate therapy with her psychologist and begin treatment with him. During her next session she reveals this to her psychotherapist.

Figure 11.2. Continued.

9. A 45 year old psychologist is consulted by a young man who appears in a "homosexual panic." The psychologist discloses to the client that he is himself a homosexual, and that he is willing to counsel the client toward understanding and accepting his homosexual desires.

10. After several sessions with a married, 32 year old female, who is requesting therapy due to "mood changes," the psychologist notes increased agitation, excitability and hyperactivity being manifested in session. She is unable to concentrate on any one particular subject and is quite distractible. The therapist calls the patient's husband, who states that this is not uncommon behavior for her and that her mother and brothers have this problem. The psychologist arranges for sessions to be three times per week, and sets up a home token economy to help the client develop more stable and appropriate behavior.

11. During the initial group session the group leader discusses the value of group, how "it" works and some of the techniques which may be used. About 3 weeks later a member exits from the group because a friend of his, who was taking a course from the group leader at a local college, saw him on a video tape of group process, that was shown in the college classes.

12. A busy psychologist makes it a practice to give a prescribed battery of psychological tests to all new clients. Because of his busy schedule and lack of space in his office, he often will send the M.M.P.I. and the Edwards Personal Preference Schedule home with the client to be completed there.

Note: Reprinted by permission of the author, Dr. Thomas Baldick.

In summary, although during the last decade, books and articles have been devoted to ethics, few have been devoted to ethical training (Baldick, 1980; Bernard, 1987; Corey, Corey, & Callanan. 1987; Pelma & Bergers, 1986). Instead administrative and clinical supervisors seem to have assumed that supervisees will be sufficiently exposed to ethical issues through their association with professional role models and supervisors. Yet evidence indicates this assumption is invalid. In fact, based upon existing evidence, the indications are that a need exists to provide ethical information to supervisees before ethical problems and/or violations arise.

REFERENCES

Alexander, D. (1976). Legal issues in guidance. In T.H. Hohenshil & J.H. Miles (Eds.), *School guidance services.* Dubuque, IA: Kendal/Hunt.

Allen, V.B. (1986). A historical perspective of the AACD Ethics Committee. *Journal of Counseling and Development, 64,* 293-294.

American Association for Counseling and Development. (1988). *Ethical Standards.* Washington, D.C.: American Association for Counseling and Development.

Baldick, T. (1980). Ethical discrimination ability of intern psychologists: A function of training in ethics. *Professional Psychology, 11,* 276-282.

Bartlett, W. (1983). A multidimensional framework for the analysis of supervision of counseling. *The Counseling Psychologist, 11,* 9-19.

Bernard, J. (1979). Supervisory training: A discrimination model. *Counselor Education and Supervision, 19,* 60-68.

Bernard, J. (1987). In L.D. Borders and G.R. Leddick, *Handbook of counseling supervision.* Washington, D.C.: Association for Counselor Education and Supervision.

Borders, L., & Leddick, G. (1987). *Handbook of counseling supervision.* Washington, D.C.: Association for Counselor Education and Supervision.

Boyd, J. (1978). *Counselor supervision.* Muncie, IN: Accelerated Development.

Bradley, L., Brian, T., & Richardson, B. (in press). The initial counseling supervision interview. In J. Eddy & M. Altekruse, *Counseling: Theory, practice, and training.* Lanham, MD: University Press of America.

Corey, G., Corey, M., & Callanan, P. (1984). *Issues and ethics in the helping professions.* Monterey, CA: Brooks/Cole.

Corey, G., Corey, M., & Callanan, P. (1987). *Issues and ethics in the helping professions.* Pacific Grove, CA: Brooks/Cole.

Cormier, L., & Bernard, J. (1982). Ethical and legal responsibilities of clinical supervisors. *Personnel and Guidance Journal, 60,* 486-490.

Denkowski, K., & Denkowski, G. (1982). Client-counselor confidentiality: An update of rationale, legal status, and implications. *Personnel and Guidance Journal, 60,* 371-375.

DePauw, M. (1986). Avoiding ethical violations: A timeline perspective for individual counseling. *Journal of Counseling and Development, 64,* 303-305.

Falvey, J. (1987). *Handbook of administrative supervision.* Washington, D.C.: American Association for Counseling and Development.

Goodyear, R., & Sinnet, E. (1982). Current and emerging ethical issues for counseling psychology. *The Counseling Psychologist, 12,* 87-98.

Gove, P.B. (Ed.). (1981). *Webster's Third New International Dictionary.* Springfield, MA: Merriam Company.

Hart, G. (1982). *The process of clinical supervision.* Baltimore, MD: University Press Park.

Hayman, P.M., & Covert, J.A. (1986). Ethical dilemmas in college counseling centers. *Journal of Counseling and Development, 64,* 318-320.

Herlihy, B., & Sheeley, V. (1987). Privileged communication in selected helping professions: A comparison among statutes. *Journal of Counseling and Development, 65,* 479-483.

Hess, A. (Ed.). (1980). *Psychotherapy supervision.* New York: John Wiley.

Kaslow, F. (Ed.). (1986). *Supervision and training: Models, dilemmas, and challenges.* New York: Haworth.

Loganbill, C., Hardy, E., & Delworth, V. (1982). Supervision: A conceptual model. *The Counseling Psychologist, 10,* 3-43.

Mueller, W., & Kell, B. (1972). *Coping with conflicts: Supervising counselors and psychotherapists.* New York: Appleton-Century-Crofts.

Newman, A. (1981). Ethical issues in the supervision of psychotherapy. *Professional Psychology, 12,* 690-695.

Pelma, D., & Bergers, S. (1986). Experience-based ethics: A developmental model of learning ethical reasoning. *Journal of Counseling and Development, 64,* 311-314.

Richardson, B., & Bradley, L. (1986). *Community agency counseling: An emerging specialty within counselor preparation programs.* Washington, DC: American Association for Counseling and Development.

Shaw, S. (1969). Privileged communications, confidentiality, and privacy: Privileged communications. *Professional Psychology, 1, 59-69.*

Shaw, S. (1970a). *Privileged communications, confidentiality, and privacy: Confidentiality. Professional Psychology, 1,* 159-164.

Shaw, S. (1970b). Privileged communications, confidentiality, and privacy: Privacy. *Professional Psychology, 1,* 243-252.

Siegel, M. (1979). Privacy, ethics and confidentiality. *Professional Psychology, 10,* 249-258.

Stadler, H. (Ed.). (1986). Professional ethics (Special issue). *Journal of Counseling and Development, 64.*

Stenack, R., & Dye, H. (1982). Behavioral descriptions of counselor supervision roles. *Counselor Education and Supervision, 23,* 157-168.

Stoltenberg, C., & Delworth, U. (1987). *Supervising counselors and therapists: A developmental approach.* San Francisco: Jossey-Bass.

Talbutt, L.C. (1981). Ethical standards: Assets and limitations. *Personnel and Guidance Journal, 60,* 110-112.

Upchurch, D. (1985). Ethical standards and the supervisory process. *Counselor Education and Supervision, 25,* 90-98.

Van Hoose, W.H., & Kottler, J. (1978). *Ethical and legal issues in counseling and psychotherapy.* San Francisco: Jossey-Bass.

Wolman, B. (1982). Ethical problems in terminations of psychotherapy. In M. Rosenbaum (Ed.), *Ethics and values in psychotherapy: A guidebook.* New York: Free Press.

CHAPTER **12**

SUPERVISION TRAINING: A MODEL

Loretta J. Bradley, Ph.D.

Peggy P. Whiting, Ed.D.

Recent books (Borders & Leddick, 1987; Falvey, 1987; Hart, 1982; Hess, 1980; Kaslow, 1987; Mueller & Kell, 1972; Stoltenberg & Delworth, 1987) and articles (Bernard, 1979; Borders & Leddick, 1988; Bordin, 1983; Bradley & Richardson, 1987; Hansen, Robins, & Grimes, 1982; Hart & Falvey, 1987; Hess & Hess, 1983; Lambert & Arnold, 1987; Loganbill & Hardy, 1983; Williams, 1987; Worthington, 1984) describe models of supervision training. After examining the models, it becomes apparent that supervision is a complex process yet an important learning experience for both administrative and clinical supervisors.

In this chapter is presented a model for training supervisors. The model is composed of three major components originally suggested by Loganbill, Hardy, and Delworth (1982): conceptual, experiential, and integrative. The model separates the supervision process into stage components and thereby provides a viable method for isolating and teaching techniques germane to each specific stage. This model provides, especially for inexperienced supervisors, the discovery that supervision can be learned in smaller, logical segments. Additionally, training in logical segments allows time for the supervisor to identify and understand the segments prior to their implementation in actual supervision settings.

Although alarming, apparently even though supervision training is advocated, only a few counselor education programs and agencies provide supervisory training (Borders & Leddick, 1988; Hart & Falvey, 1987; Holloway, 1982; Richardson & Bradley, 1986). Borders and Leddick (1988) reported that only one-third of the counselor preparation programs provide training in supervision. Similar results were obtained in earlier studies by Hess and Hess (1983) and Richardson and Bradley (1986). Thus, this chapter addresses the need for supervision training by providing a training model. The model demonstrates how didactic and experiential components may be integrated to provide effective supervision training.

SUPERVISION TRAINING

What is Supervisory Training?

Blocher (1983) stated that "the purpose of supervision in counselor preparation programs is obviously the education of a competent, ethical and responsible professional person" (p. 27). He further stated:

> supervision is a specialized instructional process in which the supervisor attempts to facilitate the growth of a counselor-in-preparation, using the primary educational medium, the student's interaction with real clients for whose welfare the student has some degree of professional, ethical, and moral responsibility. (p. 27)

Although most of the literature on supervision training discusses the needs of the student in training, also a need exists for training for the supervisor in the field so as to increase and improve supervisory competency areas. In addition supervision training can be a requisite for employment because many agency directors in filling vacancies request experienced supervisors. Whether in an administrative or clinical setting, supervisory training is needed. Experience alone can not qualify one for supervision.

Initial Planning

Prior to the initial supervisory training session, a meeting is needed with the supervisor to provide an overview of the supervisory training session(s). During this initial meeting, background information should be obtained to be sure the supervisor has the requisite background and interest to participate in the training sessions. The supervisor should be informed of the anticipated structure and format of the training session(s). Additionally the supervisor should understand the expectations and requirements for successful completion of the supervision training. Further the following topics should be discussed: amount of time anticipated for completing the supervisory training, information about who is responsible for the training session, responsibilities for the supervisor in training, overview of evaluation procedures, clarification of how satisfactory and unsatisfactory performance will be determined, and a discussion of confidentiality issues that impact on the supervisor in training. The preceding list of topics is intended to be exemplary not comprehensive as topics will vary depending on the individual needs of the supervisor in training. The important emphasis is that an initial meeting should be planned before the actual supervision training is begun so as to lay the cornerstone for future training.

Goals

Four major goals guide the planning of the supervision training:

1. to provide a theory or knowledge base relevant to supervisory functioning,

2. to develop and refine supervisory skills,

3. to integrate the theory and skills into a working supervisory style, and

4. to develop and enhance the professional identity of the supervisor.

In Figure 12.1 is presented an overview of supervision training. As illustrated in Figure 12.1, the four supervisory goals

Goals	Instructional Mode	Instructional Outcome
Theory	Didactic	Listens and understands lectures on supervision models Demonstrates knowledge about supervision models Acquires information about supervisory roles Obtains information about effective and ineffective supervision
Skills	Didactic & Experiential	Knows and understands supervisory techniques Exhibits knowledge about supervisory skills Develops skill-mastery appropriate to direct supervisee
Integration	Experiential	Integrates skills into supervisory style Demonstrates the integration of theory and skills training via live supervision, videotape, audiotape, and role-play Organizes, understands, and translates knowledge into actual practice Effectively assumes supervisory role with supervisee
Identity	Didactic & Experiential	Advocates and uses effective principles endorsed by the profession Implements professional supervisory terminology Develops professional supervisory maturity Internalizes the identity of the profession Exhibits professional and emotional maturity

Figure 12.1. Overview of supervision training.

can be achieved through a combination of didactic and experiential learning modes. In providing a synthesis of conceptual and experiential exposure, the overview presents an integrative training component. The training is similar to that described by Loganbill and Hardy (1982) "integration allows conceptual material to become more than mere intellectual data, [it becomes] meaningful input which can organize and make sense of the experiential" (p. 38). The instructional events listed in Figure 12.1 offer opportunities for theoretical solidification, clarification of personal supervisory style, internalization of supervisory identity, and peer feedback.

Training

A recent study on supervision training was conducted by Borders and Leddick (1988). The researchers mailed a survey to the 450 counselor programs listed in *Counselor Preparation* (Hollis & Wantz, 1983). A total of 60 counselor education program administrators responded to the study. From the 60 respondents, 47 indicated their program offered a supervision course. The authors received 35 course syllabi with 23 syllabi containing a course outline. The authors reviewed the course syllabi and classified them into class topics. In Figure 12.2 is presented the topics specified in the supervision course syllabi. The authors concluded that a variety of supervision models were taught with syllabi indicating that supervision models were taught more frequently than supervision techniques. Additionally evaluation, ethical and legal issues, and the supervisory relationship were frequently discussed. Other popular topics included the history and definition of supervision, research on supervision, group versus individual supervision and administrative supervision (p. 276).

Overview

After incorporating the information obtained from the Borders and Leddick (1988) study, a model of supervisory training components is presented in Figure 12.3. The model is based on the premise that the goal of supervision training is development and supervision training is a process that develops over time. Similar to the definition provided by Williams (1987), supervision is depicted as "a process of incremental learning,

Class Topics Specified in Supervision Course Syllabi

Topics	Frequency
Supervision models and theoretical approaches	
Instructional or behavioral	12
Developmental	11
Client-centered or personal growth	10
Psychoanalytic	10
Skill training and development	9
Integrative-integration	9
Microcounseling	4
Cognitive-behavioral	3
Eclectic	3
Adlerian	2
Co-therapy	2
Social learning	2
Systems	2
Existential	1
Multimodel	1
Triadic	1
Vertical	1
Supervision techniques	
IPR	7
Live supervision	1
Evaluation of supervisee (general)	10
Preparing for and giving feedback	2
Evaluation instruments or rating scales	2
Initial assessment of counseling skills	1
Characteristics of effective counselors	1
Quality control issues	1
Ethical or legal issues	10
Relationship issues (general)	1
Parallel process	4
Counselor-supervisor relationship	3
Client-counselor supervisor relationship	1
Supervision versus therapy	2
Supervisee resistance, games	3
Supervisee "problems with learning"	1
Concerns of beginning supervisees	1
Supervisee anxiety	2
Supervisee expectations	1
Expectations of on-site staff	1

Note: From "A national survey of supervision training" by L.D. Borders and G.R. Leddick, 1988. *Counselor Education and Supervision, 27,* 271-283. Copyright 1988, American Association for Counseling and Development. Reprinted by permission.

Figure 12.2. Class topics specified in supervision course syllabi.

Figure 12.2. Continued.

Topics	Frequency
Sex role, racial, ethnic, and social class issues	3
Supervision in particular settings	
Schools (elementary through college)	4
Community agencies	4
On-campus counselor training programs	2
Private practice	1
Rehabilitation agencies	1
State Department of Education	1
Supervision of specialized counseling	
Marriage and family counseling	6
Group counseling	2
Counseling adolescents	1
History of supervision	6
Definition of supervision	
Roles or role conflict of supervisors	5
Responsibilities of supervisors	2
Purposes of supervision	3
Transition from counselor to supervisor	1
Research on supervision (general)	
Components of effective supervision based on research	2
Group versus individual supervision	5
Administrative supervision (e.g., staff development, organizaitonal goals, policies, procedures)	5
Consultation	2
Training for supervisors	2
Case conceptualization skills	1
Emergency procedures	1
Intake responsibilities	1
Paraprofessionals	1
Standards for counselor education programs	1

adjusted to the differential, developmental needs of trainees" (p. 253). Since the training is planned in incremental stages, it can be implemented as a seminar or practicum for students enrolled in clinical supervisory training or as an in-service workshop for administrative supervisors. The model therefore addresses training needs for both administrative and clinical supervisors.

Supervisory Development

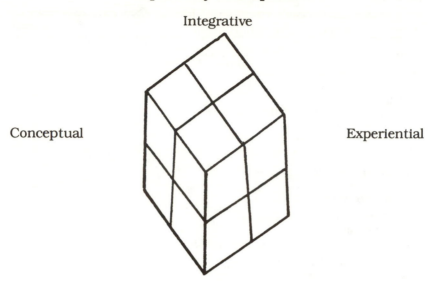

Figure 12.3. Supervisory training components.

In Figure 12.4 is presented a model of supervision training. The model contains the four goals identified earlier in this chapter. As is illustrated in Figure 12.4 the training components incorporate conceptual, experiential, and integrative learnings with the teaching modalities using didactic presentations, modeling, simulation exercises, and supervised practice. Five major content areas are in the training model: (1) conceptualizing the supervisory function, (2) orchestrating a supervisory relationship, (3) focusing supervision goals toward mastery and maturity, (4) facilitating a supervisory learning environment, and (5) developing a theory base, supervisory technology, and personal style. Evaluation consists of a knowledge, practice, and personal component and is conducted throughout the training process.

SUPERVISION TRAINING MODULES

Conceptualizing the Supervisory Function

Supervisors in training need to have a clear understanding of what supervision is and how it differs from counseling.

I. **Goals**

   A. To provide a theory knowledge base relevant to supervisory functioning
   B. To develop and refine supervisory skills
   C. To integrate the theory and skills into a working supervisory style
   D. To develop and enhance the professional identity of the supervisor

II. **Training Components**

   A. Conceptual
   B. Experiential
   C. Integrative

III. **Teaching Modalities**

   A. Didactic presentations
   B. Modeling
   C. Simulation exercises
   D. Supervised practice

IV. **Content Modules**

   A. **Conceptualizing the supervisory function**
      1. Supervision defined
      2. Supervision differentiated from other counseling roles
      3. Portrait of an ideal clinical or administrative supervisor
      4. Supervision as pacing leadership
      5. Ethical and legal considerations of supervision

   B. **Orchestrating a supervisory relationship**
      1. Relational dimensions between supervisor and supervisee
      2. Supervision as a working alliance
      3. The establishment of goals and means
      4. Progression of the supervisory relationship by stages
      5. Group supervision
      6. Environmental/agency context for supervision

Figure 12.4. A model of supervision training.

Figure 12.4. Continued.

C. **Focusing supervision goals toward mastery and maturity**
   1. Developmental issues of supervisees
   2. Roles of supervisors which promote development
   3. Supervision aimed toward processes of professional identity solidification and autonomy

D. **Facilitating a supervisory learning environment**
   1. The interaction of a learner and a learning environment in supervision
   2. Blocher's developmental learning environment— the seven basic dynamics
   3. Supervisee's development
   4. Supervisors stimulate maturity

E. **Developing a theory base, supervision technology, and personal style**
   1. Theoretical approaches to supervision—psychotherapeutic, behavioral, experiential, developmental, systems
   2. Multi-techniques for supervisors
   3. Supervisory interventions based on developmental level
   4. The development of a justifiable personal style of supervision
   5. Integration of theory, skill and style

V. **Evaluation**

   A. Evaluation of knowledge component
   B. Evaluation of practice component
   C. Evaluation of personal component

Perpetuation of the belief that supervision is the mere application of sophisticated counseling techniques must be avoided. To avoid this error, a working definition of supervision needs to be provided. A good beginning is to simply ask: What is supervision? As supervisors respond to the question, three columns might be listed on the board or easel. The first column should be labeled effective supervision, the second ineffective supervision, and the third counseling. What generally is most effective is to first clarify what constitutes good (effective) supervision. Then good supervision (column 1) can be contrasted with poor supervision (column 2). The information in columns 1 and 2 should provide the impetus for what is counseling (column 3). Supervisors should be challenged to identify differences, major differences do exist, between supervision and counseling. Supervisors in training should also realize that one can be a good counselor and know nothing about supervision. Distinctions between supervision and counseling are important and must be understood in order for supervision training to be successful. This portion of the training session should conclude with an agreed upon working definition of supervision. A definition similar to that provided by Hess (1986) is suggested:

> A supervisor is a lecturer who conveys global schemes and techniques, a teacher of specified content and skills, a case reviewer to explore ways of thinking and conceptualizing cases, a monitor to ensure at least minimal levels of competence, a therapist to nurture growth and a colleague to give support and provide a different view. (p. 58)

After supervisors in training have a clear conception of what supervision is and is not, the training can focus on a portrait of an ideal supervisor, clinical or administrative. Carifio and Hess (1987) synthesized the research and described the ideal supervisor as "high-functioning supervisors perform with high levels of empathy, respect, genuineness, flexibility, concern, investment and openness" (p. 244). Herein lies the thesis that regardless of role differences between administrative and clinical supervisors, these primary personal characteristics are primary to any supervisory function. These authors continued to describe ideal supervisors as "appearing to be knowledgeable, experienced and concrete in their presentation. . . [and] use appropriate teaching goal-setting and feedback techniques during their supervisory interactions (Carifio & Hess, 1987, p. 244). Loganbill et al. (1982) described the ideal supervisor as being at a higher competence, maturity, and experience level than the supervisee. These qualities impact on the authoritative nature of supervision. The authoritative role of supervision with its evaluative component is more likely to be accepted if the supervisor is perceived (by the supervisee) as having achieved a higher level of competence. While the ideal supervisor may effect and help produce several changes in the supervisee, the primary goal for the supervisor to achieve is the development of the professional competence of the supervisee even to the exclusion of other considerations (Sansbury, 1982).

Another function of the supervisor is the pacing of the supervisee. As the term implies, the supervision and related activities are to be paced so as to occur at the appropriate time. That is, it is important that supervisory methods not be presented too quickly or too slowly to the supervisee. Another concept involving pacing is proposed by D'Andrea (1984) in which counselors are viewed as pacers in the development of their clients. This idea is applicable to supervisors in that master supervisors should provide provocative, stimulating, and psychologically challenging leadership for promoting the development of their supervisees. The opportunity for pacing occurs in both administrative and clinical supervision for the need to influence the development of effective supervision occurs in both settings.

The final component of this module is the ethical considerations involved in supervision. Supervisors must attain the knowledge necessary for good ethical practice. In an article by Upchurch (1985), the author stressed that "ethical standards for the supervisory process are necessary for the protection of the client, the supervisor, and the supervisee, all of whom are vulnerable in different ways" (p. 17). These same principles apply for administrative supervision with the added component of promoting sound ethical behavior congruent with organizational accountability. The content of ethical training in either administrative or clinical settings cannot be complete without attending to the legal implications with its statutory trends and implications for practice (Herlihy & Sheeley, 1988). Since supervision is a relatively new professional activity, supervisors, more than likely will have had little if any professional training and limited experience in dealing with the lawsuit arena. In this module both ethical and legal issues relating to supervision should be provided to present an integrated understanding of ethics and the supervision process. Such concepts as confidentiality, duty to warn, due process, dual relationship, and informed consent should be stressed. A more complete description of ethical training can be found in Chapter 11 of this book. Other information about ethics is provided by Corey, Corey, and Callanan (1988); Cormier and Bernard (1982); a special issue of the *Journal of Counseling and Development* (Sadler, 1986); and professional codes of ethics.

Ethical training should be presented during the first supervision training module to allow the trainee to understand and incorporate sound ethical practice into the supervisory role. One method for teaching about ethical issues is described in Chapter 11 of this book. Basically it involves a demonstration of ethical dilemmas via videotapes. Supervisors in training describe the ethical dilemmas and by referring to ethical principles and codes of ethics, supervisors discuss the correct ethical behavior. This training approach incorporates a demonstration-discussion-feedback training format.

Although the model for conceptualizing the supervisory function is one of five proposed in the supervision training model, it is important for it provides the foundation for the remaining aspects of the supervision process. In summary, the content for this model includes the following:

1. a clear definition of supervision and delineation of the supervisory function to facilitate professional growth, and to assure quality service delivery;

2. a portrayal of an ideal clinical or administrative supervisor;

3. a clear differentiation between supervision and counseling;

4. a perspective of supervisory leadership whereby the supervisor serves as pacer; and

5. a conceptualization of supervision as an ethical responsibility with legal ramifications for practice.

Instructional approaches in this module include assigned readings from books and journals, viewing audio and videotapes depicting supervisory functions, conducting role-playing with other supervisors in training to illustrate different supervisory roles, reviewing case studies, and viewing vignettes of actual and potential ethical dilemmas.

Orchestrating a Supervisory Relationship

Holloway (1987) stated that "the supervisory relationship itself creates a trainee's initial vulnerability and final independence" (p. 215). Holloway further stated "the trainee's feelings are not intrinsic to becoming a counselor or establishing a professional identity but are the result of being in an intensive, evaluative, ongoing and demanding relationship" (p. 215). Throughout supervision literature, attention is devoted to the supervisor's ability to form a working relationship with the supervisee. Clearly knowledge about the activities of supervision can not substitute for understanding the feelings which emerge within the supervisory relationship.

The second training module is focused upon the relational dimension between supervisor and supervisee. Because Chapter 2 of this book is devoted to the supervisory relationship, this discussion will focus on the training techniques involved in the supervisory relationship for it becomes the vehicle by which learning is facilitated or hampered.

Bordin (1983) presented a good model of the relationship and referred to it as the "supervisory working alliance." He described the supervisory working alliance as a relationship targeted toward supervisee goals including mastery of specific skills, enlargement of the understanding of client concerns and of process issues, awareness of the impact of self on the therapeutic process, and initial translation of theory into practice. In this module an important procedure is to establish a working understanding of the nature and purpose of the supervisory relationship (Bordin, 1983; Ekstein and Wallerstein, 1972; Loganbill, Hardy, & Delworth, 1982). The supervisor must realize that the relationship develops over time and in stages. Ekstein and Wallerstein (1972) described a beginning unfamiliar stage, a middle game, and an end phase while Mueller and Kell (1972) described a beginning trust phase, a working phase, and a termination phase.

The most logical place to begin this module is to have the supervisor and supervisee discuss their expectations about the supervisory relationship with the understanding that new expectations will develop with time. After expectations are understood, then means for completing expectations should be discussed. Within this module, attention should be devoted to anxiety. The mere fact that the relationship is uneven (supervisor higher, supervisee lower) suggests that anxiety may be present especially since the supervisor at some time will be in an evaluative role. Resistance and conflict also should be discussed. Figure 12.5 provides a listing of some of the fundamental tasks necessary for an effective supervisory relationship.

In training supervisors for clinical and administrative settings, the relationship should not be envisioned as only one-to-one between supervisor and supervisee. Supervisors must be educated to conduct group supervision. This is particularly important in administrative supervision where supervisors may be realistically unable to supervise every subordinate. Educators also must attend to the need for clinical supervisors to be exposed to group supervision with supervisors in training supervising three or four supervisees.

Within this module, the impact of the environmental or agency context within which the supervisor operates must be considered. Environmental issues such as time, policy, agency procedures, client population, facilities, and organizational stresses can and often do impact on the quality and nature of the relationship offered by the administrative supervisor. Similarly, clinical supervisors must attend to the influence of environmental factors on their supervisees.

In the relationship module, the imparting of knowledge can occur through didactic and experiential learning. Readings and group discussions should be an integral part of training. In this

Achieved	Fundamental Tasks
————————	1. The supervisor and the supervisee address their respective expectations.
————————	2. The supervisory function is clearly articulated in terms of content, context, boundaries, and opportunities.
————————	3. The supervisor and supervisee establish mutual goals, respective tasks, a timeline for their alliance, and a statement of confidentiality.
————————	4. The evaluative means are clearly specified and the supervisor addresses with the supervisee the anxiety associated with performance and assessment.
————————	5. The supervisor and the supervisee engage in a trust building phase of their alliance which is facilitated by affirmation and structure.
————————	6. The supervisor attends to supervisee resistance which may stifle the working alliance.
————————	7. As the alliance solidifies, the working phase emerges wherein mastery of skills, understanding of issues, and focus on goal attainment are targeted.
————————	8. The supervisor delivers feedback in a sensitive yet challenging fashion.
————————	9. Supervisee feelings are explored and addressed within the supervisory alliance.
————————	10. The supervisor addresses the impact of the environmental context within which the supervisee operates.
————————	11. The supervisor evaluates the supervisee through the means that have been previously established.
————————	12. The supervisee has the opportunity to deliver feedback to the supervisor about any aspect of the supervision experience.

Figure 12.5. A checklist of fundamental tasks involved in the formation of a supervisory relationship.

module, students can progressively move from cognitive information about the supervisory relationship to (1) case studies illustrating the working relationship; (2) observations of other supervisors via live supervision, videotape, and role-play modeling; and (3) actual monitored supervisory practice. In summary, this training module includes the following:

1. primary attention is focused on the relational dimension between supervisor and supervisee;

2. the supervisory relationship is illustrated as a "working alliance";

3. the supervisory relationship begins by addressing the expectations brought into the relationship by both persons, expectations which continue to be articulated as the relationship progresses;

4. the supervisory relationship is characterized as developing in predictable, identifiable phases;

5. supervisee resistance is managed sensitively as a manifestation of performance and evaluation anxiety; and

6. the working relationship is orchestrated using both individual and group supervision modalities.

Focusing Supervision Goals
Toward Mastery and Maturity

Explicit in the formation of a supervisory relationship is the mutual agreement of goals for the supervisory experience. Although specific goals of supervision will be tailored to the needs of the individual supervisee, the global aims of supervision can be viewed as the development of supervision mastery and of professional identity (maturity and autonomy). This third training module focuses on the developmental issues of supervisees and the roles of supervisors in promoting developmental progression. A more complete perspective of developmental supervision is provided in Chapters 7 and 8 of this book.

Hess (1986) described four processes of professional development that seem common to various stage theories of supervision. First, a time exists of "inception" involving the induction of the professional into his/her roles and tasks. The move is from the unfamiliar to the more familiar. This perspective could find application to transitions from theoretical learnings to performance applications that occur with novice practitioners as they become supervisees and later as they assume supervisor positions. Fear, often felt as crisis, is characteristic of this process. Both professional identity and autonomy are unrealistic in this introduction period. Second, a process of "skill development" follows wherein the supervisor in training, understanding more clearly his/her expected roles and tasks, begins to accumulate some tools of practice. Professional identity and autonomy begin as the supervisor risks assuming the roles and performing the tasks. Third, a "consolidation" period occurs as the professional emerges in self-definition, refines skills, and develops competence. Finally, a process of "mutuality" is developed whereby the individual can function as an independent, autonomous professional with an integrated sense of identity. Here is where supervisors in training are transformed into supervisors with leadership capacity. Professional development has matured although it is never completed.

Stoltenberg and Delworth (1987) described supervision development by stages. The beginning supervisor is described as one lacking in professional identity and skills. The beginning supervisor needs training that is structured with opportunity to practice the new learnings. Beginning supervisors, especially those with little experience, need concrete information about how you supervise. At this stage, global anxiety and power playing are often present. Often the power playing centers around the expertise and evaluation elements. At this stage a discussion of feelings of anxiety and issues related to the mechanics of supervision and evaluation is important. Direct instructional supervisory roles are less effective as the supervisor moves to the second stage. At this stage, the supervisor is beginning to develop competence and a belief in his/her ability as a supervisor. As the supervisor becomes more experienced and mature, the supervisor becomes more committed to the growth of the supervisee, and maturity and competence emerge within the supervisory style. At the last stage, the supervisor has an integrated supervisor identity and is perceived as more secure and competent. The supervisor permits the supervisee's agenda to dominate the supervisory sessions. Assuming the supervisee has the competence, the supervisor will employ a more collaborative and consultant role, one that is in keeping within the developmental needs of the supervisee.

In Module 3, the broad goals are mastery and maturity. The training module entitled "focusing supervision goals toward mastery and maturity" includes the assignment of reading materials to illustrate developmental supervision. Simulations are presented to illustrate different supervisory roles. Using case studies, supervisors in training are asked to conceptualize and defend their supervisory role. Effective supervisors are often asked to demonstrate and explain their rationale for supervision with a supervisee. In summary, Module 3 incorporates the following content emphases:

1. the global aims of supervision are viewed as mastery and maturity, processes involving professional identity and autonomy;

2. supervisors develop by stages moving from dependence, confusion, and ambiguity to independence, self-direction, and competence;

3. maturation progresses and increases in conceptual complexity, emotional expression and professional awareness and judgment; and

4. the choice of supervisory role is aimed at promoting mastery, and maturity is based on the developmental level of the supervisee.

Facilitating a Supervisory Learning Environment

Lambert and Arnold (1987) concluded that both skills and attitudes are affected during supervision and that "the most efficient way of maximizing learning [of these]. . . is to systematically structure their acquisition" (p. 222). In this training module, the successful supervisor creates learning conditions that are optimal for the supervisee. The supervisee's development is the central issue, and supervision tasks are sequenced to provide for that development.

Blocher (1983) proposed a learning environment that is composed of seven dynamics: (1) challenge, (2) involvement, (3) support, (4) structure, (5) feedback, (6) innovation, and (7) integration. The dynamics of Blocher's learning environment address interaction between the supervisor and supervisee. In either administrative or clinical supervision, the supervisory experience is the environment and the person in supervision training (student at university, supervisor at agency) is the learner. Regardless of setting, the supervisory experience is directed by a master practitioner who attends to the needs of the supervisee.

The training module in this section of the chapter incorporates Blocher's seven principles for providing a learning environment. Similar to the components described by Loganbill et al. (1982), the module creates conceptual, experiential, and integrative opportunities. Although readings are assigned, the main feature of this module is the modeling of a learning environment. Adequate conditions of structure and support are built into the module with the intent that the supervisor will carefully monitor the learning environment and will increase and decrease the structure and support in accordance with needs of the supervisee. The intent of this module is to provide the impetus and opportunity for the development of the effective supervisor in either an administrative or clinical setting. In Figure 12.6 is provided questions that may be used in assessing the presence of an optimal learning environment. An optimal experience will yield a "yes" response to each question.

In summary, the training module includes and incorporates the following content:

1. the supervisory experience provides a model learning environment;

2. within the supervisory learning environment, the supervisee's development is the core issue;

Achieved	Components of Optimal Learning Environment
_____	1. Is the level of challenge great enough to sufficiently motivate the supervisee?
_____	2. Is the dissonance realistically resolvable for the supervisee?
_____	3. Does the supervisee possess the skill and/or maturity to meet the demands of the task?
_____	4. Is the supervisee invested in the learning process and tasks?
_____	5. Does the supervisee have a sense of worth and esteem that is separate from his/her perceived professional success or failure?
_____	6. Does the supervisee have a felt sense of warmth, empathy, and support within the supervisory relationship?
_____	7. Is the amount of support proportional to the amount of challenge?
_____	8. Is the experience structured so as to specify the supervision goals and means?
_____	9. Are the evaluative means objective, accurate, relevant, and interpretable?
_____	10. Is the supervisee able to process feedback?
_____	11. Does the supervision experience allow the safety necessary for practice attempts at new skills and behaviors?
_____	12. Does the supervisor assist the supervisee in integrating mastery with the development of professional identity, autonomy, and maturity?
_____	13. Is the termination of the alliance managed purposefully so as to identify progress, delineate further concerns, and address the interpersonal experience of the supervisory relationship? Are issues of professional identity, autonomy, and competence emphasized?

Figure 12.6. An evaluation of the dynamics of a supervisory learning environment.

3. the seven basic dynamics described by Blocher (1983) provide the foundation for stimulating the supervisory learning environment in both clinical and administrative settings; and

4. within the learning environment, supervisors will learn to facilitate levels of challenge, involvement, support, structure, feedback, innovation, and integration which collectively stimulate professional maturation.

**Developing a Theory Base,
Supervisory Technology, and
Personal Supervisory Style**

The last training module emphasizes the development of a theory base, supervision technology, and personal style. The process of professional maturation, autonomy, and identity requires a synthesis of science (theory) and art (practice) which translates into a identifiable and justifiable personal style of supervision. Thus the goal of this module is to help the supervisor mature to the extent that he/she can transfer cognitive and experiential learning into future situations and take ownership of the knowledge and skill. This module is based on the premise that the knowledge base presented in the previous modules is fundamental and therefore provides the foundation for this module.

While the knowledge base presented in this module is considered basic for both clinical and administrative supervisors, the content might be focused differently to accommodate the needs of clinical and administrative settings. Additionally theoretical approaches and case illustrations might be focused toward specific supervisor roles. For example, for the administrative supervisor, the systems model might focus on organized objectives, demonstrated effectiveness, program efficiency, and problem-solving potential. In contrast, the clinical supervisor while needing to know about systems theory might benefit more specifically from case illustrations adapted from various theoretical approaches often applied in clinical settings.

Supervisors must be exposed to a variety of theoretical approaches and supervisory techniques otherwise they will be unable to provide effective supervision to their supervisees. Secondly, supervisors must be aware of a wide range of supervisory technology which in turn will allow them to select and decide from among the various approaches. In the end, this knowledge base and selection process will allow them to own a particular supervisory style.

This module therefore advocates a "macroscopic" or "multi-modal" approach to supervision. The skill repertoire needed for the multi-modal (multi-techniqued) approach includes skills related to developmental assessment (of both the individual and the learning environment), relationship building (with both individuals and groups), confrontation (the compassionate presentation of discrepancy), and case conceptualization (the selective attention given to themes and patterns which collectively form a prescription for action). In addition to the references previously cited, the *Handbook of Counseling Supervision* (Borders & Leddick, 1987) and the *Handbook of Administrative Supervision* (Falvey, 1987) are recommended as good reading resources.

In summary, this module includes the following content emphases:

1. supervisory maturation requires a synthesis of theory and application which can be translated into an accountable personal style of supervision,

2. a supervisory knowledge base is identified and taught and this base must provide exposure to a variety of approaches,

3. supervisors must be armed with an encompassing supervisory technology to insure that choice of intervention in accordance with the needs of the supervisees and with the dynamics necessary to promote an effective learning environment, and

4. supervisors in training must be able to integrate training and practice and translate this into a personal supervisory style with evidence of personal identity and demonstrated competence.

EVALUATION

The evaluation portion of the supervisory training model contains three components: the knowledge component, the practice component, and the personal characteristics component. Whether in an administrative or clinical setting, the three should be evaluated. In Figure 12.7 is illustrated the three components which should be viewed as interrelated.

Personal

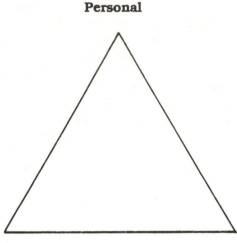

Knowledge   **Practice**

Figure 12.7. Evaluation components.

While evaluation can present an uncomfortable situation for the supervisor in training, evaluation does not have to be an uncomfortable process. Careful planning prior to the beginning of supervisory training can help to reduce the anxiety associated with evaluation. Prior to the first training session, the recommendation is that means for evaluation be described. Evaluation should be described as directly and accurately as possible. If forms are going to be used in the evaluation process, supervisors in training should know the content of the forms and, if possible, be given a copy of the evaluation form(s). If written materials (supervisory theory paper, case conceptualization) or direct observations by an educator or agency site supervisor are a part of the procedure, the supervisor in training should be provided with as much concrete information as is available. Issues related to confidentiality and its impact on evaluation also should be provided. Basically, the supervisor should be given as much information as is available for the evaluation procedures. Anxiety usually decreases in direct proportion to the amount of information provided. Discussion should be directed to insure that the supervisor in training understands that the aim of evaluation is to enhance the learning experience and in no way is it intended to "put down" or make the supervisor feel inferior.

Knowledge Component

In this component, the intent is to assess whether a knowledge base of the supervisory process has been acquired. Examples of competence areas include supervision models, supervision techniques, knowledge of ethical and legal issues related to supervision, supervisory intervention strategies, supervision research, supervisory organizational structure, and individual and group supervision strategies. Methods for assessing competence include examinations (including cognitive and experiential components), writing or verbally presenting one's supervision theory, preparing a paper that compares and contrasts administrative and clinical supervisory roles, developing an in-service workshop on the basics of supervision, creating ethical supervision dilemmas for class discussion, and demonstrating (written, verbal) knowledge of the rationale for and the appropriate supervisory methodology to implement with supervisees at different stages of development. A more extensive listing of possible course requirements is provided in a recent article by Borders and Leddick (1988).

Practice Component

The practice component encompasses an evaluation of how supervisors in training deliver supervision. In essence the practice component involves the actual demonstration of the total realm of supervisory learning. Audiotapes, videotapes, and direct observation represent three frequent methods used for evaluating the implementation of supervision skills. A combination of verbal and written feedback is needed in evaluating the practice component. Especially in instances where negative feedback is given, a written summary should be provided. The summary should include suggestions for improvement and additionally it should be signed and dated by both the supervisor and supervisee. The signature of the supervisee indicates that he/she has received and read the evaluation. In Figure 12.8 is presented an example of an evaluation form that may be used in evaluating supervisory skills. Before the written evaluation is given to the supervisee, a verbal summary should be presented. A highly recommended procedure is for the two to occur in the same session. The written evaluation should never be given without an accompanying verbal evaluation with ample opportunity for questions to be asked by the supervisee. Many supervisors-in-training at universities and agencies are often supervised by an on-site supervisor. Since the on-site supervisor is usually involved in supervisory training, consultation should occur with the on-site supervisor to obtain that individual's input and evaluation about the performance of the supervisor-in-training. In Figure 12.9 is presented an example of an evaluation form that may be completed by the on-site supervisor. The on-site supervisor should both discuss the evaluation with and give a copy of the evaluation to the supervisor-in-training. Both the on-site supervisor and supervisor-in-training should sign and date the form. A copy of all evaluation forms and other information related to evaluation should be kept in the supervisee's training file. Additionally an evaluation by the supervisee(s) can provide insight into the supervisor's service delivery.

In evaluating the practice component, it is advisable to obtain information from a variety of supervisory activities. For example, evaluative information should be obtained about the supervisor's delivery in both group and individual supervisory sessions. Direct observation of the supervisor supervising at an agency or with a group of pre-practicum or practicum students can provide information on several supervisory practice elements.

The evaluation of the practice component usually centers on **what** supervisory function is to be implemented and **how** that function is being implemented. The "what" in supervision refers to the behaviors in which the supervisor in training engages and the "how" describes the way in which the supervisory behaviors occur. Supervision tasks including how

(Continued on p. 476)

Supervisor-in-training's Name _____

Evaluator's Name _____

Date _____

Directions: Rate the following supervisory functions using a scale ranging from 1 (low) to 5 (high). A score of 1 (one) indicates poor with 5 (five) indicating excellent skills. A rating below 3 indicates supervisory standards were not met. (Ratings may be made in quartile increments).

Rating Scale	1	2	3	4	5
	Poor		Acceptable		Excellent

_____ 1. Supervisor-in-training greets supervisee in warm, friendly, manner and opens supervisory session with appropriate amount of structure.

_____ 2. Supervisor-in-training provides overview of supervisory process (goals, roles, expectations, length of session meetings, time & place for meetings, ethics, confidentiality, evaluation, etc.).

_____ 3. Supervisor-in-training is accepting, understanding, and exhibits interest in supervisee.

_____ 4. Supervisor-in-training listens to and encourages supervisee to discuss counseling issues.

_____ 5. Supervisor-in-training attends to both verbal and nonverbal behaviors of supervisee.

_____ 6. Supervisor-in-training tracks supervisee accurately . . . does not lead or lag behind.

_____ 7. Supervisor-in-training responses accurately reflect both the content and affect of supervisee's message.

_____ 8. Supervisor-in-training accurately employs supervisory roles (teacher, counselor, consultant, etc.).

_____ 9. Supervisor-in-training understands supervisory functions and does not overly control the direction of the supervisory session.

_____ 10. Supervisor-in-training exhibits good knowledge of supervision theory.

Figure 12.8. Form for evaluation of supervisor-in-training.

Figure 12.8. Continued.

_____ 11. Supervisor-in-training understands supervisory techniques.

_____ 12. Supervisor-in-training effectively integrates supervisory theory and techniques and implements these in actual supervisory practice.

_____ 13. Supervisor-in-training effectively promotes the development of the supervisee.

_____ 14. Supervisor-in-training exhibits a personal supervisory style.

_____ 15. Supervisor-in-training develops professional maturity and identity.

Comments: _____

_____

_____

_____

Evaluator's Signature _____

Date _____

Supervisor-in-training's Signature _____

Date _____

Date _____

Supervisor-in-training's Name _____

Evaluator's (on-site Supervisor) Name _____

1. Please rate (using an "x") the following supervisory functions using a scale ranging from poor to excellent. If you have not observed the supervisor performing a function, please indicate by marking N/A (not appropriate).

	N/A	Poor	Good	Excellent	Comments
Individual Supervision	—	—	—	—	_____
Group Supervision	—	—	—	—	_____
Consultation	—	—	—	—	_____
Relationships with colleagues	—	—	—	—	_____
Participation in Supervisory Training	—	—	—	—	_____
Interest in Supervision	—	—	—	—	_____
Acceptance of Supervisee	—	—	—	—	_____
Understanding of Supervision Theory	—	—	—	—	_____
Understanding of Supervisory Techniques	—	—	—	—	_____
Implementation of good Supervisory Skills	—	—	—	—	_____
Overall Performance	—	—	—	—	_____
Potential as future Supervisor	—	—	—	—	_____

2. If you were in a position to employ this person, would you employ him/her as supervisor?   Yes _____   No _____

   Comments _____
   _____
   _____

3. Please provide any additional comments
   _____
   _____
   _____

Evaluator (on-site Supervisor) _____
                                        Signature

   Date _____

Supervisor-in-training _____
                                        Signature

   Date _____

Figure 12.9. Form for on-site supervisor to evaluate supervisor-in-training.

one determines a rationale and theoretical basis for supervision, how supervisees are supervised, and how supervisory goals are planned and achieved are representative areas for supervision evaluation.

Personal Component

In the personal component, the intent is to evaluate characteristics that indicate whether the supervisor has developed into a competent supervisor. In this component, information should be obtained about the quality and nature of the supervisor's personal characteristics. Evaluation about the supervisor-in-training's professional maturity and identity and ability to promote the development of the supervisee(s) should be assessed. Additionally assessment about such personal tolerance traits as being flexible, accepting, empathic, fair, sensitive, objective, and honest should be made. Further assessment should be made about the supervisor-in-training's ethical beliefs and behavior.

The personal component can be difficult to assess because of its qualitative nature, and therefore many supervisory training programs conduct a cursory if any evaluation of this area. This component is an important component and therefore should not be overlooked. Supervisors-in-training should understand from the onset of training that a knowledge base of supervision and skills can never substitute for the personal component.

Effective personal characteristics must be modeled and demonstrated throughout the supervisory process. The supervisor-in-training's supervision of supervisees provides a direct means for assessing the personal component. Information about the supervisor-in-training's personal characteristics also can be obtained during in-service training in agency settings, classroom training in supervision courses, and feedback from supervisees, on-site supervisors, and other colleagues.

The explicit goal of the evaluation component is therefore the assessment of information about the development of the supervisor-in-training's mastery of supervisory knowledge, implementation of supervisory skills, and demonstration of effective personal characteristics throughout the supervision process. Evaluation should include both quantitative and qualitative data, direct and indirect observations, and formal and informal methods of assessment. The overall intent of the evaluation is to determine whether the supervisor-in-training has reached professional competency.

SUMMARY

In summary, in this chapter was presented a model for supervision training. Administrative and clinical supervisors were characterized as catalysts for helping supervisors-in-training develop greater counseling competence. The model proposed a means for equipping the supervisor-in-training with a knowledge base and skill repertory for implementation into actual supervisory practice.

Five training modules and an evaluation component were presented. The five training modules were (1) conceptualizing the supervisory function, (2) orchestrating a supervisory relationship, (3) focusing supervision goals toward mastery and maturity, (4) facilitating a supervisory learning environment, and (5) developing a theory base, supervisory technology, and a personal supervisory style. The evaluation component addressed: (1) knowledge component, (2) practice component, and (3) personal component.

In summary, the training of supervisors must consider three essential components (Figure 12.10)—*model, setting,* and *modality.* Several supervisory models are listed in Figure 12.10. From exposure to several models supervisors can be motivated to sort through the models and integrate the knowledge into a workable supervisory style.

Supervisory training is viewed as a basic on-going need for supervisors in either an adminstrative or clinical setting, the second component. Clearly many supervisory skills and techniques are shared by administrative and clinical supervisors, and yet administrative and clinical supervision differ. The focus of administrative supervision is therefore on the tasks that directly affect the organization whereas in clinical supervision the focus is on the supervisee's clinical interventions that directly affect the client.

Modality, the third component, is composed of interaction and means. Interaction refers to mutual or reciprocal action or influence. While individual is usually the modal type, interaction may be achieved by co-supervision, group or peer supervision. At least four means (methods) are available; academic, observational, experiential, and supervisory training. Depending upon experience, expertise, and work setting, supervisory training may vary its focus on the three essential components. The ommission of one component can have a serious impact on the other components and in turn, the overall success of counselor supervision. The supervisory training model proposed in this chapter and throughout the book is based on the premise that supervision is a process that can be enhanced by training if its essential components are understood and incorporated into the overall supervision training process.

Model	Setting	Modality
—Cognitive-behavioral	—Administrative	Interaction:
—Developmental (Person-Process)	—Clinical	individual
—Eclectic		co-supervisor
—Gestalt		group
—Humanistic-Existential		peer
—Integrative		
—Personal Growth		
—Person-Process		Means:
—Psychoanalytic		academic
—Psychotherapeutic		observational
—Social Learning		experiential
—Systems		supervisory
—Transactional Analysis		

Figure 12.10. Modal, setting, and modality—three essential components of counselor supervision.

REFERENCES

Bernard, J.M. (1979). Supervision training: A discrimination model. *Counselor Education and Supervision, 19,* 60-68.

Blocher, D.H. (1983). Toward a cognitive developmental approach to counselor supervision. *The Counseling Psychologist, II,* 27-34.

Borders, L.D., & Leddick, G.R. (1987). *Handbook of clinical supervision.* Alexandria, VA: American Association for Counseling and Development.

Borders, L.D., & Leddick, G.R. (1988). A national survey of supervision training. *Counselor Education and Supervision, 27,* 271-283.

Bordin, E.S. (1983). A working alliance based model of supervision. *The Counseling Psychologist, II,* 35-42.

Bradley, L.J., & Richardson, B. (1987). Trends in practicum and internship requirements: A national study. *The Clinical Supervisor, 5,* 97-105.

Carifio, M.S., & Hess, A.K. (1987). Who is the ideal supervisor? *Professional Psychology: Research and Practice, 18,* 244-250.

Corey, G., Corey, M., & Callanan, P. (1988). *Issues and ethics in the helping profession* (3rd ed.). Pacific Grove, CA: Brooks/Cole.

Cormier, L.S., & Bernard, J. (1982). Ethical and legal responsibilities of clinical supervisors. *The Personnel and Guidance Journal, 60,* 486-491.

D'Andrea, M. (1984). The counselor as pacer: A model for revitalization of the counseling profession. *Counseling and Human Development, 16,* 1-15.

Ekstein, R., & Wallerstein, R.S. (1972). *The teaching and learning of psychotherapy* (2nd ed.). New York: International Universities Press.

Falvey, J.E. (1987). *Handbook of administrative supervision.* Alexandria, VA: American Association for Counseling and Development.

Hansen, J.C., Robins, T.H., & Grimes, J. (1982). Review of research on practicum supervision. *Counselor Education and Supervision, 22,* 15-24.

Hart, G.M. (1982). *The process of clinical supervision.* Baltimore, MD: University Park Press.

Hart, G., & Falvey, E. (1987). Field supervision of counselor trainees: A survey of the North Atlantic Region. *Counselor Education and Supervision, 26,* 204-212.

Herlihy, B., & Sheeley, V. (1988). Counselor liability and the duty to warn: Selected cases, statutory trends and implications for practice. *Counselor Education and Supervision, 27,* 203-216.

Hess, A.K. (Ed.). (1980). *Psychotherapy supervision: Theory, research and practice.* New York: Wiley.

Hess, A.K. (1986). Growth in supervision: Stages of supervisee and supervisor development. *The Clinical Supervisor, 4,* 51-67.

Hess, A.K. (1987). Psychotherapy supervision: Stages, Buber and a theory of relationship. *Professional Psychology: Research and Practice, 18,* 251-259.

Hess, A.K., & Hess, A.K. (1983). Psychotherapy supervision: A survey of internship training practice. *Professional Psychology, 14,* 504-513.

Hollis, J., & Wantz, R. (1983). *Counselor preparation 1983-86.* Muncie, IN: Accelerated Development.

Holloway, E. (1982). Characteristics of the field practicum: A national survey. *Counselor Education and Supervision, 22,* 75-80.

Holloway, E.L. (1987). Developmental models of supervision: Is it development? *Professional Psychology: Research and Practice, 18,* 209-216.

Kaslow, F.W. (Ed.). (1987). *Supervision and training: Models, dilemmas and challenges.* New York: Haworth.

Lambert, M.J., & Arnold, R.C. (1987). Research and the supervisory process. *Professional Psychology: Research and Practice, 18,* 217-224.

Loganbill, C., & Hardy, E. (1983). Developing training programs for clinical supervisors. *The Clinical Supervisor, 1,* 15-21.

Loganbill, C., Hardy, E., & Delworth, U. (1982). Supervision: A conceptual model. *The Counseling Psychologist, 10,* 3-42.

Mueller, W.J., & Kell, B.L. (1972). *Coping with conflict: Supervising counselors and psychotherapists.* New York: Appleton-Century-Crofts.

Richardson, B., & Bradley, L. (1986). *Community agency counseling: An emerging specialty in counselor preparation programs.* Washington, DC: American Association for Counseling and Development.

Sadler, H. (Ed.). (1986). Professional Ethics [special issue]. *Journal of Counseling and Development, 64.*

Sansbury, D.L. (1982). Developmental supervision from a skills perspective. *The Counseling Psychologist, 10,* 53-57.

Stoltenberg, C., & Delworth, U. (1987). *Supervising counselors and therapists: A developmental approach.* San Francisco: Jossey-Bass.

Upchurch, D.W. (1985). Ethical standards and the supervisory process. *Counselor Education and Supervision, 25,* 90-98.

Williams, A. (1987). Parallel process in a course on counseling supervision. *Counselor Education and Supervision, 26,* 245-254.

Worthington, E.L., Jr. (1984). Empirical investigation of supervision of counselors as they gain experience. *Journal of Counseling Psychology, 31,* 63-75.

INDEX

INDEX

A

Abels, N. 77, 120
Abels, P. 4, 27, 232, 254
Accountability 14-6
  definition 15
Activities
  adjunctive, *Figure* 145-6
  consultation 16, 18-20,
    Figure 17
  counseling 16, 20-2, *Figure* 17
  counselor supervision 16-26
  evaluation 16, 25-6, *Figure* 17
  instruction 16, 22-4, *Figure* 17
  sequence of 411-5
  supervision 301-69
  training 16, 22-4, *Figure* 17
Affective Sensitivity Scale 106
Akamatsu, T. J. 23, 27, 165, 179
Aldrich, L. 353, 369
Alexander, D. 424, 444
Allen, G. G, 23, 27
Allen, G.J. 103, 118, 351, 369
Allen, V.B. 423, 444
Alonso, A. 3, 22, 27, 46, 48, 59
Altekruse, M.K. 161, 180, 444
Altucher, N. 35, 36, 41, 54, 59, 65,
    66, 68, 74, 82, 119
American Association for Counseling
  and Development (AACD) 3, 423,
  424, 425-30, 432-3, 435-6, 438,
  444
American Association for Marriage
  and Family Therapy (AAMFT)
  423-4
American Personnel and Guidance
  Association (APGA) 197, 423, 424
American Psychiatric Association
  424
American Psychological Association
  (APA) 424
American School Counselor Associ-
  ation (ASCA) 132
Amidon, E. 293, 295

Analysis
  skill 130-55, *Figure* 131 &
    138-47
  system 232-5
  tasks 232-5
Anchor, K.N. 105, 121
Anderson, M.W. 126, 160, 183
Angyal, A. 376, 397
Anxiety
  anticipatory 55
  approval 43-4
  avoidance 353
  dependency 55-6
  dominance 45-6
  excitement 55
  performance 43-4
  risk-taking 353
  supervisor 46-9
Anxiety management 340-1
Appraisal
  self 159-61
Approach
  developmental model 257-95
  psychobehavioral 197-203
  psychotherapeutic 128
Arbuckle, D.S. 36, 59, 65, 83, 119,
    161, 180
Archer, J. 79, 106, 119
Ard, B.M. 284, 295
Arieti, S. 293, 295
Arndt, G.M. 167, 182
Arnold, D.L. 11, 28, 201, 225
Arnold, R.C. 447, 465, 480
Asbury, F. 411, 418
Assessment
  categories, *Figure* 131
  counseling skills, *Figure 319-21*
  skill 130-55, Figure 131 &
    138-47
  teaching skills, *Figure* 319-21
Association for Counselor Education
  and Supervision (ACES) 3, 4, 5, 22,
  28
    Committee on Counselor Effec-
    tiveness 229, 254
Association for Specialists in Group
  Work (ASGW) 411, 413, 417, 424

Attitude
    peer supervisor 162
    reflection 152, 153
Austin, B. 161, 180
Austin, M. 4, 28, 230, 254
Authier, J. 169, 180, 197, 225, 336, 371
Authority 353
Avery, A.W. 195, 196, 226
Avila, D.L. 411, 417
Awareness 81, 89
    dynamic 73, *Figure* 101
    treatment 172-3
Awareness, dynamic
    unstructured therapeutic supervision 85-7

B

Baker, E. 46, 61
Baker, R.D. 119, 226, 259, 296
Baker, S. 23, 28
Baker, S.B. 164, 167, 180, 189
Baldick, T. 439, 444
Balzer, F. 411, 418
Bandura, A. 163, 165, 180
Barker, E.N. 68, 69, 83, 121
Barmann, B. 23, 30, 74, 121, 196, 227, 335, 371, 410, 418
Barrett-Lennard Relationship Inventory 103, 106
Bartlett, W. 427, 444
Bartlett, W.E. 200, 226, 335, 369
Bartunek, J. M. 267, 292, 295
Baum, D. 339, 369
Bauman, W.F. 51, 59, 69, 119, 353, 369
Beck, A. 230, 238, 254
Beck, A.C. 25, 28
Beck, A.T. 171, 180
Beck, T.D. 25, 34, 43, 62, 353, 373
Becker, H.S. 10, 28
Bednar, R. 400, 419
Behavior
    factor, *Figure* 356
Behavioral model
    supervision 125-79
Bell, G.E. 107, 123, 163, 176, 187
Bellucci, J.E. 167, 180

Benjamin, D. 74, 122, 160, 185, 354, 372
Berenson, B.G. 84, 123, 192, 226, 227,
Bergers, S. 444, 445
Bergin, A.E. 163, 172, 180
Bernard, J. 6, 29, 426, 427, 428, 430, 437, 444, 445, 459, 479
Bernard, J.M. 6, 20, 23, 28, 200, 226, 302, 305, 369, 447, 478
Bernier, J.E. 65, 119, 410, 417
Bernstein, B.L. 158, 170, 180. 229, 254
Berven, N.L. 354, 369
Betz, E.L. 137, 189
Betz, R. 410, 421
Beutler, L.E. 105, 119
Biddle, B.J. 186
Birk, J.M. 104, 107, 119, 176, 180
Bishop, J.B. 161, 180
Black, J. 4, 28
Blane, S.M. 163, 181, 196, 226
Blass, C.D. 196, 226
Blocher, D. 410, 416, 417
Blocher, D.H. 3, 6, 11, 21, 22, 28, 37, 38, 39, 41, 59, 162, 182, 200, 226, 229, 231, 254, 366, 370 448, 466, 468, 478
Block, P. 20, 28
Bloom, B.L. 20, 28
Blumburg, A. 293, 295
Bonney, W. C. 414, 417
Borders, L. 3, 4, 23, 25, 28
Borders, L.D. 28, 55, 59, 311, 317, 318, 321, 325, 333, 335, 339, 352, 369 426, 432, 444, 447, 448, 451, 452, 469, 471, 479
Bordin, E.S. 6, 23, 28, 36, 41, 60, 84, 119, 447, 460, 479
Bowman, J.T. 159, 181, 195, 226
Boyd, J. iv, 31, 61, 114, 120, 126, 167, 169, 170, 172, 176, 181, 184, 195, 201, 226, 302, 317, 325, 339, 369, 430, 444
Boylston, W. 339, 369
Bradley, F. 25, 30
Bradley, F.O. 201, 227
Bradley, L. 23, 28, 336, 372, 427, 446, 447, 449, 480
Bradley, L.J. 23, 32, 158, 167, 187, 410, 419, 429, 444, 447, 479

H

I

V

Validation 406
Van Hoose, W.H. 424, 437, 446
Van Noord, R.W. 106, 124
Vance, A. 164, 165, 188
Video models 169
Vitalo, R.L. 109, 124, 196, 228

W

Wade, P. 158, 170, 180
Wagaman, G.L. 159, 182
Wagner, C.A. 161, 189
Walker, J.R. 23, 33
Wallace, W.G. 164, 189
Wallerstein, R.S. 11, 29, 36, 27, 42, 60, 65, 83, 120, 308, 335, 352, 353, 270, 460, 461, 479
Walters, R. 411, 418
Walton, J.M. 161, 189
Walz, G.R. 160, 164, 189
Wampold, B.D. 77, 121
Wampold, B.E. 310, 371
Wantz, R. 451, 480
Ward, G.R. 106, 124
Ward, G.W. 310, 373
Ward, L.G. 166, 189
Warner, R. 21, 30
Wasik, B.H. 407, 420
Wassmer, A.C. 65, 119, 200, 226
Weathersby, R.P. 267, 291, 292, 295, 298
Weaver, S. 25, 33
Webster's Third New International Dictionary 16, 33
Wedeking, D.F. 109, 124
Weinrach, S.G. 175, 189
Weiss, S.D. 107, 123, 163, 176, 187
Weitz, L.J. 105, 121
Wessler, R.L. 335, 373
West, J.D. 23, 33
Whiteley, J.M. 100, 124, 263, 297
Whiting, P. 447
Wiener, N. 376, 397
Wilbur, M. 22, 23, 410, 421
Wiley, M.O. 308, 310, 373
Williams, A. 447, 451, 480

Williams, B. 6, 23, 27
Williams, B.D. 103, 118
Williams, B.E. 351, 369
Winborn, B.B. 229, 256
Windle, C. 245, 256
Winter, D.E. 107, 123, 163, 176, 187
Wisconsin Relationship Orientation Inventory 106
Wise, F. 172, 173, 187
Wolleat, D.L. 357, 371
Wolman, B. 433, 446
Woody, R.H. 198, 228
Woolsey, L.K. 100, 124
Worthington, E.L. Jr. 6, 23, 33, 34, 262, 298, 351, 373, 447, 480
Worthington, W. 23, 34, 310, 325, 330, 373
Wrenn, C.G. 8, 34

Y

Yager, G.G. 43, 62, 170, 184, 353, 373
Yalom, I. 403, 404, 414, 421
Yeager, G. 25, 34
Yogen, S. 284, 298, 410, 421
Young, D.W. 166, 189
Young-Eisendrath, P. 416, 421

Z

Zander, T. 410, 419
Zeran, F.R. 229, 230, 235, 245, 255
Zerega, W.D. 159, 182
Zerface, J.P. 10, 34
Zimpfer, D.G. 164, 185
Zucker, P.J. 351, 373
Zytowski, D.G. 137, 189

CONTRIBUTORS

John D. Boyd, Ph.D., is a Clinical Psychologist in the Independent Practice of Clinical Psychology in Charlottesville, Virginia and an Associate Clinical Professor of Behavioral Medicine and Psychiatry at the University of Virginia, Charlottesville, Virginia. Dr. Boyd's early research interests focused on the preparation of doctoral students as counselor supervisors. His research led to the publication of *Counselor Supervision,* one of the early books published on the training of supervisors and a book that provides the theory base for this book. Dr. Boyd maintains a continuing interest in supervision and currently focuses on supervision involving the independent practice of clinical psychology.

Michael D'Andrea, Ed.D., is Assistant Professor and Research Coordinator at Meharry Medical College, Nashville, Tennessee. In addition to his interest in developmental supervision, Dr. D'Andrea has conducted research on ego and moral development with adolescents and unwed Black pregnant teenagers.

Mary Deck, Ph.D., is an Assistant Professor in the Counselor Education Program at the University of Alabama, Tuscaloosa, Alabama. She received her Ph.D. at the University of Virginia. Her special interest focus is the preparation of doctoral students as supervisors.

Richard L. Hayes, Ed.D., is an Associate Professor in the Department of Counseling and Human Development Services, College of Education, University of Georgia, Athens, Georgia. A Harvard college graduate, Dr. Hayes received his doctorate in counseling psychology from Boston University. He is a past-president of the Association for Specialists in Group Work and a former editor of the *Journal of Humanistic Education and Development.* His present research interest includes the application of human development theory to counseling practice especially in group settings.

Ruth C. Meredith, Ed.D., is an Assitant Professor of Counselor Education in the Department of Educational Leadership at Western Kentucky University, Bowling Green, Kentucky. Besides her interests in counselor supervision, Dr. Meredith works closely with school and community agency counseling programs.

Jim M. Morrow, Ph.D., is a Coordinator of Counselor Education at Western Carolina University, Cullowhee, North Carolina. Dr. Morrow completed his Ph.D. in Counselor Education from the University of North Carolina at Chapel Hill. In addition to his interest in the supervisory relationship, other special interests are career development, career counseling, and career assessment. He is especially interested in the application of the Holland theory/model in the person-environment and interpersonal interactions.

Julius Seeman, Ph.D., is a Professor Emeritus in the Department of Psychology and Human Development at George Peabody College of Vanderbilt University. He is currently a Professor of Human Development Counseling at George Peabody College. His major research interests focus on personality integration and models of positive health. Prior to his affiliation with George Peabody College, he was affiliated for six years with Professor Carl Rogers at the University of Chicago.

Peggy P. Whiting, Ed.D., is an Assitant Professor in the Human Development Counseling Program, George Peabody College of Vanderbilt University, Nashville, Tennessee. In addition to counselor supervision, she focuses her research efforts in the area of the impact of personal loss and grief upon development throughout the life span.

LORETTA J. BRADLEY

Loretta J. Bradley, Ph.D., is an Associate Professor of Counselor Education at Texas Tech University, Lubbock, Texas. Prior to affiliating with Texas Tech University in 1987, she was an Associate Professor of Human Development Counseling at Peabody College of Vanderbilt University (1978-87). Other university affiliations include Temple University and Purdue University. Dr. Bradley earned her Ph.D. in counseling and Student Personnel Services at Purdue University with Dr. Bruce Shertzer as major professor.

Dr. Bradley's previous publications have focused on micro-supervision and the clinical supervisor, practicum and intern-ship supervision requirments, community agency counseling, developmental assessment, career assessment, career develop-ment, hi-tech and the work force, and issues facing ex-offenders. Her efforts in community agency counseling were recognized when she and a colleague received the 1985 ACES Research Award and the 1987 AACD Research Award. Other awards include the 1983 Peabody Innovative Teaching Award, 1983, SACES Outstanding Program Award and the co-recipient of the 1986 SACES Individual Achievement Award.

Dr. Bradley is a National Board Certified Counselor, National Certified Career Counselor and a Licensed Professional Counselor. She has served on the Editorial Board of *Counselor Education and Supervision* (1978-1984) and the *Journal of Counseling and Development* (1984-1987). Currently she serves on the Editorial Boards of the *Journal of Humanistic Education and Development* and *Human Development and Counseling.*